THE BOOK OF SAINTE FOY

University of Pennsylvania Press
MIDDLE AGES SERIES
Edited by
Edward Peters
Henry Charles Lea Professor
of Medieval History
University of Pennsylvania

A listing of the available books
in this series appears at the
back of this volume

THE BOOK OF
SAINTE FOY

translated with an introduction and notes by
PAMELA SHEINGORN
The Song of Sainte Foy translated by
ROBERT L. A. CLARK

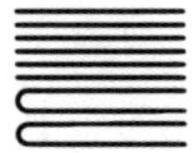

University of Pennsylvania Press
Philadelphia

Printed in the United States of America
Second paperback printing 1996

Library of Congress Cataloging-in-Publication Data
Liber miraculorum sancte Fidis. English.
The book of Sainte Foy / translated with an introduction and notes by Pamela Sheingorn ; the Song of Sainte Foy translated by Robert L. A. Clark.
p. cm. — (University of Pennsylvania Press Middle Ages series)
Chiefly a translation of the medieval Latin text of the Liber miraculorum sancte Fidis; Song of Sainte Foy translated from Provençal.
Includes bibliographical references and index.
ISBN 0-8122-3283-6. — ISBN 0-8122-1512-5 (pbk.)
1. Foy, Saint, ca. 290–303. 2. Christian saints, Juvenile — France — Conques — Biography. 3. Conques (Aveyron, France) — Religious life and customs. 4. France — Religious life and customs. I. Sheingorn, Pamela. II. Clark, Robert L. A. III. Chanson de Sainte Foy. English. IV. Title. V. Series: Middle Ages series.
BX4700.F37L52 1994
270.1'092 — dc20
[B] 94-24676
CIP

Cover: Historiated initial S from beginning of *Passio*, Sélestat, Bibliothèque Humaniste, folio 33r. Photograph by permission of the Bibliothèque Humaniste, Sélestat.

For Mark

Contents

Figures

Preface

The golden majesty of Sainte Foy has fascinated me ever since Professor Marilyn Stokstad showed a slide of her reliquary-statue in my first art history class. As I learned more about relationships among art, liturgy, drama, and hagiography in graduate school and later, my thoughts often returned to a figure that seemed to stand at the intersection of so many strands of medieval culture. Ilene Forsyth's magisterial book *Throne of Wisdom* made me aware of the *Liber miraculorum sancte Fidis*, and her short quotations from it whetted my appetite for the whole. Surely, I thought, there is even more information about the reliquary-statue to be gleaned from that text. Being one of those people who begins at the beginning, I acquired a copy of the Latin text and, having made a commitment to keep my medieval Latin supple through use, I began to read it with my Latin reading partner, Marcelle Thiébaux. Soon I was in Sainte Foy's thrall and kept translating until I had a draft of most of the text. Kathleen Ashley convinced me that I should put these entertaining, informative, and often surprising stories into publishable form and gave me crucial moral and intellectual support along the way. I also began to present papers in which I explored various aspects of Sainte Foy's impact on medieval culture, and Kathleen Ashley and I have since joined forces to work on interpretive studies of Sainte Foy's cult.

I am indebted to many people for the encouragement I needed to complete this volume. The Friends of the Saints, an informal gathering of scholars interested in various aspects of the saints, listened to samples from an early draft with forbearance and enthusiasm; over the years their meetings have been for me an on-going seminar in hagiography. Floyd Moreland and Rita Fleischer were the best possible teachers of Latin. Marcelle Thiébaux and I worked closely together on a first draft of portions of the *Book of Miracles*; she has generously allowed me to make use of her work. Mark Sheingorn and Carol Weisbrod reacted with graciousness and patience when I turned our summer home into "medieval camp" for weeks at a time. C. Clifford Flanigan generously and characteristically gave time and expertise to working through parts of the translation with me. It is an immense sorrow to me that he did not live to see the fruits of his labor in print. Stuart Kane worked long, hard, and, I believe, successfully to improve the accuracy of my translations from the Latin. Robert Clark made a crucial contribution to this volume with his translation of the *Song of Sainte Foy.* Richard Emmerson, that rare and treasured combination of good friend and critical reader, improved the introduction, as did historian and fellow Foy enthusiast Amy G. Remensnyder. Sharon Kraus meticulously read the entire manuscript and saved me from numerous stylistic infelicities. Marilyn Deegan's photographs, as well as her infectious enthusiasm for Conques and its saint, have enriched this work. I am very grateful for the enthusiastic responses and helpful suggestions of the readers for the Press, Thomas Head and Benedicta Ward. Above all, I am indebted to Kathleen Ashley for encouragement, for the complementary qualities that make collaborative work so rewarding, and for being the perfect traveling companion.

I would also like to thank the people who gave me the opportunity to lecture on various aspects of the Sainte Foy materials: Martin Stevens, C. Clifford Flanigan, Elisabeth Parker, Thelma Fenster, Caroline Bynum, Tom Heffernan, Irene Winter, Marcelle Thiébaux, Ruth Evans, Roger Ellis, Jody Enders, Cynthia Brown, Paula Gerson, and Annie Shaver-Crandell.

Much progress was made on the first draft of my translations during a year spent as a fellow in the Department of Art History and Archaeology at Princeton University. I especially appreciate my warm and supportive friends, the staff, former and present, of the Index of Christian Art there. The National Endowment for the Humanities provided crucial time for concentrated work with a year-long fellowship for college teachers. Released time for research, granted by the Dean of the School of Liberal Arts and Sciences at Baruch College, CUNY, has been most helpful, as have the awards from the PSC-CUNY Research Program that enabled me to make two pilgrimages to Conques.

Research for the introduction and notes to this book was greatly enabled by the generosity of Pierre Lançon at the municipal library of Conques in making accessible the valuable materials he has collected there. Hubert Meyer, Conservateur at the Bibliothèque Humaniste, Sélestat, made my study of the manuscript of the *Liber miraculorum* in his keeping thoroughly pleasant. Amy G. Remensnyder graciously allowed me to use her unpublished dissertation and shared her expertise in the medieval history of southern France. Finally, I have benefited greatly from the vast amount of scholarly work devoted to various facets of Conques and its saint, but above all from the huge compendium published by Bouillet and Servières at the beginning of this century. For me, to redo some of their work is not to diminish their contribution. And, after all the assistance I have received, errors that inevitably remain in this text are certainly my own.

Introduction

As a compilation of texts that make up the dossier of a saint, this book resembles what medieval people would call a *libellus*, a "little book" about one saint. And it is appropriate that this should be so, for almost all the texts translated in this book appeared in manuscripts solely concerned with Sainte Foy (see Figure 1). These manuscripts exemplify a type not so well known as the great compilations of stories or *legenda* about many different saints, such as the *Golden Legend*, that proliferated in the later Middle Ages.[1] One crucial way that *The Book of Sainte Foy* differs from a *libellus*, however, is in its inclusion of this introduction, which is intended to provide enough background to allow readers to understand these texts, background for which the original owners of the manuscripts, medieval Christian communities devoted to Sainte Foy, had no need. In this introduction I first offer some general material on the origins and development of the cult of saints and of the kinds of texts generated by and for such cults. I then turn more specifically to a discussion of Sainte Foy, her cult, and her monastery at Conques. I also introduce each of the texts translated here, describe some of the manuscripts in which these texts are preserved, and offer some information as to the methods and aims of the translator.

The Development of Christian Hagiography

Derived from *hagios*, the Greek word for "holy," the term hagiography—"the broad range of literature produced for the cult of saints"[2]—accurately characterizes all the texts gathered in this book. Individual hagiographic texts range widely, from short accounts of a martyr's death to massive compilations of miracles worked from beyond the grave. Not so long ago, this vast body of literature was undervalued by scholars. Historians found hagiographic texts unreliable as documents for reconstructing the past and students of literature neglected them in favor of what they considered to be more aesthetically pleasing and consciously crafted texts. But there has

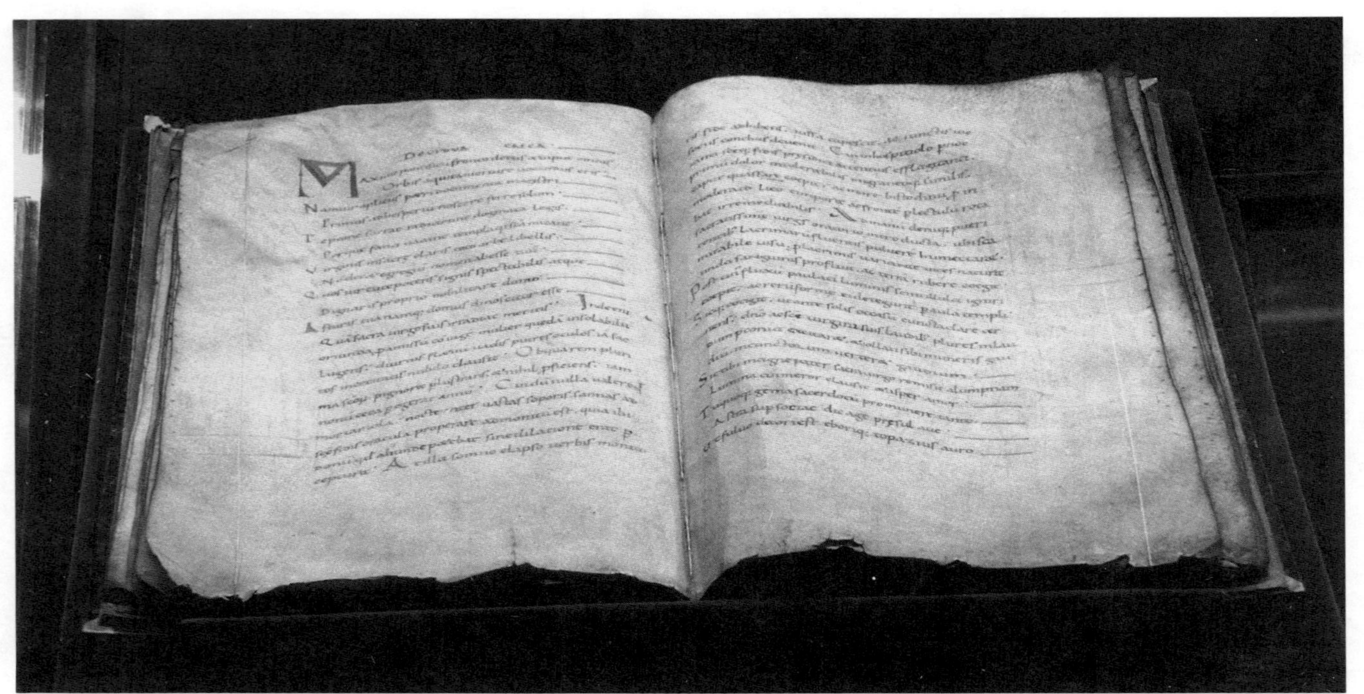

1. *Book of Sainte Foy's Miracles,* Conques, Abbey Church of Sainte Foy, treasury. Photo: Marilyn Deegan.

been a sea change in attitudes toward these materials as new approaches based in social history, history of mentalities, cultural studies, gender studies, and interdisciplinary studies have come to the fore. During the last few decades, hagiographic texts have found new audiences who have given them intense attention and employed them to answer a great variety of new questions.[3]

The cult of saints for which hagiography was composed can be traced to the early Christian martyrs.[4] Martyrdom shaped the concept of sanctity that became dominant in the early Christian period. A Christian martyr (literally, "witness") gave public witness by dying at the hands of the Roman legal system as a result of refusing to recant belief in Christianity. The Christian community apparently obtained and preserved copies of official transcripts of the martyrs' trials and incorporated them into fuller accounts of their last days and deaths.[5] Such an account of the suffering and death of a martyr came to be called a *Passio* (Passion), a term that underscores the way that the pattern of the martyr's life and death repeated that of Christ. On the anniversary of a martyr's death, understood as his or her birthday into an eternal life, the Eucharist was celebrated at the martyr's tomb.

But in addition to their understandable impulse to honor the dead, early Christians remembered and revered the martyrs because of the power they were believed to have. Recalling the words of Jesus to the good thief crucified with him, "Today you shall be with me in Paradise," early Christians concluded that the souls of martyrs ascended directly into the presence of God. From their places near God's throne, these martyr-saints were ideally positioned to intercede on behalf of still-living Christians. Theologians eventually distinguished between the veneration (*dulia*) that the saints deserved as channels through which God's grace could flow to humankind and the adoration (*latria*) reserved for God alone, and they emphasized that miracles were worked *through* the saints *by* God. Many Christians, however, focused directly on the more accessible and tangible wonder-working saints.[6]

Tangibility was provided by the saints' physical remains, or relics. Christians clung to the comforting idea that, although saints' souls had joined the ranks of the blessed and were in ideal positions to act as intercessors with the divine, their bodies that remained behind offered especially effective channels of communication through which living Christians could direct their prayers and petitions; it was as if some of the saints' power had adhered to their mortal flesh. Shrines were erected over the burial places of martyrs; some of them eventually became churches. The Eucharistic celebration on a saint's day evolved into a liturgy for the saint that could include the reading of the saint's life or Passion, the preaching of sermons holding up the saint as an example for living Christians, and special prayers and hymns.

Saints' bodies were often moved from one place to another, usually either for safety or to provide relics for a church without them, since from early Christian times the church had insisted that an altar should contain a relic. In the early Middle Ages the western church frowned on the practice of moving bodies. In Rome itself, however, the relics of early Christian martyrs were transferred from the catacombs in the eighth and ninth centuries, an action that cleared the way for the widespread movement of holy bodies in subsequent centuries. (When no other method of acquiring relics suggested itself, monks like those of Conques resorted to theft.) Rather than being reburied, such relics were usually housed in containers called reliquaries. Initially box-shaped and usually made of metal, reliquaries later took the form of the body or body part enclosed in the reliquary. Such reliquaries embellished altars and were carried in processions into the surrounding countryside.

Saints' relics received all this attention because of their wonder-working powers. Those in control of the relics, whether bishops or monks, wanted to expand the territory in which their saints held sway. Accounts of miracles were therefore collected, written in narrative form, and compiled into miracle books. Such a manuscript might well contain the saint's life or Passion and other texts used in the performance of the liturgy on the saint's feast day. The texts translated in this book come from such manuscripts, and their collection here forms a *libellus* of Sainte Foy, early Christian child martyr and patron saint of the monastery at Conques.

The Cult of Sainte Foy

Though it reached its high point as long ago as the eleventh century, the cult of Sainte Foy at Conques en Aveyron[7] still attracts a great deal of attention today. A site that preserves an intact pilgrimage road church in a charming village located in the rugged but picturesque countryside of south central France, Conques is, as it was then, a magnet for travelers (see Figure 2). Whoever chose this location, a level area shaped like a mussel shell (*concha*) that gave its name to the place, made a most fortunate choice. Nestled into

2. Village of Conques from the far side of the gorge in which the Ouche River runs. Photo: Marilyn Deegan.

the sloping side of the deep valley where the River Ouche flows on its way to meet the Dourdou at what is now the outskirts of the village, Conques enjoys brilliant sunshine along with its view of the misty valley below. Fresh water flows from a spring that made life easier for inhabitants of both monastery and village and was a boon to medieval pilgrims. With its multiple towers and sonorous bells, the medieval abbey church dominates its surroundings (see Figure 3), which include a carefully reconstructed cloister and a richly furnished treasury.

But it is surely the rare visitor who realizes that, in addition to these most impressive physical remains of Sainte Foy's cult—including a reliquary-statue of virtually hypnotic power—there are significant textual remains. This book contains translations into English of some of those texts.

Historical Overview

Texts and artifacts throw only a dim light on the early history of Conques. Shards of Gallo-Roman pottery indicate occupation in the first few Christian centuries but do little to substantiate the claim made in the monastery's chronicle (written in the late eleventh century and added to in the twelfth and thirteenth) that in the early Christian period large numbers of hermits inhabited the region. The chronicle reports the massacre of a thousand hermits by pagans late in the fourth century; repopulation followed by Frankish devastation in the sixth century; another refoundation, destroyed by Saracens in the eighth century; and a fourth, enduring foundation by Pippin the Short, father of Charlemagne, later in that century, in cooperation with a hermit named Dado. The chronicle insists not only on Charlemagne's direct interest in the monastery, but also on his high regard for it as indicated by gifts. Though some scholars have dismissed the earliest parts of this "history" as apocryphal, fragments of an object in the monastery's treasury that may date to the Merovingian period leave open the possibility that the monks who wrote the chronicle may have been embellishing their past rather than manufacturing it out of whole cloth.[8]

They were certainly on firmer ground with the hermit Dado and the patronage of the Carolingian royal house.[9] Both appear in a poem in praise of Emperor Louis the Pious written between 826 and 828 by Ermoldus Nigellus,[10] who had been exiled from the court of Louis's son Pippin I, king of Aquitaine. According to Ermoldus, while Dado was away fighting Saracens, they captured his mother. When he tracked them down, the Saracen leader offered to trade Dado's mother for his warhorse, but Dado declined and saw his mother killed. Later, overcome by remorse, he became

3. Abbey Church of Sainte Foy, Conques, from the south. Photo: Marilyn Deegan.

a hermit. Hearing his story, Louis the Pious called him to a royal audience, and together they founded a monastery, presumably on the site of Dado's hermitage, to which Louis himself gave the name Conques.

Although Ermoldus has been criticized as a poor historian, documents indicate that Louis was indeed directly involved with Conques, granting the monastery gifts of churches and immunity in a royal diploma of 819 that mentions Dado. Further gifts, including land, market rights, and immunities, were bestowed by Pippin I in 838, as recorded in a royal diploma of that year. He may also have presented the imperial crown later used to adorn the reliquary-statue of Sainte Foy (see Figure 4). Pippin's gifts to Conques indicate its stature at this early date,[11] as do other documents in the monastery's cartulary, a collection of charters recording legal transactions, mostly gifts of land and property to the monastery.[12] The earliest charter is dated 801, at which time an abbot named Madraldus presided over the monastery, which was following the Benedictine Rule.

Pippin I apparently thought he was helping the monastery when, as part of the diploma of 838, he made possible a move to a more accessible location at Figeac, about forty kilometers north and west of Conques on the Célé River. The monastery at Figeac was to be called New Conques. Some of the monks refused to move, and a rivalry grew up between Conques and the increasingly prosperous foundation at Figeac. Pope Urban II issued a bull in 1084 that attempted to resolve the dispute, and at some point the monks of Figeac forged a diploma, supposedly issued by Pippin the Short in 755, giving them control over Conques.[13] Probably both this document and the chronicle of Conques, which refutes its claims, were products of the high point of the dispute in the eleventh century. A final resolution did not come until 1096, when the council of Nîmes definitively separated the governance of the two monasteries.

The dispute with Figeac, which was flourishing while Conques's resources dwindled, also helps explain why the monks of Conques sought Sainte Foy's relics: Conques needed a power base of its own in order to maintain its independent existence, and the appropriate power base in the ninth century was a miracle-working saint. Not having such a saint, the monks determined to acquire one through theft, and eventually set their sights on Foy. Foy's *Passio* vividly describes her martyrdom as a child in Agen during a Roman persecution of Christians at the beginning of the fourth century. Subsequently her body was enshrined in a church in Agen dedicated to her, where she rested in peace until monks of Conques successfully plotted the theft, which seems to have taken place on January 14,

4. Detail (from the back) showing Carolingian crown, reliquary-statue of Sainte Foy, Conques, Abbey Church of Sainte Foy, treasury. Photo: Marilyn Deegan.

866.[14] The story of this relic theft was eventually given written form in the *Translatio* included in this book.

Foy's presence at Conques resulted in both a new statue and a new church. In the last quarter of the ninth century, a piece of Foy's skull was enclosed in a reliquary-statue of a type apparently familiar to a large part of southern France, but unknown elsewhere (see Figure 5).[15] Large scale three-dimensional sculpture was still quite rare in this period, at least partly because of early Christian fear of idols reinforced by Carolingian repugnance toward what was understood to be worship of icons in the Byzantine east. In Book 1, Chapter 13 of the *Book of Sainte Foy's Miracles*,[16] Bernard of Angers writes of his own distrust of religious statuary, the making and honoring of which he identified as indigenous practice of the region around Conques.

Around 900 a number of donations came to the monastery at Conques, possibly attracted by the newly acquired relics of Foy, and a new church dedicated to the Holy Savior was built between about 940 and about 980. Then came the event most responsible for Conques's rise to glory: the miracle in which Sainte Foy is credited with replacing a man's eyeballs that had been ripped out a year earlier. Thereafter the man was called Guibert the Illuminated. The importance of this miracle is recognized by both the length and the placement of the chapter in the *Book of Miracles* devoted to it (1.1). Probably taking place in 983, the miracle of Guibert stimulated a great flood of donations, grants of land and churches, which enabled the creation of a new golden altar frontal (see Figure 6). Gifts continued to flow unabated until the early twelfth century. As Gournay meticulously documents, their sources changed. Through the mid-eleventh century, it was the local castellans, feudal tenants, and peasants who made Conques wealthy. After 1065, the donors were people of power and authority—bishops and archbishops, counts and countesses, even kings—and represented a wide geographical distribution.

Not only did Foy's unusual miracles attract donations—some of which the monks spent late in the tenth century in renovating her reliquary-statue—they also drew the fascinated attention of Bernard of Angers, who made three pilgrimages to Conques early in the eleventh century, and recorded and then drafted in Latin what were to become the first two books of her miracle collection. Foy's reputation brought Bernard to Conques and he in turn contributed to that reputation by disseminating the stories of her miracles in northern France, primarily to learned churchmen. During its heyday in the eleventh century, pilgrims made Conques the goal of their

5. Reliquary-statue of Sainte Foy, Conques, Abbey Church of Sainte Foy, treasury. Photo: Marilyn Deegan.

6. Christ in Glory, possibly part of a tenth-century altar frontal, Conques, Abbey Church of Sainte Foy, treasury. Photo: Marilyn Deegan.

journeys, leaving behind gifts and taking with them stories of Sainte Foy's amazing miracles. On their return home, some of them established foundations in honor of the saint.

One of the four routes to the shrine of Saint James at Santiago de Compostela in northern Spain, the one called the *Via Podensis*, which started at Le Puy en Velay, passed through Conques as early as the mid-eleventh century and brought considerable prosperity to the northern Rouergue, the county in which Conques is located. The guidebook for pilgrims to Santiago instructed them to stop on their journey to visit Conques, where Sainte Foy's "very precious body" was enshrined.[17]

During the course of the twelfth century Conques lost its position as the chief destination of pilgrims, becoming instead simply one of many stops on the great pilgrimage to Santiago de Compostela. There were other reasons as well for the decline of the monastery's fortunes in the course of the twelfth century. For example, the new monastic orders, which grew rapidly in the Rouergue, diverted both attention and donations from the traditional Benedictine abbey to fund their own aggressive expansion.

SOCIAL CONDITIONS

During the later ninth century the system of government put in place by the Carolingians slowly collapsed in southern France, with the result that there was little secular government of any effectiveness until the rise of a centralized monarchy in the thirteenth century. Though there were people with nominal authority over the area around Conques, for example Raymond II, Count of Rouergue from about 961 to about 1008, the moral of the story told in the *Book of Miracles* 3.5 is that this count's attempts to exert authority over the monastery at Conques resulted in his death. The monastery had been granted immunity by Louis the Pious and again by Pippin I in the ninth century, and was also free of a bishop's supervision. In effect, the abbot ruled over his territory with exclusive authority.

The monks, who followed the Benedictine Rule, came from families of some means who were able to provide donations to the monastery. Some entered as children; others had significant experience in the secular world and had even led armed men into battle.

Although the monks appear as characters in the *Book of Miracles*, its stories center on a society in which two classes, the *milites* and the peasants, are very much at odds with one another. Building on the work of Georges Duby,[18] Gournay delves deeply into the range of meanings that this text and the cartulary assign to the word *miles*. A person so designated definitely used weapons and rode a horse; *milites* lived in castles, and so probably had a certain nobility and wealth (though none of the refinement associated with later chivalric society). Armed followers of a lord called a *miles* might also be called *milites*. In the absence of a strong central power, the countryside was dominated by such men: mounted warriors who left their castles to attack one another, raid the small farms of the peasants, loot the goods of the Church, take captives for ransom, and, in general, spread terror and destruction among the populace. Bernard of Angers rails against these depredations and employs cautionary tales of Sainte Foy's vengeance to discourage their perpetrators.

The castles of late tenth- and eleventh-century Rouergue were not surrounded by moats and high walls. Rather they were stone towers built on outcroppings of rock chosen for the steepness of terrain and inaccessibility of location that were essential aspects of their defenses (see Figure 7).[19] Such castles either had or improvised a place to hold prisoners captive, usually bound in chains. Castles housed a castellan and his armed retainers (all of whom were *milites*); in the *Book of Miracles* there is little mention of families living in these armed encampments, though some of them had small chapels. In this period there is no evidence of settlements growing up in the areas around these castles. Bonds between a castellan and his garrison of armed men may have resembled vassalage, a term that is used a few times in the *Book of Miracles*, and some castellans were apparently vassels of more powerful lords, but though this system may have been widespread, it did not result in social order, as was often the case during the height of feudalism elsewhere.

In addition to castellans and their retainers, the countryside of the Rouergue was populated by peasants working the land. Most seem to have lived in isolated farmsteads. Some are described as "Sainte Foy's peasants," meaning they worked land belonging to the monastery, but many others held their own small parcels of land. These peasants do not seem to have been dependents of the castellans, but rather potential victims of their raids.

It was to combat the breakdown of social order, as well as the destruction of its own property caused by these castle-holding raiders, that the Church instituted the interrelated movements that came to be known as the Peace of God and the Truce of God. Frederick S. Paxton offers a concise summary of Georges Duby's interpretation of the social effect of the Peace: "The Peace was directed both from above and from below at the free class of mounted warriors, the *milites*. In its earliest stage, the Peace movement acted to separate the mounted horsemen from the unarmed—that is the increasingly servile peasant class and the clergy (to whom it prohibited the use of arms)—and added to the sharpening of distinctions between laity and clergy in general."[20] At least one of the councils mentioned in the *Book of Miracles*, the one held at Rodez not long after the year 1000, was probably associated with the Peace of God movement, and the presence of Sainte Foy's reliquary-statue at that council indicates that the monastery at Conques participated actively in the movement against the lawlessness of the mounted warriors. Not only did the monks organize military retaliation, they also created a territory around the monastery that was a safeguard, extending the right to provide asylum beyond the monastic grounds so that a small settlement of peasants grew up around the monastery. In this way the village of Conques came into existence.

Some of these peasants, and many others who owed gratitude to Sainte Foy, donated land to her. Thus the monastery accumulated land through gifts of allodial holdings, that is, land owned in such a way that the

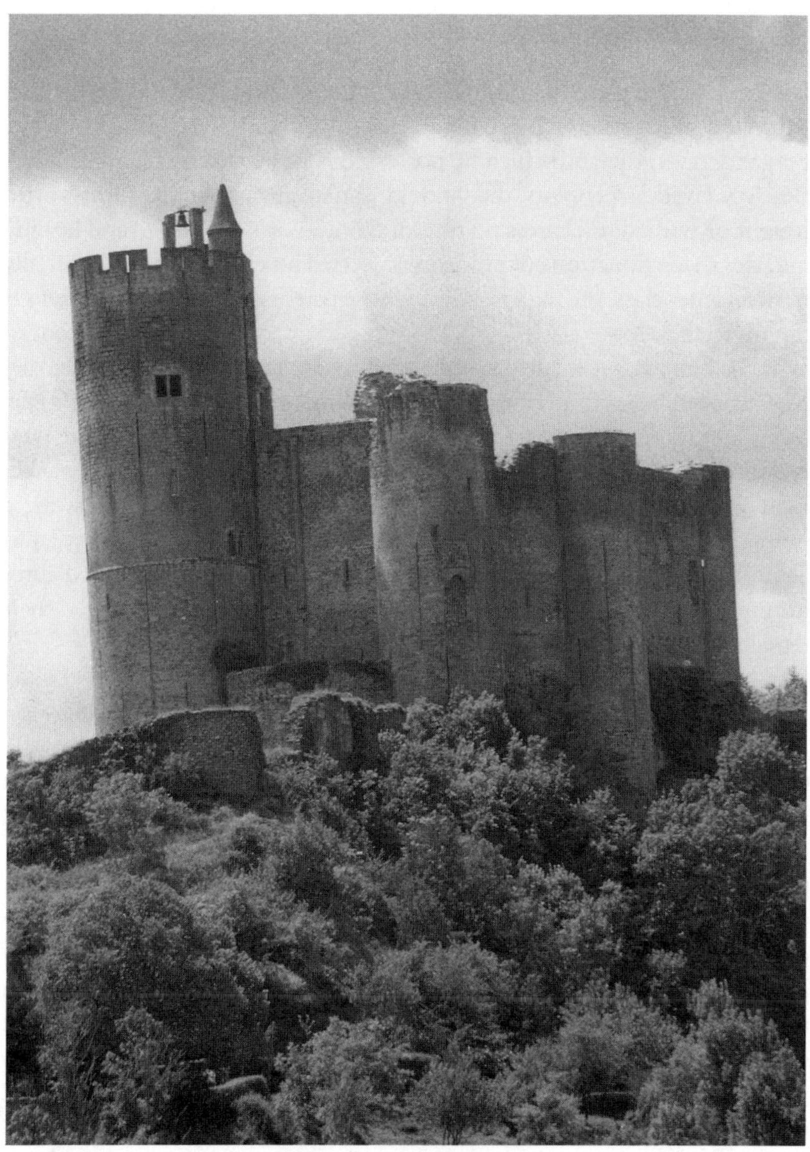

7. Castle of Najac, Aveyron. Photo: Marilyn Deegan.

owners had the right to dispose of it permanently. Families sometimes contested such gifts, as can be seen in 1.5 of the *Book of Miracles*, where Bergand gave Foy land which he possessed allodially but which his family clearly viewed as property that should remain in the family. Others who sought or wished to express thanks for Sainte Foy's protective and healing miracles made donations of precious objects. These donors came especially from another class, the high nobility, whose patronage the *Book of Miracles* is careful to mention.

Women are especially prominent in these stories: Countess Bertha, who amused her noble companions by calling one of Foy's miracles a *joca*, using the peasants' word for Foy's practical jokes; Countess Arsinde, who bargained with Foy to trade her gold armlets for a guaranteed pregnancy; Lady Beatrice, left in charge of the castle while her husband was away; a peasant woman who found Countess Richarde's gold brooch and gave it to Sainte Foy, knowing better than to keep it; women who demanded cures for their desperately ill children. And it was often women who urged their recalcitrant husbands to yield to Sainte Foy before it was too late.

Relics and Reliquary

According to the *Translatio*, the mid-eleventh-century text describing Conques's acquisition of Foy's relics, the relics of Sainte Foy in her church at Agen were kept in a place covered with a stone held in place by iron seals. The text names Arinisdus as the monk who stole these relics from Agen and transported them to Conques in "a small sack that was very clean." At Conques the monks placed the relics "in the most fitting place under the most diligent guard," presumably somewhere in their church. By the end of the ninth century, a piece of the skull had been enshrined in the head of a reliquary-statue. Just under three feet in height, the statue represented the saint seated in a stiff, frontal posture (see Figure 5). The statue itself was made of yew wood and, in place of a head, ended in a cylindrical projection over which a gold head was fitted. Not made in Conques or for this statue, the head portrays an adult male and came from a late imperial portrait bust, probably of the fifth century, which must have been a royal donation. The statue itself may have been sheathed in gold from the beginning; in any case the gold was in place at the time of the monk Gimon (around 930–960; 1.26). During the late tenth century and after the miracle of Guibert the Illuminated, the statue underwent a renovation in which it received a crown, ecclesiastical garb, and a throne. Various other modifications have taken place through the centuries.

Statues of this type, called "majesties,"[21] could be found in various places in southern France in this period. By enshrining relics, that is, some part of the saint's physical body, in the three-dimensional form the body once had, these statues blurred the distinction between image and reality, between memory and presence. Thus, to many pilgrims, the reliquary-statue *was* the living saint who could hear and see them and, most important of all, could grant their petitions. As Michael Camille observes, "The animate aura of such cult images as . . . the statue of Ste. Foy at Conques stemmed from their articulation of a whole set of hieratic conventions associated with power and magic—such as the glaring eyes, potent and penetrating to the beholder—that go back to imperial portraiture. Medieval optical theory judged *spiritus* to emanate from the eye like a ray, illuminating the world around so that the beholders could literally be trapped by the gaze of the image."[22]

The Churches at Conques

Perhaps a modest church or oratory served the needs of the hermit Dado and his followers after their arrival in Conques in the late eighth century, but no details about it are known. A new church dedicated to the Holy Savior was built in the tenth century during the abbacy of Stephen, who was also bishop of Clermont, and was standing when Bernard of Angers visited in the early eleventh century. His eyewitness description is recorded in 1.31 of the *Book of Miracles*. In spite of his northern sophistication, Bernard found this church quite impressive, not least for the abundance of iron grillwork made from chains and fetters brought to Sainte Foy as offerings of thanks from prisoners whom she freed. Two pieces of stone carved in relief, one patterned with ivy leaves and the other with interlace, survive from this church and indicate its importance.

Excavation in the late nineteenth century revealed that the tenth-century church had been on the same site as the present one and had been about half its length. These excavations uncovered a circular foundation at the east end; it may be the remains of the separate building described in the *Translatio*, to which the saint's relics refused to be moved, or it may simply be the apse of the church. The *Book of Miracles* (1.26) suggests that Foy's reliquary-statue stood near the high altar of this church, protected behind locked doors, presumably iron grillwork through which the saint could be seen. A monk kept watch in the church during the night to keep candles lit.

The success of Sainte Foy's cult made a rebuilding of her church not only possible, but necessary in order to accommodate large numbers of pilgrims. By 1050, or possibly a few years earlier, the monastery had both the need and the means to rebuild its church, a project that was launched under Abbot Odolric. By his death in 1065, parts of the eastern end, constructed of rather large blocks of red sandstone from a local quarry, were complete. The chronicle reports that the ceremonial transfer of Foy's relics from the old church to this new sanctuary took place under Odolric; a large number of bishops attended. Scholars have suggested that the *Translatio*, the story of the original acquisition of Foy's relics, and the *Song of Sainte Foy*, an account of Foy's Passion in Provençal verse, may have been composed for the festivities surrounding the transfer of her relics.

Differences in the stonework and in the style of the carved capitals indicate that Odolric's sanctuary was reconstructed later in the eleventh century; the need for rebuilding is alluded to in the *Book of Miracles* (4.24), which vividly describes the unstable condition of the structure. Construction also moved forward toward the completion of the church, though it is impossible to reconstruct a detailed chronology. Scholars do not agree on a date by which the building was finished and the great tympanum of the west façade was in place, but the financial condition of the abbey strongly suggests that there was no construction after roughly 1120, and work may have been completed as early as 1110.[23]

The church of Sainte-Foy at Conques ranks as one of the great pilgrimage road churches (see Figure 3), meaning that the style of its architecture, similar to that of Saint-Sernin of Toulouse and Santiago de Compostela, met the needs of the pilgrims who poured through Conques. Using the side aisles and ambulatory, pilgrims could progress through the church to view, through the protective iron grillwork, the reliquary-statue reigning over the choir. They could also crowd into its spacious nave and transepts for special occasions such as the saint's feast day. Constrained by its site, the church of Sainte-Foy is not so large as its sister churches, but its height rivals theirs. Its simple geometric forms, harmoniously grouped, are realized in a warm yellow limestone.

The dramatic conclusion to the grand building program and the first sight that presents itself to the gaze of approaching pilgrims is the sculpture of the great tympanum over the west door of the church (see Figure 8).[24] A representation of the Last Judgment, the tympanum seems to speak in the voice of Bernard of Angers in his angry conclusion to 1.11: "Hear, you plunderers and ravagers of Christian property, how inevitable are the scourges and just judgments of God. His vengeance yields to no power, and if it spares for the present it will strike more heavily in the future. If it

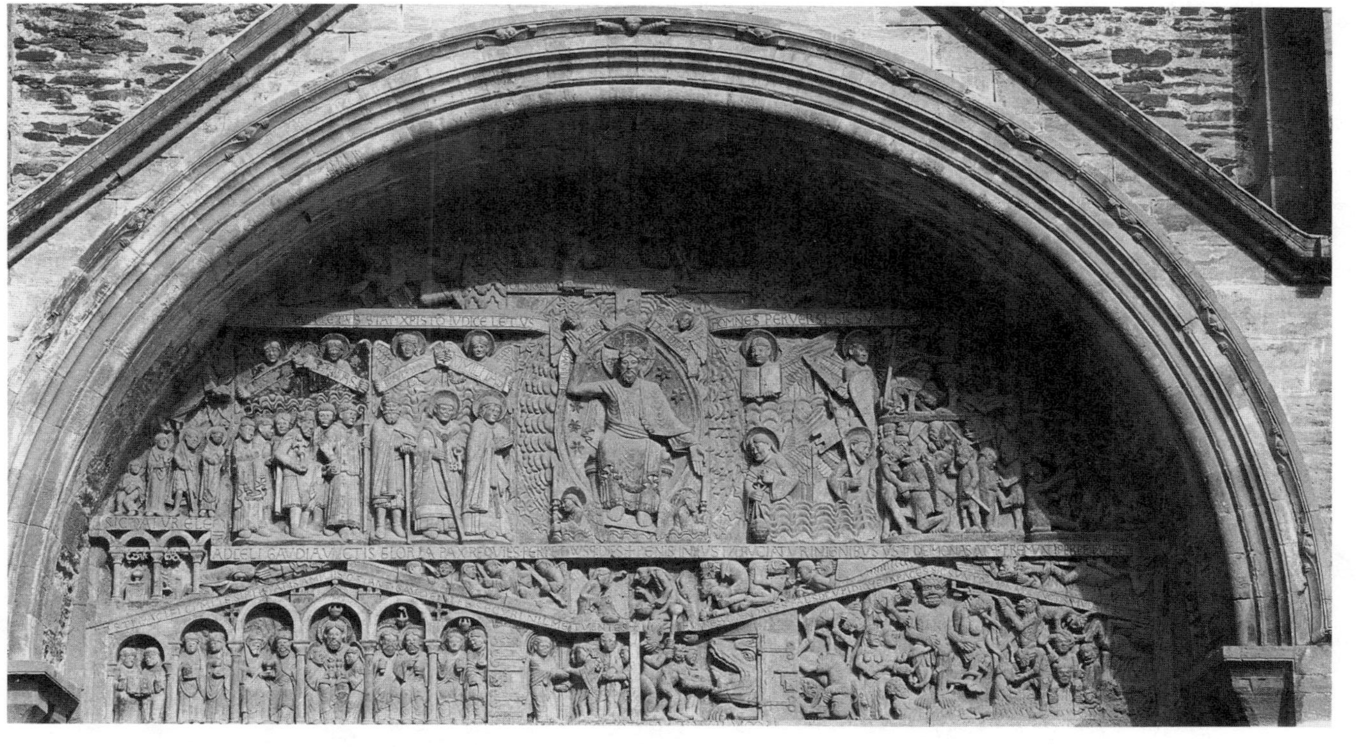

8. Tympanum, Conques, Abbey Church of Sainte Foy. Photo: Marilyn Deegan.

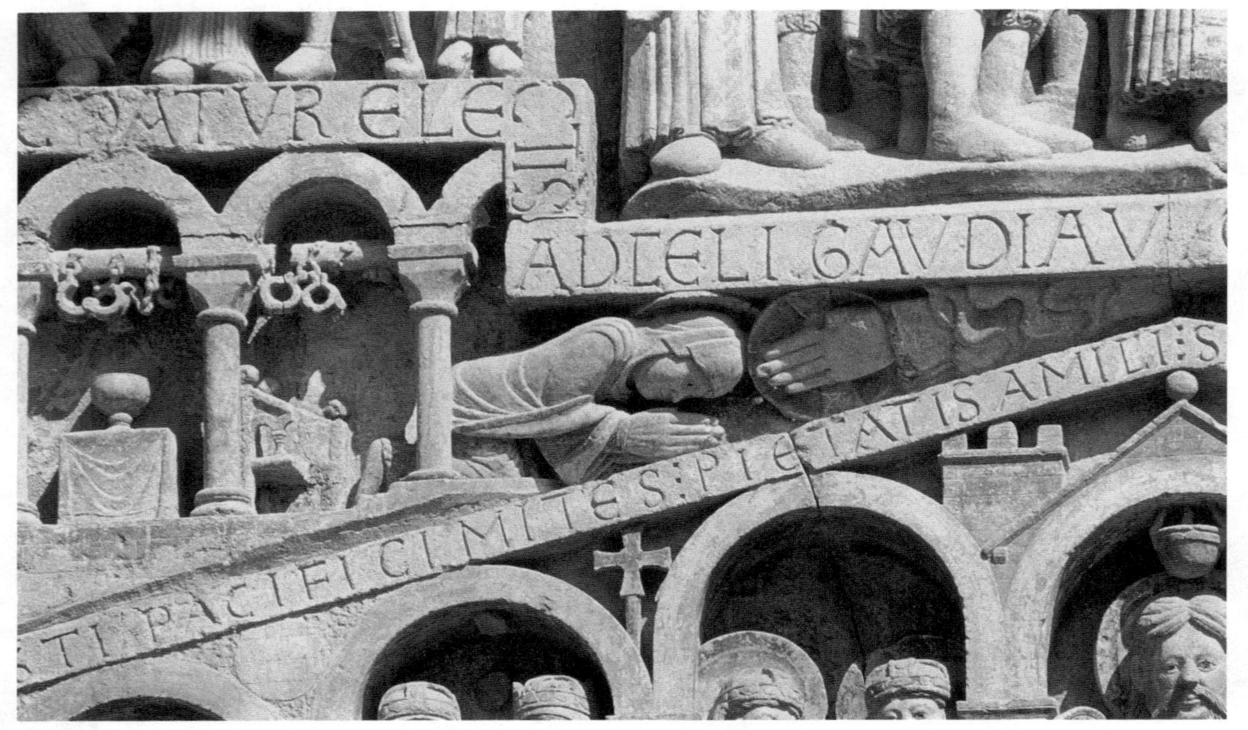

9. Hand of God recognizing Foy as intercessor, detail of tympanum, Conques, Abbey Church of Sainte Foy. Photo: Marilyn Deegan.

forbears to punish in this world, a harsher and more effective punishment awaits you in the eternal fires." As Gournay observes, the monks would have understood the "plunderers and ravagers of Christian property" to be the castellans and their retainers, bands of armed horseman who swooped down on innocent monks; it is no accident that the tympanum's sculpture shows such a figure plummeting into hell. Yet this is no simple screed against a single group, for monks may also be found among those suffering hell's torments. To avoid eternal punishment, the anxious viewer turns to Sainte Foy, represented on the tympanum just as she is so often in the miracle stories, interceding to win God's favor toward those who invoke her (see Figure 9). Peace, order, and harmony on the side of the tympanum associated with heaven contrast sharply with the chaos of hell. Abraham calmly presides in heaven, cherishing the souls of the blessed in his bosom. Above and over all reigns Christ the Judge, frozen in his great gesture of separation, rejecting the damned and welcoming the blessed.

The Texts in This Book

Passio: The Passion of Sainte Foy

The earliest surviving reference to Sainte Foy is in a martyrology, a list of martyrs according to the dates of their martyrdom, compiled so that the early church would know when to honor its saints. A version of the *Hieronymian Martyrology* dating to the end of the sixth century notes without elaboration Foy's martyrdom in Agen on the sixth of October.[25]

The story of Foy's martyrdom, her *Passio*, may have been written down as early as the fifth century. Of the various versions that survive, the one translated here, the oldest extant, may incorporate material from this putative fifth-century original, as Louis Saltet argues.[26] But the Benedictines of Paris in their multi-volume study of saints' lives and feasts conclude that a first, no-longer-extant *Passio* text can be dated only shortly before the earliest surviving text, which is in a tenth-century manuscript. Two tenth-century manuscripts preserve this text: Paris, B.N. MS lat. 5301, fols. 328r–329v, and Montpellier, Library of the School of Medicine, MS H 152, fols. 231v–237r. I have translated the edition in Bouillet and Servières (707–711 and 394–404), which follows the Paris manuscript but uses occasional variants from the Montpellier manuscript and adds to it a last section on the translation of the relics found only in the Montpellier manuscript.

Amplifications and revisions of this *Passio* were made at Conques, including a version in leonine verse composed in the mid-eleventh century. Many more manuscript copies of these later versions remain. The *Passio* text in the Sélestat manuscript (Bibliothèque Humaniste MS lat. 22; formerly Bibliothèque de la Ville MS lat. 95) is divided into numbered sections for use in the liturgy, that is, for reading in the Office, and introduced by a historiated initial that shows a monk with a book witnessing a scene from Foy's Passion (see Figure 10). André de Mandach has argued that this version could have been accompanied by mimed performance when it was read on the saint's feast day and on other occasions.[27]

Liber miraculorum sancte Fidis: The Book of Sainte Foy's Miracles

Though word of mouth might effectively spread the news of a saint's miracles, preservation in writing was obviously desirable and became more common as the culture moved from oral toward written preservation of events. Books of miracles had become the most popular kind of writing about the saints by the eleventh century. Such books had several functions. Circulated among the clergy, and especially to places where the cult of Sainte Foy was celebrated, a book recording some of her miracles could be used as a source for sermons preached in the vernacular to the laity.[28] But, as Jean Hubert and Marie-Clotilde Hubert write of *The Book of Sainte Foy's Miracles*, "It presents itself as a work of edification, but also of propaganda, intended to spread the renown of the sanctuary where wondrous cures and other miracles were effected. The descriptions of a multitude of pilgrims pressed into the narrow space where the statue was displayed were very likely intended to attract new dévotées."[29]

The organizational principle introduced by Bernard of Angers, the writer of the first two books of the *Book of Miracles*, and followed more or less faithfully by the writers of the later books, was to group the miracles by type. Within each type, organization is generally chronological; thus Bernard begins Book One with the foundational miracle of the cult, the restoration of Guibert's eyes, and follows it with a number of other miracles involving eyes and blindness. As Pierre-André Sigal observes, a simple chronological organization that indiscriminately mixes types of miracles is much more usual for miracle collections.[30] Bernard's desire to organize his material by subject may reflect his education at the School of Chartres.

Most of the miracles reported in the *Book of Miracles* fall into previously existing types; they are the kinds of miracles, such as healing the sick, freeing prisoners, and punishing transgressors, that were expected of a

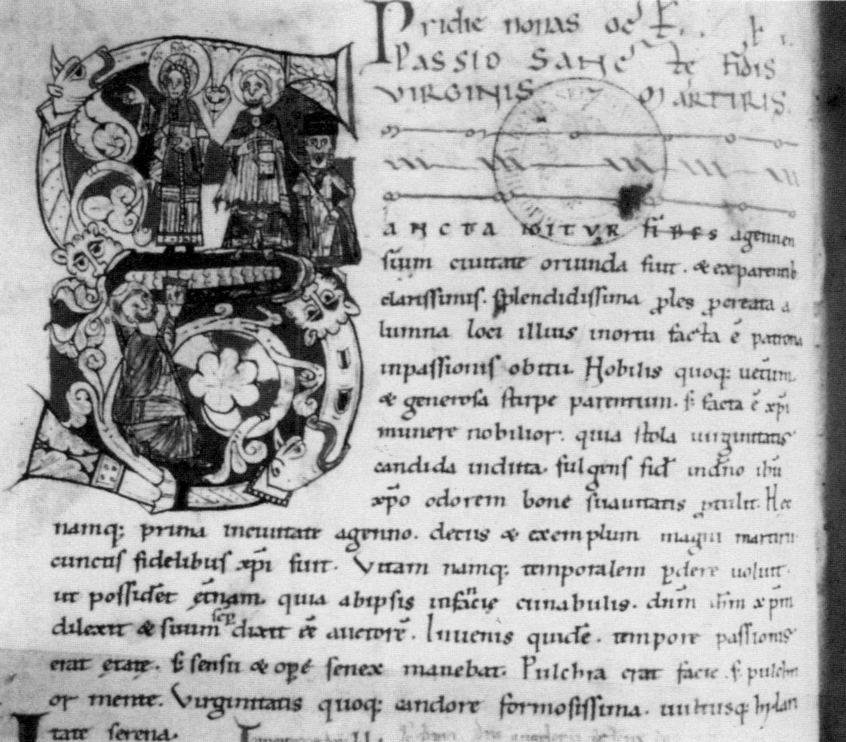

10. Historiated initial S from beginning of *Passio,* fol. 5v, Sélestat, Bibliothèque Humaniste, MS 22. Courtesy of Bibliothèque Humaniste, Sélestat.

patron saint. Yet, as Remensnyder has shown, Bernard emphasizes Foy's "unheard of and new miracles," by which he seems to mean the literal replacing of eyeballs that had been torn out, the resurrection of animals, and the *joca* and *ludi*, jests or practical jokes played by the saint, who displays some of the qualities associated with a trickster throughout the *Book of Miracles* (see, for instance, 1.23 or 4.23). Bernard of Angers feels especially defensive about miracles in which animals are revived from the dead; apparently such stories had caused the saint to be mocked. To substantiate his reports, Bernard employs a device common to hagiographers for underscoring their truthfulness, namely, insisting that at least one of the witnesses is still alive.[31]

Bernard of Angers, the author of the first two books of the miracle collection, emerges from his text as a clearly defined personality. In spite of the numerous topoi Bernard wields so well, he reveals curiosity, enthusiasm, persistence, and wit, as well as skepticism.[32] He holds opinions on many subjects—certainly on the danger that works of art can become idols—and is quite touchy when criticized. He seems to have been an indefatigable interviewer and note-taker as he documented miracles worked for and in the presence of others, but he really wanted to see one for himself and was terribly pleased when this finally happened (1.9).

Little is known about Bernard other than what he tells us. The beneficiary of one of the miracles he records (2.13) was his brother, who may have been Robert, abbot of Cormery.[33] Bernard studied at the School of Chartres and speaks as if he had spent a great deal of time in the presence of Fulbert, who was associated with the cathedral school during Bernard's years there.[34] It was during his stay at Chartres that Bernard became intrigued with the cult of Sainte Foy and determined to test the truth of the miracle stories that were circulating by traveling to Conques himself. Instead, probably in 1010, he moved to Angers at the behest of its bishop, Hubert of Vendôme, to head the new cathedral school Hubert had founded there.[35] Three years later Bernard managed to get away from his burdensome duties at Angers and made his first journey to Conques, accompanied by one of the teachers in his school, Bernier.

Bernard reports that the monks of Conques "received me with proper hospitality and provided everything I needed to carry out my vow, even assigning me excellent servants who obeyed my orders as long as I was there" (1.9). Before long they were bringing him witnesses and begging him to write up more of their miracles. It was an unusual opportunity for Bernard, since the miracles of a saint were usually redacted by a local author.[36] Though Bernard was cognizant of the monks' interests, his real audience, in his own mind, seems to have been the clerics of northern France whom he names in the last chapter of Book 1 (1.34). He wanted to make his mark among his peers.[37] His text reveals that he was familiar with the classic texts of western hagiography—Gregory the Great's *Dialogues* and Sulpicius Severus's *Life of Saint Martin*. He names the *Psychomachia* of Prudentius as something scholars would have read.

Bernard returned to Conques sometime between 1013 and 1020 and subsequently wrote up a group of miracles that he apparently intended to stand as a second book. In 2.6 he mentions that not long thereafter he was at the court of William V of Aquitaine on business; in 2.7 he relates a third trip to Conques in 1020, when he was accompanied by his secretary, Sigebald. This time, he says, he had no intention of collecting further miracles but had hoped to see once more the subject of his first chapter, Guibert. The miracles he was prevailed on to record during this visit, which may have once been considered a third book, form the second part of Book Two in the manuscript translated here.

The prologue to Book Three clearly announces the death of Bernard and a change of authorship. The monks of Conques now took charge of their saint's stories. It appears that the monk-author of Book Three had Bernard's notes in hand and used them to write up some of the stories Bernard had collected. This book has been dated between 1020 and 1050; Gournay states forcefully that it is closer to 1020.[38] Book Four seems to have been written around the middle of the eleventh century for the most part, and several authors drafted its stylistically diverse chapters. In these later books the interest of the monastic community is often a central concern; the point of view is that of the insider, in strong contrast to Bernard's ethnographic perspective. Concerned to display their learning, the monk-authors laboriously worked in classical references; as one would expect, they had also read standard Christian texts like Gregory of Tours' *Glory of the Martyrs*. In the miracle stories the monk-authors wrote to impress their peers, monks at other monasteries including their own priories; in contrast, their cartulary, the compilation of documents regarding their land holdings and intended mainly for internal and local use, frequently displays a simpler, even ungrammatical Latin with an admixture of local dialect.

The expectation that the title *Book of Miracles* implies a standard text is a modern construct. In fact, of the manuscripts discussed below, no two contain the same stories in the same sequence. Choices were made depending, presumably, on the needs of a specific audience or on the availability of texts to be copied. Bouillet's edition of the *Book of Miracles*, the one translated here, is based on a manuscript at Sélestat in Alsace where there was a priory of Conques (Bibliothèque Humaniste MS lat. 22; formerly Bibliothèque de la Ville MS lat. 95; fols. 15r–104). Miracle stories found in other manuscripts but not in the one at Sélestat were grouped by Bouillet in an appendix. Here they are gathered as "Other Miracles of Sainte Foy."

Translatio: The Translation of Sainte Foy

The earliest extant text describing the secret theft of Sainte Foy's relics from her church at Agen by a monk of Conques was not written until the eleventh century, sometime between 1020 and 1060. It provides more details of the early removal of her relics from their original place of burial to the church built by Dulcidius in Agen than does the brief sketch at the end of the *Passio*. A poem on Foy's *Translatio* composed sometime after 1060 seems to be based entirely on this prose text.[39]

The translation into English offered here is of the text printed in the *Acta Sanctorum* October (6), III, 294–99, which is based on Vatican MS Reg. lat. 467, fols. 6–14. The original manuscript, of which Reg. lat. 467 is a part, was a compilation of materials related to the cult of Sainte Foy. It is described below.

The Song of Sainte Foy

The story of Sainte Foy's Passion was recounted again, in the vernacular, in the Provençal verses of a song known by the title *Chanson de Sainte Foy*.[40] Soutou has argued convincingly that it was written in the Rouergue, most likely at Conques, in about 1065–1070. The language of the *Song* evokes the world of the secular or heroic chanson de geste, for example, in the way that the bonds between Foy and her God are constructed as feudal bonds. Sainte Foy's story is recast into the language of the newly emerging feudal and chivalric society. This poem precedes the earliest known chanson de geste by twenty or thirty years.[41] The probable occasion of its writing returns us to the history of the monastery, for it may well have been written for the transfer of Sainte Foy's relics to the choir of the new church that Abbot Odolric had begun. Marcel Durliat's careful study of the sculptural decoration of this still extant church shows that its eastern parts were completed in the eleventh century.[42] For those with no understanding of Latin, this song could have substituted for the reading during the liturgy of Sainte Foy's

Passio. Some scholars have concluded that mime would have accompanied its performance.[43]

The translation of the *Song of Sainte Foy* in this book was made by Robert L. A. Clark of the Department of Romance Languages, Kansas State University. It is of the only surviving manuscript version, that in the Leiden manuscript (Bibl. univ. Voss. lat. o.60). Clark based his translation on Hoepffner's edition, and consulted the edition by Thomas as well.

Manuscripts and Translation[44]

The manuscript at Sélestat (Bibliothèque Humaniste MS lat. 22; formerly Bibliothèque de la Ville MS lat. 95) is the most complete compilation of texts for Sainte Foy's cult that is still intact. André de Mandach concludes that its oldest portions were written near (if not in) Conques in the late eleventh century, and that additions were made later at Sélestat. Included in the manuscripts are texts useful for the liturgical celebration of the feast of Sainte Foy, such as an Office, prayers, sermons, hymns, and the *Passio*, *Translatio*, and the longest version of the *Book of Miracles*. Denis Grémont has argued that the liturgical texts in this manuscript are different from those used at Conques and are specific to Sélestat; if so, then this manuscript preserves evidence that liturgical practice could differ even in a foundation with a direct relationship to Conques.

Other manuscripts contain different selections of miracles from that of the Sélestat manuscript. The most important of these, and the only one that contains the *Song of Sainte Foy*, suffered dismemberment and is now dispersed among four libraries (Orléans, Bibl. mun., MS 347 [296]; Leiden, Bibl. univ., MS Voss. lat. o.60; Paris, B.N. MS n. a. lat. 443; Vatican, MS Reg. lat. 467). Grémont recognized that these fragments belonged together and described the original contents of the manuscript, which contained materials pertaining to the cult of Mary Magdalene as well as the *Passio*, *Translatio*, chapters of the *Book of Miracles*, and an Office for Sainte Foy. Three miracles unique to this manuscript are translated here in the chapter "Other Miracles of Sainte Foy," where they are numbered V.1 to V.3. It seems most likely that this *libellus*, or book containing materials for a saint's cult, was written at Conques or a daughter house late in the eleventh century and taken to Fleury sometime in the twelfth century.

The abbey at Conques still holds one of the manuscripts of Sainte Foy's miracles, now preserved in the abbey treasury (see Figure 1). It was probably made at Conques not long after Book Four of the *Book of Miracles* was written. Little can be said about the original contents of this manuscript, for most of it is lost; only twenty-seven leaves of Book Four survive. Five miracles recorded there that are not found in Sélestat 22 are translated as C.1 to C.5 in "Other Miracles of Sainte Foy."

Four other miracles numbered here A.1 to A.4 are unique to a manuscript from the Abbey of Saint Peter at Chartres which is now Chartres, Bibliothèque de la Ville, MS lat. 1036. This manuscript, which was completed in 1373, was badly damaged in modern times. Gournay tentatively suggests that these stories were composed in the second half of the eleventh century.[45]

Two fragmentary miracles, once part of a larger manuscript, survive on a parchment leaf used in the binding of a sixteenth-century manuscript made at Conques. This leaf, along with another from the same manuscript, is now designated Rodez, Arch. dep. de l'Aveyron, 2 E 67.4.[46] According to Lemaître this manuscript was produced at Conques in the twelfth century.[47] Gournay suggests a date of about 1100 for the composition of the miracle stories.[48] In "Other Miracles of Sainte Foy" these fragments are R.1 and R.2.

The most recent miracles of Sainte Foy translated here are found in an English manuscript of the second half of the twelfth century (London, B. L., MS Arundel lat. 91). They were probably composed in the first half of the century. Here they are designated L.1 to L.6.

The Translation

Though all the texts translated here (except the *Song of Sainte Foy*) were originally written in Latin, they differ from one another in many ways, including style, grammatical correctness, and vocabulary. In general, they follow the evolution of the language from more classical to more medieval forms.

Bernard of Angers wrote good Latin; he had a fairly clear understanding of the subjunctive, and wrote sentences replete with dependent clauses, eschewing the paratactic structure of much medieval Latin. His vocabulary contains few neologisms and employs very little vernacular. His letter to Fulbert of Chartres that introduces his text follows the formulae in use for letter-writing. As is probably to be expected in addressing his teacher, Bernard writes more complex Latin than in any of his miracle stories. He is concerned about the quality of his writing and chides the monks for allowing some of his chapters to circulate before he had put them in final form. The monks writing later in the eleventh century in Books Three and Four are less skillful in their manipulation of the language.

The *Translatio*'s distinctive style makes frequent use of relative pronouns and of the subjunctive. The vocabulary employs nouns that are formed from classical Latin verbs but are known only in medieval Latin.

By the time we reach the miracle stories in the Chartres, Rodez, and London manuscripts, the Latin in use follows a simpler sentence structure and has no regard for correct use of the subjunctive. The rhetorical flourishes so dear to Bernard have completely disappeared. The writer of the miracles in the London manuscript cannot resist punning on the saint's name.

Throughout, I have used first person singular where the text uses first person plural, in order to avoid the artificial connotations of the "royal we" in English. I consistently translate the name Sancta Fides as Sainte Foy because she is so imbedded in local culture. Some wordplay is thereby lost in translation, as, for example, in 4.22: "Saint Faith, perceiving his faith . . ." but it is rather surprising how seldom this obvious pun is made.

Biblical quotations are from the Vulgate, either my own or the Douay-Reims translation, which I have sometimes modified for clarity.

As discussed above, the word *miles*, *milites* is used in the *Book of Miracles* to designate men who live in castles, and can refer both to the castellan and to his men; I have translated it occasionally as "lord," more frequently as "warrior," and rarely as just "man." I have avoided the later meaning of "knight" because it suggests a chivalric code of behavior foreign to this society. The word *villa* referred originally to a large country estate owned by a wealthy Gallo-Roman family. By the time our texts were written, the term may simply designate the contiguous territory that once belonged to such an estate. In translation I have used either "country estate" or "territory." Where places can be identified, their names have been given in modern French.

Notes have been supplied to identify named persons and places and when necessary for the understanding of the text. I have tried to avoid excessive annotation so that the reader may approximate to the medieval experience of these miracles, that is, as narratives, stories rather than as historical documents burdened by apparatus. I have found the notes in the edition of Latin text and the French translation in Bouillet and Servières very useful and have relied on them heavily.

A translator offers one reading from what often seems a bewilderingly

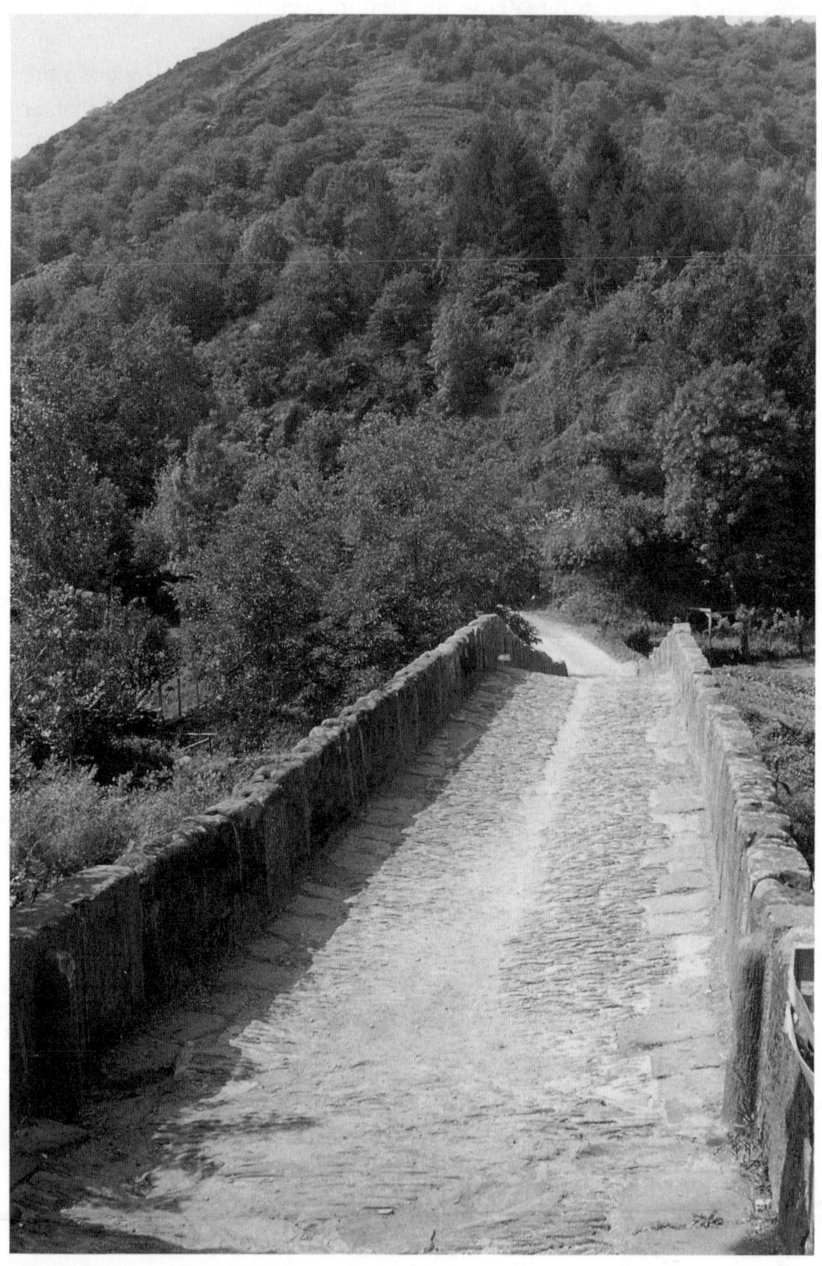

11. Bridge over which pilgrims left Conques on their way to Santiago de Compostela. Photo: Marilyn Deegan.

large number of choices. Only by consulting the text in its original language can the reader judge whether these choices represent a consistent and reasonably faithful rendering of the author's words. This book will have served its purpose if it motivates some of its readers to search out those words.

Conclusion

In the late twentieth century a visit to Conques remains a memorable experience. Preserved as a historical site of the first class, Conques manages, to a surprising degree, to stand apart from the clatter and confusion of today's urban life. Tourists come, great numbers of them, but pilgrims always came, and Conques receives them graciously and lends them its tranquil beauty for the duration of their (usually) short stay. Walking its steep, narrow cobblestone streets that offer memorable vistas onto the church and across deep gorges at every turn, tracing the steps of medieval pilgrims over the ridge and down into the village, across the Romanesque bridge spanning the Dourdou River (see Figure 11), the visitor feels not so much the collapse of time into the past, for too much has changed for such easy access even in so special a place, but a moment when the Middle Ages seem not quite so remote, the otherness of those distant centuries diminishes just a little. This book offers the experience of text, not of place, but with the same goal in mind.

Passio: The Passion of Sainte Foy

The sixth of October, the Passion of Sainte Foy, virgin and martyr.[1]

When it comes to relating the merit-filled Passions of the great and illustrious saints Caprais[2] and Foy, words do not suffice to lavish on them the praises they deserve. Out of envy for Christian religion, antiquity wished to remain silent about their deeds and miracles rather than to leave behind any monuments with inscriptions that would commend them to some human memory thereafter. I have found a great deal of information in narratives of their acts, and I have briefly related a few things about them in a stammering style. But where shall I begin, when I know so many praiseworthy things about these most blessed martyrs? I could neither attempt nor complete such a glorious task if I hadn't been fully supplied with the authoritative opinions of the Fathers of the Church and set aflame by the splendor of the ancient poets. For it is easier to recognize the merits of the martyrs Caprais and Foy through their powers than to set forth their praises. My talent is so feeble and barren that I am disheartened, but the intense devotion rooted deep in my heart holds these saints before me as inspiring models. And if my tongue stops performing its function, that is, praising the saints, it shall still be my will to serve them with faithful devotion. Therefore this text of their blessed Passion honors their deeds insofar as God's abundant gifts have allowed me to reach that goal. I have selected a few outstanding things from the great many pages that have been written about them at various times, and I have presented these things with the same faith and devotion with which knowledge of the martyrs was handed down to us. For the deeds of these saints have not fallen into oblivion but have been remembered by being told. And if particular cities and places consider themselves outstanding because they possess particular martyrs, this is only just, because these martyrs gave up their lives for the Lord Jesus Christ.

Sainte Foy was born of noble parents in the city of Agen.[3] Through her birth she became a very illustrious daughter of that place, but through her death she became its patron. She was noble because she came from an old and high-born family, but she was made more noble by Christ's gift: the glistening white garment of virginity and faith in her Lord Jesus Christ, in which she shone brightly and fragrantly. She was the first in the city of Agen to receive the crown of a martyr's Passion; she was its glory and its model of a great martyr. She wished to lose her earthly life in order to have eternal life because from her early childhood she loved the Lord Jesus Christ and said that He had created her. It is reported that she was a young girl at the time of her Passion, but both in her understanding and her actions she seemed to have the maturity that belongs to advanced age. She was beautiful in appearance, but her mind was more beautiful.

When a judge came to a city, it was customary for him to promise his favor and good will to idolators and to persecute vigorously any Christians that were found. During that time a prefect named Dacian[4] entered the city and immediately ordered that blessed Foy be summoned; he directed that she be led into his presence.

But when blessed Foy was being brought by his wicked servants she prayed to the Lord, saying, "Lord Jesus Christ, You Who always aid Your own in every circumstance, be present now with Your handmaiden and supply acceptable words to my mouth, which I may give in answer before this tyrant." And she armed herself with an unconquerable shield, making the sign of the holy cross on her forehead, mouth, and heart, and so she went on with her spirit strengthened.

But when Foy stood in the prefect's presence, he spoke gently to her, saying, "What is your name?"

Sainte Foy felt no fear. She answered, "I am called Foy."

The prefect said, "What faith do you follow?"

Blessed Foy replied, "From my earliest youth I have been a Christian, and I serve the Lord Jesus Christ with complete devotion."

The prefect said, "Take the advice required by your beauty and your youth and abandon this religion. Sacrifice to holy Diana, because her cult suits your sex, and I will enrich you with many gifts."

But Sainte Foy was filled with the Holy Spirit and said, "I know from the teachings of the Fathers that all the gods of the heathens are demons, and you wish to persuade me that I ought to sacrifice to them?"

The prefect's anger was aroused when he heard this, and he said to her, "Since you have dared to say that our gods are demons, either sacrifice to the gods, or I shall see to it that you die in all kinds of torments."

But when Sainte Foy heard these threats, she understood that she would be honored with the great glory of martyrdom. She was desirous of migrating from earthly life to heavenly glory and she burst out with these words: "For the name of my Lord Jesus Christ I have been prepared not only to be threatened but to suffer all kinds of torments."

Then the prefect burned with great fury. He ordered his men to carry in a bronze bed[5] and place Sainte Foy on it. And he commanded that she be stretched out to its four corners and that fire be set underneath so that her tender body might be broken to pieces by a torture so cruel.

Seeing this, those who were present cried out in one voice, "O wicked and unjust justice! She is innocent, a worshiper of God. She stands out among people of high rank. Why is she being punished when she hasn't committed any crime?"

For there were many whose names we do not know who saw Sainte Foy's constancy that day. They believed in the Lord Jesus Christ and acquired a martyr's glorious crown.

During this time, Saint Caprais, whom God had chosen, was moving about from hiding place to hiding place, along with the other Christians in that land, because the idolator's persecution raged fiercely. Outstanding among those who worshiped God, Caprais anxiously examined all these hiding places and hastily settled on a rock shelter lying not far from the northern part of the city. Still stunned by what was happening, he was deep in thought as he turned over all his secret plans in his mind. Then he saw Sainte Foy being tortured by an uncountable number of wicked punishments. And so he lifted up his eyes and gazed heavenward; he poured out many prayers to the Lord, asking Him to grant the victory to His own handmaiden in her present contest. Again Christ's athlete looked up to heaven with complete mental concentration, and again he prostrated himself on the ground and asked the Lord to show her His heavenly power. Then Caprais saw above Sainte Foy a crown, decorated with bright, glittering gems and celestial pearls, and a dove descending from the clouds placed the crown on Sainte Foy's head. And he saw the blessed martyr adorned with a brilliant snow-white garment radiant with bright light. Then he understood that she had already attained the palm of triumph and the prize of victory, which was eternal salvation. And when Caprais had seen all the miraculous power of God manifestly in his own sight, he rejoiced because of the joys of eternity. Then Saint Caprais grew fearless; he was going to go to glory with merits equal to hers. With his right hand he struck the rock that had sheltered him and at once a spring of water arose, which flows without fail to the present day. Because of the holy martyr's merit, God has deigned to make His power so abundantly present there that whoever drinks from that spring who had been possessed by any kind of illness receives healing medicine.

Joyful, eager, and undaunted, Caprais slipped away without being seen and unexpectedly went to the place of martyrdom where Sainte Foy had been taken and where she was undergoing torture. At once the wicked tyrant ordered that Caprais be brought before him, but Caprais came eagerly into the prefect's presence. The prefect asked him his name, what country and what family he was from. Blessed Caprais answered him, saying, "The principal and outstanding thing about me is that I am a Christian. I was reborn when I was baptized by a priest who confirmed my name of Caprais."

The prefect wanted to persuade Caprais with flattery, so he said, "I see that you are an extremely handsome young man; if you heed my words you will be able to be called the first in the palace and you will obtain the friendship of the ruler as well as great gain for yourself."

But Saint Caprais kept in mind the heavenly miracles he had seen and said, "My desire is to live in the palace of Him Whom I have loved since my baptism, and I know that He is the Redeemer of all who believe in Him."

The prefect said, "I want to deal with you in such a way that you receive the gains for yourself that I have already promised."

Saint Caprais said, "I believe that whoever is faithful to His words and holy in all his deeds receives from Him gain without end."

Now the prefect saw that neither Caprais's mind nor his words could be changed, so he said to his men, "I am afraid to dispute with this man any longer, for I have a forboding that if I go on he may tire me and win the day."

Then he ordered his attendants to seize Caprais and to rend his flesh without pity. And when this was done, Caprais bore the pain bravely. Everyone there who saw the youth tortured with every kind of cruel torment was filled with distress. Their eyes were wet with tears and they cried out, "What a wicked and unheard-of judgment!" because the blessed martyr Caprais was beloved by all and he had an angelically handsome face. But no force was strong enough to overcome the spirit of this glorious martyr, neither verbal disputation, nor flattery, nor torture. And so the prefect ordered that he be led to a temple and along with the blessed Foy he was crowned with the glory of martyrdom, for their struggle was completed when their heads were struck off.[6] In this way their lives, which had been beautiful, worthy of respect, and pleasing to God, were more beautifully and unfadingly happy in the fellowship of the martyrs. We count the city of Agen a worthy and joyous place, for it merited to be the birthplace of martyrs, the site of their glorious struggle and burial.[7]

He wishes us to rejoice over and to retell the Passion of these martyrs on the day before the nones of October, He Who glories in His saints, the Lord Jesus Christ, to Whom is honor and glory forever and ever. Amen.[8]

At that time in the place where she was martyred the pagans were inflicting such terror that Christians feared to bury a body in the ground. She did not not receive a worthy grave, for it seems that the martyr's venerable and holy relics were not exactly buried but rather hidden,[9] and so remained until Saint Dulcidius became bishop of the city of Agen.[10] At once he devoted himself to the task of building a beautiful basilica in which the body of the holy martyr would be buried. With his meritorious support it was constructed swiftly. But when the time came for the service of venerating and transferring the martyr's relics, Dulcidius was hesitant. This was not due to his own unbelief; rather, out of reverence for her honor he did not presume to open such an important tomb nor to move the holy relics for fear that he would injure them by losing some part of her body. Therefore for a long time Dulcidius turned this problem over in his mind until a dream gave him to understand that he should not unfaithfully neglect what he had faithfully believed. He saw that moving the relics would bring honor to the martyrs and salvation to believers, and he was strengthened in his resolve by the counsel of his own monks and many other people. So blessed Dulcidius came to her venerable resting place accompanied by a crowd. All agreed that they wanted the holy relics to be moved, so they made an attempt, applying their hands to complete the task.

But then a shudder of awe and terror ran through all the Christians; they were in a kind of mental stupor and all their voices stuck in their throats. Therefore all the people standing there, both men and women, together with the priests, threw themselves down onto their knees in prayer. When Bishop Dulcidius rose from prayer he set his hand to the task of moving the glorious martyr's tomb and—marvelous to report!—he lifted it with just his own hand. The litter on which they bore her arrived at the agreed-upon place in the basilica so swiftly and speedily that the strong men who were there to carry it seemed to follow along rather than to bear any weight. There she was entombed so beautifully that afterward everyone agreed that she had demanded it herself for her own benefit.[11] The place of her first burial did not lose its holiness, but acquired the grace of sanctification through an effusion of blood, a gift that celebrated the holy body's presence there. Then her tomb gained the same benefit and merit, so that when anyone invoked her faithfully, she was at hand as an intercessor before the Lord Jesus Christ, to Whom, with the eternal Father, is glory forever and ever. Amen.

Liber miraculorum sancte Fidis: The Book of Sainte Foy's Miracles

The beginning of the book of miracles of holy and most blessed Foy, virgin and martyr, related by Bernard, a teacher,[1] master at the school of Angers.

A letter to the lord Fulbert, bishop of Chartres.

To the holiest and most learned of men, Fulbert, bishop of Chartres, Bernard, the least of teachers, sends a gift of supreme blessedness.[2]

During the time when I was at Chartres, where I had the benefit of your sound conversation,[3] I often visited the little church of the martyr Sainte Foy located outside the walls of the city, either to write or to pray there. I also remember that many times when we had gathered for discussion we happened onto the subject of Sainte Foy and her miracles, which took place constantly with the help of Christ omnipotent in the monastery at Conques where her sacrosanct body is reverently venerated. Partly because it seemed to be the common people who promulgated these miracles and partly because they were regarded as new and unusual, we put no faith in them and rejected them as so much worthless fiction. Nevertheless, what was true through God's will could not be suppressed and belief in its truth was already spreading through all Europe.

Little by little a plan took root in my heart, and although I kept it secret I couldn't forget it; it was a plan to go to the holy martyr's dwelling-place to fulfill my desire to learn about her. Finally the matter returned to my mind so forcefully that I marked down in a little notebook the time and day by which I vowed to go there, so that I wouldn't forget. Meanwhile I had a reason for moving to the city of Angers, for the bishop of that city had implored me to come.[4] For almost three years I wasted time there that should have been used for study on behalf of stupid good-for-nothings — I may as well admit the truth—and the date by which I had vowed to visit Conques passed by. I thought that I was waiting for a good opportunity, but since I was increasingly involved in various duties, I was actually deceived by false hope. I was just like a fish caught in a net—the more I tried to become disentangled, the more entangled I was by increasingly serious problems. Finally, however, lest I should seem to be using the excuse of adversity as a pretext for idleness—although I was becoming more and more aware that these hidden and almost inescapable snares had been prepared for me with diabolical trickery and, in short, that through the skill of the Enemy I was being discouraged from planning to implement my good intentions—all at once I put off the business at hand and with God's guidance I succeeded in reaching my goal, the mausoleum of the glorious martyr.

Since the time of my arrival here I have begun to inquire diligently about Sainte Foy's miracles. Such a great number of miracles have poured forth from various narrators that if my mind had not been burningly eager to hear them my brain would have been overwhelmed with weariness. But I myself have been fortunate enough to see the very man whose eyes were violently plucked out by the roots and afterward restored to their natural state, intact and whole. And I can see him even as I write this. Since he himself asserts that this really happened and the whole province attests to it, I know that it is true. Therefore I think that his story ought to be introduced first as the basis for reading the rest of the miracles, and not just my interpretation of his meaning, but word for word as I hear it from his lips;[5] not abbreviated, but in a narrative long enough to satisfy my readers. To his story I have decided to append only a very few miracles so that I can return home quickly. As to the other miracles that remain, I have noted down the more beautiful ones swiftly and with the greatest brevity, but only those that are not older than our own time, and whose eyewitnesses told me not an invented tale but the clearest truth. I am resolved, with God as my guide, to carry these notes back home with me. When I have leisure time for more careful work, I shall make a fuller text for the future reader out of this material.

Therefore, most learned of mortals, when you have received these miracles, correct only the way in which they are written. For, although I am unlearned and ignorant in the art of composition, nevertheless I was not gullible when I listened and I did not easily believe what I heard. But it may seem to you that my foul pen is unequal to the material and has sullied it. If so, you will not offend me by adopting such a noble and glorious theme as your own; you will embellish with a noble and glorious style, since all agree that you stand alone at the pinnacle of wisdom. For if the truth in these stories has been corrupted by my bad style, readers will turn away in disgust and this best of subjects will have been debased. To write up such excellent material myself, thereby degrading those wise scholars who could have done it better, would have been the height of wickedness and presumption if the very fact that I have made the material widely available does not protect me from the charge of harmful boldness. Let me state the case more clearly: it is better that miracles from heaven be committed to writing now, while they are recent and cannot be doubted, no matter what the style, by a scholar however unlearned save in knowing the truth, than to leave this material waiting for the unlikely possibility that a writer who would convey their message with indifference might appear from some unknown part of the world. Therefore I do not judge myself to be so culpable if I strive to the best of my ability to record the works of divine grace on behalf of humankind, when the very scarcity of writers strongly insists that I do it.

And, future readers, I warn you not to be thrown into confusion by the way this work is organized and not to look for a chronological sequence of events. The urgent necessity of returning to Angers did not permit me to complete my investigations in Conques, so I have limited myself to those miracles whose omission would do harm to the results. Therefore here in the writing of this book about Sainte Foy's miracles, which I begin to put together with God as my fellow-worker, the miracles will be grouped not in chronological sequence but by the similarity of their subject matter. I have very diligently investigated to determine the inviolable truth of these miracles. Because there is nothing truer, I implore you to bring faith wholeheartedly to my narration so that later you will not regret that you disparaged a holy martyr. Better yet, if the unusual novelty of the miraculous content disturbs you, I prostrate myself on the ground to beg this of your brotherhood: that after my return you also come here, not so much to pray as to gain knowledge through experience. For through lack of experience you might prematurely judge something false whose truth, once you have seen it for yourselves, you will proclaim thereafter.

The end of the letter.

The First Book of Sainte Foy's Miracles

1.1. How Guibert's Eyes Were Restored by Sainte Foy After They Had Been Torn Out by the Roots
1.2. A Similar Miracle About Gerbert
1.3. How a Mule Was Revived from Death
1.4. Another Miracle like the Preceding One
1.5. How a Man Was Killed in a Headlong Fall While He Was Attacking One of Sainte Foy's Monks
1.6. How Divine Vengeance Acted Against Those Who Wanted to Steal the Monks' Wine
1.7. A Commentary That Confirms the Preceding Narratives
1.8. How Guy Died
1.9. About a Widow's Blind Daughter
1.10. How Celestial Vengeance Struck a Man Who Attacked Sainte Foy's Pilgrims
1.11. How a Man Who Was Slandering Sainte Foy Was Destroyed by the Sudden Collapse of a Roof
1.12. About a Man Who Perished When He Was Struck by Lightning
1.13. How It Should Be Permitted That Statues of Saints Are Made Because It Is an Ineradicable and Innate Custom of Simple People, and Especially Because It Detracts Nothing from Religion; and About Divine Vengeance
1.14. About a Man Who Wished That the Image Would Fall
1.15. About a Girl Who Was Scornful of Standing for the Image
1.16. The Miracle of the Golden Doves
1.17. How Sainte Foy Collected Gold Everywhere for the Fashioning of an Altar
1.18. How a Ring Was Denied to Sainte Foy and Later Handed Over to Her
1.19. About Golden Bracelets
1.20. About a Pilgrim Who Gave Sainte Foy a Ring so That She Would be Freed from Her Pains
1.21. About a Pilgrim Who Wanted to Exchange a Ring Promised in a Vow
1.22. About a Woman Who Wrongfully Seized a Ring That Another Woman Had Bequeathed to Sainte Foy When She Was Dying
1.23. How a Falcon Was Found
1.24. A Dishonest Merchant

1.1: How Guibert's Eyes Were Restored by Sainte Foy After They Had Been Torn Out by the Roots[6]

Up to the present time in the district[7] of Rouergue where the most blessed virgin Foy rests, in the neighborhood of the village of Conques, there dwells, still alive, a priest named Gerald.[8] This priest had a blood relative who was also, according to the sacrament of confirmation administered by the bishop, his godson.[9] His name was Guibert; he was Gerald's household servant and vigorously managed his business affairs. Once Guibert had made his way to Conques for the feast day, and after the nighttime activity of the vigil was completed according to custom, on the next day, that is on the feast day itself, he was returning by the same road on which he had gone. Then he had the bad fortune to meet his master, who was aroused by a secret hatred against him that was motivated by jealousy. When the priest saw Guibert close at hand in a pilgrim's garb, his initial approach was peaceful:

"Look at you, Guibert, you've been made a *romeus*, I see," for that is what they call pilgrims of the saints in that country.[10]

And Guibert answered, "That's right, master, I'm returning from Sainte Foy's feast."

Then Gerald, pretending to be friendly, inquired about some other matters and gave Guibert permission to depart. But although he went on himself a little way, the priest — as treasonous as a Jew![11] — (if it is right that a man is called "priest" who corrupts the priesthood with sacrilege), turned back and ordered Guibert to wait for him for a little while. Coming after Guibert, Gerald ordered his men to hold him and they soon boxed him in on both sides.

When Guibert saw what was happening he began to tremble with great fear, and he asked of what crime he was being accused. The treacherous man gave this menacing answer:

"You have done a wicked thing to me, and you are preparing to do worse; that's why I'll be satisfied with nothing less than your very own eyes as punishment."

But he did not describe the kind of crime more clearly and pretended that this was out of a sense of decency. For surely it is disgraceful for priests to render judgment based on their own jealousy. In fact the cause of this trouble had arisen from the suspicion of debauchery with a woman.[12] Guibert was quite confident that he could offer an explanation for anything for which he was blamed, so he said, "Look, master, if you would accuse me openly of any crime of which you suspect me, I am prepared to defend myself according to law. I don't think anything can be found for which I deserve to incur your anger and that of your followers."

Gerald replied, "You might as well stop defending yourself with useless double-talk, for all is lost already. I have pronounced the sentence — you lose your eyes."

Guibert saw that Gerald was determined to be his executioner and that the inexorable hour of his destruction was at hand. He perceived that no room was left for any pleading but, even though he despaired of his safety at that moment, he cried out, "Master, I beg you, spare me, if not because of my innocence, at least for the love of God and Sainte Foy — it's for love of her that I'm wearing a pilgrim's sacred garment at this very moment."

But this fierce monster, who thought highly neither of God nor of His saint, gnashed his teeth, roared with savage fury, and spewed out the blasphemous poison he had held in for a long time in the form of these sacrilegious words: "Neither God nor Sainte Foy will free you today, and you won't succeed in escaping from my hands unpunished by calling on them. And don't think there's a chance that I'll view you as reputable and protected from attack out of respect for pilgrim's clothing, when you have been so wickedly unjust to me!"

Then he ordered that Guibert be thrown down headlong and that the eyes of this innocent man be torn out violently. He couldn't persuade any of his men to commit such a crime (they were only three and I pass over their names because of my distaste for barbaric language), but he at least succeeded with his order that they hold Guibert down. Then Gerald suddenly slid off his horse and, with the very fingers with which he usually touched the sacrosanct body of Christ, he violently tore out the eyes of his own godson and tossed them carelessly to the ground. But divine power was not absent, for it does not leave unheard those who importune heaven's care; it is always present near those invoking it in truth and renders a favorable judgment for those suffering injury. Those who were there were fortunate enough to see that a snow-white dove appeared instantly (or, as the perpetrator of the crime tells it, it was a magpie). The magpie or dove at that very hour took up from the ground the wretch's eyes, which were covered with fresh blood. The bird flew above the mountaintops and appeared to descend to Conques with its burden.

Don't be amazed that God entrusted the rescue of Guibert's eyes in the wilderness to a winged magpie, for in time past He used ravens to send food to Elijah in the desert.[13] Or perhaps, in accordance with divine will, an ambiguously marked bird came, which could be clearly recognized neither as a magpie nor as a dove. But the men who saw the bird didn't see any ambiguity. The others in fact perceived a dove clothed in white, but Gerald asserted that he had seen none other than a magpie adorned with black and white. Just as God will seem terrifying to the wicked but gentle to the just, it could also have happened that the form had seemed to be white to those innocent men who groaned inwardly at the sight of the crime, while to the criminal it had seemed to be of mixed colors.

Nevertheless, when the sacrilegous Gerald saw the bird he was led to repentance and began to weep profusely. One of his companions told him this weeping was in vain and too late. Then Gerald departed, and from that time forward the scoundrel didn't undertake the celebration of the holy mass, either because of the crime he had perpetrated or, as seems more likely, because he neglected it altogether in favor of secular business.

But Gerald's mother was moved by strong feeling for the innocent, wounded man. She took Guibert into her house and very kindly supplied everything he needed until his health was restored. His living in her house at that time was scarcely at the behest of his master but rather was to avoid his ferocity, for Gerald had continued to be stirred up against Guibert by the same gossip that had originally pierced his heart with the wound of false jealousy. At last Guibert regained his health and during that year sought his living with his skill as a jongleur. He received such a profit from it that—as he is in the habit of saying—he didn't care to have his eyes thereafter because both the lust for wealth and the enjoyment of income delighted him so much.

And in this way a year unfolded and the day of the feast was at hand. On the day before the vigil, while Guibert lay in a deep sleep, a little girl of indescribable grace seemed to stand near him. Her appearance was angelic and quite serene, and her countenance was a dazzling white, besprinkled drop by drop with a rosy blush.[14] The lively expression on her wondrous face exceeded all human charm. Her size, in truth, was what it is said to have been at the time of her Passion, that is, she had the stature of a young girl, not yet advanced in age. Her clothing was very flowing and interwoven with the most elegant gold throughout, and delicate, colored embroidery encircled it. Her long sleeves, which hung down to her feet, had been delicately gathered into very tiny pleats on account of their fullness. And the band entwined in a circle about her head gleamed with two pairs of translucent, glossy white pearls. Indeed the form of the little body seemed to me to signify nothing other than what is said regarding the time of her Passion, that is, just as I already indicated, that she was young.

However, the character of her face and her marvelous style of dress—insofar as it was possible for Guibert to discern them—were, I think, not without a reason, for these things carry in themselves a very clear portent. If we are able to accept her clothes exceeding the measure of her person as the armor or protection of abounding faith, then the golden radiance of her clothing figures overtly the illumination of spiritual grace. Why the delicacy of the embroidery or the pleating of the sleeves if they do not reveal that she was clothed in divine wisdom? And, rightly, on the principal part of the body, that is, on the head, four gems were seen, through which we are able to observe clearly the quadrivium of the cardinal virtues: prudence, justice, fortitude, and temperance. Sainte Foy, because she had understanding of these and perfection in them, and because she was deeply inspired by the Holy Spirit, also cultivated most perfectly in her heart the remaining virtues that are derived from these. She pleased the Almighty in every way and therefore was not unacquainted with the highest good. To holy martyrdom, to Christ, she offered herself as a sacrifice, a voluntary and pure holocaust.

As to her face, I mentioned it first in my description because I learned of it first from my informant. Nevertheless I place it last in my exposition, because in her face I see a figure of the aim and pinnacle of her whole life, for

I perceive that the whiteness of her face signifies charity. As a matter of fact, it is appropriate that through whiteness, which conquers other colors by its own radiance, charity, the most perfect of virtues, is understood. I mentioned the whiteness of her face before describing her blush (which implies martyrdom), as did my informant, not inappropriately, because there is no way to attain to the grace of martyrdom without the preeminence of charity. Foy, God's dearest and most beloved, held to this virtue invincibly, since for love of it she eagerly sought out the untimely bitterness of death.

But soon—I return to my subject—this same most blessed Foy, leaning on the bedpost and slowly and sweetly reaching out her hand toward the right cheek of the sleeper, spoke:

"Are you sleeping, Guibert?"

"Who are you who calls me?"

"I am Sainte Foy."

"What is the reason, my lady, that you come to me?"

"None other but to see you."

Guibert thanked her, and Sainte Foy asked him in turn:

"Do you recognize me?"

But he identified her as if he had already seen her and seemed to answer in this way:

"Indeed I see you clearly, my lady, and I recognize you perfectly well."

"Tell me also how you are situated," she said, "and how your affairs prosper."

"Most satisfactorily, my lady. Fortune advances my affairs and all things, thanks to God, go prosperously for me."

"And what do you mean 'prosperously,'" she said, "when you do not see the light of heaven?"

For, just as people sometimes perceive themselves differently in dreams from the way they actually are, Guibert thought he could see. This last question reminded him of his missing eyes:

"And how," he asked, "could I see? I am the wretch who lost his eyes to the violence of an unjust master when I was returning from your feast day a year ago."

"The man who condemned you to bodily harm without cause," she said, "has greatly offended God and seriously provoked the anger of the Highest Creator. But if tomorrow, the vigil of my martyrdom, you go to Conques, purchase two candles, and place one in front of the altar of the Holy Savior and the other in front of the altar where the clay of my body is enshrined, you will have a proper reason to rejoice because your eyes will be wholly restored. I raised an immense outcry on account of the injury inflicted on you, and with it I swayed the goodness of the Heavenly Judge to mercy. I importuned God for your health with the diligent presence of my prayer so long, until He returned a favorable and sympathetic outcome to my pleas."

After she had given Guibert these instructions she began to insist repeatedly that he should set out and that he should proceed energetically and swiftly. Since he was unsure about finding the money for the wax necessary to his healing, she instructed him more firmly and advised him in this way:

"A thousand people whom you have never seen," she said, "are going to give you alms. But so that you may complete the present business more easily, before that, go speedily at today's dawn to the church of this parish" (doubtless this was near the place where he had lost his eyes; it has been called Spariacus since ancient times)[15] "and hear mass. You will find a man there who will give you six deniers."

But while Guibert was expressing to her the gratitude she deserved for the kindness of her consolation, this divine power returned to heaven. Now awake, Guibert immediately sought out the parish church and recounted the whole vision in sequence to all who were present. They thought it was absurd nonsense, but Guibert didn't give up. He kept canvassing those crowded around him, one by one, asking them to pledge twelve deniers. Finally a man named Hugh came forward and put into Guibert's open money-pouch a donation of six sols and one obol, which just exceeded the amount mentioned in the vision.[16] Then Guibert remembered the divine vision and became more certain that its promise would be fulfilled. What more do I need to say? He went to Conques, he related the vision to the monastic officials, he bought the candles, he placed them in front of the altars, and he kept the vigil near the most holy martyr's golden image.

At about midnight it seemed to Guibert that he saw two light-filled globes like berries, scarcely larger than the fruit of the laurel tree, which were sent from above and driven deeply into the sockets of his excised eyes. The force of the impact disturbed his brain and in a state of bewilderment he fell asleep. But when they were singing the praises of matins he was awakened by the choir and the loud voices of those chanting the psalms, and it seemed to him that he could make out the shadowy forms of shining lamps and people moving about. But because of the pain in his head he had almost forgotten who he was. Since he could hardly believe the truth, he thought he was dreaming. Finally the dullness that had taken over his brain gradually disappeared, and he began to make out the shapes of things more clearly. Scarcely returned to full consciousness, he recalled his vision, and reaching up with his hands he touched the windows of his reborn light with their perfectly restored pupils. Immediately he summoned witnesses and proclaimed the immeasurable greatness of Christ with boundless praise. Therefore there was unutterable joy, unimaginable gladness, incredible bewilderment. They didn't know what to think, especially those who had known Guibert before—should they understand such an unheard-of miracle as the fancy of a dream or as a true event?

In the midst of all this something happened that was amusing and richly deserving of laughter, for, since Guibert was a very simple and unsophisticated man, unnecessary and fearful anxiety crept into his heart. He was afraid that by chance the man who had once wrenched out his eyes had attended the liturgical celebration (which, as usual, was public), and that, if he should encounter the priest, then Gerald, relying on his greater force, would once more destroy the renewed glory of his eyes. Because of this fear and because the confused racket of the crowd reacting to the miracle made it possible, he slipped away secretly. The bewilderment of it all had taken such possession of him that he wasn't yet fully certain about the gift of regained sight. In the press of the crowd converging on the church, now in clear daylight, he bumped against a donkey standing in the way. When he had looked at it, he scolded severely: "Hey there, whoever you are, you fool, get your donkey out of the way or people will stumble over it."

This was when he fully accepted the truth of what had happened.

Then Guibert fled swiftly to a warrior he knew, whose castle was located on a high cliff. Nature had fortified it on all sides so that it seemed inaccessible to every kind of siege machine. This stronghold was not more than sixteen miles from Conques. Guibert took refuge there because of the protection of its impregnable walls, and only with difficulty and with many a prayer was he extracted by the monks. He returned only when he was assured of complete security. Because of the unusual miracle, a great many people from both near and far flocked to see him, vying with one another in their haste. As they left they demonstrated their joy by conferring on him many pious donations. And, as I said, this is what Sainte Foy told him when she appeared to him in the vision, "A thousand people whom you have never seen are going to give you alms." As is customary in the Scriptures, she used a definite number to indicate an indefinite one.

In order to provide easier access to the miracle and to give Guibert a more established place to live, Abbot Arladus of blessed memory, with the unanimous consent of the brothers, put him in charge of selling wax, a large amount of which was sold there due to the bountiful hand of God. From these sales he received much profit and he began—for it is in the nature of humankind—to grow arrogant. He found a likeminded and unchaste woman, and immediately he forgot the greatness of the miracle done for him. But then, so that he shouldn't go unpunished for profaning the miracle, suddenly the holy virgin's avenging displeasure was at hand. She blinded him in one eye, but did not utterly destroy it.[17] Then she led him back to the cure of repentance and healed him for the second time with renewed sight. But when he slipped back again and again into his habitual hog wallowing, divine vengeance soon followed: he lost the sight of one eye and repenting, recovered.[18] For every time this happened, I would have been able to write a little chapter of miracles, if I hadn't avoided a taste for redundancy. But finally, because he had fallen into the same behavior without interruption, Guibert lost the service of the other eye. Then, in order to repent of his faults more completely, he shaved his beard, had his head tonsured, and, seeking to become a monk, gave himself over to the order. Although he did this as an ignorant and unlettered person, nevertheless it pleased divine mercy so much that he was fortunate enough to regain his eyesight. But even after so many chastizing scourges Guibert was still unable to restrain his lust. It is reported that he sank into the same mire, although no bodily punishment followed. Now he is an old man, impoverished and held in contempt because of his shameless activity. He lives on the common dole provided by the brothers and is content with very little, very often just with an evening meal. He rejoices merely in easing his hunger, safe from the trouble of all his folly.

I bear witness to Divine Providence that in writing this text I have kept to the truth as I received it from Guibert himself. It is free of any deceitful lies, and I haven't added more than is proper to render it suitable. Moreover I don't imagine that I would be able to escape unpunished if I thought that Sainte Foy herself—beloved and perpetual friend of God—would rejoice at praise from a lying pen, when it is undisputed that she underwent the grievous sentence of martyrdom on behalf of the truth which is Christ. Finally, it is well known that many whose authority is generally accepted were content to skillfully describe marvelous events much previous to their time, when the source was only one oral informant who wasn't even present when the thing happened. Then why should I allow something that happens in my own time to go unrecorded in the accounts of history when I even see it myself with my eyes, and Auvergne, the Rouergue, the Toulousain, and all the rest of the people offer their unshakeable witness to it? I must consider my duty as a teacher, especially when, as I said before, the very indifference of writers—which is the reason that such an insignificant little man as myself presumes such perilous and difficult material—vehemently compells me. For if even a rare literary scholar is found anywhere in this country, he either disdains to write down material like this for his own reasons or he does not appreciate the nature of the material and disregards it entirely. Or it could be because of slothful laziness or ignorance in composition. And even supposing that there were a great many people who took pride in the expression of their skill, those who assert that they are highly skilled reveal themselves, by the very act of self-praise, to be the least competent.

Therefore I have resolved rather to be blamed for daring too much than to incur the guilt of negligence. I will devote myself to putting in writing only recent and true events, which, if they were left to be written by those who come later, could never be considered free of doubt, and truth would thereby be injured. And so that there should be no uncertainty about believing this story, when Guibert was deprived of his eyes God in His mercy did not heal him immediately but, as mentioned above, He left Guibert blind for a whole year. He called the attention of a good many inhabitants of the province to the blind man through Guibert's skill as a jongleur, and, after all of the people were aware of his blindness, then God healed him. This miracle is in no way inferior to the one told in the Gospel about the man born blind, and in fact it is much more marvelous by far, since Truth herself, who is Christ, promised that His followers would certainly do greater things than He, for He said: "He who believes in me shall also do the works that I do, and greater than these, because I go to the Father."[19]

1.2: A Similar Miracle About Gerbert

God in His goodness causes desire for what is morally right and He always goes beyond what faithful people long for. That is why Divine Providence ordained that, as incredible and beyond hope as it may seem, I saw another example of the kind of miracle I had wanted to see in the first place. This was after I had searched out the first one. That is, I saw that the maimed face of Gerbert had been restored by the strange phenomenon of a miracle equal to that granted to Guibert. No one should doubt this miracle because I didn't mention it in the previous letter. I was writing about Guibert first, whom I sought out by name, and I didn't want to hear the story of another miracle until I had been freed from the obligation to write the first one. As it so happened, almost immediately after I finished the first one the monks presented two men to me: a man who had no precise knowledge about a miracle and this Gerbert. Of course Guibert's miracle is much more widely known, since about thirty years have already passed from the time in his youth when it took place. But the other man, whom I'm going to discuss now, claimed that he had experienced his miracle not more than three years before.

Since I was concerned about the truth of this miracle, I tracked down so much evidence that it is too boring to go over all of it. For in addition to the testimony of those who presented themselves to me, prepared either to swear on the holy martyr's relics or to undergo ordeal by fire, you may still see the old marks of Gerbert's scars and the horrid disfigurement caused by cuts in the skin around his eyes. The deed was done as night was falling and it was growing dark. Gerbert was rolling his head back and forth and trying to pull away from the hands of his tormentors. Therefore the wounds that he received then, before his eyes were gouged out, lend greater credence to the words of the witnesses I mentioned before. With all this evidence, no one should doubt that this is a true story, nor should anyone think that I relate things not carefully researched, nor that I make up false stories out of my own imagination, nor that I substitute imaginary spirits where I ought to attribute actions to God. Actually, it would be more satisfying to me to be completely silent than to corrupt God's word with deceit. This is what I have to say:

A man named Guy, a very brutal man with an extremely fierce nature, ruled a castle called Calmilliacum[20] in the district of Velay. Once Guy, with his usual oppressive cruelty, was unjustly holding captive three men from the land of the church of Santa Maria Anicia. With a shameless oath Guy swore resolutely that they weren't going to escape from there soon unless it were to the gallows. But, as the outcome of the affair will soon show, he swore falsely. It happened that Gerbert, who was well known because of his high rank, was passing by alone in front of the contrivance that bound the feet of the three captives. They knew him to be a man of mercy, since for the love of God alone he had ransomed several people in this same situation with his own money, so they all cried to him. They begged him, for the love of Christ and of his holy mother Mary together with the love of Sainte Foy martyr, that if he could find any way at all he should come to their rescue as soon as possible before they perished.

A year earlier, while he was passing through the Rouergue on a journey, Gerbert had made a detour in order to go to Conques. His purpose was not, however, to pray, but to see Guibert with his restored eyes. He had heard of Guibert's reputation long before, but had never seen him. When he did, he gave Guibert alms, for his means were ample. From that time forward Gerbert especially cherished Sainte Foy deep in his heart more than all the saints. And so when these men cried out to him with such distress and made mention of Sainte Foy, he could do no other than to hurry to relieve them to the extent that he could, even at the risk of his life. So much did the effect of her sweet name reach into the innermost recesses of his heart that his whole being was moved by compassion and his face was wet with tears. He hastened to their aid as quickly as he could.

Gerbert acquired three very sharp little knives, hid them in his cloak, and carried them to the captives. He gave them lengths of rope that would enable them to scale the wall, imposing only this condition: that if they were captured again they would not confess who had helped them and thereby condemn him. But these men were impatient by nature, so they went into action immediately, before the friendly cover of darkness could settle, instead of waiting as they should have. They cut their fetters and recklessly fled for their lives, but they were easily seen in the hostile daylight and recaptured. When one of them was asked under torture who was responsible for their freedom, he revealed Gerbert's name. Therefore, as I would say in my own words, Gerbert was detected in a good crime. The wicked lord accused him of plotting to seize the castle for himself. What more is there to say? Guy couldn't bear to wait until the next day, but menacingly and unrelentingly ordered that right then, at twilight, Gerbert's eyes be violently cut out of their sockets. At once Gerbert was hedged round by men who had once fought by his side. Nonetheless they overcame their reluctance to act against him and threw him to the ground. He resisted for a long time, for he had outstanding strength, and twisted his head vigorously. Finally with great difficulty his eyes were mutilated. In the struggle Gerbert was slashed so many times around his eyes by the unsteady hands of his attackers that it is easy to believe in the miracle just from the evidence of his scars. As for the men who were recaptured, through the grace of God they were not harmed in any way, and they don't deny that it turned out so well for them through Sainte Foy's kindness.

Right away the wretched Gerbert, who now despised his life, went into the countryside. His plan was to drink goat's milk, for people say that if anyone who has recently been wounded drinks goat's milk the person will be undone by death on the spot. But no one would take the responsibility of giving Gerbert goat's milk. Therefore he decided to starve himself to death, and for eight continuous days and nights he ate nothing, but went hungry and kept the night vigil. By the last night he was in a kind of trance, in which he could forget his situation a little. In that state he saw what seemed to be a ten-year-old girl. She had a charming and indescribably beautiful appearance, and wore attire adorned with gold and embellished with embroidery made with inestimable skill. She looked at him rather closely and with her right hand she seemed to implant eyes in his ruined sockets while she cradled his chin in her left hand. Gerbert awakened immediately and quickly leapt out of his bed. At once he tried to prostrate himself at her sacred feet. But when he realized that she had vanished and could by no means be found, he cried out in his misery and filled the whole inn with his loud lament. His two servants awakened and asked what he wanted for himself with this kind of plaint. Gerbert told them that he, their master, had seen the shape of a young girl who had restored his eyes to him, and that because of this he was going to go to Conques immediately. But they burst into jeering laughter, for they thought this idea of his, that he would have his sight restored the way Guibert's had been, was the height of stupidity. Nonetheless, when Gerbert rose at dawn the next day, the cloud of total gloom had been completely driven away from him. He became so cheerful and joyful that it was easy to believe in this vision from heaven. At once he demanded food and, eating, regained his strength.

Gerbert certainly didn't forget his vision, and after a few days he asked to be taken to the holy monastery of the monks at Conques. But, as I've said, the servants considered their lord's undertakings to be nonsense or, more likely, they held him in disdain, so they neglected the blind man's commands. Finally they abandoned him, since they felt that he had been struck down and his good fortune had fled. Therefore it is true that adverse fortune uncovers the false faces of friends. Nevertheless Gerbert put his complete trust in God's mercy. With the help of some friends he was able to make the desired journey. He arrived at the monastery, invoked the aid of the Almighty, and then returned to his lodgings. He had already begun to regain his sight a little, but when he sensed the miracle and began to boast indiscreetly about God's gift he was enveloped in shadows again before the midday meal was finished. After this he devoted several days to prayer and his eyes were healed by Sainte Foy's very kind intervention; his face was thus perfectly restored to its former handsomeness.

From then on Gerbert repeatedly strove with great effort to return to his former life as a mounted warrior, but was immediately hindered from heaven. At last, he was persuaded by the illustrious Theotberga, wife of Count Pons,[21] that if he ever wished to become well he should not abandon Sainte Foy nor refuse the yoke of her service.

"Because it is evident," she said, "that Sainte Foy did not work such a great miracle for you so that you could return to the turmoil of a fighting man's worldly life, where you would also be in danger, but so that you would cling to her as a permanent member of her household and in this way be saved and rise to the gate of perpetual glory."

After he had been so strongly rebuked by the wise matron and so beneficially confirmed in his faith, Gerbert completely abandoned his resistance and made no further efforts to thwart the divine will. Therefore he serves God and His saint now in that very monastery with the most devoted obedience, content with a monk's daily allowance of food. He is a man of calm character and a simple way of life, measured by our times and our ways of doing things. Thus the authorities of the monastery have treated him well up to the present time, and he obeys them in all things and cherishes them with a deep affection. You might see that the jewels of his pupils sparkle in the midst of the old marks of his scars. Though their restoration was contrary to nature, his eyes shine now just as they did before, not like glass but like flesh. But to prevent the happenstance that he might be corrupted by arrogance or by the seductive counsel of those near him—for human nature is frail—and might wish to return to secular life, through divine will the sight of his left eye began to disappear almost completely afterwards.

In this, O Sainte Foy, the praiseworthy compassion of your goodness is revealed. You who heal them in body are just as concerned to heal them in spirit, and for this reason you removed light from the exterior eye of the body, in order that the inner spirit might become brighter. And you, faithful people, inscribe this miracle on the tablets of your hearts, praise the kindness of the martyr Sainte Foy, try as hard as you can to imitate her in the performance of good works, hasten to her tomb and claim with assurance the salvation of your souls. For it does not lie hidden from the comprehension of the human mind that she who grants so abundantly the benefits of health to the lower part of man, that is to the body, will bestow them even more abundantly on the higher part, that is, on the soul, to anyone who asks in the right way.

1.3: How a Mule Was Revived from Death

The miracle that God's omnipotence worked through Sainte Foy by reviving an animal from death should be made public, since it is as praiseworthy as her other miracles. For it is unseemly that a rational creature should feel ashamed to tell about something that it did not disgust the High Creator to make. To the reader or listener it may seem absurd to hear about a creature that has to lift its ears in order to understand another creature, but it should not seem so unusual since the merciful Creator of the physical world watches over His manifold creation. And so it has been written: "You will save both humans and animals, O Lord."[22] Here is the story I have to tell.

A mounted warrior from the Toulousain named Bonfils (whose son is still living and bears the same name), was coming to the virgin's holy monastery. When he was not more than about two miles from Conques, the mule he usually rode was struck down by some kind of disease and fell to the ground lifeless. Therefore Bonfils hired two peasants and ordered them to strip the hide from the body. But he went on to pray to the holy virgin, for whose love he had made the journey. Prostrate on the earth, he gave voice to his prayers, fulfilling the vows he had made. Afterward, in front of the sacred martyr's golden image, Bonfils complained bitterly about the loss of his mule. Since the mule had been so outstanding and almost beyond compare, Bonfils bore the sad loss very hard, especially because the Enemy had inflicted the injury himself, attempting thereby to discourage Bonfils from his good work. It seems that the steadfastness of Bonfils's faith ought to be highly praised, for when he stopped praying the mule repulsed the peasants on either side of him by repeatedly kicking the feet they were already grasping as they prepared to flay him. Marvelous to report!—alive again, the mule sprang up and eagerly followed the tracks of its fellow animals through the mountaintops until it burst forth into the town. As those who were present tell me frequently, you could see the animal staggering with joy at its recovered life, according to the measure of its brutish understanding. Up and down through the marketplace in front of the church it ran. And you could tell that in a certain way it felt the kindness of the doer, and so with a repeated braying it gave thanks to God, "who gives food to the animals and to the young ravens who call upon Him."[23]

The peasants ran in pursuit of the mule, carrying their bloody knives, and told the miracle they had seen to those still hesitant to believe it. And, so that firm belief in the truth of the miracle might be based on more than the oral testimony of those who saw it, there was also a certain kind of clear writing to banish every wavering uncertainty, for on its two hind legs the mule had the furrows of fresh wounds. And as long as the mule lived it possessed evidence of its resurrection, for in that very hour the wounds healed and were soundly joined together. Like the oldest of scars they even had gray hairs. Bonfils offered a gold piece to God and His saint as an expression of thanks and returned home. He sent the mule back to Sainte Foy and for many years afterward he dispatched many donations to her.[24]

1.4: Another Miracle like the Preceding One

A mounted warrior named Gerald, scarcely an obscure person,[25] lived in the district of Rouergue, in a country estate called Vialarels, about six miles from Conques. Once when Gerald was returning from Rome, it happened that a mule that had been loaned to him by his brother Bernard, a cleric, had been weakened by some illness and began to falter. But Gerald remembered the miracles of Sainte Foy, who was his neighbor, so he vowed to give her a candle the length of the mule in return for its recovery.[26] But the mule didn't recover; it became weaker and weaker and died. When he saw what had happened, Gerald sold the hide to his innkeeper. The wicked innkeeper offered a price to Gerald that was as low as possible, reckoning that even if he gave nothing he would still get the hide. This made Gerald immensely angry, so he plowed the flank of the body lengthwise and crosswise with several cuts. That way, after he left there, the perfidious innkeeper would not have the joy of an intact hide. Finally Gerald grabbed up his own walking stick, pierced the dead beast's eye with its point, and cut off its tail. Beside himself with rage, he said:

"What a loss Sainte Foy would suffer now, if, while she was giving other gifts of healing, she cured this mule, for she would receive a candle only this long as her due! Now, wretched man that I am, I've been hit by a double loss—I have to continue my journey on foot and when I get home I have to pay a hundred solidi to my brother." For the brothers had agreed between themselves to this value for the mule, if it happened to encounter danger or death.

And scarcely had Gerald finished saying these very few words when the mule came back to life, leapt up very agilely, and stood firmly on all fours. And to prevent anyone from concluding that the mule had not actually been dead, at that very moment the mutilated skin grew into intact scars as if they were being painted on. They were no longer fresh wounds running with blood, but, as I said about the other mule, they had a healthy glow of downy hair, as if they were very old. After this happened, Gerald rejoiced greatly and returned home. He gave huge thanks to God and His saint and spoke everywhere about the novelty of the miracle. Both Gerald's noble character and his faith were observed by all, for if anyone seemed to suggest that the miracle was mere babble or happenstance, he had the mule, marked by its wounds, brought into that person's presence.

The monks themselves told me this, and so did several others who saw Gerald afterward more than a thousand times. But, although I am sufficiently convinced of its truth by hearing this miracle, I wouldn't leave it at that if Gerald were still living. I would turn aside to see him on my return journey. Since he was an inhabitant of this region[27] it wouldn't take me much out of my way.

For, although I am both frail in understanding and weighed down by sin, and thus unworthy of this duty, I am not so deceitful that I willfully report falsehoods. Nor would I have exposed myself to widespread contempt by relating such a strange and wondrous thing if I didn't know that there was undeniable truth in it. For it would indeed be wicked to hide Christ's truth because of human fearfulness. I fear greatly for those who do such things, for Christ before His Father in heaven will consign them to oblivion. For He said, "Whoever denies me before men, him will I deny before My Father Who is in heaven."[28] He spoke the same truth elsewhere: "Whoever is ashamed of Me and My words, the Son of Man will be ashamed of him when He comes in His majesty and that of the Father and of the holy angels."[29] Christ, may I never be ashamed to acknowledge Your truth to people and to write it in my book, lest You are ashamed to acknowledge me before Your Father Who is in heaven and You delete me from the book that You have written. But I should end this now. What madman will doubt any longer the future resurrection of humankind, when already in the present even animals rise up?

1.5: How a Man Was Killed in a Headlong Fall While He Was Attacking One of Sainte Foy's Monks

The miracle I am going write next ought to be emphatically recalled by the faithful and dreaded by the enemies of God.

There is a monk named Bergand who is a member of Sainte Foy's monastic community. Before he took up the sacred monk's habit, Bergand turned over to God and Sainte Foy his hereditary rights in his share of the family property.[30] Recently, in this very year at harvest time, Bergand was making his way to this property to issue a legal challenge to someone who had wickedly taken possession of it. That same day it so happened that Rainon from the castle of Aubin,[31] located in the district of Rouergue, had hurried out with thirty of his horsemen because of some pressing need. When he was about six miles from Aubin, Rainon chanced to see the monk in the distance. Bergand, accompanied by an escort, was riding on the same road that Rainon was traversing. Rainon asked the people standing there who the passersby were. After he found out, he quickly manufactured a reason for laying hold of their horses; he turned pale, gnashed his teeth, and muttered shameless threats. Of course, Rainon had already been excommunicated long before by the community of monks at Conques because of the monstrous evils he had inflicted on them, and he continued to be held fast in the grip of their curse. But why should I delay by telling about the brashness of his words and the violence of his threats when you have been waiting so long to hear how it turned out?

The ill-fated Rainon was dazzled by wretched greed and carried away by contemptible pride. He ranted and raved irrationally with furious passion, showing respect neither for God nor for His saint. Suddenly he spurred his horse violently forward, and with frenzied speed this utter savage rushed headlong toward the innocent men. He was hurrying to attack them as quickly as he could when divine vengeance intervened. Rainon's horse kicked its hind legs high into the air, plunged its neck downward, and fell to a sad death. And the rider, who was flung a good distance beyond the horse, died for nothing, with a twisted neck and a fractured skull.

And so the one who was in a hurry to injure the good and obedient monk or to cheat him completely of his life received the death sentence himself first by divine judgment and was sent down to hell, where he became the companion of the dead or the prey of demons. One of Rainon's friends had swiftly followed him, intending, it is said, to prevent Rainon's attack. But he took a dangerous fall from his horse in the same place, even though it was a plain. However, only his sword was broken and both he and his horse escaped unharmed because God saw his good intentions.

You should rejoice, scholar, that now Pride, not in imagination as you have read in Prudentius's *Psychomachia*[32] but actually and in human form, was overpowered by the whirlwind of her own speed and lay there dead. Thrown down headlong from the lofty height of her vainglory into the bottomless pit of the abyss that the deception of sin had secretly prepared, Pride was irrevocably cast down.[33]

Although the monk had seen the incident from a distance, he was unaware both of the cause and of the outcome of the matter in which his death had been intended. He went safely on his way, quickly completed his business, and retraced his steps back to the monastery. Later Rainon's brother Hector made unrelenting threats to tear the monk to pieces limb from limb, just as if he were seeking to punish a murderer. But heavenly vengeance prevented this and Hector died suddenly in a war.

Understand these things, you who have proud hearts. Now is the time to come to your senses from your wickedness and learn to do right. For otherwise the untimely arrival of the hour of judgment may prevent you, or death may unexpectedly overpower you before you have repented. For injustice does not always have the upper hand and divine judgment is not a trifling matter.

1.6: How Divine Vengeance Acted Against Those Who Wanted to Steal the Monks' Wine

This next does not deserve to be considered a lesser miracle than the preceding one. At a different time the goodness of God worked it through Sainte Foy near the castle named Cassagnes, which is eight miles from Conques and in the same district.[34]

Three years ago Hugh, who ruled over that castle, seized an opportune moment and ordered two of his servants to carry off the monks' wine, which was kept at the country estate called Molières.[35] This estate is only about two miles from Cassagnes. The two servants hurried off in different directions on separate paths, searching through the peasants' barnyards for carts that they could use to convey the wine. The first of them, named Benedict, received an earnest warning from a simple peasant not to carry out the evil task he had begun. People say that Benedict replied with blasphemy like this:

"Does Sainte Foy drink wine? What foolishness! Don't you know that whoever doesn't drink doesn't need wine?"

The wretch was unworthy of the meaning of his name[36] and unaware that those who offend the servants of the saints show that they have insulted the saints themselves. They do injury not only to the saints but even to Christ the Lord, Who feels the pains in the body of another, and Whose saints are nothing other than limbs consubstantially forming an organic whole with Him. Benedict was told that the keeper of the storeroom key was not there. In response Benedict boasted that he carried the key at the end of his foot, and that there weren't any doors anywhere strong enough that he couldn't break them with one kick. As he said this, he struck a great blow, shaking the wall of the building where he stood. He meant to demonstrate, of course, the potent strength he was going to use to assail the cellar doors, for at this point he was en route and still very far away from the storeroom. Then the haughty man lifted up his foot to strike a second, powerful blow and bent his knee back toward his body. At that very moment his muscles lost their ability to move and stiffened completely; the wretch lay paralyzed on the ground, his arms and legs drawn up to his body. In addition, his mouth was stretched back to his ears and gaped obscenely, and the filth that streamed foully from his entrails manifestly revealed how harshly and distressingly he had been afflicted. So the wretch, tortured with wretched torture, scarcely extended his wretched life, wretchedly, for more than two days.

Now that the violent death of the first servant has been described, let me turn in this section to the other, who was named Hildebert. He had used force to steal a shoulder of pork from a peasant and refused to return it. Neither the tear-filled petition of the poor peasant nor reverence for the saints moved him, and the haughty man disdainfully said:

"I'll have chunks of this meat scattered over glowing-hot charcoal and very carefully roasted. After I've been well fed with the meat, then I'll open my throat and consume the monks' wine just like a hawk that finds a stupid chicken after it has gone without eating for a long time. After seizing the chicken and carrying it off from the farmyard, the hawk eviscerates it with taloned feet, and after its appetite has been sated it glides freely on the breezes wherever it pleases, exulting in winged flight through the clear air."

When he had finished speaking, the servant began to hit his head in agony,[37]
And then a tremendous inflammation gradually filled up
His gullet and his swelling throat and his proud neck.
Nor did the pain abate until—wretched sight—
His inflated neck had grown wider than his head. You would have been able to see

That the whole of this glutton had become one insatiable gullet,
Filled with the foul rottenness of sudden disease.
He dragged out his worthless life no more than three days.
Thus the wretch perished, snatched away by the wrath of the
Heavenly Judge.
Thus the hawk's throat learned to stretch for its enormous meal.
Thus Sainte Foy shrewdly fed his gluttonous beak with the deadly
meat of her food.
Now he is learning to suffer his punishment,
For he despised of learning pity for a poor man,
And had no fear of provoking the beneficent saints.
Now the wretch is pursued by the tortures of the underworld.
The news of such a miraculous portent swiftly reached the castle,
Where it was told in all its detail.
But the lord of the castle was not afraid and did not abandon his
endeavor.
Infuriated, he threatened to go out and seize the wine himself.
His wife Senegund opposed the crime, calling it
An outrage, a detestable deed.
The good woman urged him not to begin this,
Not to touch the consecrated wine of the monks,
For fear that the condemnation of death would come suddenly,
And that he would perish, struck down by the holy virgin's wrath.
Far from complying, the savage unleashed his blind greed,
And in a fit of wild rage struck her with his fists.
Blood poured from her mouth and stained her clothing.
Then the lord leapt up from his seat,
He descended from his high stronghold in a passion.
The villain hurried to finish the undertaking,
And when he was rounding a turn in his descent of the steep steps,
His anger unbalanced him, his legs tottered, his feet slipped.[38]
He fell on his side and broke two ribs.
His body fell to the bottom and began to rot.
The criminal experienced the just wrath of the Judge.
He lay senseless in punishment for his offenses,
And his servants brought him back half-dead.
They watched over him as he lay in his bed for three months,
With no expectation that he would regain consciousness.
But he recovered through the merits of his good wife.

I believe that this faithful woman brought her unjust husband back to life
By urging him to visit the virgin's holy shrine.
This time he trusted in her advice,
And soon he went to the saint to give his best thanks,
And after he returned he was no longer rebellious.

1.7: A Commentary That Confirms the Preceding Narratives

The second half of the preceding miracle [1.6] is composed in verses, contrary to my usual practice of writing in prose. A monk named Arseus persuaded me to write them with his insistent pleas. But lest the second half should seem to be out of harmony with the first, I have chosen to set those verses on the page like prose. I feared that the meaning would be lost if the rhythmical measure of the scansion confused the reader's expectations.[39]

The miracles written above are the only ones I prepared while I stayed for three weeks and four days in the village of Conques. What I had written I left there, and I very strictly cautioned them not to allow copies to be made of this unfinished and imperfect volume. I wanted them to wait until more of the remaining miracles had been included and the finished book had been read and very scrupulously corrected by a discriminating scholar. After this emendation, my book might be able to gain a place in the ranks of authentic writings. I had noted down these extraordinary miracles hastily and briefly, as I said earlier, on pieces of parchment, just as I heard them from eyewitnesses. I have brought my notes with me and now I am very diligently revising them into a clearer text, fleshing out accounts. But I am adding only what is essential. In fact, for the sake of brevity I am leaving out much of what I heard, for writers receive the most praise when they have the skill to select outstanding historical events. For if kind readers judge that the miracle stories I have chosen to set down in writing deserve their highest admiration, surely they will not doubt that an infinite number of the more humble miracles survives. And if an immense library of them were to be heaped up, what else would result if not boredom? It seems therefore more adviseable and more reasonable either to finish my abundant material in a concise way or to select for the reader from the many miracles those that must not be ignored. Moreover, by the grace of God I myself merited to see some miracles, even in the short time that I was there; these are not in need of another witness. I shall relate them more suitably in their appropriate place. But before I write a word of the next miracle, there is a great and almost inevitable necessity that I loosen the reins a little and turn back to discuss the miracles I have already entered in this book.

Recently some of my fellow Angevins set out on a pilgrimage, intending to offer prayers at the churches of that well-known and populous city commonly called Le Puy de Sainte-Marie; its ancient name has been almost entirely forgotten, but, unless I am mistaken, it seems to have been Anicium.[40] There the compatriots whom I mentioned met an impious and heretical man who said that he lived near Conques. When he had learned that they were Angevins he said, "You must know that Bernard who came to Conques this year. Bah! How many lies about Sainte Foy he wrote down there! For how could any reasonable person believe things about eyeballs torn out and afterward restored, and animals brought back to life? I have heard of other kinds of miracles that other saints and—rarely—Sainte Foy worked now and then. But mules! For what reason, for what necessity, would God bring them back to life? No one who is mentally stable can or ought to expound such things."

Oh, what a blind and foolish man! Oh, the stony heart of this man, who made darkness of the light that he had in himself! This wretch did not cleanse himself through baptism of the sinful condition in which he was born; no, after what should have been a spiritual rebirth he continued in that same condition, and grew far worse. If this man had lived in the time of our Lord's Passion, he would undoubtedly have joined the Jews in denying that Lazarus was resurrected or that the soldier's ear struck off by Saint Peter was restored. Truly this man was a son of the devil, an enemy of truth, a minister of Antichrist. He was not of God, because he had not heard the words of God.[41] Rather he was someone that the Devil, who envies good works, tried to use, as he so frequently does, to sow the seed of error in this very small, pious work of mine.

But why should I be surprised if a peasant, a stranger to all wisdom, completely unfamiliar with every divine virtue, and what is worse, a liar with a depraved and perverse mind, should fall into such grave and perilous error? For even the Pharisees themselves and those experts in the law who boasted that they were descended from the holy blood of the prophets, from very illustrious lineages, did not recognize Christ, Who had been promised to them in signs and miracles. Although they had seen ever so many of His miracles, either they denied them completely or they strove futilely to twist them into their opposite. This empty-headed little man was so completely like them that he rivaled them in his deceitful faithlessness.

This same Devil had tried to impede me from setting out for Conques in a thousand ways, but he failed to thwart me since God was defending me. Nevertheless, he regained his strength somehow and used this man to raise doubts in the minds not only of inexperienced people, but also in my own, even though I ought to have been an unconquerable defender of this truth. He was trying to deflect me from my plan of writing the remaining miracles. With the subtle skill of his crafty trickery he even diminished my resolve a little. But I give thanks to the Author of Truth for this, that the only man the Enemy sent for this wicked task was illiterate and ignorant of all good. Nevertheless, it seems that this happened in accordance with the purpose of the Highest Creator, because through it He made true defenders ever more vigilant to destroy heretical depravity.

Oh, if only sometime I were able to discover this man who has such a good grasp of things among the inhabitants of Conques! I witness to God, Author of all Truth, before Whose eye no falsehood finds a hiding place, that I would find it an easy enough contest, if I had upright listeners, to cause them to call him a Pharisee rather than a Christian.

Although his notions are absurd and filled with the wickedness of total depravity, and I find nothing fouler and more detestable anywhere, they provoke me to respond. Therefore I will explain the reasons that God worked this kind of miracle, insofar as the Holy Spirit will deign to inspire my sinner's heart. If I don't do this, it may happen that some simple Christian will think that such a miracle lacks reason or necessity. In short, this kind of miracle may not be believed because I have written about brute animals rising from the dead rather than men, when brute animals are of a lesser concern to the Creator and men are far more valuable in His eyes. But it actually seems to be much more necessary and reasonable that animals, which were created only for human use, should live again, but that men, who have been called for the purpose of earning eternal life and for whom the present life is nothing other than death or a passage to the future, should rest after death in the hope of the Resurrection. This should not distress good people, because if they breathed again they would only return into the exile of this troublesome life. Concerning the hope of future resurrection the prophet David, who had knowledge of the future through the Holy Spirit, rejoiced with indescribable joy and exclaimed: "Therefore my heart has been glad, and my tongue has rejoiced; moreover, my body shall also rest in hope."[42]

In addition, we maintain our hope of human resurrection with greater certainty if we see that animals, which are inferior to men, are sometimes raised from death. Besides this, if there are eras when the condition of religion has grown so perverted that human corpses are not thought worthy of resurrection—and we read that there were people who thought this in the times of the Holy Fathers—it follows that through such a miracle in our time faith in human resurrection is also restored to the faculties, so that the authority of Holy Scripture does not seem fictitious due to lack of faith. And furthermore, human beings who see that lowly beasts are raised up from death, and don't recognize that they themselves are images of God, learn deservedly how much they have fallen away from the old faith. They also learn that they need not worry about God's concern for them when the resurrection of the flesh is revealed to them with so evident a portent. Nevertheless, if God had worked that miracle only because the travelers on their holy journey needed the help of those animals, this cause could appropriately be accepted as one of reason and necessity.

Therefore there is nothing in this kind of miracle that is lacking in reason or necessity. But if the peasant who attacked my work has in fact been refuted by this reason and necessity, and still complains that my argument lacks the support of authority, I answer that I am not reporting something unheard of, for there are reports of the same kind of miracle in the books of our religion. Furthermore, we believe that once an ox came back to life through the prayers of Saint Silvester.[43] If this ignoramus still doesn't understand for what reason or necessity God worked this miracle, he should look it up in the old texts. But if he is illiterate and can't verify it there, he should understand that in comparison to wise men he is a brute animal wholly unworthy to dispute concerning divine reasons. And I can report something more unheard-of and more astonishing than the revival of an ox. In our own time Berenger of Reims, a medical doctor with an insolent attitude, blasphemously compared Saint Martin of Tours to a donkey, and people say that the vengeance of the Omnipotent turned Berenger himself into a donkey for awhile. In memory of this monstrous transformation, verses with an amusing theme have been inscribed above his tomb:

> Here let men lament by braying like donkeys,
> Since this one person had two different forms.

And more lines follow, which were apparently composed by the monk Azolin, a student of the very wise Gerbert.[44] However, I am of the opinion that the story about Berenger doesn't have to be wholly doubted or wholly accepted. But I have no doubt as to the source from whom I got the story I told. Actually, it is difficult not to believe what I have received, not from fictitious report or apocryphal text but faithfully from the mouths of a thousand eyewitnesses. I am as convinced as I would be if I had been fortunate enough to see it with my own eyes.

But perhaps someone will charge that proof by authority is not credible. Let it be so: yet I need no other authority than the will of God which has certainly been able to take the place of precedent. For if we believe no miracle unless we can prove that the same kind of miracle happened before, then we wish to confine the omnipotence of the High Creator to the mode of human reason. Moses wouldn't have believed that the sea was going to be divided, as God foretold, if he had been looking to compare it to a similar miracle, for God hadn't parted the sea that way before. Nevertheless Moses believed that the Red Sea was going to be divided before it was done. And we now believe that it was divided, although nothing similar had been done at any earlier time. Therefore, why should a false accusation be tolerated when God brings about something that is unfamiliar in accordance with His rightful use of His own will through the goodness of His own saints? For it has been written: "Whatever the Lord pleased, that He has done, in heaven and in earth, in the sea, and in all the depths."[45]

If, through Sainte Foy, Omnipotent God revives mortal animals with the breath of life, both for the health of the animals and as a basis for faith, this miracle must be accepted without hesitation. After all, He entrusted to Noah in the ark those creatures that had to be saved, so that they did not die in the Flood, and He did this for the health of our bodies and the service of our needs.

Finally, if hearing what I have said about mules that were resurrected does not satisfy the malicious attack of my enemies, then seeing would not have satisfied them either, for a blind spirit has dull bodily sight.

However, whoever does not believe the stories that I, a Christian, have told about people whose eyes were torn out by the roots and that I saw restored in the same faces, let them go and see. After the beneficiaries of these miracles have described the events and the whole province has corroborated them, let such people put aside all their unbelieving arguments then and there. I saw those men who were healed myself, I invited them to meals, I gave them money, and there will never be a day when I am dissuaded from the truth of this opinion. If I wished, I would be able to keep on writing a great many miracles about them. For when they begin to sneak off to worldly affairs, divine power immediately hinders them. Either by blinding an eye or by disabling a limb, God forces them to stay where they are. Moreover, Guibert, just as I said above, was unable to control his lust, and every time he was sullied with a prostitute he experienced the retribution of divine vengeance.

But may that impious man perish who constrained me to such a great digression, detaining me for a whole day while I directed my course in other ways, away from the correct path of the narrative. I was led off rather far in rivulets of eloquence. Now let me cling closely to the bed from which the stream of my narrative strayed, weaving the themes of miracles in the sequence I had intended.

1.8: How Guy Died

And so my narration will continue at this point with the story of the infamous Guy's death.[46] I heard it from Gerbert, whom I have often mentioned, and I will tell it now.

Guy had heard very frequently of the great marvels of the omnipotent Christ revealed through Sainte Foy, but they did not provide him with sufficient reason for giving up his insolent stubbornness. When anyone referred to the restoration of Gerbert's eyes, Guy is reported to have answered with such great blasphemies that with his shameless mouth he even slandered Sainte Foy herself, she who restored Gerbert's sight. Following the example of the perfidious Pharisees, when Guy couldn't deny a divine miracle he turned it in a perverse direction. This is the reason that, some time later when his utterly wretched soul departed, in accordance with the Prophet's saying that "the death of sinners is evil,"[47] all who were there found the stench unbearable. A huge snake shot out from the dying man's bedcovers into the midst of the crowd that was present and wound this way and that in slimy circles, slithering in agile, sinuous movement until it fled and ceased to be seen. And so the wretch who had shown himself to be a blasphemer against the saint clearly perished both in body and in soul. Obviously he was led to hell by the demon that he had imitated as his teacher in evil-doing.

1.9: About a Widow's Blind Daughter

Since the Lord favored me by letting me see something that had a divine cause, as people say in the celebrated monastery at Conques, I will describe it here in the middle of my work.

Among the floods of pilgrims who had poured into Conques from various regions, one woman, a widow, kept vigil through the night to pray that her blind daughter would be healed. While the daughter was keeping the night's watch in prayer with her mother, during the first vigil of the night the eyesight she had lost was wholly restored through the power of Sainte Foy. The monks who watched over the relics and some of the monks who were taking their turn officiating at night, according to the custom there, saw what had happened. At once they all began to run swiftly to my lodgings. And because they knew that I longed to witness a new miracle, they exhausted one another in their eagerness to report it to me.

"Look! For you, fortunate Bernard, a miracle, a miracle from Sainte Foy!" they said. "This is what you have been praying for, what you wished would be shown to you before your departure. You thought it wasn't fair that, when you came so far intending to write miracles, you weren't seeing any yourself."

For I had explained the reason for my pilgrimage to the monks when I arrived. They received me with proper hospitality and provided everything I needed to carry out my vow, even assigning me excellent servants who obeyed my orders as long as I was there.

I quickly leapt out of my bed, for I had already lain down, and in my joy I hurried out at what, I confess, was not a decorous pace. I entered the monastery, and I saw that the girl could see and could make out the lights of candles. And she even noticed my hand, in which I offered a denier to that impoverished girl. When she saw it, she received it with thanks.

It is not in my power to describe how many and what kind of miracles happened there continually in regard to various infirmities through divine compassion. A little while before my arrival, eleven people who were gravely afflicted with a variety of ills were completely restored to health in only one night. If I had heeded all the miracles worked there daily for the sick, I would have gathered a huge library. I have concentrated on the miracles that were worked to take revenge on evil-doers or on those that are in some way new and unusual, and have greatly abridged them in order to bring out a small but precious volume. But there may be some miracles that I chose to leave out in my eagerness to be brief, or some that I will hear later that need to be included. If so, I shall add them to my second book.

1.10: How Celestial Vengeance Struck a Man Who Attacked Sainte Foy's Pilgrim

In the days when I was a visitor at Conques, there was another miracle that was quite terrifying. Although I could have seen it, I did not witness it myself. But the man who publicly reported it to me solemnly swore that he knew it to be true. For as long as God preserves for me my senses and my reason, I will not knowingly and willingly insert anything that is false into these sacred pages. I know that God does not rejoice in idle talk, and He is not misled by empty flattery. Besides, I possess no reward for business like this, nor do I hope for one other than my trust that Sainte Foy will aid me in life's trials.

A warrior named Gerard, a native of the Limousin, had made a very devout pilgrimage to Sainte Foy. An enemy of Gerard's named Gerald acquired information about Gerard's return journey and, with the aid of fifteen armed Franks,[48] attacked him while he was returning home. Gerald had respect neither for God nor for His saint, for he laid an ambush for her pilgrim. He attacked Gerard, who had put up as a guest in a peasant's hut. When the pilgrim realized that he was surrounded by enemies, with a worried heart he began to call on heaven to defend him since he had no one with him except one servant. Then a great crashing noise sent from heaven struck terror into the men who had begun to assault the little house from all sides, and they ran off in unsteady, headlong flight, leaving behind only one of their companions in the siege. Gerard, who had been confined inside the hut, expected nothing but death. He grabbed up the peasant's version of a sword and quickly sprang through the doorway, for he was armed with the same spirit that Moses had when he fought against Egypt and Samson had against the Philistines. Running the man through, he killed him. Then he overcame another, Gerald himself, and led him home as his captive.

What Gerard did with his captive after that, no one could tell me. All I know is that the country estate where it is said to have happened is named Sulpiac, which is thirty miles from Conques.

And so the snare came unawares upon the one lying in ambush, the enemy of God, and the ambush that he set caught him, and the sinner fell into the snare that he had stretched out for the innocent.[49]

I.11: How a Man Who Was Slandering Sainte Foy Was Destroyed by the Sudden Collapse of a Roof

Here is another miracle of divine vengeance that was worked at a different time, before I arrived in Conques. It should intensify dedication to divine worship in men of the Church and in those who serve devotedly in the house of God, but it should thoroughly frighten those who violently steal goods from God's holy Church, or those who appropriate, as if it were legally their own, property that the saints have inherited, and unjustly claim the rents and services due its owners. For at this time there are a great many people who deserve to be called Antichrists.[50] Blinded by their greed, they dare to seize what rightfully belongs to the Church; in so doing, not only do they show no respect for officials of the sacred ministry, but they sometimes even assault them with insolent abuse and beatings. Sometimes they murder them. I have seen canons, or even monks and abbots, driven out of their positions, deprived of their goods, and violently slaughtered. I have seen bishops, some condemned by being outlawed, some driven from their episcopal sees without cause, others slaughtered by the sword and even burned to death in cruel flames by Christians for defending the rights of the Church. But it is not right that those people are even called Christians who fight against the order of the Christian religion, whose every act identifies them as opponents of Christ and enemies of truth. As things are now these men undergo no punishment, so they haven't the least dread of divine vengeance; on the contrary, they don't anticipate that it will ever come. They have no belief in the future judgment because they always succeed in their evil-doing, and after they get what they want they escape unharmed and unpunished. No trace of divine vengeance can be seen in their lives, and therefore they think that what they hear about Christ's return as avenger in the future is false. And so it is necessary that God the Avenger punish some of them while they live on this earth. Otherwise it may seem that God is not easily moved to anger toward those who have grown insolent because they have enjoyed excessive freedom from punishment. And it is necessary that the folly which runs riot, which shirks the sweet yoke of Christ and spurns the warnings of saintly correction, be curbed by the punishment of pain in the present life. Then these impious people will either impose limits on their own evil-doing to avoid more severe punishment or they will repent completely, and once they have reformed they will return to spiritual health. Then those who have prepared themselves to commit similar misdeeds will be thoroughly frightened by such examples, repent of their evil intentions, and hasten as penitents to the fellowship of the sons of light. But I have said these things by way of preface; now let me reach the end toward which I set out.

A noblewoman named Doda ruled over the castle called Castelnau, lying above the Dordogne River in the district of Quercy.[51] While this woman was alive, she had unjustly seized one of Sainte Foy's manors, a farm that they call Alos.[52] However when Doda had reached the very end of her life and was already failing, she was troubled and concerned for the cure of her soul, so she returned the estate to the abbey of Conques. Doda's grandson Hildegaire, her daughter's son and the lord of a famous castle called Penne in the Albigeois, had inherited from her both great wealth and high social position.[53] Nonetheless he dared to seize the same farm again, wrenching it away from the monastery of Conques. For this reason the monks decided that the holy virgin's venerable effigy should go to that farm, as is the custom, carried in a procession of the people, so that through divine intervention they might recover from the hand of that violent marauder what was rightfully theirs. As for the image, it may seem to be an object surrounded by superstitions, but later I will explain in detail what I think of it.

Meanwhile it happened that one of Hildegaire's men, whose name has slipped from my memory (it isn't possible now for me to make a quick trip to Conques to ask what it was), was feasting gaily on the day of the Lord's birth. He was sitting at a banquet in the midst of a magnificent train of armed retainers and servants, and, as happens frequently over wine, he was ranting brashly about a variety of subjects. Among other unnecessary remarks he made bitterly hostile comments about those who served Sainte Foy and said openly in very foul and abusive language that they were a pile of shit. He even asserted that he would not care a straw if the monks carried her statue, which he thought of as a demon that should be ridiculed and spat upon, to that estate over which both parties were wrangling. No such method would scare him away from defending his lord's rights very forcefully and vigorously. Actually it seemed to him that it would be very easy to trample that statue underfoot, because it was a complete and total abomination. The rogue repeated the same things three or four times, accompanied by so much mockery and raucous laughter that it is boring to tell it.

Then suddenly the air resounded with the fearful din of a windstorm sent from heaven. With an abrupt crash the solarium of the house was completely destroyed, the structure of the upper story collapsed, and the whole fabric of the building, both above and below, fell in ruins. Nonetheless not one of the multitude of people perished except that shameless man and his wife along with their five household servants. And to insure that no one would think it pure chance that the house collapsed, or that people died only because of that accidental collapse, rather than because they were struck down by a blow from heaven, the bodies of those seven people were thrown through the windows and found a great distance from the house. Their ashes are buried in the cemetary of Saint-Antonin in the Albigeois.

Hear, you plunderers and ravagers of Christian property, how inevitable are the scourges and just judgments of God. His vengeance yields to no power, and if it spares for the present it will strike more heavily in the future. If it forbears to punish in this world, a harsher and more effective punishment awaits you in the eternal fires.

1.12: About a Man Who Perished When He Was Struck by Lightning

Raymond [II], count of Rouergue, was the son of that Raymond, who, unless I'm mistaken, was later massacred while he was traveling on pilgrimage to Saint James.[54] Before Raymond [II] undertook the journey to Jerusalem on which he died, he had given Sainte Foy twenty-one silver vessels, well-engraved and embossed with designs, and gilded lavishly, as a goldsmith's taste requires. He also gave her a saddle he had used when riding, which he had as booty after winning a battle against the Saracens. It was estimated to be worth at least a hundred pounds. The saddle had been taken apart into separate pieces and made into a great silver cross without breaking or damaging the Saracen engraving, which is so subtle and ingenious that among our goldsmiths no one tries to imitate it and there isn't even one who has the discernment to appreciate it. And he far surpassed these gifts by relinquishing to Sainte Foy his hereditary rights to an estate called Pallas with a very good saltworks.[55] The estate and saltworks are located in Gothia, on the seashore where the Spanish ocean flows around the Mediterranean islands. After the death of Raymond [II], a woman named Grassenda, who belonged to a very eminent family and was the wife of a man called Bernard the Hairy, began persistently and wickedly to misrepresent this gift. She claimed that the estate had once belonged to her first husband, Raymond, son of Rodegar, count of Carcassonne, but that it had been violently stolen from him by Raymond. She further claimed that, since Raymond was dead, the rights to and ownership of this property ought to return as part of the patrimony owed to her own son William, the child of her first husband. When the parties to the dispute had attempted to reach a judgment at Conques in regard to this property there was not much agreement between them; they arranged to go to the disputed manor itself to have the matter decided.

On the appointed day Abbot Airad[56] and the senior monks, escorted by a noble band of armed riders supplied by their benefactors, set out honorably to that place.[57] Bernard the Hairy and the false accuser, his wife, presented a pompous appearance with their strong band of vassals. A place was prepared for hearing the case, the seats were arranged, and the speakers for both parties took their places. The proceedings began as one would expect when the arbitrary judgments of humankind are considered to be equivalent to laws: the speakers each argued for their own point of view; there was a confused racket as shouting voices mixed together; it was difficult to judge what was true and what was false. Finally Bernard,[58] who held firmly to what was right and just, gave a verdict for the monks' party and rebuked the offensive opposition party with threatening authority. But they became more vehemently insistent and raved like madmen. Finally the lord's opinion prevailed; he calmed the mad raving and forced them to return to the matter at hand. He didn't dismiss the step-son's case until he was satisfied that he had found the truth, which he then proclaimed openly. The two sides began to reach something of an agreement because the woman was willing to give up her wicked and malicious charge in return for a payment in money. But then a young man named Pons, who was very belligerent and bombastic but nonetheless noble and quite powerful, was goaded by the barbs of Tartarean Furies.[59] He rudely interrupted the proceedings by leaping into their midst and proclaiming that he'd had enough of mutual concord. He said:

"What sluggards we are! Have we been taken in so completely by the stratagems of these flatterers that we are going to let our lord's son give up his paternal right without retribution? Let one of their fiercer and braver men come forward now, and the two of us will fight it out on equal terms. Let's assign the settlement of the affair to arms. For I shall win the day, and then afterward neither Sainte Foy nor those utterly corrupt servants of hers will dare to demand again the right and ownership of our fief."

Pons had said this with pallid face, rolling eyes, gnashing teeth, and flailing fists, seeking combat with such wild outbursts that he disrupted everything. And he so incited the minds of his comrades-in-arms that they even rushed to arm themselves. In this way the settlement was undone, a sudden outbreak of violence was barely repressed, and the negotiations were dissolved. And now nothing seemed more beautiful to those who had come from Conques than to preserve their own lives by retreating in great haste to avoid the insolent Antichrist in their midst. But with the aid of God and the very present intervention of Sainte Foy, it was going to turn out differently than they thought and their trembling hearts were going to be filled with hope once again. The heavenly armies were at hand where human frailty was inadequate. So why am I delaying further? Why am I waiting so long to tell you the ending you yearn for?

When the two parties broke off their negotiations, as I have told you, it so happened that the defiant Pons received permission from his lord to take the same road by which the monks had planned to return to Conques. He set out ahead of the monks, accompanied by fifty of his own armed men and, riding apart with only two members of his household, he spoke of his plans for the monks' death, saying, "What sluggards we are! When these men are so unprepared, how can we let them get away unpunished? Alas, wretched me! It torments my mind, it distracts me with intolerable pain, to see such impunity for these scoundrels and to consider our cowardice. But if the lady follows my counsel, she will avenge her injuries by massacring them before they pass our borders, and she will appease my anger."

The wretch uttered such things and others like them just as foolish, for he was beguiled by false security and mindful neither of God nor of His saints. But God wisely settled what was going to happen and it was quite contrary to Pons's ideas, for the result was the death of this man who was God's adversary. Pons had not yet finished speaking when suddenly, with a turbulent convulsion of the air, a spherical cloud veiled the serene sky and, after a sudden horrifying and menacing rumble and a huge flash of fire, an arrow from heaven pierced the man's brain. Thus the wretch ended the last day of his wickedness, burning with fire from heaven. He left behind his burnt-up corpse, reduced to a piece of charcoal. He was like the trunk of a huge oak that aggrieves a poor farmer because it has occupied a well-cultivated field for a long time. The farmer exerts himself with all his strength in the struggle to turn it and uproot it, but he is conquered by its massiveness, so he finally sets a huge fire all around it,

> And in the end he leaves a blackened tree trunk in the middle of his fields.[60]
> Just so, the wretched corpse looked horrible, its limbs burned off on both sides.
> And the mule of the wicked rider perished as well,
> And his spear was splintered into tiny pieces.
> Great shudders left his two companions virtually dead;
> They lay near the animals they were riding.

This threat from heaven threw the rest of Pons's men into disarray. In such a dangerous situation they didn't know where to turn, so they wandered off in disorderly haste, not even staying close to one another.

Oh, bold fighter, oh fearless warrior, oh, most outstanding of men, you who exalted yourself up to the heavens, you who considered the very saints of God as if they were nothing, where is your power now?[61] Where your strength? Where your vigor? Where the violent storms of your threats? Where your unconquerable force?

> Say, where are the imposing muscles and your strong arms,
> That you used to lift up in the air when you tried to provoke battles,
> Troubling the heavens? Where your wicked, insane spirit,
> And your pride in broad shoulders and a ferocious body?
> You called, "To arms!" and you eagerly desired armed combat, and
> in war you perished.
> For from heaven's citadel, from His high throne,
> The Warlord fought you to the finish,
> He who threw Zabulon down headfirst,[62]
> Justly struck you with His lightning from heaven.
> Behold, you lie dead, wretched, thrown to the ground.
> And so you have been reduced to nothing.

Your corpse can't even serve as food for wild animals and birds. What happened to you? What torpor has invaded you? What forgetfulness of mind captured you? Why are you listless? Aren't you defending yourself with your shield? Brandishing your lance? Hurling up your arrow? Baring your dagger? Stirring up a brute with your heels? Turning your foaming horse around in spinning leaps? Perhaps you dispute with the most high God and not with a cowled monk. Your business is with the Omnipotent One and not with a common person. Such a person, I grant you, may be lowly, but not so worthless that he doesn't have God Himself as his defender and advocate. It is not advisable to lie to Him and it is not possible to deceive Him. Whoever strives against His will, will not rejoice in a favorable outcome, for to Him human strength is feebleness and the wisdom of the world foolishness. Therefore give up the attempt now. Stop now, stop harrying the servants of Christ, carry out obediently the duty imposed upon you. The harbinger and precursor of that most degenerate and most recent Antichrist is in the pit of eternal perdition. If you were perchance unaware that he is going to be destroyed at some future time, you have been able to learn of it from the forewarning of your own horrifying death. Now you see how fitting it will be that he will be put down from the throne of his own pride by the forces of good. But now I have ridiculed this most wretched man enough. Since he was a human being, it would have been more fitting to lament. I'll hurry to end this overly long text.

When the hard-hearted woman discovered what had happened to

Pons, she was stricken with fear of divine vengeance and sent envoys to call back the abbot, for he had started his journey. It was scarcely necessary for her to report these things to him, since he had come upon his enemy (who, as I said, preceded him) thrown down in the road. And when the monks returned to Conques they had acquired double joy, because they were enriched with the recovered fief and avenged upon their worst enemy.

1.13: How It Should be Permitted That Statues of Saints Are Made Because It Is an Ineradicable and Innate Custom of Simple People, and Especially Because It Detracts Nothing from Religion; and About Divine Vengeance

Divine justice works very many, terrible punishments, so numerous I can't describe them all, on those who slander Sainte Foy. Shortly I will relate one such case, a powerful miracle, after I have said a word about the image of the holy martyr.

For in fact there is an established usage, an ancient custom, in the whole country of Auvergne, the Rouergue, and the Toulousain, as well as in the surrounding areas, that people erect a statue for their own saint, of gold or silver or some other metal, in which the head of the saint or a rather important part of the body is reverently preserved. To learned people this may seem to be full of superstition, if not unlawful, for it seems as if the rites of the gods of ancient cultures, or rather the rites of demons, are being observed. And I was no less foolish, for I also thought this practice seemed perverse and quite contrary to Christian law when for the first time I examined the statue of Saint Gerald placed above the altar, gloriously fashioned out of the purest gold and the most precious stones.[63] It was an image made with such precision to the face of the human form that it seemed to see with its attentive, observant gaze the great many peasants seeing it and to gently grant with its reflecting eyes the prayers of those praying before it. And soon, smiling at my companion, Bernier[64] — to my shame — I burst forth in Latin with this opinion:

"Brother, what do you think of this idol? Would Jupiter or Mars consider himself unworthy of such a statue?"

Bernier had already been guided in forming his judgment, so he mocked the statue ingeniously enough, and beneath his praise lay disparagement. And not at all undeservedly, for where the cult of the only high and true God must be practiced correctly it seems an impious crime and an absurdity that a plaster or wooden and bronze statue is made, unless it is the crucifix of Our Lord. The holy and universal church accepts this image, in either carved or modeled form, because it arouses our affective piety in the commemoration of Our Lord's Passion. But the saints ought to be commemorated by displaying for our sight only truthful writing in a book or insubstantial images depicted on painted walls. For we allow the statues of saints for no reason other than very old, incorrect practice and the ineradicable and innate custom of simple people. This incorrect practice has such influence in the places I mentioned earlier that, if I had said anything openly then against Saint Gerald's image, I would probably have been punished as if I had committed a great crime.

After the third day we finally arrived at Conques. When we had entered the monastery, fate brought it about, quite by chance, that the separate place where the revered image is preserved had been opened up. We stood nearby, but because of the multitude of people on the ground at her feet we were in such a constricted space that we were not even able to move forward. Although it is grievous to me now that I did such a thing, I stood looking at the image and spoke the words of a prayer exactly like this: "Sainte Foy, part of whose body rests in this likeness, help me on the day of judgment."

And, with a sidelong smile I looked back at Bernier, my scholarly companion,[65] thinking it absurd, of course, and far beyond the limits of reason that so many rational beings should kneel before a mute and insensate thing. In truth my empty talk and smallmindedness at this time did not arise from a good heart. For the holy image is consulted not as an idol that requires sacrifices, but because it commemorates a martyr. Since reverence to her honors God on high, it was despicable of me to compare her statue to statues of Venus or Diana. Afterwards I was very sorry that I had acted so foolishly toward God's saint.

In this regard, among the other reports of miracles, the lord Adalgerius (then dean, and afterward, as I have heard, abbot),[66] a venerable and upright man, told me about a certain cleric named Odalric, who was considered a prig and held himself somewhat above the others. One day when the sacred image had been carried to another place for some necessary reason, that man so subverted the people's hearts that he completely dissuaded the crowd from making offerings. He was greatly dishonoring the holy martyr and spreading some silly foolishness or other about her image. On the following night, when he had given his drunken body over to quiet rest, he had a dream in which a lady of terrifying authority seemed to stand before him.

"And you, worst of criminals," she said, "why have you dared to disparage my image?" After she said this, she applied the rod that she seemed to carry in her right hand and she left behind a beaten enemy. He only survived long enough afterward to be able to tell the story the next day.

After that no room was left for argument as to whether the shaped image of Sainte Foy ought to be held worthy of veneration, because it was manifestly clear that he who criticized the statue was punished as if he had shown disrespect for the holy martyr herself. Nor did any doubt linger as to whether the image was a foul idol where an abominable rite of sacrifice or of consulting oracles was practiced. The image represents the pious memory of the holy virgin before which, quite properly and with abundant remorse, the faithful implore her intercession for their sins. Or, the statue is to be understood most intelligently in this way: it is a repository of holy relics, fashioned into a specific form only because the artist wished it. It has long been distinguished by a more precious treasure than the ark of the Covenant once held, since it encloses the completely intact head of a great martyr, who is without doubt one of the outstanding pearls of the heavenly Jerusalem. Because of her merits, divine goodness performs such great feats that I have neither known nor heard that their like was done through any other saint, at least not in these times. Therefore Sainte Foy's image ought not to be destroyed or criticized, for it seems that no one lapses into pagan errors because of it, nor does it seem that the powers of the saints are lessened by it, nor indeed does it seem that any aspect of religion suffers because of it.

1.14: About a Man Who Wished That the Image Would Fall

Now that I've explained some things about the holy image, I want to add another miracle about it.

Once in a famine (I don't know what caused it), the revered image in which the holy martyr's head is preserved was carried out-of-doors in a huge procession. It happened by chance that a man coming toward the procession passed by very near to the statue. When he saw the effigy radiant with glowing reddish gold and blazing gems, he was blinded by a cloud of greed and said, "Oh, if only that image would slip from the shoulders of the bearers and fall to the ground! No one would gather up a greater portion of the shattered stone and broken gold than I."

While the foolish man was muttering these words, the mule on which he was sitting bent its head down between its front legs and kicked up its hind legs so that they flew over the rider's head. The man ended up in the mud under the heavy hindquarters of the mule. Some people ran quickly to keep him from suffocating and freed him from the calamitous weight. Then all gave thanks to God, Who protects His own saints even from silly chatter.

1.15: About a Girl Who Was Scornful of Standing for the Image

Just as I shouldn't leave out lesser miracles, I also shouldn't fail to add more about the powerful miracles worked on behalf of the sick.

Because a triple miracle was worked for her, I'll speak now about a poor girl who had been crippled in all her joints and had been carried to Sainte Foy's monastery. There she had been so completely cured that no trace of her illness remained. Afterward she spent some time in the settlement near the monastery working to pay for her food, for she was poor. Soon, the severity of vengeance followed after the work of pity; heavenly truth punished what proud willfulness did wrong. Therefore this case is not out of harmony with those I have already mentioned.

For while the girl was living there a fast had been declared because of some calamity, and the venerable image was carried out-of-doors and followed in procession by an enormous crowd of both sexes. And according to the custom there all the people rushed out of their houses and fell prostrate before the image. Almost all the inhabitants of the village gathered hastily in preparation for the image's arrival. The woman who employed the girl as a weaver began to caution her firmly and then to scold her vehemently, telling her to leave her work and to stand up for the procession. But the girl was not moved by fear of God, nor did she take pleasure in the sound of those singing divine praises; she completely ignored the chiding voice of her employer, as if she were deeply devoted to her work. And immediately, in that very hour, the destroying fury of heaven acted. The girl began to be made pathetically deformed throughout her whole body. She became so misshapen that it was just as if she had never been healed but had remained bent and crooked, wholly deprived of the function of her muscles. Her body was completely drawn together and she didn't have the strength to let go of the tools of her loom—the very shuttle was held fast in her clenched fist.

The girl had shown arrogant disdain for the saint, even though her cure had been effected through the immense kindness of God. Now this very girl, who could speak only hoarsely because her condition greatly restricted her voice (though she had been able to speak normally before), humbly confessed that she was guilty of offending Sainte Foy. Nonetheless, her torments did not cease, even a little, for the whole time that she was carried behind the golden reliquary box through the complete route of the procession and back to the monastery. There she kept holy vigil for several nights and through the glorious martyr's just intercession she was transformed a second time from a cripple to a person who could stand upright. In her case every slander against the image was purged, for the image cannot be discredited without harm to the slanderer. Now no one should be surprised if that little object is considered worthy of honor out of respect for the relics of such a great martyr, for the worthiness of such a holy martyr beautifies even the ranks of the angels.

1.16: The Miracle of the Golden Doves

Long before the events in the preceding chapter, yet in our own time, the excellent miracle of the golden doves took place. If you kindly people have time to listen and will allow a true story to enter the secret places of your hearts, then I will tell you at once about the fashioning of the famous image that the inhabitants of the monastery call the Majesty of Sainte Foy.[67]

It is made of the finest gold and becomingly adorned with gems delicately and carefully inserted on portions of the garments, as the judgment of the craftsman thought best. The band about the statue's head also displays gems and gold. She wears golden bracelets on golden arms and a low golden stool supports her golden feet. Her throne is made in such a way that only precious stones and the best gold are to be seen there. Also, above the tops of the supports that project upward at the front, two doves made of gems and gold adorn the beauty of the whole throne. Now I am going to relate a miracle about these doves.

Bernard, who was then abbot of Beaulieu and was afterward made bishop of the city of Cahors, once owned the doves.[68] Sainte Foy warned him in dreams to give them to her. Since he refused to do this, she tried to persuade him again and again in the same way. Finally Bernard sensed that the warning came from God, so he took other gold of the same weight as the doves and set out for Conques. There he offered this gold to God and His saint. Then he returned, certain that Sainte Foy was pleased because the weight of his offering was equal to what she had demanded. But after his return, one night while he was sleeping the same vision appeared. She was no less insistent than before that the doves be given to her and she declared that he wouldn't be able to satisfy her in any way, even if he paid out all his gold, unless he gave her the doves as well. Finally the reluctant man was compelled to deliver the golden doves, just as though they had only been entrusted to him for safekeeping, and he placed their remarkable beauty on the supports of Sainte Foy's throne.

And since Sainte Foy made a great search for gold of this kind, it is appropriate to demonstrate this more clearly in the following miracles.

1.17: How Sainte Foy Collected Gold Everywhere for the Fashioning of an Altar

The monastery of Conques was dedicated in honor of the Holy Savior. Long ago the holy martyr's body was secretly carried away from the city of Agen and brought to Conques by two monks. After that Sainte Foy's name prevailed there because of her more numerous miracles. Finally, in our own time, after the renown of the great miracle worked for Guibert (called "the Illuminated") flew across the whole of Europe, many of the faithful made over their own manors and many other pious gifts to Sainte Foy by the authority of their wills. And though the abbey had long ago been poor, by these donations it began to grow rich and to be raised up in esteem. In the time before Guibert's era the place was not adorned with so many golden or silver reliquary boxes, nor so many crosses or great basins (there was only one made entirely of gold with all kinds of stones, and two of silver), neither with candelabra nor with thuribles; there was not even an altar frontal, nor so many kinds of ornaments. The most outstanding of the ornaments then was the splendid image, which was made long ago. Today it would be considered one of the poorer ornaments if it had not been reshaped anew and renovated into a better figure. If this restoration had not taken place, then, besides the things I've mentioned, a huge crucifix would be preeminent. It is made entirely of pure silver, with the exception of the diadem and the loincloth, and I remember that it seemed to me that the gold they were made of was superior to all other gold in its vibrant redness. In addition, there are a good many silver frontals, embellished in places with gold and stones. There remains the golden frontal of the high altar, which is not less than seven feet and two fingers in length—not in geometrical feet, but as the peasants are accustomed to measure, with both hands spread out and the thumbs linked at the upper joint [see Figure 6].

Saint Martin of Tours has two that are larger, but not more lavishly adorned with gems and engraving. Moreover, when you see for yourself that there are very many things yet undescribed — there are so many crowns, just as many chalices, and furthermore vessels of various shapes — you will not think that I am lying. I am leaving out most things. For if I speak of altar cloths or copes, and other things of that kind, I will digress too much from my subject.

As I have said, many people had granted to Sainte Foy great farms and many possessions of manors, as many from the natives of the region as from religious pilgrims. They also made innumerable, lavish contributions of gold or silver, and also of precious stones. And for this reason the abundant accumulation of gold inspired the senior monks with the idea of building a new frontal for the high altar. But because such a great quantity of materials was required for the large size of the frontal that they planned, what they had on hand did not suffice. The gold was all used up first. There was a need for a greater supplement of gold and of precious stones. And this is the reason that few people are left in this whole region who have a precious ring or brooch or armbands or hairpins, or anything of this kind, because Sainte Foy, either with a simple entreaty or with bold threats, wrested away these same things for the work of the frontal. She appeared to each one of them in a dream just as if she were a beggar, in the form of a very beautiful not yet adult girl. She demanded no less from the pilgrims who pour in from every direction.

And so a frontal so beautiful and so large was produced with the gold and the stones that I've seldom been able to see a better elsewhere. But I've not yet passed the Jovian heights, and in heaven there may be many things made with greater skill. A great quantity of gold was left over, which was later adapted to sacred uses.

1.18: How a Ring Was Denied to Sainte Foy and Later Handed Over to Her

A noblewoman who heard of the renown of Sainte Foy's miracles decided to go to Conques. After she had already gone a short distance on her journey, she recalled that Sainte Foy had a habit of appearing to pilgrims in dreams and asking for their rings. So she turned back, drew her own ring from her finger, and entrusted it for safekeeping to the chambermaid whom she had summoned.

"Hold this," she said, "and keep it safe until I return, for Sainte Foy may snatch it away from me if I take it to Conques."

Now, of course, she thought she was being clever—as if to think that any kind of precaution would be able to deflect the foreknowledge of God, Who foresees all things before they happen!

What more is there to say? The woman went to Conques, she said the prayers she had promised to say there, and she returned home in peace. On the following night, a maidenly shape appeared to her while she was sleeping. When asked, she said she was Sainte Foy and, without pausing, warned with imperious authority that the ring had best be given to her. When the woman denied that she had a ring, Sainte Foy reminded her that she was the very woman who, when leaving for Conques, had entrusted her ring to a chambermaid in order to avoid giving it to Sainte Foy. When morning came and the woman awoke she decided that the divine vision had only been a fantasy, a meaningless dream. But how much longer will I delay the end of my story? Immediately the woman began to burn with such a fiery fever through her whole body that she could scarcely rest for even an hour. After three days of fever she realized what was happening, remembered her offense, and confessed that she had slighted Sainte Foy. While she was ordering that a horse be saddled so she could make a return journey the excessive surge of fever abated. And so the woman set out healthy and returned rejoicing, counting it not a small gain to exchange a ring for her health.

1.19: About Golden Bracelets

The Lord has already deigned to work so many miracles of this kind through Sainte Foy that no one could have preserved all of them, and there isn't enough time for anyone to write out those that have been preserved. Nonetheless, I want to add a few miracles from those that I noted down as they were told to me, because I don't want to appear too taciturn by remaining silent, or too annoying by being wordy. I know the proverb from before our time that says everything uncommon is precious. And this is why, in comparison to all the remaining miracles, I write the uncommon miracles, because they are precious. Therefore Christ will pardon me for knowingly omitting a great many miracles.

Arsinde was the wife of William, count of Toulouse, brother of the Pons who had later been treacherously killed by Artaud, his own stepson.[69] She owned golden bracelets, which should really be called armlets, since they reached up to the elbow. They were embellished with marvelous craftsmanship and with precious gems. Once when Arsinde was lying alone on her own fine couch she had a dream in which she saw what appeared to be the form of a very beautiful girl passing right in front of her. Because Arsinde admired the girl for her very great elegance, she addressed her with a question: "Tell me, Lady, what are you?"

Sainte Foy answered the humbly inquiring voice: "I am Sainte Foy, woman, don't doubt it."

Arsinde meekly begged: "O holy mistress, why have you deigned to approach a sinner?"

At that moment Sainte Foy made the inquisitive woman familiar with the business on which she had come: "Give me your golden bracelets. Go to Conques and place them above the altar of Saint Savior. This is the reason I have sought out your presence."

But the prudent woman wouldn't allow such a great gift to leave her hands without some advantage for herself, so she said: "Oh holy mistress, if through your intercession God grants that I conceive a male child I will carry out your command with pleasure."

Sainte Foy answered her: "The Omnipotent Creator will do this quite easily for His own handmaiden, if you do not refuse what I ask."

On the next day Arsinde, who was motivated by the saint's reply, conducted an eager and thorough search to determine in what district the village called Conques was located, for only rarely had news of the miracles at Conques passed beyond its own borders. When Arsinde had learned this from those who knew, she performed the duty of a pilgrim herself. She carried the golden bracelets to Conques with the highest devotion and offered them to God and His saint. And there the worthy woman spent some days of the Lord's Resurrection honorably and adorned the ceremonies with her gift. Then she returned home. As the divine vision had promised, she conceived and bore a son. And she became pregnant again and gave birth to another. Their names were: the firstborn, Raymond, the second, Henry.[70] Afterward the gold of the bracelets was used in the work of the altar frontal.

1.20: About a Pilgrim Who Gave Sainte Foy a Ring so That She Would be Freed from Her Pains

It delights me to disclose another occasion on which Sainte Foy wrested a golden ring away from a woman.

Although her husband had forbidden it, this woman had come to Sainte Foy out of her great devotion. When she had left the monastery and returned to the guesthouse she met with such sudden pains, for she was near childbirth, that she seemed about to die. The wretched woman didn't know what to do. She had no hope of giving birth at the right time, and if she gave birth prematurely she wouldn't dare to return to her husband. In her great sorrow and anxiety she began to appeal to Sainte Foy with repeated cries, imploring the saint to be well-disposed toward her. But in the end, when the pains did not ease, she was carried back into the monastery by faithful porters and there she drew her ring from her finger and offered it to God and His saint on behalf of her health. The intervention of the merciful martyr, so powerful and so efficacious, brought prompt help to the little woman and relieved her pain immediately. And so she walked out of the church on her own feet in that very hour, as merry and healthy as she had been but a short time before. She went back to the guesthouse and, before she could be prevented by the birth that was at hand, she returned joyfully to her home.

1.21: About a Pilgrim Who Wanted to Exchange a Ring Promised in a Vow

A young man named William, a native of Auvergne, was worried about a distressing situation and filled with unbearable anxiety, so he vowed to Sainte Foy his best ring, which was set with a brilliant green jasper. Things turned out for him better than he had hoped in the matter, and everything else was prospering as well, so William went to Conques because he was concerned to fulfill the vow he owed. But when he had approached the sacred majesty, William brought out and presented three gold coins, for he calculated that he should be able to redeem the promised gift with one that was larger even though it was different. When he was already about six miles from Conques on his return journey, William suddenly felt drowsy, so he stretched out on the ground and fell asleep for a little while. He soon awakened, but he didn't see his ring, which until then he had worn on his finger. Then he searched his companions thoroughly and very closely but he didn't find it anywhere, and he looked in his own clothing and found nothing. He even proceeded to untie his belt once more, thinking that by chance it might have slipped through an inner fold of his clothing, and there was nothing. What, then, should he do? Downcast and filled with confusion he turned his mount back toward Conques. He returned very quickly to the saint and prostrated himself at the foot of her image. There, in a tearful voice, he complained bitterly about the loss of his ring in this way:

"Oh Sainte Foy, why have you taken my ring from me? Give it back to me, I implore you, and be satisfied with receiving the ring as a gift. I will give it to you and won't think it lost, but rather safe. I have sinned, I confess, I have sinned before God and before you, but, Lady, do not look to my transgression but to the customary compassion of your kindness. Do not cast me, a sinner, into sadness, but forgive and make a gift return with joy."

While William was constantly repeating these and other similar pleas, he looked to the side. Marvelous to report! but believable to the faithful, he saw his ring lying on the pavement. Immediately he snatched it up and returned it to the holy virgin, rejoicing greatly, and those who were standing there marveled at the sight, for they saw Sainte Foy's power even in trifling matters.

1.22: About a Woman Who Wrongfully Seized a Ring That Another Woman Had Bequeathed to Sainte Foy When She Was Dying

There is a small castle bordering on the village of Conques, which a man named Austrin (whose successor I have seen myself) governed under the authority of the monks.[71] The miracle I am beginning here happened in our own time.

Austrin took a ring that his dying wife Stephana had promised to Sainte Foy and with it married another woman, named Avigerna, for he had dismissed his first wife's words as those of a person in delirium. Avigerna, a shameless and heedless woman, ostentatiously displayed her finger decorated with gold that had been solemnly promised by oath to another. But afterward she was punished by divine justice and that very finger developed an intolerably painful swelling. Then a pustule puffed up over the swollen flesh, and her finger swelled so much that it almost entirely covered the ring. It was clear that an implement could not be inserted nor the ring cut off without damage to the finger. So when they despaired of the remedies offered by the doctors they had summoned to arrest the force of the illness, and Avigerna could no longer bear the intense suffering at all, they had recourse to the help of divine aid. They made an open confession that they were guilty of wrongdoing and the feeble woman was led to the holy martyr's sacred reliquary. There she spent two nights keeping constant vigil; during the third, which was Sunday, the strength of the pain afflicted the suffering woman so grievously that the pitiable sound of her screams did not cease all night long. At last, when the monks were already intoning the praises of God at matins, divine mercy benevolently descended from the high-throned seat of the highest majesty. He did not allow such heavy crosses of punishment to vent their rage on human flesh any longer, nor did He wish the penitent's tears to reach the point of complete despair. For when the sorrowful woman happened to blow her nose, the ring flew off without hurting her fingers, just as if it had been hurled from the strongest siege engine, and gave a sharp crack on the pavement at a great distance. And for this reason there was a joyous celebration that Sunday, in which all the people of that region took part, because they saw that their compatriot and neighbor had been saved from grievous torment through the help of Sainte Foy.

And certainly many, virtually innumerable miracles like this one are reported about Sainte Foy even throughout the various places of the earth, so that now there is no one capable of recounting them let alone writing them. For it is impossible either to explain in spoken words or to describe in written words all the feats of Sainte Foy.

1.23: How a Falcon Was Found

Even in regard to the smallest of problems a great many miracles were performed, and such miracles the inhabitants of the place[72] call Sainte Foy's jokes, which is the way peasants understand such things. Since she has Christ as her fellow-worker, Sainte Foy performs so many miracles like this that no one can even say how many there are. And if some of them are told, they are not easily believed because of their novelty. But the truth cannot easily be stifled or extinguished; the more harshly truth is torn to pieces by the treachery of unbelievers, the more effectively it retains its strength and force to continue in existence. And just as a burning lamp shines with a greater tail of beams under the onslaught of a raging gale, so also out of the uproar of detractors truth advances in a straight line from out of the whirlwind, and the more it is slandered, the more ardently it holds to its purpose. When the same lamp is protected and defended, it may escape human notice in the more open light. But if the kind of people exist who don't want to believe these miracles, it makes no difference to me. God, Who created me and gave me life for the task of writing them, knows who the people are, and where and when it will be granted to them to believe these miracles and, by believing, to benefit.

In this wicked age of ours the greater part of humankind have turned astray from the former condition of religion, so much so that they wander in pursuit of their own desires. Nevertheless, the Creator of all good things does not allow any ages or times to pass without evidence of His goodness; moreover, He unceasingly carries out His powerful deeds through His saints, even if they are rather infrequent because of human sins. And just as His wisdom is unsearchable and inexhaustible, so also the quality of His powers cannot be comprehended or judged by anyone at all, and if He wishes He works new and unusual miracles. For, as Boethius says, it is not possible either to comprehend all the stratagems of divine work by natural ability or to explicate them in words. But I am going to speak about the least important matters or, if it is permissible to call them this, Sainte Foy's jokes—so let me turn my straying pen back to the beginning.

I mentioned a warrior named Gerald, who lived near Conques, when I spoke about the mule a short time ago.[73] Gerald, who was very highly skilled in all the military arts, went to the city of Rodez and asked for the loan of his lord's best falcon.[74] His lord did not hesitate to grant his petition at once. Nevertheless, the agreement was made and confirmed that if Gerald happened to lose the falcon he would be deprived of all his property. This kind of condition pleased both of them. It was especially pleasing to Gerald's lord, who was the more cunning of the two, since the result of such an occurrence would be to fill up the insatiable gullet of his own avarice through the devastation of another's goods; but it also pleased Gerald, since, at least for a moment, he could enjoy the esteem of having such a great bird.

Gerald set out for home, but before he arrived he turned aside into the Albigeois for some reason. While he was there, he sent the falcon out for the first time with an unsteady throw and the bird strayed off and disappeared into the vast sky. Although Gerald followed her for a long time, he had no success in calling her back. He arrived home, very downcast and exhausted from his great efforts to retrieve the falcon. Sadly he reported what had happened. No doubt he was well acquainted with the cruelty and implacable anger of his merciless lord.

"Alas, wretched me," Gerald said, "how tightly I have been bound to an unhappy fate and how I am forced to suffer the ferocity of my stubborn lord. What remains now, oh shame! oh disgrace! but that I will be stripped of my goods and left in the deepest dishonor! Wretched me! It seems to me that I can already see that day when I have been deprived of my goods and counted as a beggar by those who wish me ill."

And when the members of his household, who gathered around him to soothe his sorrow, poured forth words of consolation, for a long time Gerald didn't heed them, nor did he find relief in anything at all. He only complained with even more anguish for the rest of the day and refused to eat the food that had been prepared. Finally, his good wife approached him and spoke forcefully.

"My love, why are you tormenting yourself? Why are you distressing yourself? Why are you visited with so much grief? Why do you banish your happy expression with weeping? Why is it that you uselessly heap up such great wails and complaints over something that can't be recovered? Nevertheless, if you commit yourself with a solemn vow to go barefoot tomorrow morning to Sainte Foy and offer her a candle, I hope that in this matter God will be your helper. Do it manfully and let your heart be strengthened. Don't let yourself doubt that God's mercy can result from Sainte Foy's intercession. Get some life into your face, put on a happy expression, and take your place at the table among your people for the meal with your usual good cheer. For it is not difficult for God to make you get up from there a happier man. Doesn't it seem that a wise woman has given you good advice? Anyway, in a tight spot nothing is more offensive than mistrust."

Gerald was greatly strengthened and soothed by these words. And so, after he had made a generous vow, he sat down to a sumptuous meal as if he had endured no sorrow, for he was already somewhat aware that he would be gladdened by divine assistance and he had a presentiment of great joy. But while this was happening—what a beautiful thing it is to report!—a tame goose flew in from outside and disturbed the company at table. Immediately the lost falcon followed the goose as it circled the dining room and threw itself on the fowl with a rapid attack. And this was the sign of an excellent miracle, that, as if intentionally, the winged creature returned from another district to a place that it didn't know. What joy, what happiness there was, how much thanks offered on high, because he had regained his hope of retaining his property rather than yielding it to his lord. This made the miracle even more glorious. And so on the next day, grateful for God's goodness to him, Gerald hurried to fulfill his vow to God and to Sainte Foy.

1.24: A Dishonest Merchant

A merchant, an inhabitant of Auvergne, came to Sainte Foy to offer prayers. He noticed that there was a very brisk trade in wax, and, with such a throng of pilgrims offering candles, the price seemed far too low to him.[75] At once the merchant remembered the skill for which he was known as a businessman and thought to himself, "What an easy profit! How stupid I am! If I had learned this before, I could have put my business on a sound footing and made myself rich! But now I'll make up for my ignorance! Frequent trips to and from Conques will make me a wealthy man in no time! It's time to act like a man and get this business underway."

And so the merchant approached the waxseller, made a hard bargain for a great quantity of wax, and and paid ten gold coins for it. Then he took possession of all the wax and stored it in sacks. And he was already rejoicing, for he saw that his profit would be at least four times what he had paid for the wax. He thought to himself, "Yes, yes, I'm off to a good start. And what if I come back many times?"

But now let's get to the ending quickly. A beautiful candle had been left out because it didn't fit into the merchant's sacks. The greedy man slipped it into his clothing in such a way that the larger part of it projected below his belt and the smaller part jutted up toward his beard through the opening in his garment. But the avenging omnipotence of all-seeing God didn't allow the robber's presumption to stay hidden. For the wax taper held beneath his belt was suddenly set afire by divine flame and began to scorch him badly beneath his garments. Steam, belching flames, and billows of smoke poured out. Then a ball of flashing sparks hurled itself upward, his huge beard blazed, and, with a crackling sound, the hair on his head was consumed. Nor were the flames confined to the front of his body: they encircled him and burned his backside as well. You would have been astonished at his horrible bellowings as the flames drove him mad, at the noises he emitted as he kicked, at the grating of his teeth, at his wildly rolling eyes and the uncontrolled contortions of his whole body. In his unbearable pain, the wretch seemed to be propelled back and forth in headlong movement. He was like a snake that receives a sudden, hard blow; sometimes it coils up and contracts itself into a ball and sometimes it stretches out quick as a flash and drags itself forward, reaching out its twisting neck to take flight. But it is weakened by the blow and turns again to threaten the one who struck it, hissing, and rolling its blood-red eyes.

That's the way the wretched merchant looked, running up and down, here and there, driving himself back and forth, first bending forwards, then backwards, unable to breathe in any position, kept on the move by a strong force. Nevertheless, a remaining vein of human emotion brought the wretch to repent. Calling out loudly, he ran at once to the holy martyr's tomb and dumped all his wax there, and just as swiftly the penal fire vanished. He didn't complain about the loss of the money as long as he had escaped from torment.

Since things like this happen, I don't think I would offend anyone by asserting that Sainte Foy's goodness is praiseworthy and marvelous also for this: that to prevent vile commerce from weakening her pilgrims, she punished greed and avarice.

1.25: How Gerbert the Watchman Returned Sainte Foy's Gold Against His Will

I won't be slow to tell you what happened to a young man named Gerbert before he became an employee of the monastery.

When Gerbert was strolling one day in front of the smithy where the golden altar frontal had been made, he happened to discover among the ashes discarded from the furnace the earthenware vessel in which the craftsmen had melted the gold.[76] That vessel had been softened by the intense heat required to liquify the gold and a swollen hollow space had formed in its very bottom. Particles of the metal had run down into this space and lay hidden there. And so when Gerbert caught sight of a tiny gleam shot forth by the hidden gold, which had been somewhat uncovered already and was sparkling brightly, he came closer. He decided to see what it was. And after he broke the vessel he found in the little hollow a ball of the purest gold, nine deniers and one obol in weight by the impartial scale. Gerbert rejoiced greatly over his find, as a person would who had never owned any gold. He thought he should hide it with a friend of his.

Some days later Gerbert was lying down in his bed, for one of his eyes had developed a rather serious inflammation. It seemed to him that Sainte Foy appeared to him in a vision, not in the form of a girl but, contrary to her usual custom, in the form of her sacred image. She rather severely demanded the gold Gerbert had hidden away; then she seemed to leave, as if she were angry. On the next night she seemed to appear again in the same terrifying way, and to leave as threateningly as before. This time Gerbert made her a solemn promise that he would return the gold the next day.

When he nonetheless persisted in his hardheaded stubbornness, the same vision, but far more terrifying, came to threaten the naysayer on the third night.

She said, "Tell me, you worst of criminals, why haven't you returned my gold to me when I've demanded it back so many times?"

Together with this verbal reproof she thrust toward his sore eye a hazel wand that she seemed to carry in her right hand, as if she were about to strike him. Gerbert turned his head away in another direction as if to avoid a very swift blow and, in a higher voice than he was usually able to speak, he cried out asking for mercy over and over. And the greedy man had been struck down by such great fear that he carried the gold back to God and Sainte Foy the next day. After that, as he told me himself, he suffered no injurious punishment.

1.26: How the Monk Gimon Fought Courageously Against Sainte Foy's Enemies

In the same vein I want to add another of the kind of miracles I've already mentioned, those that inhabitants of the place call Sainte Foy's jokes, which is the way peasants understand such things. What I venture to tell is marvelous to report and, although it may seem more incredible in every way than the miracles that have already been set forth here, nothing truer has been heard about all the powers of the saints. I know that my hostile readers especially will not find this material sufficiently convincing; they can slander anything by interpreting it badly. But when the task is to reveal proven truth, it is a profanation of what is sacred to cater to fawning flattery and an offense against moral law to falter before the attacks of enemies. Therefore the Christian, and I am a Christian, should be susceptible neither to the exhilaration that comes from applause nor to the dejection that comes from disparagement, but remain calm and even-tempered. How could I ever use deceit to corrupt God's word or pretend to write the truth while cheating my readers by lying—it would cost me my salvation!

Many people knew Gimon, a monk and prior of the monastery,[77] and they told me miraculous things about him that are, I believe, quite unheard-of. When he lived in the secular world Gimon had a fierce and manly heart, and he didn't leave it behind when he entered the monastery, but applied it entirely to vengeance against evil-doers. In addition to his other garments, which were suitable for clothing a monk, Gimon kept in the dormitory a cuirass, a helmet, a lance, a sword, and all kinds of instruments of war. These were placed above the foot of his bed within easy reach for use, and to the same end he had a fully equipped war-horse in the stable. Then, whenever wicked men invaded the monastery with hostile intent, Gimon himself immediately took up the duty of defender. He rode at the head of his armored ranks, leading the campaign, and with his own daring he heartened the spirits of the fearful, giving them strength to face manfully either the reward of victory or the glory of martyrdom. He declared that they had a much greater obligation to vanquish false Christians who had attacked Christian law and willfully abandoned God than to subdue those pagans who had never known God. He said that no one who wanted to be worthy of leadership should become cowardly, but rather, when necessity demanded, should battle forcefully against wicked invaders so that the vice of cowardice would not creep in disguised as patience.

Many who attacked the monastery's property were so frightened at the thought of Gimon's arrival that they often fled before he could come to fight them. At the same time, those who resisted in their rash rebellion and took confidence from their numbers were nevertheless overcome by a smaller force than their own through the ever-present power of Sainte Foy. But if by chance—and this was seldom—such a large and destructive enemy force fell violently upon the monastery that the weaker forces on the side of good mistrusted their own frail humanity and their courage to do battle slipped away, then immediately, as was his custom, Gimon approached the martyr's holy tomb with the greatest trust. There he pled his case before Sainte Foy in his down-to-earth way of addressing her. Undoubtedly his confidence was based on experience—he knew that she never found it easy to ignore him. For he threatened to flog the sacred image and even to throw it in a river or well unless Sainte Foy avenged herself on the evil-doers immediately. And yet in the very midst of his angry, threatening outbursts, Gimon wouldn't stop pouring forth humble, pleading prayers and repeating them over and over. And I think that God Himself had engendered this manner of praying in Gimon and that God did not consider the harsh words to be sinful, since in all other things Gimon's mind was sound and filled with moral excellence. For God does not judge people by their manner of speaking, but by their intentions or actions. And just as a flattering manner of speaking doesn't acquit a hypocrite, so a harsh manner of speaking doesn't condemn a worker of true justice. It seems that this thought accords with the proverb that is recorded in the Gospel about the father who had two sons. He did not reward the son who answered obediently, but failed to make the words good with deeds. Rather he rewarded the son who answered disobediently and harshly, but soon hastened to carry out his father's command. And again, in order that false flatteries might be confounded, God Himself says this: "Not everyone who says to me, Lord, Lord, shall enter into the kingdom of heaven, but the one who does My Father's will."[78]

Therefore it is my considered opinion that Gimon ought not to be blamed for his harsh manner of speaking when I've heard his deeds described as irreproachable in every way, except that he used to go on expeditions armed. But if people understood this behavior of his correctly, they would be able to ascribe it more to moral excellence than to an assault on the monastic rule. For he will not be judged except by the motives he was understood to have. If only lazy monks would put aside their cowardly sloth and act as bravely to the advantage of their monasteries! Instead they parade the handsome habits of their order on the outside, while making a hiding-place for iniquity on the inside! For it is clear that there are men like Antichrists, who live for nothing other than to speak against the truth and to attack anything that has any good in it. They seize the goods of the saints as plunder, laugh at the bishop's interdict, think the legal position of the monks is a pile of shit, and even rail against the army of the living God like insolent Philistines. If God's avenging omnipotence should employ the hand of any of His own servants to strike down and slaughter one of these Antichrists, no one could call it a crime.

Don't we read that after Saint Mercurius had already been martyred he punished the emperor Julian the Apostate by piercing him through with a lance?[79] Therefore He Who raised Mercurius from death in revenge against His own adversary was also able to arm Gimon well in defense of His own Church. God could not be prevented from an action that He previously thought fit to perform through a dead man if He wanted to do it again by the hand of a living man. If such a thing ever happened to Gimon, it is my considered opinion that the same penance ought to be imposed on him—indeed, I would impose it—as King David paid in the matter of the Philistine.[80] That man will not be regarded as a murderer whom the Lord Saboath and King of Armies and Powers destined to be the sole protection of his own monastic community, as if he were another defender-angel. For just as a prophet is not able to prophesy other than what God places in his mouth for him, so Gimon was not able to do other than what the spirit of virtue and power had suggested to him in his heart. Truly the good protector and defender of the good was zealous on God's behalf and disdainful of the sons of Belial.[81] No one could doubt that his bravery was pleasing in the eyes of God. For whenever a party of evil men lay in wait with their battle-line strongly deployed against him, at once, as I've said, Gimon resorted to his usual defense of prayer, and Heaven heard him. He used to extort divine assistance for himself as much by upbraiding as by imploring, and whatever he hadn't been able to accomplish with his armed men he managed to get God to do. Further, a great many of those evil-doers at that time were said to have perished due to various misfortunes. Some threw themselves from the highest rocks, others choked to death on food, others inflicted death on themselves with their own hands, and for whomever the hour of judgment had come the means of death was always nearby.

In addition to his responsibility for guiding the monastery in its obedience to the Rule, Gimon was also the guardian of the sanctuary. At that time Conques was quite isolated, no throngs of pilgrims came there, and there wasn't such a great abundance of lights—only one candle served the high altar. Since it went out rather often, the guardian rose constantly to restore it. And many times when Gimon was weighed down by sleep because his labors had made him weary or because he had prayed a very long time, he felt a hand gently touching his cheek and at the same time he heard a sweet voice admonishing him to adjust the light. And immediately he would leap up, vigorously shaking off his drowsiness, but, before he could reach the candlestick and touch the candle itself, which he could see had gone out, he would see that it had been lit again at that very moment from heaven. Or if by chance, as happened frequently, he carried it to the fire, before he reached the coals the light would revive by divine power right there in his hands. Again, when he had returned to his bed and was already beginning to sleep, the same vision returned three and four times, as if she were playing with him. This would force the old man to rise up reluctantly from his bed and hurry back to the candlestick. By this time he was thoroughly enraged, for he had a fiery temperament. He would rail against Sainte Foy just as if she had been disturbing him and making sport of him. He scolded her and called her names in his native tongue. Then the miracle would cease and he escaped again to his bed.

More often on such an occasion he would take up the meditative activity of chanting the Psalms and spend that whole night sleepless. It is said that Gimon meditated in this way at other times so intently and steadfastly that his uninterrupted murmuring almost made day continuous with night. On several nights when he was in the monastery devoting himself to a holy vigil, Gimon would hear the golden statue moving with a rattling sound.[82] Instantly he would understand that this movement was supernatural and hurry to the light, just as I have described. It was, moreover, now habitual for him and repeated with a frequency far beyond general human experience to enjoy conversations in which he received various kinds of divine instruction. It is no wonder that he was considered worthy of this kind of good, for he was a person in whom no impurity of body or mind could dwell. He was always prepared to undertake every labor for the advantage of his monastic brothers and he was second to none in the virtue of obedience. His impatient anger was in accordance with the teaching: "Be angry, sin not."[83] But how much he truly excelled in the preeminence of virtues can be judged from this: that he would tame everyone, not only the other monks, but even the abbot himself, as if they were under the yoke of discipline; and this was due not to his erudition in letters, but to his fortitude of spirit.

1.27: Because Sainte Foy Loves the Chaste, She Spurns the Unchaste

Many other good things have been reported to me about Gimon, but let what I've already said suffice for devotees of Sainte Foy. As was shown in his case, she loved her devotees with eternal charity, and most greatly of course she loved those whom she saw persevering in the virtue of chastity.

An inhabitant of that village told me that if at any time after sexual intercourse, even if it was legitimate, he passed beyond the first set of iron grills without having washed himself, he would never complete that day unpunished. That was how vexed Sainte Foy became at anyone who thoughtlessly dared to frequent her sanctuary while in a defiled condition. Such was the lofty and wondrous merit of this one girl, to whom the great favor of miracles had been granted in matters both great and small.

And I have heard that her actions in regard to feudal tenants are excellent and filled with much compassion. If wicked overlords unjustly take what belongs to their tenants and the tenants ask for Sainte Foy's help, they are immediately restored to the good graces of their superiors through divine intervention.

It delights me to include this, not because I am unable to discuss some greater matters—which I omit purposely—but because when I heard it, it pleased me greatly. And so I offer thanks to divine goodness, which deigns to bring relief to the oppressed even in needs like these.

1.28: How Sainte Foy Performed Her Remarkable Miracles at Councils and About a Boy for Whom a Four-Part Miracle Was Done

I don't think that I ought to pass over this: that in the midst of the many relics of saints that are carried to councils according to the custom of that province, Sainte Foy shines forth as if she is preeminent among them because of the glory of her miracles. Since there were so many, and I may seem to be writing a volume that is too boring, I judge that it is enough to record two of these miracles.

The most reverend Arnald, bishop of Rodez, had convened a synod that was limited to the parishes of his diocese.[84] To this synod the bodies of saints were conveyed in reliquary boxes or in golden images by various communities of monks or canons.[85] The ranks of saints were arranged in tents and pavilions in the meadow of Saint Felix, which is about a mile from Rodez.[86] The golden majesties of Saint Marius, confessor and bishop, and Saint Amans, also a confessor and bishop, and the golden reliquary box of Saint Saturninus, and the golden image of holy Mary, mother of God, and the golden majesty of Sainte Foy especially adorned that place.[87] In addition to these, there were relics of many saints, but I can't give the exact number here. There, in the midst of all the rest, the goodness of the Omnipotent deigned to glorify His own handmaiden by the working of a remarkable miracle.

A boy, blind and lame, deaf and mute from birth, had been carried there by his parents and placed close beneath the image, which had been given an elevated and honorable position. After he had been left there for about an hour, he merited divine medicine. When he had received the grace of a complete cure, the boy stood up speaking, hearing, seeing, and even walking around happily, for he was no longer lame. And when the common people responded to such an amazing event with uproarious joy, the important people at the council, who were seated together a little farther away, began to ask each other: "Why are those people shouting?"

Countess Bertha[88] replied, "Why else should it be, unless Sainte Foy is joking as usual?"

Then all of them were flooded with both wonder and joy because of the exquisite miracle. They called together the whole assembly to praise God, recalling frequently and with very great pleasure what the respectable lady had said—that Sainte Foy was joking.[89]

1.29: Another Miracle About a Person Who Was Blind and Lame

At that same synod a man who was blind and lame spent the night in vigil before the image of Saint Marius the Confessor in order to be cured. Many people considered Saint Marius's wondrous miracles, which had been worked in many places, to be the most celebrated. When it was already growing light, the man was suddenly overcome by deep sleep and he seemed to hear a voice saying to him, "Go to Sainte Foy. For your infirmity won't be healed unless it is through the power she has earned."

This answer awakened the weary man and he began to search out that place with the strength he could muster. When he arrived, the holy martyr's intercession immediately dispensed with further delay. For when the man rushed into the entrance of the pavilion, at once his blood vessels regained strength and his muscles were invigorated. What had been bent became straight. Also the veil over his pupils split apart, and after a sudden and violent discharge of blood came very clear light. And then he was completely healthy, for the right hand of the heavenly doctor had treated his body.

1.30: How a Man Was Freed from Hanging on the Gallows Through Sainte Foy's Aid

Among all the other miracle stories that were told to me about Sainte Foy so far, while I was energetically pursuing various informants as if I were hunting with the greatest desire, everyone was speaking joyfully and very often about the miracle I begin now. And after I had verified it more certainly by consulting those who were present, I recorded it so it will be remembered.

A very noble man named Hadimar of Avallène (for this is what the mountainous region of the Limousin is called) had had among his vast household a retainer who stole some horses from him and fled. Finally on another occasion Hadimar unexpectedly came upon this man. At once he tore out the man's eyeballs, like little plums, and then allowed him to go free. But there was another man, a close friend of the thief, who had not been a participant in the villainy. Hadimar bound him with the most miserable restraints as if he were equally guilty of the crime. Though he struggled and denied knowledge of the theft, nothing did any good. On the contrary, when he cried out in protest to Sainte Foy, his cruel captor responded like this:

"What else do scoundrels do when they have been apprehended but immediately invoke Sainte Foy as their patron? But, without a doubt, that clamor will have to be punished with torture."

And so Hadimar carried the fettered man home on his galloping horse and confined him in a deep storeroom that served as a dark, underground prison. The next day he was to be delivered to the gallows for hanging. What could the wretch do? Through the whole night fearful and distrustful in the horror of total darkness, he remained a stranger to sleep. He never stopped appealing to God and His saint with some words that he knew. About the middle of the night, he noticed that a girl of indescribable beauty was coming toward him from the direction of the door. He supposed that she was some chambermaid, but she was surrounded by a glowing light even though she was carrying neither a candle nor any other source of light. Approaching him, she began as if she knew nothing to ask him insistently why he was being held prisoner. When he had explained it all to her and afterward had inquired as to her name, she replied that she was Sainte Foy.

"And do not," she said, "stop what you have been doing or have any lack of confidence, but always have on your lips both the name and the cry of Sainte Foy. Nevertheless, as they have threatened you, tomorrow you will undergo the gallows. But the Omnipotent One lives and He will call you back from the gaping jaws of death."

She followed these words with more like them, and then this powerful personage returned to heaven. Although the prisoner spent the rest of the night in violent shuddering caused by this unusual vision of divinity, his mind could be troubled no longer, because he had been visited by the side of the good.

Early the next day he was led out from his prison and brought before the tribunal. But the more frequently the prisoner spoke Sainte Foy's name, the more swiftly malicious thoughts hastened him toward the gallows. And so the prisoner was taken to the place of punishment. It was not enough for the lord to order his own servants to commit the wicked deed. Accompanied by a great band of horsemen, he departed with them. While the bound man was being hanged, he never forsook the name of Sainte Foy but obeyed the command he had been given until his throat was constricted so tightly by the noose that his voice was choked off. Soon thereafter they left him hanging. When they were already a little distance away on the return journey, they looked back and saw the gallows empty. With a great clatter they returned and lifted the bound man up high again, more roughly this time. As they turned toward home again, they looked back and saw with astonishment that the gallows-bird had slipped to the ground a second time. And already some of them were saying that it was the power of Sainte Foy, when their cruel beast of a lord menacingly thundered down his reproaches on them and forced them to keep silent. Then he renewed his efforts and throttled the man's throat much more roughly and brutally, and as long as he watched the hanging man he thought without doubt that he had been strangled to death. Nevertheless when Hadimar had begun to descend through a sloping passage of the mountain on his return, he was badly troubled in his mind and could not resist turning his fierce eyes back. And when he had seen the miracle, he returned in a hurry. Finding the man free and unharmed he hesitated, not knowing what to do. But all the others now openly declared with one voice that it was the power of Sainte Foy. They cried out that their own lord was guilty of a very wicked deed and that they weren't going to endure such a scandalous crime any longer. Seeing that a miracle had been worked, Hadimar became remorseful and began to beseech the man to forgive him. But the man had no trust in him at all and said that he would rather make his way to Sainte Foy and relate this wrongdoing to to her. Then Hadimar saw that the man was obstinate and, taking fifteen young men of his own household with him, he hastened to the holy virgin unarmed and barefoot. You could see both Hadimars (for they each had that name) arguing before the holy image as if before a tribunal, this one accusing, that one admitting his own sin and offering reparation. But the senior monks of the monastery interceded, prescribed the legal reparation for a person's death, and restored harmony between them.

As I have said, I had already heard this miracle everywhere from the common people. Later, the monks confirmed it and related it to me more accurately. To intensify my faith with words, they summoned as witness a young man who was a first cousin of the celebrated Hadimar and had come with him to Conques after he had been saved from hanging. But I would also have been able to see Hadimar himself if there had been time for me either to wait for him after sending messengers for him or to travel to see him. They said that not more than five years had passed since the miracle had happened, and that he was still alive.[90]

1.31: How Sainte Foy Frees Prisoners Who Cry Aloud to Her

One kind of miracle above all others is specifically associated with Sainte Foy, for which she is best known and most highly renowned. This miracle is that she frees prisoners who cry aloud to her and orders the freed prisoners to hurry to Conques with their heavy fetters or chains to render their thanks to the Holy Savior. It makes no difference whether a person is held in prison justly or unjustly. For if the prisoner keeps up a persistent outcry she soon shows how much grace God bestows upon His own handmaiden. The locks to shackles and the fastenings to barred doors are undone and iron door-bolts burst apart, as divine compassion unlocks what the sin of human cruelty had confined. The captives step out of their bonds to freedom, displaying the burden of their useless chains. Freed, they hold the shackles with with they were bound. They are reborn from the prison, even though it did not engender them. Those whom arrogance had once lured into crime come forward from confinement into the light, reformed. Preceded by the tokens of their triumph, the pitiable men are restored to the bosom of the holy martyr's church. And those who have long been confined in the dark, foul horror of prison afterward drink in the joyful light of heaven. In the midst of a rejoicing church, they return thanks and praise to God and His saint.

This miracle kept happening with such great frequency that the immense quantity of the iron fetters they call "bracelets" in the language of that district was beginning to hold the monastery prisoner. Therefore the senior monks decided that this great mass of iron should be hammered out and converted into various kinds of doors by blacksmiths.[91]

From the outside, the basilica is made up of three forms by the division of the roofs, but on the inside these three forms are united across their width to shape the church into one body. And thus this trinity that fuses into unity seems to be a type of the highest and holy Trinity, at least in my opinion. The right side was dedicated to Saint Peter the apostle,[92] the left to Saint Mary, and the middle to the Holy Savior. But because the middle was in more frequent use due to the constant chanting of the Office, the precious relics of the holy martyr were moved there from the place where they had been kept. There is scarcely any opening in this church full of angular passageways that doesn't have an iron door fashioned from fetters and chains. To tell the truth, they would seem to you more marvelous than the whole edifice of the basilica, with the exception of the beautiful furnishings, whose abundance, whether of gold, of silver, or of rich fabrics, together with precious stones, provides a pleasing variety.

And when I chided the senior monks because they had not kept written records of the freed prisoners—their names, families, homes—they said that it would have been very difficult. Furthermore, they had not expected a writer like myself just now, for whom they would have kept brief descriptions of these things that could have been used to write a fuller text. And, as they shamelessly admitted, all these miracles happened daily, to the point where they loathed them—in short, they had become indifferent. They were even completely ignorant of the name of the man whose fetters—a huge quantity of them!—I myself have seen hanging below the carved paneling of the ceiling. Since the miracle had happened so recently, the iron had not yet been melted down for the uses I have described above. But the castle where he had been in captivity was called Broussadel, and I have learned that the name of its lord was Aimon.[93]

1.32: About a Man to Whom Sainte Foy Brought a Small Hammer so That He Could Pound His Iron Fetters to Pieces

Now I return to my narrative to relate a very renowned miracle about another man, which all the monks reported to me the same way. While this man was wasting away in a long imprisonment he cried out incessantly to Sainte Foy. She appeared to him while he was keeping vigil. When he asked the saint who she was, she named herself with the word "Foy" and immediately presented him with a small hammer that was very old; its whole surface was corroded with rust. She ordered him to use it to strike off his fetters. Next she commanded him to set out quickly for Conques, bearing the heavy burden of his smashed chains. He carried out her instructions, finding that the passage out of the prison lay open. No one stopped him and, trusting to divine protection, he directed his course on the right path to Sainte Foy. Grateful for the great kindness done for him, he returned great thanks to God and His saint.

The little hammer had hung in that place about three years and as the sign of such a great miracle it was an attraction to pilgrims. I was extremely angry that it had been destroyed in the making of the iron grillwork. But what a wondrous thing! Where do you think Sainte Foy got a physical hammer? But we shouldn't judge divine work with human reason; we should firmly believe that it was done.

1.33: About a Man Who Was Counseled by Sainte Foy to Escape Through the Window of a Tower; and About a Miraculous Donkey

As I am about to recount for all future generations a miraculous and memorable occurrence—and I'll do it concisely, especially for squeamish readers—I faithfully entreat God, the living font of wisdom, that He may deign to pour a flood of divine wisdom into the secret places of my heart and to saturate my parched understanding with the dew of the Holy Spirit. Then I will be enabled to bring forth what is true in a text that is both appropriate and correct, one that will benefit my audience. Let not my thought stray from the correct path so that I begin to turn toward worthless ideas and hold to what is not true.

A warrior was in captivity in the fortress of Castelpers in the Rouergue,[94] which was under the command of the high-born lord Amblard. The man gave sureties for himself and then, as if he were going to do other business, he went secretly to Sainte Foy. Then he kept his word and returned to captivity. How his escape from there some time afterward was enabled by a divine visitation must be told. But first I ought to say a few words about the location and nature of that region.

It is a thoroughly mountainous country, and indeed in many places the rocky cliffs thrust up so high that one can see vast distances because of the great height. But where there happens to be a plain between these cliffs, the yield of the crops makes it so fruitful that no land seems to me to have been more fertile in rich grain and excellent wine, the gifts of Ceres and Bacchus. I think that the fertility of this land came about for this reason: it is more elevated than our regions and therefore harsher because of the brutality of winter's cold, and it is nearer to the sun—as is natural since it is located in the south—and for this reason hotter because of summer's heat. Of course in the summer on account of the nearness of the sun it blazes up excessively with torrid heat. But just as the south wind rules with a free rein in the summer, in the winter, on account of the altitude of the land, it is stiff with ice and snow because of so many cold spells. Therefore, the more the contraries of diverse nature weigh upon that soil, the more faults are burnt away and harmful moisture sweated out. And because of this the land became a producer of richer and sweeter fruit. But, as I have said, it contrasts with our region in having high mountains and cliffs. This is why the structure of the fortress of Castelpers, which is built on the solid platform of a very steep, rocky cliff, soars higher into the spacious void than we can imagine. Furthermore, there is a dwelling for the inhabitants on the part that seems flatter and more suitable for habitation, and a stronghold was erected in a higher place, at that part where the cliff drops more abruptly. There in the highest story of the tower was the lord's chamber, where the lord himself, with his household, enjoyed quiet slumber and placid dreams. Outside of this chamber on the same level, but on the side facing the rest of the castle, the prisoner I've mentioned was bound up with a heavy weight of iron around his lower legs and kept under observation by a guard of three serfs.

He had been crying out to Sainte Foy in a plaintive voice for a long time and had almost given up hope. One night after the guards had fallen asleep, Sainte Foy appeared to him visibly and in physical form. When he asked her, "Tell me, who are you?" she answered that she was Sainte Foy. At once she added that she had been worn down by the earnestness of his prayers, or rather, constrained by his prolonged wailing. And so she had been sent by God and had come to set him free.

"Why," she said, "are you delaying so long? Rush right through the chamber and slip out through the highest windows of the tower."

The prisoner began to crawl toward her admonishing voice when the lord of the castle, awakening and apprehensive, turned toward the sound of the jangling iron. Then he woke a female servant and gave her a stern order to shake up the drowsy guards. When she had done this, she closed the small door and shut herself in the chamber. After some hours had passed, behold! Sainte Foy appeared again, encouraging the prisoner to begin the plan. He immediately complied but found that the door into the chamber was closed and returned from his vain effort. Again the lord of the castle was awakened by the clash of iron and sent the female attendant as before. When she returned after carrying out her master's order, through the will of God she left the door of the cell open. Later, when all had been overpowered by a much deeper sleep, behold! Sainte Foy, clearly visible for a third time, criticized the prisoner's faint-heartedness more harshly and severely. Then he offered the closed door as his excuse and said that he didn't take it lightly that he had already been tricked twice.

But she said, "Don't hesitate, because you'll have a way out and God will help you."

He trusted completely in God and began to move with as much of a stride as he could manage. And finally with great difficulty he got himself into the chamber and stopped short at the windows, for he was greatly frightened by the height. Then Sainte Foy, who had accompanied the man of faltering mind this far, went in front of him as if to show him the way and began to exhort him spiritedly, saying:

"Have confidence! Quick! You won't be able to escape another way now. You are just like the Israelites, for the Scriptures tell us that they had been given a divine command to conquer the tribe of Benjamin in revenge for the crime committed in the Benjaminite city of Gibeah, yet they had to make a third attempt before they won the victory."[95]

His situation had reached a deplorable crisis. At last he took courage and putting his life in danger thrust himself feet first through the window, trusting himself entirely to the vast height. But never did his own feather bed caress Sardanapalus more softly and more sweetly[96] than those very rugged cliffs caught the prisoner. Divine power supported him so well that this man to whom nature had denied wings seemed not to fall but to fly. Gaining confidence from this miracle, he did not hesitate to make a leap to a far lower cliff. And then he made a third leap from the very high cliffs upon which the whole structure of the fortress rested and, rushing past the lower parts, he glided along to the firm earth. Marvelous to tell and terrifying to hear, with what daring a human mind was ever able to plunge into so much danger! For I confess that even in telling such things I tremble all over with great dread. But He Who wished to glorify His own saint with a miracle like this protected the man from fear of such a great fall. It is true that he received no injury, but the crashing sound of the fetters during his first leap reached the ears of the sleeping lord. Awakened by the noise and enflamed with burning rage he told his servants what had happened, found them guilty, and judged them to be worthless dogs. Finally he ordered them with threats to follow after the fugitive as soon as possible. They thought these orders were ridiculous and promised that they would collect the pieces of his battered corpse on the next day at quite the proper time. But he didn't give in to them at all and told them that torches and lamps must be lit, and that runners must go ahead swiftly, on a path where the descent was easier, to apprehend the man.

When the escaped man saw the light of the pine torches and at the same time heard nearby the clamor of those pursuing him, he didn't know what to do, for he was weighed down by the enormous mass of iron attached to both of his feet. Nevertheless, as quickly as he could he crawled towards an escape-route provided by a small wood, which, through the providence of God, nature had produced near the castle. He worked with all his strength, striving to reach his goal. There was no need for anyone to force him when necessity itself commanded him. Nor should his slowness have been rebuked, although it seemed to him that he was walking more slowly than a tortoise. And as he was straining in this anxious, critical moment and was already pulling himself into the dense shrubbery somewhat, in a marvelous way he stumbled upon a donkey. When he had knotted his belt in the donkey's jaws to serve as a halter, he sat on its back with his legs turned to one side, the way women ride. In this he followed reason rather than custom, putting aside his honor as a man. The fugitive would have been done for, without a doubt, if this donkey had kept him waiting for the space of one hair's breadth. Never did a war-horse or a royal steed move with a more agile or more gentle trot than did that donkey, as it traveled right through the middle of the region into that area where the fugitive supposed that they would be least likely to look for him. Meanwhile the rider, not yet daring to believe he was safe, kept listening and holding his breath. He kept on looking back to see if by chance he could hear or see anyone. Finally when he had traveled almost eight miles, he felt that he was safe for the moment.

It was already growing light, and the gleaming dawn was urging weary mortals to the practice of their labors. Then the fugitive tied the donkey to a shrub in a place where he saw hard stones and turned away from the path a little. He struck his iron fetters against these rocks, and they broke as easily as ice. But while he was busy with this, the celestial donkey vanished. Looking back, he saw neither the animal nor its tracks; no matter how much he investigated, he could find absolutely nothing. But as a proof of the miracle he found the belt, just where he himself had tied it. Therefore he proceeded with his journey on foot, taking the right path to reach Sainte Foy.

Never had a more beautiful or more splendid sight entered the basilica of the Holy Savior before that day, and the populace of Conques has never seen anything more delightful than this shining example of a noble man with the lofty stature of a very handsome body, bearing a heavy mass of iron on his shoulders, rushing forward to the saint's tomb through the surrounding crowds of worshipers. He was just like a lion who had broken out of its cage, its neck burdened with a great weight of chains, seeking the native refuge of the forest. Then before all the people the man deposited his burden there; the hostile load which he had carried on his neck as if it were his captive, he gave to freedom. He had been brought back from imprisonment to a joyous welcome, and the senior monks of the monastery, along with the entire populace, rejoiced because it was such an unusual miracle. The minds of his friends, who had been held in a long dread-filled suspense, were flooded with gladness at his unexpected return. Afterward he did not grow despondent as a result of his captivity, for he escaped both financial loss and bodily harm.

But what do you think we ought to conclude about that donkey? Was it not a powerful and good angel, manifested in the more humble figure of a beast of burden? The Savior himself rode on such an animal to humiliate the proud and defiant behavior of worldly pomp. He preferred a means of conveyance more associated with the common people, even though He was "Lord high above all nations; and his glory above the heavens."[97]

Oh, the great merit of one girl! Oh, the wondrous gift granted to one woman! Oh, the wondrous and ineffable grace invested in one virgin! The pen does not suffice to write down her miracles, nor the human tongue to relate them! For Sainte Foy works miracles, not only there where her body rests but also, as I have learned from those who witness her miracles daily, on land, on the sea, in prisons, in infirmities, in many dangers, and, as I have also learned partly through my own experience, she responds to all kinds of needs. If anyone appeals to her with a pure heart, that person feels her presence. And wherever Sainte Foy is named, there her power is also, to the praise and glory of Christ Omnipotent, Who controls all things with the reins of His own omnipotence and rules with the Father and the Holy Spirit in co-eternal unity that endures forever and ever. Amen.

1.34: A Letter Intended for the Abbot and Monks, Which is Considered the Conclusion of the First Book

To the most reverend and serene Adalgerius, abbot of the holy congregation of Conques,[98] and to the other brothers in God ministering to Sainte Foy, Bernard, the least of scholars, sends a perpetual greeting in God.

A new edition of the miracles of Sainte Foy has been made, just as you asked. In the midst of so many gyrations of adverse fortune that scarcely allowed my grief-stricken mind to breathe again for quite some time, it was due to the way that divine grace relieved my discouragement, I am sure, that I was able to carry my task through to the end. And lest at any time even by a slight chance this book is criticized as inauthentic, I do not wish to suppress the title identifying the author. Moreover, as much as I am inferior to Sulpicius Severus,[99] that much more am I inclined to reveal my name. For relating the life of Saint Martin it was not possible to find a better writer anywhere on earth than Sulpicius Severus. Nevertheless, so that he might escape the slur of being called a conceited person, he erased the title on the front and gave instructions that the page remain mute. But I, on the other hand, have given my name at the beginning and in the middle and at the end, lest material so unknown should produce doubt and through this doubt the very great works of Sainte Foy should be held in contempt.

A controversy has been produced by certain people that greatly confuses a clear reading of the word "Fides," for they want it to be inflected in the fifth declension. But I have paid attention to the long tradition of the ancient writings and I say that it ought to be "Fides, Fidis," as, for example, in "nubes, nubis" and "soboles, sobolis." Unless I am mistaken, Master Fulbert, bishop of Chartres, most learned of almost all mortals in this our age, will agree with this assertion. At Fulbert's altar of the martyr Sainte Foy, on the day of the birth of that same virgin, I myself have seen and I have read that "Fidis" not "Fidei" was expressed as the genitive two or three times. For, if we change this rule, it will seem that we mean the virtue named Faith, or the Faith who was martyred with her two sisters, Hope and Charity, at Rome under the emperor Hadrian. And so I admonish you amiably that you abandon the practice you have followed up till now and make the name of our Faith a word of the third declension.

And as regards these miracles, I myself took them down from you or from the inhabitants of this village in your own words. They should be returned to you in recompense, so receive these miracles back again with kindness toward the poverty of my talent, which rendered them into some feeble sort of Latinity. And for the love of Sainte Foy, exalt and praise them highly and frequently, not because of the unlearned way of speaking, but because they contain the unadulterated truth and because the narrative sequence of those who told me these miracles has been faithfully observed to demonstrate clearly that they were actually present at so many miraculous deeds. Do not think that my humble little additions to this book have been confirmed by me alone and rest only on my authority. I wasn't able to go afterward for help to Master Fulbert, whom I just named above and to whom the first letter is addressed, because of all kinds of disruptive troubles. But it happened that I showed this little book to my highly revered teacher, Reynold, master of the school of Tours, a man who is highly educated in the liberal arts.[100] He considered my book to be of such great value that when he was afflicted with a serious illness while in my house he had it placed on his head just as if it were the text of the holy gospel and trusted that he would recover through Sainte Foy's power. But even before that time, when the opportunity presented itself I showed this book, which was not yet completed, to two brothers, my friends Wantelme and Leowulf, canons of Saint-Quentin in the Vermandois, men distinguished as much by the reputation of their ancestral stock as by their own refined wisdom. Their diligence, along with the very renowned accoutrements of their wealth, has spread their precious fame far and wide through the broad spaces of the earth. They themselves received it with such avid hearts that they almost tore it away from me violently, asserting that in a certain way it was rightfully theirs, because in their city, Noyon, of course, a new church of Sainte Foy was then being established, due to the new reputation of her powers. But because I did not have a copy in another place they left empty-handed, insistently pleading with me to send one to them without delay.

What if this book were to be given to John Scotus, not he of old but one living now, a blood relation of the above-mentioned Reynold, who was his tutor from boyhood and lived in his household? He would never indulge in either heretical deception or uncritical admiration. There is no one in our time of whom more outstanding deeds can be reported, unless John's works were attributed to him. In his close friendship he is so favorable toward my humble work that he dares to number me among the wise. Doubtless he bears towards me the kind of love that a doting mother feels. For although she distinguishes forms clearly enough, using the natural discretion that is innate in the human mind, the face of her son, no matter how much more unsightly it is than others, seems more handsome to her. For John Scotus displayed such favor toward me that he asserted I was not inferior to the genius of the writers of antiquity. But although his generous honesty may be exaggerated, I won't fall under this spell. I won't be so deluded as to think myself their equal, since, as I have said so often, I seem more like a monkey than a man in comparison to them. Nevertheless, it is fitting that a teacher praise a student, because the encouragement increases mental abilities, but it is also fitting that the disciple see himself as less than he is, so that he doesn't come to grief through excessive praise. Moreover, some famous men have read my book and their opinions differ only a little from those mentioned above.

Also many respected people have heard of Sainte Foy for the first time through my writing and through me her previously unknown miracles become known to many. Among them is my lord Hubert, bishop of the city of Angers, an unusually kindhearted man[101] who pursues a cultured way of life. In the cathedral he himself rebuilt from the ground up, he will declare the perpetual memory of Sainte Foy by dedicating an altar to her. And furthermore lord Gautier, the very reverend bishop of Rennes,[102] has seen the reputation of Sainte Foy's outstanding miracles. And so in speaking with me he promised that a secondary altar will be built in honor of Sainte Foy in the basilica dedicated to Saint Thomas the Apostle, which that very notable man is building in that city. And then there is that very estimable man, Guy, priest of the church of the Holy Mother in Angers that I mentioned above, who is a wealthy man and to no small extent endowed with all moral uprightness. He has been consumed with such love for Sainte Foy that he arranged for a glorious oratory to be made to the holy martyr in his own church. This was the church that, in an extraordinary effort, he renewed from its very foundations in honor of Saint Martin of Vertou. I could name many more people who have become devotees of Sainte Foy, but I have thought that to include them in these pages would result in a repetitive and very boring text. Until recently these people had hungered for banquets of such miraculous and renowned deeds. It is as if my promulgation of the miracles revived them with rich food. They thank God that I (although they greatly magnify the value of a sinner) took such great care and diligence and was eager to preserve with the service of my pen the great deeds of Sainte Foy, lest time pass and they be forgotten.

As a recompense for my work, I ask above all things for a reward like this: that when my very wretched and sin-filled soul passes from this life I may deserve to have Sainte Foy, whom I call upon among all the saints as my special patron, to be my invincible champion against the servants of iniquity, so that, since Christ our most gracious redeemer has atoned for my sins, I may be a partaker in Christian redemption with you, oh, Sainte Foy. In the place where the joy of the saints endures forever, may I possess eternally even the smallest portion of your glory. Amen.

The end of the first book of miracles of Sainte Foy, virgin and martyr.

The Second Book of Sainte Foy's Miracles

Rescued with Sainte Foy's Help and Regained His Lost Property After His Return

2.3. How Sainte Foy Healed a Man's Eye on the Sea; and the Miracle of the Creaking Ship

2.4. About the Large Number of Miracles Worked by Sainte Foy During a Procession in Auvergne

2.5. How Sacred Vessels Were Preserved Intact in a Fall; and How Hugh Was Killed by Divine Providence

2.6. How a Pilgrim Who Was Captured and Enchained Was Suddenly Freed with Sainte Foy's Aid

2.7. How Sainte Foy Miraculously Healed a Man Who Was Struck by a Sword

2.8. What Happened to Abbot Peter on a Journey to Rome

2.9. How Abbot Peter, on a Journey to Sainte Foy, Was Freed from Enemy Ambush by a Four-Part Miracle

2.10. About the Miracle of the Golden Clasp Denied to Sainte Foy by Countess Richarde

2.11. How a Thief Returned a Horn That Had Been Stolen

2.12. About the Miracle of the Double Doors of the Church and of the Inner Doors, Which Stood Open of Their Own Accord Because of the Clamoring Pilgrims

2.13. How Sainte Foy Miraculously Cured Bernard's Brother, Whose Limbs Had Become Contorted

2.14. How a Man Recovered with Wondrous Swiftness After He Called upon Sainte Foy

2.15. How a Psalter Was Found Through Sainte Foy's Power

2.1: Another Miracle About Gerbert

Let's remember Gerbert, whom I mentioned in the first book. There I described the restoration of his sight after his eyes had been torn out, a miracle worked in the same way as that by which Guibert was enlightened. Earlier Gerbert had congratulated Guibert for his miraculous healing, and when he first saw Guibert he said that Guibert's miracle was considered to be greater than any other and called him blessed. It was, of course, through the provident and miraculous dispensation of the Supreme Creator that the same miracle was later performed for Gerbert himself, and he rejoiced with a similar joy, for it was beyond his wildest hope. I wrote how afterward, so that Gerbert wouldn't become puffed up by arrogance at some future time and presume to revert to the wicked life of a fighting man, which he had abandoned, the just plan of God brought it about that he lost the sight of one restored eye. But the substance of the eye remained unimpaired and he retained the sight of his right eye. As a result he led a pure and tranquil life, without uneasiness of mind about returning to his former ways. On my previous journey I took down a precise rendering of this miracle as I did for others, just as I heard and saw it, but in a very abbreviated form. After I returned to my own country, I expanded and corrected what I had written. But during the years that have passed (as I said a little before) in which I had neither returned to Conques nor sent a representative, a miracle happened to this Gerbert scarcely unequal to the first.

One day when Gerbert was walking around in the open space in front of the church, he was holding a lambskin in his hand and playfully waving it in the air. Soon a townsman,[1] Bernard Pourcel, leaped on him furiously. Bernard had lost a virtually identical skin the previous day and he was convinced—though it was a false impression—that Gerbert was the thief. Since he was completely drunk, this very wicked man gave the matter no considered thought, but immediately assaulted Gerbert with verbal abuse and accused him of having stolen his property. Although he had no legal evidence he tried to avenge the crime at that very moment. But Gerbert couldn't bear a false charge wrapped in insults—for rare indeed are mortals who aren't provoked when they are discredited even deservedly. He replied in kind, not ceding any point to Bernard's words. And so the conflict escalated on both sides, with all kinds of cursing and abuse flung back and forth, to the point where it came to blows. For a short time they fought evenly and neither backed down. But then Bernard, who was goaded by a more savage fury, rushed away from the fight he had begun, armed himself, and began to run back in a hurry. Moreover, as commonly happens at a critical moment when haste is of the essence, weapons weren't close at hand when required. All he found was a spit for roasting meat. When he took up the fight again, he inflicted a deep cut on Gerbert's healthy eye and drilled a hole in the pupil. Then the violent man hacked the rest of the eye into tiny pieces. Finally the men were separated by the crowd of bystanders.

Gerbert's clothing was stained with fresh blood and he was now blind in both eyes. With a stranger to lead him, he hurried into the church. Repeatedly he cried out to heaven and called on Sainte Foy for help. For three whole months, he continued to keep vigil in the sanctuary through every single night, wearying everyone with his incessant outcries and scolding Sainte Foy quite insistently: "Oh, Sainte Foy, Lady of Conques, why didn't you protect the eye you gave back to me after it had been torn out by the root? Why didn't you defend the wretched man whom you gained as a special servant because of your beneficial deed?"

He never stopped pressing her with persistent questions like these for the whole time until the feast of Saint Michael was at hand. And on that night preceding the vigil, behold! Sainte Foy appeared in a dream and seemed to speak to him: "Tomorrow after vespers go with the procession of monks in front of the altar of Saint Michael, and there God will restore your eye to you."

On the next day, at the hour that she had commanded, Gerbert was very mindful of the divine vision. He accompanied the procession into the chapel of Saint Michael. There, when they were singing an antiphon from the Gospels in honor of the coming feast day, the heavenly Creator Whose wisdom finds nothing difficult deigned to make good the loss of that which He had made. He did not allow the suffering man's prolonged tears and supplicating prayers to pour forth in vain any longer. God formed for a third time the substance of the eye that He had already restored twice. Although that eye will be reformed a fourth time at the last day in the great resurrection, in that last resurrection Gerbert will not have more eyes than nature gives to other mortals.

Gerbert turned the gaze of his new eye in all directions and clearly discerned the forms of things around him. Before he burst out in a voice of great joy, first of all he hastened to the bellropes, running wildly up the steps to the gallery at the entrance of the church, which was below the vaults over the altar of Saint Michael.[2] The servants whose duty it was to ring the bells followed him at once. Certain that the miracle had been revealed from heaven, they rang the whole peal of bells, and at the same time all the monks chanted "Te Deum Laudamus" and praises to God. There was great tumult and unspeakable joy. Nothing in the affairs of humankind can be called its equal.

A little time passed, during which Gerbert joyfully basked in his new glory and offered good witness to the ineffable miracles worked for him. Then he reached the end of his life. He was undoubtedly borne away to that eternal life in which the holy virgin and most glorious martyr Foy enjoys perpetual happiness. There she even has Gerbert for a companion; after she healed his mutilated head, she didn't wish to be separated from him for long.

Therefore I was not able to see him on my second journey, because he had died. But I saw Guibert, whose healing miracle was older than Gerbert's. He was called "the Illuminated" because of the miracle and was still living at the time by the grace of God, though I saw that he was very old. He wept profusely over my return and said, "Now you are returned, lord father, you who helped me with both material and spiritual things. My time is nearly over and I am worn out by old age. I know that I don't have enough time left in this life to see you again. May God and Sainte Foy reward you, for you alone undertook the task of coming here from far away to hear and record her miracles."

In honor of the outstanding miracle I kissed his eyes warmly three and even four times and, saying farewell to him, I left. I was no less struck by compassionate emotions than a person who travels across the sea, leaving behind sweet children or a dear spouse, uncertain as to whether he will ever see his own once again. If only God would ever, through His mercy, let me come back to Conques again and Guibert should still be living then! Only if I now held him in low regard or didn't care about him at all, could I be prevented from handing down the record of his very celebrated miracle to perpetual memory and making him memorable to every generation. How could I not preserve this miracle, when it is apparent that this worst age has been glorified by such a great miracle we would not otherwise have heard of? But because of too many digressions this lengthy text is already keeping me from those miracles that remain, so let me bring this chapter to a timely end.

2.2: About Raymond: How He Was Shipwrecked, Held by Pirates, and Carried Away into Foreign Countries; and How He Was Rescued with Sainte Foy's Help and Regained His Lost Property After His Return

It seems fitting to tell about a man named Raymond, who came from the Toulousain and was highly renowned for his lineage and wealth. The castle that Raymond held in that district was called Le Bousquet by the locals. Once this man set out on a pilgrimage to Jerusalem. When he had traversed most of Italy and had reached the city of Luna (known by this name since antiquity),[3] Raymond had a ship made ready for crossing the Mediterranean Sea, for he believed that he would be able to reach the territories of Jerusalem more swiftly and directly by sea. But after they had crossed most of the way on a calm sea, while they were cleaving the placid, blue waters a storm arose suddenly. Their ship was dashed against the cliffs and destroyed. Smashed to bits it left behind the helmsman himself, who was swallowed up with the others by the savage whirlpools. Only two barely survived: Raymond, of course, and one faithful servant whom he had brought with him. The servant, clinging to a very small fragment of the ship, was cast up on the Italian shore.

The servant thought that his master was undoubtedly dead, slain by the waves of the sea. So he went back to the person to whom his master had entrusted a part of his money, as is the custom of pilgrims. There he received his master's money and brought it back to his master's wife as his only remains. He related his own experiences to her and explained his master's apparently fatal end. She feigned grief for a while, but did not turn it into a matter of heavy weeping or long sighs as is the custom of good women. Instead, she quickly made herself an elegant spectacle for men and threw herself with unbridled passion into faithless and untrustworthy love in its many and varied forms. In this way she found a man unequaled in debauchery and acquired him; he was a fit companion for her lust. She even gave the castle to him, and she would have done the same with the remaining territory. Because she was lost to blind lust, she would even have deprived Raymond's daughters of their inheritance. But a man named Hugh Excafrid, who was an old friend of Raymond's, opposed her on behalf of the girls, who were suffering loss because of their mother's actions. And lest they be reduced to disgrace because they were not provided with dowries, assiduously and on his own authority Hugh recovered and kept for them half of all their father's holdings, except the income from the castle. And the marriages of the young women were not long in doubt, since he decided that each sister should marry one of his own sons.

I'll return now to my story. Raymond had clasped one broken beam of wood the same way his servant had. The waves propelled him not to Italy but to some part of Africa. The whole time he unceasingly called on Sainte Foy for help; her name was never absent from his lips. And by the time the third day had slipped by, during which he had seen neither man nor sea monster, he had become so dazed and stupified by the raging sea that except for the instinct to save his life, which is innate even in brute animals, he had no judgment left at all. Then behold! suddenly there were hosts of pirates bearing down on him. They were coming from the region of Turlanda, and were equipped with a fleet of warlike ships, with swords, javelins, shields, and arms of all kinds. They had been thirsting for plunder for a long time and that very day they had cast the lot, which told them they would find some prey for themselves immediately. So with a barbaric roar they surrounded the man they had found and asked his background and situation. But no one was concerned about his fortune, because they saw clearly that he had been shipwrecked. But, as I have said, he had been so battered by the waves that he had forgotten who he was, and his whole body had been seized by such a stiffness that he scarcely recollected he was a human being. Furthermore he couldn't have answered their questions, since he had never learned either their tongue or their customs.

Later the pirates completed their journey and returned to their own country. When Raymond had been restored a little by food and rest and they questioned him again, he answered that he was a Christian. But he denied absolutely that he was highborn and had high status. He lied, saying that he had been a farmer. And so they put a spade in his hands and forced him to dig. But due to the great tenderness of his nobleman's hands and his impatience with unfamiliar labor, he didn't do this work very well. Then the pirates began to handle him roughly and to lash him inhumanly with whips. Only in this way, compelled and unwilling, did he reveal himself and confess all the military skills he had once practiced. Immediately the pirates set up a trial and saw proof that he was very expert in arms. Aside from other demonstrations of his skills, it was shown that he covered himself with his weapons and defended himself with a shield so cleverly that only with difficulty could anyone deal him a blow. Therefore the pirates placed him in their military ranks and quite often took him on expeditions. After a short while he had gained such outstanding piratical glory that they promoted him to a higher rank.

But then, after a battle with the Berbers, the victorious Berbers killed the pirates or led them away as captives. And so Raymond was taken captive for a second time. After they had questioned him thoroughly, the Berbers began to treat him honorably and often took him on dangerous missions. But finally they were defeated by the Saracens at Córdoba,[4] and again Raymond was turned over to captors. But there those men also learned by testing him in a variety of dangerous situations that Raymond was a very fierce and strong warrior. They rejoiced with immense happiness and joy over such a great fighter, and especially because when they fought beside this ally they enjoyed success. But the recklessness of sudden joy easily turns to the punishment of sudden disaster. For in a battle with the Alabites they emerged victorious but deprived of their great warrior.

Finally there was war between the Alabites and Sancho, count of Castile, a very powerful man and a highly skilled warrior.[5] Not only did

Sancho defeat the Arabs with the help of Christ omnipotent, they also gave up an enormous number of Christian captives. But these barbaric names of peoples do not seem to have been the ones used in ancient times. Knowledge of their industrious activities has vanished through the neglect of ignorant posterity; indeed the names of most peoples are considered either to have been completely obliterated or changed because they were overrun by barbarians. Count Sancho had learned that Raymond not only was a Christian but also was of importance because of the nobility of his family. He was amazed at what had befallen Raymond and gave him his freedom along with the rest of the Christians after compensating him with all kinds of gifts. But before Raymond departed for home, Sainte Foy is said to have appeared to him in his sleep: "I am," she said, "Sainte Foy, whose name you called upon so constantly when you were shipwrecked. Go on your way easy in mind because you will recover your lost property."

Therefore Raymond arose and went back to his country. And when he was nearing his own castle he heard the news that his wife had taken another man as her husband in marriage. Then he feared to appear there openly and hid himself in the house of a poor man for some time. He was waiting to see what was going to happen to him next through God's providence. He was disguised in part by pilgrim's garb, in part by age. He had lived in exile from his country for fifteen years, so long a time that every hope had died that he would ever return. However, one day it happened that a woman who had once been his concubine was serving him by pouring bathwater over him. She recognized him by a characteristic mark on his nude body and said:

"Aren't you that Raymond who set out for Jerusalem once? People believe you drowned at sea!"

When he denied this, she went on, saying, "It's true! You can't hide your identity from me. We used to be intimate!"

And then, as secretly as she could, the woman hurried to the mistress of the castle to announce the hateful news. Thus his arrival first came to light through a low prostitute. His wife was driven into a frenzy by her husband's return and immediately began to search for any way at all to murder Raymond secretly and without scandal. But she was thwarted in thinking out a means of death, and couldn't find a moment safe enough for the crime because fortune didn't conform to her wishes. Raymond was warned in dreams, so he withdrew from the danger and worked to save his own life. He would have done that a little sooner if Sainte Foy had not ordered him by name to come to his own castle. But I believe that it was done in this way by divine assent, in order that he might discover his wife's faithlessness unmistakably. Since he had learned that his daughters had made honorable marriages, he sought the father of his sons-in-law. He described the circumstances and laid bare his wife's crime. Then Hugh Excafrid, with the help of vassals, friends, his own sons, and Raymond, soon defeated the rival and restored his old friend to his property. Moreover, it was decided that he should take back his wife, for such a thing was permissible according to customary law; there was absolutely no disgrace. For the man who had possessed her at the same time, when he had seen that the general judgment weighed against him, had yielded to justice and right, for he was prepared to abandon an inappropriate claim. Nevertheless, Raymond cast her out of his mind because of her known desire to murder him; this morally offensive plan hurt him more than her sexual infidelity.

Now, let me finish this story in a few words. People say that the first pirates gave Raymond a powerful herbal potion. When it was used with magical incantations, those who drank it were immediately so deadened by Lethean oblivion[6] that they were no longer able to remember either family or home. They say that because of heavenly compassion Sainte Foy had appeared to Raymond, aroused him from his amnesiac stupor, and called him back to his own mind. However, after that his memory was thought to be duller. Of course this was God's will, so that the evidence of his former impaired condition would bear witness and others might understand from what evils God had released him.[7]

2.3: How Sainte Foy Healed a Man's Eye on the Sea; and the Miracle of a Creaking Ship

I am going to relate this next miraculous event succinctly. When the lord abbot was already a monk but not yet abbot,[8] he made a pilgrimage to Jerusalem. As he passed through Ephesus he took as companion and guide a cleric named Peter, who had moved there from our Gaul, namely from the city of Le Puy, to make money. He knew the land and sea routes, the public roads, the ports of call, the side roads, and the customs of the peoples and their languages just as well as businesspeople who travel around the various parts of the world. Since the ocean was flowing right past them and the travelers wanted to spare themselves the labor of the road, they took to the calm sea, planning to disembark again at their intended shore. While they were sailing, Peter's eye began to hurt very painfully and to swell up little by little. The affliction kept growing worse until Peter was unbearably hot with fever. Impelled by the pain, he vowed to offer one gold piece to Sainte Foy at the Holy Sepulcher on behalf of his soul. As soon as he had spoken these words his health immediately returned. But soon he grew haughty because of his sudden good health, and he began to regret that he had made the vow, for he said that the pain had left him by chance and there was no need to lay out so much money for nothing. Although the others disagreed with him and spoke up loudly in witness, he couldn't desist from his unbelief or silence his insane and depraved thoughts.

"If, as you assert," he said, "Sainte Foy healed my eye, let her give a more evident sign so that I may believe. Let this whole ship sway and tremble. Otherwise I'm not going to fulfill my vow."

No sooner did he say this than suddenly the whole boat shook. Its frame was violently shaken and made a loud creaking noise, the way it would if the ship had been dashed against very hard rocks and were breaking up. The tremendously loud grating noise so terrified the sailors and threw them into such sudden horror that they completely forgot the steering oars of the small boat. Their high-pitched voices cried of nothing but their own untimely deaths. But this was only a divine reproach to the stupid man; at once the ship stood as before, on a tranquil sea. Those on board were deeply moved, as much by recovered life as by the joy of a miracle; they scorched the rebellious and disloyal man with appropriate enough words. With a renewed grasp on life, Peter humbly endured this abuse for his doubt.

I wouldn't have bothered to write this miracle if I hadn't been exhorted by many a petition from that same lord abbot.

2.4: About the Large Number of Miracles Worked by Sainte Foy During a Procession in Auvergne

On another occasion the image of Sainte Foy, along with the golden reliquary that Charles the Great is said to have donated and without which the sacred reliquary of her image is never borne in procession, had been carried into Auvergne.[9] The procession went to a place that the locals call Molompize, over which Sainte Foy held proprietary rights. Its purpose was to lay claim to the property for the use and sustenance of the abbey. For it is a deeply rooted practice and firmly established custom that, if land given to Sainte Foy is unjustly appropriated by a usurper for any reason, the reliquary of the holy virgin is carried out to that land as a witness in regaining the right to her property. The monks announce that there will be a solemn procession of clergy and laity, who move forward with great formality carrying candles and lamps. A processional cross goes in front of the holy relics, embellished all around with enamels and gold and studded with a variety of gems flashing like stars. The novices serve by carrying a gospel book, holy water, clashing cymbals, and even trumpets made of ivory that were donated by noble pilgrims to adorn the monastery. It is certainly incredible to report what miracles were worked in processions of this kind. But now I am constrained to write only about the procession in Auvergne.

The report of this procession had spread far and wide, and on account of it the sick from all over swarmed along the route. Such great numbers of them were healed that if those who were there were not still living there is no way that it would be believed now. At one point the bearers of the relics laid them down under a pear tree to catch their breath. I can't even offer an opinion as to how many people were fortunate enough to be healed there through Christ's mercy. I won't even mention the other people who came. The divine work never stopped for the whole distance of the long journey. And when they reached their destination, the disputed property, it is marvelous to report what a great number of miracles for still others divine grace performed there. For the whole day the monks had no opportunity to eat, because as soon as a miracle occurred it was their custom to chant a psalm,[10] sound trumpets, and strike clanging cymbals; the mingling of high and low voices yielded a very sweet sound. Finally, when evening was approaching and they were thoroughly exhausted by the day's work, they approached the tables of food. Even a small meal would have eased the fatigue of their labor. But, behold! suddenly, before anyone could lay a finger on the first dish placed before them, a miracle was done. They had to get up and sing praises, lest in the absence of the usual formal celebration the publicly displayed power should pass by unregarded. Again, when they were hurrying back to their abandoned meal, the working of yet another miracle constrained them to turn away from the returning path. Thus a third and a fourth time a miracle cut short the possibility of eating, so that they passed the day unfed all the way to nightfall.[11] Out of the thousand miracles, there are three that I especially want to explore. Each is appropriate because it is not only a jest but a model as well.

The first concerns a deaf-mute named Stephen, on whom nature herself had inflicted his defects while he was still in his mother's womb. Stephen clung constantly to the arms of the bearers who usually carried the precious image on its golden throne. Finally, in response to some sensation—I don't know what it was—he began to push his fingers into the passage-ways of his ears with great force and to rub them quite vigorously. Soon spouts of blood from these openings, along with a bloody stream that rose up from his throat, broke through the obstacles that were blocking his voice and his hearing. And these were the first words he spoke:

"Saint Mary, help me!"

But he had never heard the sound of a human voice. Therefore it is apparent that his ability to bring forth words he had never heard is beyond human understanding and had a divine cause. Then he heard the unfamiliar sound of chanting voices, along with the terrifying racket of bells and trumpets. Overwhelmed, he immediately started struggling to escape and made a great effort to break away from the hands that held him fast. He seemed to have become insane. In his frenzy nothing comforted or consoled him until the din ceased. It would have been better for him to have remained a deaf-mute but with a rational mind than to be cheated of the gift of human intelligence and turn into a madman in circumstances like these. But the miracle was perfect, for he recovered his senses and was sound both in mind and body.

What then of the little old woman whose whole body had been afflicted with rheumatism for six years and who had been imploring Sainte Foy to help her for so long? Although she had been an inhabitant of Conques from birth, she was not given a cure for her own infirmity until this procession, though many others from many other places had been healed previously. In her case celestial kindness deigned not only to work a miracle that day but also to play a clever joke on students.[12]

The old woman had been carried down to the procession in a shabby litter, for she was poor and completely without means. She was lying there in the midst of the crowds violently pushing forward to converge on the statue. Although all around her people were rejoicing as they received the gift of health, she obtained no healing at all. She was simply an obstacle to the swarms of people. Finally some mischievous young men who belonged to the community of monks, most of whom knew her, came over to this poor, wretched woman and ridiculed her:

"What are you doing here, stupid old woman? Why are you taking up space? Do you think that when boys and girls have been left behind, useful people of our age, Sainte Foy might heal a decrepit and useless old woman like you? Besides, what sort of health could be granted to you? You and your wrinkled, ugly skin and your feeble, grating voice would completely terrify a madman! Clear out of here now, you foolish woman. Don't spend the whole day deliriously cooing like a pigeon. You are already falling apart. You're in your final dotage, which is the most unhappy kind of disease — it's incurable, and now you ask to be cured!"

While they were denouncing her in this way, the old woman sprang up with a sudden leap and without any feeling of pain. She had been cured with miraculous swiftness. Walking completely upright with firm steps, she praised God. I saw her myself afterward in the village of Conques, where she lived as a servant in the house of a respectable widow named Richarde. Cheerful and healthy, she had ample strength to do her work. This miracle caused great joy for all, and even for those who were mocking her. But these must have been ignorant and stupid schoolboys if they didn't know that Christ deigned to cure an old woman who had a curvature of the spine for eighteen years,[13] and an old man who lay paralyzed in the portico of a pool for thirty-eight years,[14] both of whom had given up hope of a cure long before. As to these miracles, it seems very appropriate and in accordance with my reasoning that the Lord had delayed the healing of this woman for such a long time, either on account of her own sin, or so that His works might be shown in her. But now the Compassionate One looked on her and He wanted at least to confound those who were deriding her, so He helped her on her bed of sorrow.[15] Thus, when we pray, God in His goodness generally postpones the granting of our prayers and holds back His Providence until another more appropriate time, although we are unworthy.

Then there was a girl, a native of Auvergne, whom nature had thrust out of her mother's womb into the light blind, deaf, and mute. Also her fingers were not separated from her palms, so that her hands were perpetually closed into fists. Some time before, at Conques, Sainte Foy had granted her a triple miracle, for she transformed eyes, ears, and mouth into working organs. But she left the birth defect of her fists. After a long time had passed, the girl heard about the famous procession and she went swiftly to Molompize. There she spent the whole day before the holy image, keeping up an outcry that all could hear:

"Sainte Foy, once you gave back to me my sight, my hearing, and my speech. If you truly did this, I beg you to add to it. My hands are still curled up and useless. Bring it about that they may also perform their proper function from now on."

And her girlish voice, repeating this incessantly, moved many to pity and compassion. In addition, they say, the beauty of her form and her outstanding grace were adorned with the flower of great charm. Nor was heavenly pity unsympathetic to her plaint. As the next night was fading into early dawn, while all the others were watching, of their own accord her fists opened little by little and the fingers quivered, one by one. The hands that had been inflexible and not suited for work were unbound and reshaped by the highest Craftsman. She had not laid out her complaint before Sainte Foy's relics in vain, but rather for this small price she obtained the incomparable favor of her own reformed hands from the Lord Physician.

That procession was truly miraculous and should be spoken of with high praise. If I include those things as miracles that were done in the procession when the relics were present, how many more can I count in their absence! For people from far away who were in need of healing heard of the reputation of the procession, but were prevented by their debilities from accompanying it. Instead, after the procession had already returned home, they made their way eagerly to that tree where the relics had rested, as I have already said, and obtained cures with no further hindrance. Their number is so large that it seems infinite to me; only for God does it have a limit.

A procession made into Gothia at another time was equally celebrated for the glory of its miracles. That was the time when Sainte Foy took possession of the land and saltworks that Count Raymond had given her. In the previous book [1.12] I told about the young man who objected to this gift and was struck by lightning from heaven. The grace of the heavenly Maker never ceases to do similar things always on behalf of His own saint, both in these processions and in other processions made into other regions.

2.5: How Sacred Vessels Were Preserved Intact in a Fall; and How Hugh Was Killed by Divine Providence

This next miracle is astonishing and almost everyone refuses to believe it. Although I have kept my silence for a long time because of the murmurings of those who ask questions, truth itself has driven me to plunge into it.

It usually happens that the worst people in this earthly society obtain great standing and worldly power. So it was that in our own time the abbey of Conques was abused under the—I will not say guidance, but tyranny—imposed by Abbot Hugh. After his death his brother Peter succeeded him. When Peter died, a third brother, Stephen, who even now thrives in the flower of happy youth, became his successor not only in the abbey but also in its castles and in the wealth of all its properties. These three brothers had an uncle named Bego, bishop of Clermont, who, as long as he lived, always urged them cruelly to plunder the abbey subject to their control rather than to defend it as their patrimony.[16] But, as they say, with every crime that was committed against Sainte Foy the situation became that much more perilous. And this applied to anyone, whether a member of the monastic community or an outsider, who worked against monastic interests. And with a great abundance of material riches, the monks showed greater boldness in sinning. And so the wicked lives of the monastery's inhabitants, caused by overindulgence in debauchery and by great wealth, drove the miracles of the saints to cease. This example demonstrates that for the preservation of a morally upright life nothing is better than a mediocre talent for worldly matters, because then one is neither saddened by harsh poverty nor bloated with immoderate excess. But I am speaking of an ordinary way of life, because there is a more powerful opinion that judges the highest perfection to belong to those who have absolutely nothing in the world. But now I should end my digression and turn back to the subject I began.

Hugh, the first-born brother, was wounded in a general war. He was taken prisoner and brought into captivity at some time or other in a castle named Gourdon.[17] Although the person who held him prisoner was his first cousin, there was no way Hugh was going to be ransomed without a large sum of money. That is why Bishop Bego, backed up by a great band of his own vassals, hastened to Conques to plunder Sainte Foy's treasures; he intended to send them as his nephew's ransom. These were the four outstanding altar cloths the monastery owned, a huge silver thurible, and a very large chalice of the same metal. When they were making their way with the treasures across the precarious slopes of a nearby mountain, among their beasts was a she-mule weighed down by this booty. The mule scraped against the mountainside along which the narrow path, now frozen and glassy, was cut. Then she suddenly set her foot in a slippery spot and slid over the edge in a vast sheer drop. The mule was carried on her great downward plunge with such force that before she reached the overhanging edge of the flowing river bed whose banks were virtually the cliffs on both sides she rolled over a hundred dizzying times. Marvelous to report, it did not appear that the mule was injured, or the vessels battered or crushed, or the altar cloths even dampened by the river. It is clear from the height of the dizzying fall that these things were preserved by heaven. And there is additional evidence that it was a miracle, for the crupper was broken, the poitrel was loose, and the saddle was broken to pieces, but those much more fragile objects—the chalice and thurible—remained completely intact and unchanged. Certainly the abbot, the dean, and the necessary number of lay servants who had reluctantly accompanied these profaners of holy things were distressed about such a great loss of sacred trappings. They joined together in silent prayers imploring divine compassion, asking that in some way God return these things to the place where they belonged. These prayers were suddenly answered, since, when the baggage was found to be intact, on that day everything was carried back to the monastery. However, on the next day, in accordance with the previous arrangement, they were to be carried to none other than Gourdon Castle. But the dispensation of divine goodness was working to a far different end.

For that night a man named Stephen, a layman who watched over the candles, was sleeping in the vaulted chamber built on the right side of the church that is still used as a guardpost of this kind. Sainte Foy appeared to him in a vision, in the form of a despondent woman, very thin and wan and supporting herself with a pilgrim's staff as if she were utterly exhausted. When she called to Stephen three times he awakened. Immediately he looked about and saw her clearly, for the whole chamber was filled with a radiant light of unknown origin. He fixed his gaze on the apparition, as I said. He was totally astonished as to just how the little woman had penetrated the solid walls and iron-bound door bolted fast with iron bars to enter the chamber. He asked her, "Tell me, who are you?"

She declared that she was Sainte Foy.

Then he asked, "Where did you come from?"

She replied, "The thirteenth year has already passed since my presence has been known here."

What does this statement mean? I leave it to be interpreted by those who are wise.

But Stephen repeated the same question, "Lady, where do you come from?"

"Behold," she said, "I come from Gourdon Castle, where I myself have killed Hugh, the one whose ransom was to be paid today with my treasures. But it won't be possible to take them anywhere."

After this, she spoke again: "There remain three of the more powerful men of this country, each of whom for his own reason is preparing to oppose me with a different plot. They may be thriving and formidably strong at this moment, but since they are undertaking to shoot their arrows against me their lives will not last much longer; they will reach a premature end."

When she had said this, she disappeared. And at daybreak the next day the band of wicked men wasted no time in deliberating about whether to send the treasures again. Without any delay to take counsel they drove the mule loaded with booty onto the road when, behold! there was a messenger announcing the death of Hugh. When Stephen saw this he recalled the prophecy in his vision, which he now saw fulfilled with no uncertainty, and he began to reveal to the elders in sequence how heaven had shown all of these events to him. And he repeated word for word what the blessed woman had said about those three, whose end she had said three times was imminent. He had feared to do this just a short while before, as he was a simple and modest person. There would be many things to say about his good character and pure life if my undertaking were not hastening toward another lesson.

The elders inferred that Bishop Bego was one of the three I mentioned, he who urged his nephews to commit all these sins against Sainte Foy, for his life ended shortly after that. And they did not doubt that another was Peter, Hugh's brother. He was traveling to Jerusalem at that time, taking with him a great amount of Sainte Foy's gold, which he had violently removed from the sacred treasury. He died in a storm at sea. For the little time that he had lived, he had been like a devil and a thorn to the monks of Saint Savior's. And Raymond II, Count of Rouergue, although as I have said above he had given much to Sainte Foy, is nevertheless believed to be the third. He had threatened to destroy a whole settlement on the highest mountain ridge overlooking the monastery in order to build a fortified castle. For during the same period he also died on a journey to Jerusalem. Although he was on other occasions a most Christian and just man, it seemed that he was going to erect that structure in order to subjugate violently those who refused to offer the allegiance owed to him, and to subject them to his dominion. But in truth if the will of heaven had allowed him to do what he planned, the status and right order of the monastery would have been thoroughly and grievously transformed. And the fact is, as I said a little before, there is no more serious offense against Sainte Foy, none that will lead more surely to sudden disaster, than to intend evil against the affairs of her domain. That is how concerned the holy virgin is to trample the obstinacy of attackers and suppressers, that is how solicitous she is for the flock of the Lord. But perhaps the provident grace of the merciful Father gave this death to him not for his punishment but for his salvation, for He saved Raymond from committing a sin so that Raymond would not lose through a bad end the good that he had done.[18]

2.6: How a Pilgrim Who Was Captured and Enchained Was Suddenly Freed with Sainte Foy's Aid

As some pilgrims, natives of the Limousin, were traveling to Sainte Foy, they passed near the castle of Ebalus, which is called Turenne. By chance they met an inhabitant of that castle, an enemy of theirs named Gozbert. He was a cleric, but only in name; by employment he was a secular fighting man. At once Gozbert invented a reason for taking them all captive. It happened that Lord Ebalus had been away. When Lady Beatrice, his wife (at that time, but soon to lose him through divorce), had heard of the capture, she ordered Gozbert that if he ever wished to have a friend in her, he should allow the pilgrims[19] to leave immediately. He must not detain the people he had forcibly arrested for even one hour within the walls of the castle. Gozbert did not dare to contradict entirely the orders of his lady.

"These," he said, "I shall send on their way as my lady commands, keeping only this man. Since he is more offensive to me, I find it hard to let him go unpunished. If this isn't enough for her she might as well know that she won't succeed in a further request, for I am certain I will never release him, not even for Sainte Foy."

And so, after freeing the rest, he ordered that one man be bound with fetters, which are called "bracelets" in the local dialect. While these were being fastened with pins roughly hammered into place so they couldn't be removed later, the pins broke to pieces of their own accord and the fetters shattered as well. And when other fetters were fetched in turn, the same thing happened. The same breakage occurred a third time.

Then Gozbert said: "I see, Sainte Foy. Unless I am cunning and on my guard, she'll carry my enemy away from me by force. But I'll try my hardest to make this come out otherwise than she thinks."

Then the prisoner's upper arms were crossed in front of his chest and bound with tightly fastened coils of rope. After this each hand was brought around his neck on either side and tied down very forcefully between his shoulders. And the ropes were pulled under his armpits and tied tightly with crude knots across his belly in such a way that this unique method of binding a prisoner resulted in a constricted passage for breathing. The poor man was suffocating; he could scarcely gasp enough air to live. Gozbert ordered that his prisoner be confined in a solitary cell and firmly commanded that twelve men armed with lances remain there, men who, he knew from experience, were all equally ferocious. If they were to see their prisoner set free by a divine miracle every one of them would run him through, slaughter him on the spot, so he wouldn't survive to boast that he had escaped. After a short while the pitiably confined man grew thirsty, but he was barely able to express it in words because so many heavy chains pressed against his abdomen. Then one of the armed retainers whom I have mentioned brought him a little water. He moved the prisoner's enmeshed forearms down under his throat in order to loosen his chin so that he could put the drink in position at his mouth. The restraining knots vanished as they spontaneously untied by themselves and the cords hung loosely from his formerly bound arms.

Sensing that he had been freed by divine intervention, this extremely strong man began to flee. In accordance with their commander's orders, his guards immediately lifted up their lances to run him through. At once the great power of a divine miracle held them fast in their places, so that not one of them was even able to move or to speak at all. In this way the angel of God suddenly tied them tightly, so that they remained as immobile as if them had been stone simulacra. Only one forced the rumble of an obscenity through the suffocating tightness of his paralysis and then these words: "Bah! He's already getting away." Otherwise he remained unchanged, fixed and immobile, until the fugitive had safely reached Lady Beatrice. On the next day she assigned escorts to accompany him until he passed far beyond the territories ruled from the castle[20] and was assured of resuming his journey in safety. Finally the freed man, whose name was Peter, arrived at Conques with his companions, and there he gave thanks to God for his release. Afterward the joyful man returned home, but his bonds, which I said had remained hanging from his arms after the knots had been loosened, he left behind in witness of the miracle.

Almost a year and a half after my second return from Conques, some business affairs took me to the court of the lord William, count of Poitiers.[21] There I saw the lady Beatrice, who had been sent there by her brother Richard, count of Rouen.[22] I eagerly entered into conversation with her; then and there I began to ask her about this miracle. Her words agreed with what I had been told by all the monks at Conques. This shows how trustworthy their reports have been, if anyone should doubt the other things they told me.

2.7: How Sainte Foy Miraculously Healed a Man Who Was Struck by a Sword

In the year 1020 from the Incarnation of Our Lord, in the third year of a cycle of indiction,[23] motivated both by love for Sainte Foy and by the desire to see Guibert the Illuminated again, I returned to Conques for the third time. I took it very hard that I didn't find Guibert still alive, although I am sure that he whom God glorified here on earth with such a great miracle is on the side of the blessed in the land of the living. In the hour of his passing those who saw both his complete confession and his easy death did not despair of his salvation. His death was not sudden, because they say that he sensed the hour beforehand, although no distressful pains foretold it.

Afterward, when the customary service of prayers had been properly completed, I wished to return at once, but they began to interrupt me insistently and to implore that I should add a third book of Sainte Foy's miracles. I very strenuously refused to do this and said that it was not necessary. Not only was it the case that more powerful miracles than those I had already written could not be found, but, further, there were none even equal to those. But they insisted that it was absolutely necessary, and in order to ensnare me for their cause they said they knew such a wondrous miracle that I myself would judge that nothing in divine works should be preferred to it. When I questioned them eagerly and attentively, they said that a man named Peter, a cleric from Auvergne, a man of very distinguished family and of great power because of the high offices he held, had come a little while before to Sainte Foy. When they had shown him the new little book containing the first miracles I wrote and had mentioned the author by name, he lamented greatly that he had not known of my arrival and that I had not made a detour so as to cross his own borders. This Peter told them a remarkable miracle that deserves to be included among the most excellent.

He spoke of one of his vassals, a man named Raymond, from the town of Valières—a word meant to be plural—who had fifty men under his command. At some time while he was putting down a rebellion, Raymond had sustained a well-aimed blow from the lightning-swift sword of his opponent in battle. This blow was so strong that his nose was cut in two about halfway down, his jaw was severed on one side and on the other almost cut off to the middle, and the root of his tongue was separated from his throat. Below his eyelashes such a huge hole gaped that the sight of his divided face with the bones hanging down was terrifying. His friends and vassals carried him home and watched over him, half-alive, for almost three months. Because Raymond had sustained an incurable wound, his life was more of a loathsome burden than a pleasure to his friends. Since his mouth was no longer able to take food, they dripped thick liquids over the gaping hole that I mentioned. And so after the wretched man had dragged out his days for a long time in this horrible condition, at last he thought that he would have himself carried down to Sainte Foy the next morning. He communicated as best he could, in signs and by nodding his head. Nevertheless, when he made a vow to go to Sainte Foy he wasn't thinking about his bodily health, which seemed completely irretrievable, but that heavenly compassion would hurry to the salvation of his soul if he died either on the roads or at Sainte Foy's.

And so Raymond's mind was made up. Oppressed by sorrow and sadness, he fell into a rather deep sleep that night. And behold! Sainte Foy seemed to appear to him in the form of an elegant young girl, so beautiful, so graceful that no human lineaments could be compared to hers. When she had answered his inquiry by telling him her name, at once she added that she had come from God so that she might hasten to assist him, since he wished to fulfill his vow of going to Sainte Foy but was not strong. After she told him this, she said a prayer on his behalf speaking plainly and clearly; she added a Pater Noster at the end. When she had finished the prayer, the wise doctor seemed to thrust her fingers in the rotted mouth and to implant and reshape one by one the teeth that were already loosened and gave off the stench of putrefaction. Then she placed the palm of her hand underneath his chin and, lifting it, she healed the gaping fissure. Miraculously she brought to life the dead, shapeless mass that had been his face with divine, life-giving breath. Now that he was restored to health, she commanded him to hurry to Conques and thank the Holy Savior.

When dawn was marking the start of the day, Raymond awakened and repeatedly touched his mouth and jaws, which he found to be physically restored. To further convince himself of this miracle he decided to see whether he had regained the power of speech. He began with a loud cry to summon his servants and, because he had suffered intense hunger for a long time, he demanded food in a booming voice. Awakening, the servants thought it was some madman who asked for food so early in the morning; they were stupefied at the sound of their master's voice. Nevertheless, as soon as the voice rang out again their minds cleared. They kindled the lamps and ran to Raymond, whom they found healed beyond their wildest hopes and in unimpaired health. While they were standing there in amazement he told them of his intention the previous day and of his dream of a divine visitation. Then, refreshed and restored by food, he went to Sainte Foy and returned quickly; since he was a layperson and unlearned he did not even know that the monks ought to be told of such a great miracle. But after the lord Peter told them this miracle he sent Raymond back to them. He returned afterward not only once, but many times. Those who saw him very often testify that only the thinnest thread of a red scar marked the path of the sword.

2.8: What Happened to Abbot Peter on a Journey to Rome

During the same time that I heard these things at Conques, and in the same year,[24] I was going back to Rome. By chance Abbot Peter was making the same journey, surrounded, as always, by a company of his own noblemen seated on the best mules saddled with regal opulence. He caught up with me as I was riding with companions and asked who I was and where I was from. But indifferently, as a stranger answering a stranger, I said only that I was from Anjou. Nonetheless, I was delighted with the society of Aquitaneans, so I began to ride at the same pace and to chat. Abbot Peter had flowing blond hair; he was of medium height and broad-shouldered, and the lines of his limbs accorded with his nobility. In keeping with the unbroken custom of his region, almost all of his men wore beards, although they follow the usual monastic custom of shaving the tops of their heads. And because he was bearded I did not think he was a cleric.

Because Abbot Peter noticed a level of culture in my conversation, he began to discuss a variety of topics with me learnedly and with great courtesy. Hearing this, I asked whether he was a cleric and he said that, indeed, he was an abbot. For so he was called, not because he was an abbot of monks but because he presided over many abbots. And when he added that his own name was Peter, the thought occurred to me that perhaps he was the one I had heard of at Conques. Therefore, when each of us had asked the other the questions that remained, finally, joined in a single thought, we rejoiced at our mutual recognition. Then I received again the miracle I had heard once, and it was the testimony of a better narrator since it came from the same person who had told it to the monks. Afterward he also added a miracle concerning himself that I certainly should not omit.

2.9: How Abbot Peter, on a Journey to Sainte Foy, Was Freed from Enemy Ambush by a Four-Part Miracle

For a long time Abbot Peter had intended to go to Sainte Foy, but he had been prevented by enemy plots. Much time passed while he hesitated between love and fear but finally, mindful of his spiritual health, he yielded to love and resisted fear. He adopted a bold outlook and faced up to the reality that he would be putting his life in danger.

One of Peter's enemies who was leading a band of armed men had taken a strategically advantageous position and, contrary to Peter's expectations, appeared on the road he was traveling. Peter wasn't taking caution for himself because he was far from the borders of both of his enemies. He had no knowledge at all of their presence until the moment when a multitude of them surged forward from a road that met the one he was taking, for their scouts had determined that he would have to pass through that crossroads. They were so near that they would have been able to converse face to face; there was nothing between them but the shortest trees and they could have struck Peter down with the lances they were brandishing. But the force of celestial power hampered their fortune so that no one glanced in the direction where Peter was coming to a halt. Instead they were distracted by other inconsequential matters. Then they closely questioned travelers coming from elsewhere, asking whether they had seen pilgrims[25] like Peter passing through. Peter was badly shaken by seeing and hearing all this. His companions urged him to flee quickly. But this seemed altogether foolish to him since they were mounted on tired horses, whereas their attackers had fresh, rested horses. What should you do, Peter, in such a crisis? What thought do you grasp at first, fleeing or standing? But it is neither safe to stand nor honorable to flee, and even if flight were advantageous you would still prefer honor to advantage. They are urgently imploring you to give in and flee, but you have befitting faith and unconquered hope; you do not lack reason; you trust in the power of the saints. You explain that your enemy has been blinded by divine intervention and, scolding your companions, you urge them not to be afraid. Finally the enemies, who have been befuddled and beguiled, abandon their search and meander here and there through the meadows and faintly-marked side-roads; they wander everywhere to no purpose. But Peter used the correct road, the one on which he had set out, and when he came to a river he acquired a boat and successfully sailed across it. After a very short time his enemies returned to the public road again, exhausted from their futile search. They pursued Peter by tracking his horses but were soon stopped by the barrier of the river. Learning from the boatman that he had crossed over some time before, they turned back and returned home.

When Peter was returning from his pilgrimage, however, his enemy appeared once again without warning, though not in the same place, and overtook him with a strong band of men. Once again he saw this mass of armed men hostile to himself launch a violent attack against him, and it seemed to him that he was undoubtedly certain of dying very violently. He spurred his mount, cried out, and called to his companions with the pack-animals who were ahead of him just then, that they should neither leave the road nor stop moving. Although they were heavily laden with burdens and exhausted by the labor of the long road, divine power gave them wings of such great swiftness that neither their enemies nor even Peter himself, although he was riding a better horse, could come near them. Peter, riding furthest behind, constantly looked back at his pursuers and kept haranguing them. After the fleeing man had already covered a considerable distance, he finally withdrew into the safety of a village defended both by manpower and by walls. And Peter, who had believed just a little while before that he could only flee but not escape, was completely safe from his pursuers. From inside the walls he jeered at the enemy he had made a fool of and offered thanks to God for divine beneficence. But his sly enemy feigned penitence and called to Peter from outside the wall. He promised that one of Sainte Foy's pilgrims had nothing at all to fear from him. Managing it skillfully, he misled Peter so that he would be induced by a great sense of security to leave the village and, unsuspecting, would be captured. Unaware of this trick, Peter waited part of a day until his animals had been revived with food and rest and then went on his way, feeling safe because he thought that his enemies had disappeared. But they were lying in ambush at the slope of the next mountain, waiting to catch Peter and his party unaware from behind just after they passed by. And this would have been exceedingly easy to do if their good luck had not suddenly changed and betrayed their hopes. For after Peter passed the men waiting in ambush, he came upon others just as hostile to himself who happened to be moving in his direction on the public road. When their leader caught sight of Peter he rushed toward him as quickly as he could. He shouted threats at Peter, and he suspended his first strike in mid-air, as if he would not reap enough vengeance unless the terror of threats proceeded the actual attack. Then he thrust his lance with a steady aim, and it would certainly have struck Peter dead if one of Peter's companions had not deflected the second thrust with a plea and a sudden jolt. It was not heaven's will that he strike a third blow. For when those who were pursuing Peter from behind according to their plan saw the men whom they happened to consider enemies for a different reason, they forgot anything they had engineered against Peter and rushed headlong to attack their newly discovered enemies. And these also deserted Peter. Far from attacking him, it could now be observed how, with no third party separating them, both sides raised their shields and joined their swords. With matching fury and crashing arms, they were cruelly and horribly slashing and hacking through guts, through soft flesh, and—horrible to report!—through all parts of the body to which bloodthirsty fate directed a blow. They were tearing themselves to pieces in mutual slaughter.

It was as if there were two very ferocious lions, one of whom had found a deer first. It lets its pitiless eyes roam over the animal it has knocked to the ground. And in order to stir up the eagerness of the belly with more intense provocations it holds back the first bites, clinging to the entrails and opening its jaws very savagely, quite as if a headlong descent into slaughter would ruin its satiety. And when the lion soon flexes its claws to rend the gentle animal to pieces with all its strength, by chance it is threatened by the other lion's arrival. While they struggle, now not for booty but for their lives, the deer slips away unharmed.

So it was that, while his enemies were fighting with each other, Peter was snatched away to safety. They were battling very fiercely, now not for Peter but for their lives, and the evil they were looking for they found in full measure. They were entangled in the very ropes that they had set out as a snare, and ensnared in the same trap that they had set next to the road. Their iniquity was already coming down on the crowns of their heads and they were drinking the cup of the Lord's wrath as their deserved fate.[26] Many fell in that conflict seriously wounded, but only four died from each side due to fortune's even hand.

Peter, however, was snatched, free and unwounded, from the hunters' snare, for he had been protected by the Lord and by Sainte Foy's powers of intercession. He stayed right on the road that led him home and arrived rejoicing and proclaiming the great acts of God and the miracles of Sainte Foy.

This is the miracle that I learned from Peter's very own lips. However, now I turn my pen back to those miracles that inhabitants of Conques had already told me.

2.10: About the Miracle of the Golden Clasp Denied to Sainte Foy by Countess Richarde

This they also count among Sainte Foy's jokes, that the saint repeatedly seemed to appear to Countess Richarde in her sleep. (The countess is now a widow since the death of her husband Raymond.)[27] Foy tried to obtain from Richarde a skillfully crafted golden clasp of the kind that is called "spinx" in Latin and "spinulus"—a pin—by the peasants. It was as if the saint's girlish mind took pleasure in the things that young girls usually want and try to get for themselves. For, as I wrote in the first book, it is recorded that Foy was martyred when she was a girl.

Since Richarde was feeling coerced by the saint's frequent insistence, she confided in Austrin, son of the Austrin mentioned in the first book.[28] Following his advice she set out for Conques, where, instead of the clasp, she offered the same weight of gold in exchange. When she was scarcely more that two miles from Conques on her return journey, the royal horse she was riding was moving along with the rest at a pleasant and lively pace when the clasp that I mentioned caught on a tree branch. Although they hunted and searched for a long time, they couldn't find it. But after their departure a very Christian woman who lived at Conques found the clasp and, not knowing whose it had been, carried it back to Sainte Foy. She thought that it was more fitting to present such a gift to Sainte Foy than that she, a peasant woman, should adorn herself with it. Through this maneuver Sainte Foy was enriched by twice as much gold, not only in this case but in many others as well.

After a few days Richarde returned to Conques, for she was nearby since she was countess of Rouergue.[29] While she was prostrate in prayer she happened to see the clasp affixed to the head of the saint's image. She was amazed and asked how it got there. Then she gave thanks to God, who had punished her neglect this way.

Nevertheless the same gold was later paid out for necessary expenses. In fact it is apparent that Sainte Foy had not sought after the ornament for any other reason, since necklaces of inestimable pearls make her lovely in heaven's glory.

2.11: How a Thief Returned a Horn That Had Been Stolen

It seems to me I shouldn't leave out a story of how Sainte Foy took pity on a helpless servant's distress[30] and restored a lost item herself.

I wrote far above about the synod that was held near the city of Rodez, where among the relics of other saints Sainte Foy shone forth conspicuously because of her miracles.[31] I have already related others, but those who witnessed this one found it not only a miracle but an occasion for applause as well.

One of the servants who bore the litters in the procession—this practice has already been described several times and I need not repeat myself—had an excellent horn in his safe-keeping just then. While he was asleep it was utterly lost. When he awoke he couldn't find it anywhere, even though he searched the entire assembly. He would have been completely at a loss if he had had to find a way to replace this item of Sainte Foy's accoutrements. So he went to Sainte Foy's pavilion, which he filled with tearful plaints. Not for a moment did he spare his voice or cease his querulous lamenting until another day plainly exposed the culprit.

While the thief was coming from the city and hurrying as if pressed by some necessity, the horn kept sounding with a terrifying racket that startled and bewildered the surrounding crowd. Driven out of his mind, the thief ran right into the midst of Sainte Foy's servants. They recognized the trumpet by its shape and sound and took it away from the man, who neither offered resistance nor cried out in protest. Nor was the wicked man left unpunished, for he immediately regained his sanity. Instantly he paid the penalty of shame, which is frequently more bitter than death itself.

2.12: About the Miracle of the Double Doors of the Church and of the Inner Doors, Which Stood Open of Their Own Accord Because of the Clamoring Pilgrims[32]

It has been a custom since the old days that pilgrims always keep vigils in Sainte Foy's church with candles and lights, while clerics and those who are literate chant psalms and the office of the vigil. But those who are illiterate relieve the weariness of the long night with little peasant songs and other frivolities. This seemed to ruin utterly the solemn dignity and decency of the sacred vigil. I addressed the monks in chapter about this matter, and I made and proved a variety of arguments that this detestable and absurd custom ought to be completely prohibited. But they maintained that all these practices were valid and did not deserve censure; moreover, they asserted that it was impossible to restrain practices of this kind, which, in any case, weren't contrary to divine will.

"For in the time of that very powerful man, Gimon,"[33] the abbot said, "the senior monks of this monastery frequently forbade the unsuitable commotion made by the wild outcries of the peasants and their unruly singing, but they were unable to enforce silence. So it was decided by a unanimous resolution that the doors would be closed at night and the swarms of peasants would not be admitted to vigils. This had already been done on several occasions when it happened that one night after the meal a larger crowd of pilgrims than usual carrying candles and torches stood in front of the doors, shouting and demanding that they be allowed to come inside the walls of the monastery. And although they were denied entry to the inside of the church, behold! suddenly, while we were sleeping, the bars of the doors were spontaneously unfastened. No one pushed them back—of their own accord the bars sprang violently apart. Even the inner doors were unbarred, those that were usually kept closed in front of the shrine housing the relics in order to afford them the highest protection. No one had been permitted to enter this place except the guardian of the relics, who could admit people he considered worthy because of their special devotion to the saint. However, when we rose in the middle of the night for matins, we found the church so full of people keeping the vigil that each one of us had difficulty forcing his way forward to his own station. We were totally bewildered because we held the keys to the doors ourselves and we wondered what force had been applied by those insisting a miracle had been brought about. But after the people gathered there had described what happened, no one could find any reason for denying the miracle. I, now an old man, recall seeing this as a boy, before the miracle for Guibert the Illuminated."

"God's will expressed itself quite well through this miracle," I said. "For if I reassess my own attitude carefully in the light of what you have told me, I am satisfied that on account of the simplicity of those people, an innocent little song, even a peasant song, can be tolerated somehow. For it may be that if this custom were abolished the crowds that frequent the sanctuary would also disappear. Nevertheless, we shouldn't believe that God rejoices over a little song; it is the hardship of keeping vigil and the good will of simple people that please Him. At one time the heathen ritual of animal sacrifice was permitted to the Israelites, but such sacrifices were to be offered not to the gods but to God. Still, it was acknowledged that animal sacrifices were not fully pleasing to God, because a contrite spirit is a sacrifice to God and God accepts a just sacrifice.[34] But on account of the hardness of their hearts He permitted physical ceremonies visible to the eye to occur and to be observed, as long as they were offered only to Himself. Thus by the same principle these peasants are permitted to sing the songs that they know while their celebration is directed towards the One God Himself. But if people who are wiser feel differently about things like this, such people do not see that they have been so misled by their own high learning that they resemble something that exceeds prudence or that acts contrary to divine justice. Nevertheless, no one should think that with these assertions I wish to conclude that God wants these songs purely and simply because they are rough peasant songs. Rather, in the way I have said, God turns His gaze to the devotion of our hearts and shows good will toward human ignorance and simpleness, because God Who sustains us has a father's compassion for human frailty; He understands us because He created us; He does not seek a reason for which humankind should perish but searches out the root of salvation in sinners."

My responses, which were based on the limited ability of my small store of knowledge, were very helpful to those who had doubts about this issue. And vice versa. For where I thought to refute I was refuted by my own thoughts, just as if I had been slaughtered by my own sword in a battle, for I had been out of my senses to believe that God's goodness is subject to human judgment.

2.13: How Sainte Foy Miraculously Cured Bernard's Brother, Whose Limbs Had Become Contorted

Very recently through Sainte Foy's intercession the mercy of the highest Father deigned to work a miracle for me, though I am most undeserving. It won't be a burden to me to relate this miracle, though some may think me full of empty pride if I do so. I have a great obligation that may be absolved by telling it openly.

My brother was afflicted with a serious illness.[35] The day had long passed when the illness should have run its course. Instead he fell into such grievous and horrible physical pain—for the diagnosis had been incorrect—that the brutal wrenching of his limbs produced both grief and horror in those who saw him. The madness in his brain had left him so disoriented that the exhausted man could scarcely bring forth a rational response to repeated questioning. By then we were in complete despair as to the recovery of his health, for we were looking upon nothing other than the nearness of death, which we knew because that very year we had seen others die of similar torments. Disturbed to the heart by my brother's pain, I began to implore those gathered there to plead for Sainte Foy's help. They thought that it was completely useless, but I burst out with these words:

"Sainte Foy, how does it help me to praise your powers everywhere, if when I am myself engulfed by sorrow I am left a stranger to your beneficent aid? Restore my brother, I beg. And so no one will doubt that you are responsible for his recovery bring it about, I beseech you, that within the next day this intolerable suffering is relieved. If you do this, I promise with a vow that he will be led to you barefoot."

In saying this I confess that I acted foolishly. For to place a time limit on God's mercy and to allot to Him a day in human terms is more a provocation of divine wrath and fury than of divine compassion. Nevertheless, because I trusted confidently in His patience, I did so. And so I affirmed my solemn vow, swearing on a relic in the hand of a deacon standing there.

The holy martyr's intercession came immediately with such strength and efficacy that about two hours later that same day the cruel pains of his violent calamity were first relieved and then ceased altogether. Sleep suddenly came over him, and a health-giving sweat flowed from his open pores. And so little by little the limbs of the man who had been dying returned to life and with the passage of a few days he regained his strength.

2.14: How a Man Recovered with Wondrous Swiftness After He Called on Sainte Foy

My personal secretary Sigebald, a scholar and fellow priest, who had gone on pilgrimage to Sainte Foy with me in the present year,[36] was also seriously and miserably ill recently. Sudden pains spread through his body and the illness caused such great swelling of his brain that his eyesight was blurred. Even more unbearable was the suffocation caused by a poisonous discharge that attacked the region of his chest and the chambers of his heart. He was almost breathing his last when a memory of Sainte Foy suggested itself to his mind. He promised to make a pilgrimage to her and in that very hour he breathed freely again and recovered with wondrous swiftness, so thoroughly that no doubt remained that he had been saved through Sainte Foy's intercession.

2.15: How a Psalter Was Found Through Sainte Foy's Power

Two of my pupils were traveling toward a place about three miles from the city of Angers on a business matter. When they were about halfway there, they paused to rest in a shady forest and the younger of them forgot a psalter he had acquired as a loan from someone. The two pupils had reached their destination and set out on their return journey when night was about to fall. It was not until it was growing dark that they remembered the book. The one who had been carrying it thought it had been left behind in the place from which they were returning and wanted to turn back. But he was thwarted by the elder, who cared about getting back to the city, and he didn't dare return alone because night was falling. Since he was saddened and grieving very much, the elder pupil counseled him to promise a candle to Sainte Foy for finding the little book. Then on the next morning he should retrace their steps to the place from which they had come to see whether by chance God's mercy was guarding the little codex there to keep a stranger from finding it. On their journey back to the city they had not yet passed through the wood where they had lost the book, and the thought that it was there never occurred to them. They made their vow to Sainte Foy, recited one of the Psalms with devout solemnity, and completed their journey to the city.

On the next day the younger pupil set out to retrace the steps of the journey he had made the day before. When he reached the wood where he had unknowingly lost the book, it happened that by divine will and with no forethought he boldly shouted, "Sainte Foy, return the psalter to me."

A shepherd in the woods heard him and from a distance asked what he was seeking or what he was demanding back. When my pupil explained his purpose, he learned that the shepherd had found the book. And so he gave the shepherd a reward and returned to the city in the same amount of time it would have taken him to reach the place where he thought he would find his lost book. Very joyfully he praised God and publicly proclaimed the miracle worked by Sainte Foy.

This matter shouldn't be assigned to chance rather than to Sainte Foy's power, since the shepherd couldn't have been in another place and my pupil didn't shout out in a voice like that but once, in that very spot. Therefore we can conclude from this that even in the smallest matters God's mercy is present for those who call on Him in truth. For if anyone had lost something that brought him great honor, he would be greatly anxious about it, but it wouldn't be very essential to him. Finally it isn't even so important that it be restored to him, because worldly fortunes often purchase ruin, either temporal or eternal, and generally both together. For when anyone has been puffed up by excessive power, that person is not content with what he has of his own right, but is consumed with desire for the fortunes of others and, blinded by foolish ambition, he goes after them rather recklessly. Equanimity is never characteristic of those who have great wealth.

For if wealth is managed listlessly, then the result is sloth, but if it is managed energetically, then the result is sinfulness. Nevertheless, I know many people who were undeservedly driven out of their high positions; when they became contrite through great suffering, God eventually recalled them to their previous situations. And I know clear examples of this, both from the past and from the present. In this regard, if two of my witnesses had not disagreed on some points, though not on all, I would have added a very beautiful story and one succinct enough even for exacting readers.

The End of the Second Book of Miracles of Sainte Foy, Virgin and Martyr

The Third Book of Sainte Foy, Virgin and Martyr

The Prologue of the Third Book

No one need be surprised and search for complicated reasons to explain why a work as brief as this one has more than one preface. It could be either because this work is comprised of more than one book or because it has more than one author. Had it been written by one person, then it certainly would have been appropriate that the whole work follow behind an ascription to a single author and that the beginnings of the other books be left without such ascriptions. But because it has been necessary to burden the work with a change of author, another prologue, set in its proper place, is required. Once this has been carried out as it is here, all doubt about authorship is removed and the work of each individual follows its appropriate ascription. Had this not been done, uncertainty about authorship not only would have been sure to confuse readers, it might even have annoyed them so much that they would have neglected to read the work itself. That I might ward off such an ignominious fate from this holy work, now that Bernard has died—that man imbued to no small extent with both theoretical and practical knowledge—let it be known that I have taken up the business of continuing Bernard's text. I have collected the accounts of Sainte Foy's miracles left after Bernard's death, miracles that deserve to be widely known and written up in elegant style.

Now about Sainte Foy's *Passio*: since it was clumsily composed on the basis of early descriptions of her torments and is highly confusing and far too short, even to the point of obscurity, it has been my task to straighten out some of its confusions and correct it by casting it in a more highly rhetorical style.[1] To the *Passio* I have added a few miracles chosen from many. And I have decided to call the whole volume *Panaretos*, by which I mean "the book of all of her powers."[2] And lest I inflict some harm on this work because of the inadequacies of my manner of writing, in the place where one would expect to find the author's name only silence will be found. I have decided that the title I assigned it is the one by which it should be known forever.

The Chapters of Book Three

3.1: How a Nobleman's Wife Was Freed from Death

Through the inspiration of the Holy Spirit, wonderful and highly astonishing miracles are accomplished ceaselessly at the tombs of the saints. It is by the power of this same Spirit that the prodigious miracles of the renowned virgin and glorious martyr of Christ were shimmering through the vast reaches of the world. As is quite clearly evident in the preceding pages written by Bernard, Sainte Foy's power was traversing the farthest regions of the universe and was leaving behind no one untouched by her gifts. Nor was any needy person rejected by her assistance, for she was favorably inclined to anyone who called on her with a devout faith and a trusting heart. But why am I saying this? In any case, let me not wait any longer to narrate in an orderly fashion the main point of the following events.

There lived at that time in Normandy a warrior named Roger, who was renowned because of his noble lineage and very powerful because of the dignity of his high office. His beautiful wife Goteline was afflicted by a serious illness and lay at death's door.[3] The leading men of the realm, to whom she was related by blood, were very dejected at the prospect of her death and had gathered at her house by the order of the great Prince Richard,[4] as if they were about to hold her funeral. Relying on the careful knowledge they had gained from experience, they perceived all the signs of death in her face, and they turned their thoughts wholly to the preparation of her tomb. When they had almost completely despaired of her return to life, a bishop, perhaps inspired by a breath from heaven, addressed her husband with words like these:

"We have just learned the quickly spreading news that in Aquitaine a very holy virgin and martyr named Foy shines brightly, working miracles completely unheard of and full of wonder. If you pledge your wife to Foy's very powerful mercy with vows, I believe that she will be snatched away from the impending jaws of death and will return to you fully healthy."

Thereupon Roger, who very much wanted his wife's recovery, arranged for a relic to be placed in the bishop's hands, and he swore on the relic, solemnly vowing Goteline to the holy martyr. He also promised that he himself would conduct her to the abbey church of Sainte Foy with a great gift for the saint. Soon after this had been done, his wife let out a moan and opened her eyes wide as if returning from a long period of sleep. With an attentive gaze she began to scrutinize the faces of those standing nearby. And finally she asked why it was that she saw these princes standing near her, and she moved her body, which already lay limp in death. And so little by little as her limbs grew warm she came back to life through the intercession of the holy martyr Foy. They were not able to go to Sainte Foy's shrine[5] because Roger feared that he would be ambushed and captured by his enemies. Because of Roger's evil deeds many people had been driven from his realm and they thirsted for his blood.[6] Therefore Goteline built a church in honor of the holy martyr Foy. In this way she gave eternal renown to the saint's holy and healing name.

3.2: How a Pilgrim Was Rescued from a Huge Gorge

At about the same time an unheard-of miracle happened, one that demands reverence from all mortals. If we didn't believe that nothing is impossible for God, this miracle would seem entirely incredible.

Pilgrims were coming to the holy martyr's monastery church from the province that was called in former times Interclusana. They were going in great numbers along the fixed route through a marketplace called Saban, which is about two miles from the city of Albi.[7] In this place a river flows in the narrow channel it has carved and descends into a gorge in a series of steep falls. Churning in great turmoil, it plunges over the falls in a manner terrifying to onlookers. From these great falls the water leaps back up, forming a huge cloud of vapor that is carried on the winds. These falls are so filled with noise, with roaring, with so much mist, that they are believed by all to be more of an infernal Gehenna than anything else. People say that Saint Salvius, bishop of Albi, once cast down into this great chasm the malignant spirits that he had driven out of the city, and that the foul mistiness that fills the gorge from the bottom to the top is due to their presence.[8] The gorge is inaccessible not only to the feet but even to the human gaze. Nevertheless, travelers cross the river where it is gripped between steep cliffs that constrict it into a narrow torrent. They cross above the falls on a little wickerwork bridge placed over the river; trembling with acute fear, they hurry across swiftly.

After they had completed their prayers at Sainte Foy's abbey church, the pilgrims from Interclusana arrived at this river. While all the rest were crossing over the gorge safely, one of the donkeys bringing up the rear caught its foot up to the haunch between the lattices of the bridge and lay reclining on the wickerwork in great danger. As its master approached to help the donkey, it pulled its foot out of the hole with powerful force, struck its master in the chest with its hooves, and knocked him down headlong into the destruction of the falls. The swirling mass of water, a large whirlpool, swallowed him up and kept him immersed for an hour. All were stunned by this, both his companions and the merchants who conducted business in the marketplace there. In a packed crowd they took up positions on both banks of the river and with a great many abuses they blamed Christ's holy martyr Foy, from whose abbey church the pilgrim had been returning. They pushed forward to gain a position from which they would be able to see the limbs of his lacerated body drifting on top of the water. For beyond the gorge the river spreads out into a wide stream and slides through its bed with gentle waters. While people were standing on both sides of its banks in numbers beyond measure, one man directed his glance towards the frothing water and caught sight of the crown of a head which looked like a little bird swimming. And he soon pointed out the sight to the others with his finger. Carried along by the current, the pilgrim was soon brought near to the shore and grabbed hold of a pole that someone held out to him. And so, still very much alive and suffering no injury from his great headlong fall, he escaped the danger of death. His right arm had been entwined in the strap of the satchel he was carrying, so he did not suffer its loss, for God preserved it. When they saw this, all drenched the shores with tears of joy and praised the magnificence of God. They proclaimed Sainte Foy's omnipotent power with splendid declarations of praise. They spoke truly when they maintained that the pilgrim had been plucked out of death's abyss by her sustaining right hand.

3.3: How a Warrior Who Was Struck in the Eye by a Thief Was Restored to Health Through Sainte Foy

Not long afterward, in Auvergne, thieves crept stealthily into a castle most recently called by the name Châteauneuf,[9] freed the horses, and led them away. Although it was late at night, the watchman at the top of the fortress realized what was happening and began to shout frantically in order to awaken the soldiers sleeping both inside and outside the castle. He called out that a bandit raid was taking place at that very instant. And so, as the thieves were slipping away in hasty flight through the thick darkness of the night, one of them purposely reversed the lance he was carrying in his hand so that he would be able to wound their pursuers more quickly. A young man named Bernard from the castle called Valeilles was ahead of the others because he was riding a faster horse.[10] As he pursued the fleeing robbers by following the sound of the horses' hooves in the darkness of the foggy night, he recklessly came up close behind them and ran right into the point of the reversed spear. He was stabbed through the center of his eye with such force that the exit point of the lance was discovered behind his ear. His companions, following after, lifted up the savagely wounded youth and laid him on a bed. He was soaked with a huge outpouring of blood. Eventually the wound festered and his whole head swelled up. Since the discharge from the wound was blocked up inside, he was afflicted with intolerable pain and near to death's destruction.

His lord came to visit and comfort him. Among his other words of consolation, he urged the wounded man to send Sainte Foy a golden ring that he wore on his finger, subject to an agreement like this: that either the saint would bring him the ability to recover from this wound immediately or she would show concern for the cure of his soul in the presence of God's mercy. The wounded man gladly acquiesced to these plans. He added to the things already mentioned that if she should free him from his present affliction he would offer her a gold coin (which we call in the vernacular a *mancon*).[11] And indeed through the holy virgin's miracle a powerful intervention that assured his recovery followed soon upon this vow. For the sealed-in pus erupted from the wound with a great stench and flowed in long gushes of putrefaction until all the swelling of his head diminished and it returned to its natural size. It was declared that divine compassion brought it about. Shortly thereafter he recovered so completely that no deformity could be seen on his face except a modest scar. Without a doubt his healing resulted from the holy martyr's power, because he pledged himself to her with vows so that he would recover from his great anguish.

3.4: How a Young Man Was Freed from Fetters and a Chain

With my own eyes I saw a miracle worked at that same time, which frightened me not a little.

An inhabitant of the castle at Conques who was descended from a family native to the place, a young man named Hugh, son of the noble and powerful Siger,[12] was captured by enemies. He was taken to a different castle[13] where he was thrust out of sight in a small, dark hovel. There he became weak from starvation and the cruel weight of his chains. His throat was confined in the narrow grip of an iron collar and he was tightly bound with huge fetters. These bonds tortured him unmercifully, and in the midst of so many afflictions it was thought that he was almost breathing his last breath. A large barrel stood behind him, and the chain binding his neck had been fastened inside it, so there was no way at all for him to free himself, enmeshed as he was in chains. Placed in such cruel trouble, Hugh did not cease urgently to request Sainte Foy's help because his body was suffering unbearable injury. One night while he was in the midst of these torments sleep stole over him, and it seemed to him that he picked bunches of grapes, ate them, and hurled the weight of his chains away from himself. A vision like this, interpreted by holy Joseph, had brought consoling help to Pharaoh's cup-bearer when he was weakened by confinement in prison.[14] In the same way heavenly mercy, which Hugh had been invoking constantly through Sainte Foy's intercession, did not delay to bring him its beneficial gift. For on the following night through a dream the blessed virgin stood before him; with gentle encouragement she foretold that he would leave there.

"Rise up quickly," she said, "and depart from here in safety."

Immediately Hugh was released from the sleep that had gently restrained him. Convinced that it had been a true vision, he began to grope around with his hands, searching for a rock or something else to break the bands off of the huge barrel. His hand soon found a rock and a small piece of wood in a shape that the peasants call a tether. Working with these objects, he pried the bands loose from the grain barrel. When he had removed all of them except the one bound tightly around the base, the barrel remained intact, but he was able to remove the piece of wood to which his neck chain was fastened. Then with the tether he hollowed out a narrow space like a badger's hole under the threshold of the door and through it left the room where he had been held captive. He removed the door bars with the same tools and carried them away with him as he fled.

When Hugh was some distance away from the fortified castle, he smashed the fetter around one leg by striking it with rocks and tied it to his belt so it would be out of the way. With the other fetter hanging from his leg he made a rapid start on his journey. By chance he encountered a boy and, enticing him with many promises, prevailed on him to carry the plank fastened to his neck chain. In that way he walked as quickly as possible toward the castle where he would find the safety of his father's protection. When he had put enough distance between himself and his enemies to be less fearful, he broke the plank to pieces. Moving more briskly, he hurried to complete the journey on which he had set out. Soon he was confident of complete safety. Then he broke up what remained of the fetters and the collar with blows of a hammer and offered all of it to Sainte Foy. I saw Hugh make his expression of thanks to her, for it was due to her compassion — so readily available to those who importune her — that he was heard, and due to her counsel that he took the action that gained him freedom from his enemy's oppression.

3.5: A Similar Miracle About a Warrior

Another miracle that demands our deep reverence was also brought to completion during that same time. Since I have just related a similar story, I will compress this one with as much brevity as I can. But I will moderate the brevity somewhat, lest the story become too obscure for my readers to follow.

In the castle of Conques lived a warrior named Bernard. Although he was an otherwise admirable man, in one respect Bernard had become thoroughly detestable, and this was because he had been taken in by a devil's advice. For Bernard had a nephew named Deusdet whom he was pursuing with the hatred usually reserved for one's worst enemies, because he was obsessed with obtaining Deusdet's patrimony. And so, when Bernard came upon Deusdet by chance, he seized him forcibly and refused to release him on his word. Instead he led Deusdet away captive, wrapped him in fetters and manicles, and flung him into the dark, foul depths of the tower. But Deusdet, deprived of all help from his friends, did not cease to call on the holy martyr's assistance with querulous sobs, and concentrated completely on obtaining her mercy. His maternal uncle greatly feared that Deusdet would escape, so he removed every rock and stick from the circle within which his nephew could move, and he passed a chain from Deusdet's neck through a narrow slit in the tower wall and fastened it firmly on the outside. But he neglected to take away a pole next to Deusdet, which was long enough to reach up to the wooden flooring of the fortress. But why should I delay with so much beating around the bush?

One night while Deusdet was half-asleep, he saw a girl standing near him whose distinguished appearance and graceful beauty far excelled that of mortal beings. She repeatedly called his name and engaged him in a conversation like this:

"Why are you sleeping?"

"Who are you, Lady, tell me?"

"You ought to know that I am Sainte Foy. I have been moved by your complaints, and I have had pity on you because you have been treated so badly. I bring you a plan for escaping, and I advise you to walk out of here swiftly."

With these words she returned to heaven. Deusdet awoke and reached out his hand to the ground, where he found a hard rock supplied by the power of heaven. With a blow of the rock he easily shattered the chain from his neck that was drawn through the wall but, fearing that he would be heard, he left the fetters intact. And so with powerful exertion Deusdet climbed the upright pole and fled swiftly out to the floor above. However, when he had made his way to an opening through which a passage lay open, and hence a means of escape, he found guards lying in front of the stone wall. Risking great danger, for the guards were scattered here and there, he passed through their midst to complete the escape he had undertaken.

It had taken Deusdet so long to overcome his fright that sky and earth began to glimmer in the light-filled rays of the rising dawn and the shapes of things could be discerned. He didn't dare to return to the monastery at Conques, so he headed straight on to the top of the mountain. There he used an axe he got from a peasant whom he met en route to break one of his "bracelets" to pieces. But with the remaining one tied up securely—as he himself afterward used to report jokingly—on a swift horse he fled to the castle called Belfort.[15] There he broke off the clinging fetter and sent it to Sainte Foy. He himself followed not much later. There he paid countless expressions of thanks to the most high God and the holy martyr, and he revealed the whole story of his capture and liberation to those who stood there.

3.6: How a Blind Man's Sight Was Restored

I know of a miracle that happened in Normandy, which it would be quite shameful to pass over in silence.

There a middle-aged man was spending the night under the open sky, keeping watch over some horses. Exhausted because he had been awake so long he gave in to sleep and, deep in slumber, rested from his toil. When he awoke, he expected that he would see grazing horses, but he saw nothing at all for his sight was lost—he had become blind while he was quietly sleeping. A guide was summoned for him and he made his way home by groping. There he remained for many days. Although he knew that he deserved his blindness, it occurred to him that he ought to travel to the various churches of the saints. He thought that he might regain his sight by winning their favor. After he had tried this, he went to Rome. He assiduously completed his prayers and remained there; exhausted from the discomforts of the long journey, he fell asleep. While he was resting peacefully, he gained his answer—he was to go to Sainte Foy's church and there his sight would be restored in answer to his prayers. But he didn't put much trust in this vision; moreover, he didn't even know the location of this church. He returned home as blind as he was before and, since no remedy had been found, he remained in this condition for two whole years.

But afterward, acting more prudently, he went to the basilica of Sainte Foy, with his small son as his guide. There he prostrated himself and prayed for a long time. Engrossed in prayer he made all his needs known to the holy martyr. Then he completed his prayers and moved to a quieter part of the church to rest. There—marvelous to report!—two birds of wondrous beauty seemed to fly to him in a vision, thrust two burning candles into his eyes, and return in gentle flight on the mild breezes. Thoroughly terrified by this, he roused himself from his sleep, called his son, and was led back to the glorious martyr's altar. At the foot of her statue he completely prostrated himself. He lavishly poured out prayers in which he kept on asking for the restoration of his lost sight. Then he got up again. Struck by severe pain in his temples and other parts of his head, he leaned on the shoulder of a peasant standing next to him. Even with the peasant supporting him, he was scarcely able to stand on his feet. After this pain so much gore was seen to gush forth from each of his closed eyes that his clothing and beard were completely befouled with clotted blood. Then, realizing that a miracle had given him the gift of restored sight, he lifted up one eyelid and, as his sight increased little by little, he was able to recognize shapes and things opposite him and to point at them with his finger. He was filled with joy because of the gift he had obtained, and he remained there for some time to demonstrate the effects of the divine miracle. Then, using his own sight restored through Sainte Foy's intercession, he went back to his own home a happy man.

3.7: How Sainte Foy Restored Hair to a Warrior Who Had Been Bald for a Long Time

But while I have been expounding these awe-inspiring and almost incredible stories in praise of the most glorious virgin, other miracles more worthy of renown have been happening everywhere and I am constrained to leave in an unfinished and incomplete state the organizational plan that I had laid out. And, unless I move along more quickly by writing succinctly, I might consume the whole span of my life without finishing. I know of course that the task cannot be completed in my lifetime, yet as long as life is mine and I have sufficient strength I will never cease setting onto parchment the daily miracles of the glorious martyr as an everlasting monument to her eternal honor. Her praise will not be absent from my lips, nor will it be weakened because of my idle or lazy talent, neither will it grieve over some injury for which I am responsible. And even if my tongue is silenced it will always be my desire to praise her, because I believe that through her intercession I can be moved from the flock of goats on the left hand of the Judge to the sheep shining with white fleeces on the right hand. Since I am motivated first and foremost by the prospect of this heavenly reward, I have banished all my idleness. I will never allow that the miracles I have been granted the privilege of seeing with my own eyes are lost because of the fault of my silence. Since I am justly in debt to her, there is one miracle that I need to insert here. The agent, whose ineffable power was brought to bear through the intercession of the holy martyr, was God Himself.

In Auvergne there was a brave warrior named Bernard. Insofar as his human origins go he was a native of the castle of Gransoux.[16] After he returned from a journey to Rome, Bernard suffered a serious physical illness. Then, when he was just beginning to regain his strength, he was denuded of every lock of hair from his head, just as the leafy-tressed forests are deprived of all the beauty of their foliage by the Ides of September. He was so ashamed of his baldness, which seemed ugly to him, that he abandoned all his martial activities and stopped going to the places frequented by the noblemen who were his peers. He wanted only his mother to take care of him, just as if he were a little boy. To add the finishing touch to such great misfortune, the lords living near his lands, which he had inherited from his father, were wickedly seizing his fiefs from every side, acting with impunity and without any opposition. Because of these aggravations he began to be troubled by so much depression, which we call weakness of mind, that he thought death more desirable than life.

One night while Bernard was resting quietly beneath his bedcovers and turning over many things silently in his mind, a deep sleep crept in and dissolved all his cares. While he was in this deep sleep an old man with venerable white hair, tall in stature and handsome in appearance, stood near him and addressed him with words like this:

"Why are you lying there melancholy? Don't fear, don't be so sad. If you trust my advice you will immediately be rescued from this hideous condition. Quickly arrange a journey to the abbey church of Sainte Foy and she will restore the flower of your youth."

Since Bernard had slipped completely into the pit of despair, he considered the divine message to be nonsense and he answered that now after seven years Sainte Foy would never be able to help him recover the lost charm of his curls. When morning came he reported this vision to his mother, but, as she was a foolish old woman, she thought the divine counsel was worthless. Nevertheless, on the next night while Bernard was in the grip of a deep sleep, the same old man came near him and began to press him more urgently, repeating the same words as before. But Bernard remained disobedient to the second counsel, just as he had been to the first. Then on the third night, behold! the glorious martyr Foy came to him, and, repeating the words of her own messenger, she immediately burst forth with these commands:

"Do not delay to go confidently to the monastery at Conques. When you have arrived, make known to Abbot Girbert[17] in my name that in my memory he should celebrate the divine mystery before the shrine of my body, while you stand on his left side until the reading of the holy Gospel has been completed. After the offertory, when the abbot has washed his hands, collect that water. He should moisten your head, and after that you must go over to the right side of the altar."

Bernard awakened at daybreak, leapt up from his bed, and informed his mother about the night's vision in some detail. By now she had been strengthened in her faith and gave credence to the vision. When she had gathered provisions for the journey, she and her son traveled to the monastery. There they told Abbot Girbert about the vision point by point, but he, as is usually the case with spiritually advanced persons, immediately protested that he was not worthy of being involved in such a business. His resistance was finally overcome by their urgent pleas and he devoutly carried out everything he had been directed to do. The following night while Bernard was keeping vigil in holy prayers before the sacred virgin's mortal remains, his scalp seemed to swell with little hairs, like the head of a newborn boy. And as he was returning to his home in the morning, his head began to grow so rosy red in color that people thought the whole top of his head was stained with fresh blood. After he got home, Bernard shaved off all that hair with a razor. New hair appeared, thicker than before; he was clothed in tresses, and through the holy martyr's intercession he was found worthy of recovering the lost glory of his hair after being bald so long.

3.8: How a Young Man Was Revived from Death

I was hoping that when I had finished a concise version of the previous miracle I could hurry along to the rest, but then another, almost incredible miracle happened. Lest that miracle should be lost to silence, I have taken pains to preserve it by writing it up.

In the region the people call Ultraclausana there was a married couple with no children; they had been childless for quite a long time. They conceived a plan to seek out the holy virgin's shrine.[18] They carried out their plan, made their vows, and returned home. Soon afterward divine compassion brought it about that the woman's womb became fertile. When she gave birth she brought forth a male child into the light of day. This son was about fifteen years old when he was prematurely taken away by envious death, to his parents' grief. When they saw that their son was dead, they assailed Sainte Foy repeatedly with varied and innumerable complaints, and they demanded that she return their child to them:

"Why, O holy and glorious Lady, did you wish to gladden us with the gift of a son, when you knew beforehand that we would be more grieved by his untimely fate? We turned to you when we had already despaired of having a child. In order to have our prayer answered we sought out your holy church, we prostrated our bodies on the ground before your holy tomb, and we were found worthy of having our plea heard. We obtained our heart's desire from heaven through you, O blessed mother. What good did it do, O blessed and glorious mother, to get what we asked for if we are now reduced to ruin by permanently losing him? Be present now with your usual compassion, O virgin blessed of Christ, and restore our son to us, alive again, that son whom we received through you, for you made us fertile. We trust that you have the power to give back to us what has been taken away since you once were powerful enough to overcome nature on our behalf. By doing both you will become completely omnipotent; by doing both you will be recognized as the most efficacious of martyrs."

Burning pain without remedy tormented both parents at their dead son's funeral bier, as they incessantly repeated these words and others like them. With heavy sobs and anguished sighs they wore themselves out embracing the lifeless corpse. Even as the pallbearers were taking up the simple bier to carry it to the church for burial, the parents cried out to Sainte Foy with sorrowful voices. With ear-piercing wails they implored her to restore their lost gift to them. While they were raising their dismal cries up to the heavens, behold! the youth lifted his head from the bier as if he were returning from a deep sleep. He shook his head to free it from the gravecloth and began to wonder at the great noise that came from those standing near him. His mother, who had collapsed motionless onto the bier, soon realized that her son was blessed with the breath of life and without delay freed his face and hands from the cloth. And now she drenched her face with tears, not in sorrow but because of her great joy.

When they saw what had happened, the whole crowd assembled there stood frozen in place and the heat left their bones, for they were thoroughly frightened and amazed beyond description. After the heaviness of death had taken leave of the boy, his parents questioned him eagerly. They asked whether while he was dead his soul had been released from his body and was being led to another kingdom, or whether he had been put into a mental stupor while his body's vital heat, now returning, was slipping away. He answered that he had gone directly out of this present world and had been led down to dark places. Sainte Foy had forcibly lifted him up out of them. In order to bring him back to this earth, she had poured breath back into his body. So that both parents would be more readily believed when they related this great miracle, they led him, their Virbius,[19] to the holy virgin's monastery church where all could see him. The whole neighborhood gathered to witness the miracle, and as we marveled and moistened our faces with tears of joy his parents had him tell his story.

This deed reminds me of a miracle performed by the most holy Elisha, in which there was a very similar set of circumstances concerning a dead boy.[20] However, I think these two miracles are different from each other in this way: this mother had demanded with steadfast prayers that the holy martyr give her a child, while the Sunamite woman had no hope of bearing children because of her advanced age and feared that Elisha was mocking her when he promised her a child. But, in whatever way it came about, each woman had borne a child, and after she had received this gift each grieved deeply to have lost it in a short time. Therefore both women, driven by grief, prostrated themselves before their benefactors and berated them relentlessly to return their lost children. Both mothers roused themselves to fight forcibly, and both repeatedly assailed God's saints with urgent pleas. It was while he was still living that God's holy prophet Elisha obtained heaven's favor so that he could revive the boy. In contrast, our glorious virgin and martyr had already become a heaven-dweller and had joined the choirs of angels when she prevailed and gave the same gift to those praying to her. Because of the sanctity of her earthly life and because of the merits of her passion, there is no doubt that after her departure from this life she went to live in heaven. That is why at her sacred monument we see that through her power unclean spirits are driven out of possessed bodies again and again. These spirits are tormented, tortured, and beaten with invisible whips until they are expelled, and they cry out with great shouts that she should stop tormenting them. And these shouts are not all alike. Some of the evil spirits cry out in a human fashion, others roar in the manner of lions or pigs, while others eject their serpents' tongues with hisses as they are drawn forth from afflicted bodies through the merits and powers God conferred on Sainte Foy.

But because I reported above that the young man about whom I am writing had been led down to dark places, perhaps some people may hesitate to believe this narrative. They may ask this: since he had scarcely reached puberty and, according to the testimony of his neighbors, was not implicated in murder or any other serious crime, why was he condemned to bear such harsh punishment? To assuage all doubts about this, I have undertaken to append a brief explanation.

Among the ages of man from boyhood through enfeebled old age, two are regarded as milder. Of course these are the first and the last, and people of these ages are not so easily enflamed with all the vices of human nature. But those positioned midway in life's journey become more lascivious and more prone to every kind of fleeting pleasure. For this reason our Romans[21] used to free boys from guardianship in the fourteenth year of their lives, and they emancipated girls, who mature more quickly, in the twelfth year.

And so perhaps this adolescent had been sullied by the disease of a brutal vice. If so, he needed to expiate his sin after his death before he could go to his heavenly home. For neither a spot nor a wrinkle nor any kind of foulness is allowed in that country. Just as Christ its ruler is holy, pure, innocent, and shining white, so also its inhabitants must gleam with the brightness of sanctity in order to sojourn there. Cast out from that state of blessedness by his own sin, the young man was called back to his former life through Christ's most holy martyr mainly on this account: so that he would be seized with great zeal for avoiding the places that had so frightened him, and exercise good works out of his intense thirst for the country above. Sainte Foy wanted him to repent so that he would not again be given over to the peril of God's judgments, which he once evaded through her merits, and so that he would earn the right to participate in eternal glory when he dies again.

3.9: How a Man Trusted the Power of Sainte Foy Enough to Make His Own Sons Pass Through Fire

The miracle I am going to write next has been told frequently by many of the brothers in our monastery, and I believe them as fully as I believe the Holy Scriptures. In Périgord there was a castle called Montagrier[22] where a warrior named Elias, a powerful nobleman, was living. Since he had no children, Elias thought that his otherwise pleasant marriage was disagreeable and useless. After prolonged childlessness, he hastened to the holy martyr's church and was found worthy of receiving offspring from his spouse's womb as he had wished. His gift was a pair of sons. Elias cherished his boys with such intense love that he even used to call them not his sons but Sainte Foy's. And one time, to prove that Sainte Foy considered them to be hers, Elias had a huge fire lit in the middle of the castle courtyard. Ignoring the strong objections of those who stood nearby, Elias had the boys go through the midst of the flames with bare legs and feet. What a sight to see! The boys leapt up to obey their father and suffered no injury from the fire.

Elias decided that he ought to take his boys to the holy martyr, since she was their spiritual mother. A terrible winter had caused all the rivers to flood, and it was venting its rage with huge storms everywhere. Elias's wife and the rest of his household were persuaded that the pilgrimage ought to be postponed to another time. Completely resisting all their exhortations, Elias asserted that he was going to carry out the proposed journey, and he said that he would not delay for fear of impending storms. Not only did he have no fear of shipwreck, since the holy martyr's boys would be with him, he even promised that, trusting in their companionship, he would ride the swirling waters at the crests of the floods in a light, little boat. He accomplished all this successfully and came to the holy virgin's church. He pledged his boys with vows; he enumerated to the brothers of our holy community many, very wondrous things about them. And when he had completed his solemn prayers, he returned home happy and safe.

3.10: How a Man Attacked One of Sainte Foy's Monks

I have learned that a miracle was worked in Auvergne that I will tell you right now, in sequence but in shortened form. Where the castle named Aurouze is located, many of you know.[23] Next to it, but separated by a small plateau, is a small village that belongs to the holy martyr, which its inhabitants call Molompize. The lord of the castle, a man named Robert, attacked the monk-guardian of Molompize in a fit of anger, intending to murder him if he could. But Robert's attack was repulsed by peasants and servants and he took flight with all his men. As a result Robert's resentment grew immeasurably and he planned a night ambush, so he could avenge the indignities that had been inflicted on him. What more is there to say? Taking five accomplices with him, he clandestinely broke into the enclosure around the monk's house. In the silence of the dark night he thrust back the door-bars of his enemy's dwelling with the point of his sword. Then he stood there, in the middle of the doorway, dumbfounded and confused. When his men asked him whether he was going to enter the house, he snapped back that he couldn't see a thing, even though he stood there in the clear, bright moonlight. This exchange awakened a young man who was in the house. He swiftly leapt from his bed naked, grabbed a weapon, pierced Robert's shield, and drove him out of the doorway. Then he closed and barred the door. Robert, fully aware that he had been overcome by the failure of his eyesight, ordered his men to withdraw again, and so they all turned and fled. They were fearful that their enemies were close behind them, so when they reached the plateau I mentioned earlier, they left their lord behind in the darkness, stupefied and alone. They searched for hiding places in the sloping side of the rocky cliff, caring only about their own safety. However, when they saw that no one was chasing them, they went back to their lord. They found that his entire body had been stricken and his mouth was wrenched back toward one ear. In this repulsive condition he was carried back home on a litter.

The next morning Robert's men came to the church in Molompize and, without revealing anything about their lord's condition, humbly asked for peace and a fair truce. They were unable to find the monk-guardian because he had gone back to Sainte Foy's monastery. So they decided to carry their lord, who still remained seriously ill, to the church at Molompize, trusting in the love of the holy martyr. There they kept holy vigils by candlelight for a week.

In this way Robert was restored to his former state of health through the glorious virgin's intercession, and he proclaimed, blessed, and reverenced the power of this great martyr. Joined by members of his household, he then hastened barefoot over a rough footpath for three days to reach the holy martyr's monastery church in Conques. Robert explained the reason for his journey to the holy brothers, courteously made his peace with the monk-guardian of Molompize, and set out on his journey home a happy man. The outcome of this story was that from then on he devotedly watched over that village and looked after the church located there with due veneration, and he frequented it with a devout spirit.

3.11: How a Horse's Eye Was Restored Through a Miracle of Sainte Foy

Among the plentitude of all these miracles, one is especially marvelous. I think it should not be viewed as suspect because ignorant people disparage it. Indeed, rather than being condemned this miracle should be commended, as indisputable examples from the holy fathers show. We have learned from Saint Gregory—a man as reluctant to deceive as to be deceived—about Fortunatus, bishop of the church at Todi.[24] Because of his sanctity Fortunatus was granted this miracle: a warrior's horse that had turned ferocious was marvelously restored to gentleness when Fortunatus made the sign of the cross over it. In honor of the miracle, the owner offered the horse to Bishop Fortunatus. Lest the owner should feel any offense, Fortunatus listened to the petition that he accept the horse as a gift. Nevertheless for love of charity he paid for the horse, purchasing something he did not need. To strengthen our belief that divine mercy extends to all creatures, we need quietly to heed the saying of the Psalmist, "You save human and animal alike, O Lord."[25] Now I return to my story, in order to explain the miracle to which this chapter is devoted, for it illustrates the Psalmist's words.

In Auvergne there is a castle commonly called Miremont.[26] A warrior who lived there owned a very valuable horse. He bled the horse in the usual way, and after the bloodletting he tied it to a post with a halter. Very sharp spikes, used for hanging things, projected out from the post; they were the lopped-off branches of the dead tree. While the horse was moving unsteadily around the tree to which it was tied, it threw its head up and struck hard against one of the spikes. The blow immediately tore out one of the horse's eyes by its roots. The warrior who owned the horse was distraught. He took the eye, which was hanging down to the horse's jaws, and replaced it in its socket. Then, as the many people who had gathered around encouraged him to do, he vowed a candle the length of the horse to the holy martyr Foy. He bound up the gouged-out eye with strips of cloth and led the horse back to its stall. The warrior was deep in gloom, for that horse was incomparably swift and strong. Through the healing merits of Sainte Foy the next day the horse was found uninjured, as if it had never been hurt. At Sainte Foy's abbey church before all those present, the warrior reported this astonishing miracle accomplished through her power.

3.12: Another, Similar Miracle

Another miracle, equal to this one, deserves to be included in this little book on its own merits. Many of you know a castle commonly called Entraygues,[27] a little more than eight miles from Conques. A warrior there had a horse that was weakened by advancing old age. Whenever the sacred image of the glorious virgin and martyr had to be carried somewhere because of an urgent need, the warrior used to send the abbot this horse because of its incomparably gentle and even gait. One day when a young man was waving a stick in play, he accidently ripped out the horse's eye. It was torn up by the roots from its socket and hung down in the horse's face, as if by a thread. When the horse's owner, who was not easily angered, saw this, he first smiled and feigned a laugh. Then he began to complain gently, saying that the horse's loss was inflicted on Sainte Foy, not on himself:

"O Sainte Foy, today you have been touched by a loss that will not soon be surpassed, because this horse, your old reliable servant, has been hurt through no fault of its own. Now it is blind in one eye and useless for your service."

And when he had said these words, he replaced the eye in its socket with his own hand and led the horse toward his stables. People followed along, ridiculing them and laughing loudly. They said that the horse was already a hundred years old, had no strength, and now, to top off its troubles, had lost its eyesight. It ought to be put out as food for birds and beasts of prey rather than kept any longer out of tenderheartedness. The warrior paid no attention to their opinions but led the horse back home, as I have already said. And so that night the horse slept in its usual stall. The next day his master came to see the horse and discovered the eye in such perfect condition that there wasn't even a scar anywhere around it. He immediately recognized that this miracle had been worked through the holy martyr's intercession, and so he showed the horse, now healed, to all his the neighbors who had seen it blind in one eye the day before. In this way the prodigious feat accomplished through Sainte Foy's power became known to all.

3.13: How a Horseman's Home Was Set Afire Because of Sainte Foy's Geese

While I hasten to record in writing these great miracles of the glorious virgin — and the more recent ones are even more numerous than the older ones — it is as if I am chasing about through a flowery and pleasant meadow, selecting small blossoms of refined beauty. There I gather miracles, some more recent, others more sweetly fragrant with the aroma of virtue, those that ought to be remembered so as to demonstrate the holy martyr's powers to future generations. One of these happened near your community.[28]

In Auvergne there is a plateau from which the place called Planèze seems to have taken its name.[29] An armed man named Amblard who lived there was constantly at odds with the other men of similar standing in the vicinity, all of whom provoked quarrels and refused to yield anything to anyone. These quarrels started over questions of rank and degenerated to the point where they brought about the ruin of many people. One side would attack, then the other, and the result was that they kept destroying peasant dwellings and refuges by fire and sword. While both sides were pursuing the conflict, the peasants took steps to prevent the burning of their small huts. They extinguished their hearthfires against the chance that one side or the other would pillage the area and turn their small cottages to kindling and ashes. Since the peasants had taken these precautions, the time came when Amblard's men were not able to find a burning fireplace anywhere. They rushed into Pierrefiche, one of Sainte Foy's small villages nearby.[30] Yet they were able to carry away very little of the fire they found there. For by divine direction crackling fire jumped up over them, and tongues of flame, as if licking them, left their clothing and beards shamefully disfigured. They were forced to flee the houses. While they were engaged in swift flight one of them was overcome by gluttony and rushed into a poultry pen to snatch two geese. He was chided but not at all moved by the severe reprimands of his comrades. When he was nearly finished roasting the birds and was about ready to take them to the table, suddenly the goose fat flooded over the live coals and flamed up. Soon the flames were flying from the roof, and his house and everything he had prepared for his meal were completely consumed. All the people who barely saved themselves from the fire proclaimed with one voice that these events had happened through Sainte Foy's power, since the geese they didn't deserve to eat had been stolen from her village.

3.14: How a Man Who Rashly Wished to Attack Sainte Foy with Fifty Horsemen Was Struck Blind Along with All His Companions

In Quercy there was a piece of property that had belonged outright to the holy martyr for a very long time. Because its tenants had long held it, they had come to think of themselves as its legal owners. The brothers of Sainte Foy's monastery agreed that control of this property should be regained by the community. They unanimously decided that the golden image in which the blessed martyr's glorious head is enclosed should be carried there. When they arrived, they set down the sacred treasure in a church called Belmont,[31] which is near the disputed land. The next morning they carried it to another of Sainte Foy's manors, which a warrior named Reinfroi was claiming as his own because he had occupied it for so long. After they had done this, they brought it back to Belmont. When Reinfroi heard what had occurred he was not pleased. Gathering fifty horsemen, he hurried to the disputed property, planning to take his vengeance on the monks. But, marvelous to report! as he set foot on the holy virgin's manor, which he held as if he had the right to inherit it, he and all his men were struck blind. Reinfroi asked a peasant whom he met on the way the name of the small village where he stood. Completely astonished, the peasant answered that it was La Fargue, a place subject to Reinfroi's control.[32] Reinfroi was deeply disturbed by this reply and told all his men that he had been struck blind. They answered at once that they had been overcome by the same malady. Reinfroi said to them:

"Up till now we have acted without thinking through the consequences. Unless we come to our senses at once worse things are bound to happen."

And so Reinfroi sent a peace-making delegation to the monks, and with his men he approached the sacred relics on bare feet. Asking her pardon for his ill-considered action, Reinfroi fell to the ground before the sacred image, completely prostrating himself. He said that after his death possession of the manor would be relinquished to Sainte Foy and agreed that his sons would not succeed him in holding it unless the brothers of the sacred community should wish it. As soon as he had made this vow, his sight was restored.[33]

Not long afterward when the holy relics had been taken back to their own monastery, Reinfroi was staying in the city of Toulouse to perform duties at the court.[34] There he had a vision at night in which it seemed that the holy virgin stood near him and spoke words like this: "Do you recognize me, Reinfroi?"

To which he replied: "And how, Lady, could I recognize you when I have never seen you before?"

"I am Sainte Foy. Three days ago you relinquished to me, effective after your death, the manor that you possess unworthily. But because I know very well that you did this deceitfully, I warn you that you had better give it up now while you are still alive."

Reinfroi was stricken with terror and told her that he would do as she had commanded. However, when morning came, his greedy desire to keep the manor was rekindled. He decided that the vision of the previous night had no reality. When the warning was repeated, he again gave it no thought, as before. On the third night the blessed virgin was present again, this time frightening him with harsher threats. She declared that unless he took immediate action to give up the manor she would condemn him to eternal punishment and would pursue all of his future posterity till the end of time with accursed hatred. Totally crushed by fear, Reinfroi immediately went to the holy martyr's abbey church. There he completely appeased all the glorious virgin's rancor against him. He relinquished without condition the possession of that manor for himself and abandoned the claims of his sons and grandsons. He handed the manor back to Abbot Girbert of blessed memory,[35] and to the rest of the brothers, so that in the end the holy virgin who is beloved of God would allow him to have full enjoyment of His heavenly mansions.

3.15: How a Man Enmeshed in Chains Called on Sainte Foy and Escaped Unharmed

About that time[36] a young man named Stephen set out for the castle of Servières[37] to attack it. He had a great hatred for this castle because his father had been killed there. Before he reached the castle, Stephen captured a young man who was out hunting. This young man had had nothing to do with the murder of Stephen's father, but Stephen had contrived an ambush against him because he owned a piece of land in an advantageous location. Stephen violently attacked him, took him captive, and, when he refused to hand over the land, led him away. The young man was placed in a chamber outside the tower, and weighed down with heavy fetters. His chain was passed through an opening in the wooden wall and secured to an iron stake on the outside. Constrained in this way, the captive did not cease urgently to call on the power of Sainte Foy with supplicating vows. He utterly threw himself on her pity and mercy. In addition his devoted mother went to Sainte Foy's shrine[38] and in the presence of the glorious relics she related her fears and concerns about her son's imprisonment.

One night while he was despairing for his life, the captive was warned in a dream and behold! when he awakened there was a wooden saw lying next to him. Extracting the bolt from the bottom of the tool, he twisted it into the opening through which his chain passed to the outside, and with a repeated movement freed the iron stake from the ring that held it fast. After the chain had been pulled through the wall, he anxiously began to search for a way to escape from such a high fortress. For that tower was built atop a cliff as high as the Caucasus, and a huge chasm gaped beneath it, threatening mortal danger to anyone who even looked down. But, just as the Poet says, "One solution for the defeated is not to hope for a solution."[39]

Considering the treachery of his enemies on the one hand and the fall into the chasm on the other, he chose to die on his own terms rather than to endure his enemies' oppression for a long time. While he was poised there between hope and fear, intending to throw himself over the edge, he noticed some *balistas*[40] hanging from the wall. He pulled away the ropes and immediately tied them together. Then he securely attached this longer rope to the door post of the chamber and began to lower himself by this means. The full length of the rope did not even reach halfway to the bottom of the chasm, but he slid down as far as he could, then entrusted himself to Sainte Foy, and threw himself to what seemed certain destruction.

The guards, who were awakened by the clanging noise of his fetters, shouted to each other that the captive was escaping. At the bottom of the precipice the escaping prisoner was not yet freed from his chains, and the increasing light of dawn made him easy to spot, so he hid himself under a bundle of brushwood piled up there. Because God was protecting him, even the huge crowd of people who searched for him couldn't find him. This crowd, made up of both peasants and armed horsemen, had gathered because it was market day. Still, no one could discover the escaped prisoner, since God was hiding him. When the day was over he took flight through the protective darkness of night. He came to a country dwelling where he used an axe to break his fetters and so returned home a free man. But he soon carried his chains to the holy martyr's basilica and recounted to us the events I have recorded here. Then he completed a solemn vigil before the tomb of his glorious deliverer, devoutly and repeatedly offering heartfelt thanks to God and Sainte Foy.

3.16: How a Woman Who Wickedly Acted Against Sainte Foy Perished Through a Miracle

In the province of Quercy a marvelous thing took place. Since all-powerful God wished to work this strange miracle for love of His virgin, I consider it worthy to be inserted in this text. In that land there was a noblewoman. Either because womankind is always avaricious—as is written in books—or more likely because she was led on by a demon, she obsessively coveted the holy martyr's lands that adjoined her own fields. Therefore she subjected the farm-workers plowing the monks' field to a great deal of abuse and succeeded in driving them away. The next day she arranged to have this field plowed with her own plowshare, and she dared to make it part of her own property. And so divine power brought it about that, while she was ordering that her property line be extended to include the field and insisting strenuously, her whole body shriveled instantly and she croaked and hissed horribly as she sent her miserable soul down to Orcus.[41] The plowmen were terrified by her horrendous death and fled the field, leaving the plow behind. Out of breath and completely distraught, they scarcely managed to tell their lord what had happened. He grieved over his wife's death, sent for her body, and had it buried. And after she was destroyed in this way, the holy martyr's land was henceforth safe from all who had designs on it and remained afterwards the property of the monks.

3.17: How Siger, Who Unjustly Acted Against Sainte Foy, Met a Disastrous End

But while I was exerting myself with the greatest zeal to compile these miracles from various places into one collection, another miraculous happening came knocking at the door of my book, and no one will deny that I should allow it to enter.

In the castle of Conques[42] lived a warrior named Siger, who was characterized both by excellence of lineage and by prowess in the martial arts. But Siger diminished the dignity of his status with his great hostility to Sainte Foy. Puffed up with arrogant pride and enflamed by the fires of avarice, he stole everything he could from the holy martyr's property. He never ceased harassing her monks with vile insults, and he mutilated the men who worked on her lands. The senior monks of the monastery often rebuked him gently, but as Wisdom says, "a fool is not reformed with words."[43] Certainly he did not bring his destructive actions to a halt. Because the senior monks did not have the resources to stand up to his audacious wickedness with force, they persevered in praying to the holy martyr to help them; they implored her to free them from this incredibly cruel plague. In addition, they unfurled the banner of the Lord's victory and displayed it in the public square, along with a cross, the reliquary boxes, and the blessed martyr's holy image. They aroused all the people assembled there so that the holy virgin would be moved to stir up God's wrath against the tyrant and preserve her own territories from the violence of this cyclops.

And so it came about that the unfortunate man was struck with a wretched illness; he who deserved his punishment was handed over to hell's torments. And the Scriptures say, "the children of the wicked shall perish,"[44] which is what happened to the people of Sodom and Gomorrah, whom heaven's wrath completely annihilated. God did not preserve even one person of their bloodline because from their offspring another generation could emerge and corrupt the earth with their fathers' depravities. After Siger was destroyed, the three sons his wife had borne him swiftly took leave of their bodies, and a fourth was deformed by a paralyzing disease that forced him to follow his brothers to an ignominious death. All of them died childless. Their three sisters survived for a while, then, deservedly, because of their father, they left this life in miserable ways. The first was reviled and cast off by her husband because of suspicion and jealousy, then struck by paralysis, and finally departed from the light of this world destitute and wretched. The second along with her children contracted a disease that caused swelling and sores; they suffered great pain.[45] The third couldn't succeed her father and come into her inheritance because she took up with a serf, thereby losing her rank. And the very tower that had given shelter to this destructive group of people was shaken in all directions by a strong wind; it fell with a great crash and was completely leveled. Thus through the holy martyr's power all that pride collapsed; thus the root of evils was torn out and destroyed; thus divine vengeance delivered the holy monastery from the assault of the impious.

3.18: How a Man Overcame His Enemies Because He Was Defended by the Holy Virgin's Power and by Her Standard

The miracle that I am going to write next should be a comfort to the faithful and a severe warning to the enemies of God.

In the region of Nîmes lived a man named Fredol who was both highly celebrated for his noble character and very famous for his military prowess. A man who had fallen prey to demonic enthrallment stole Fredol's wife by deceit and—it is a sin even to speak of it—joined himself to her in marriage.[46] He set dangerous ambushes for Fredol and was in every way fiercely hostile to him. Finally he sought the aid of Matfred of Lodève and other strong men and led a band of seven hundred horsemen against Fredol. They devastated his lands with pillaging. Fredol did not have the forces to resist this army that was inflicting injuries on his holdings so undeservedly, and so with singleminded purposefulness he implored almighty God to come to his assistance. Inspired by God's grace his thoughts immediately turned to Sainte Foy and so, taking provisions with him, Fredol left his son behind to defend the castle and came as a suppliant to the holy martyr's abbey church. Before her he unfolded all the reasons for the rancor in his heart and begged her to bring him help. With his men Fredol persevered in prayer through the entire night. And as the sun was rising he gave over a manor from his own inheritance to be the holy virgin's possession in perpetuity. In return he asked the brothers of the monastery for the holy martyr's standard, because under its protection he would be able boldly to penetrate his enemy's defenses.[47]

When he had obtained the banner, Fredol hurried to his castle. Immediately he gathered his men together, a troop of one hundred and fifty horsemen. Trusting in the merits of the holy martyr, his forces fell on the immeasurably larger army of the enemy. Fredol himself carried the banner. Leading his men, he forced his way through the enemy's flanks, crying out in a booming voice all the while, "Sainte Foy, help us!" and then simply repeating her name frequently. And so with the holy virgin's aid a great part of the enemy army fell to the ground wounded, and in addition the adulterer who led them met with a sword and toppled to the earth like a fallen tree. After he had been slain, the confused multitude that remained slipped away in flight. And so without loss of his own men Fredol became the glorious victor and seized the spoils of war. In joyous triumph he returned to his castle. Then he set out on another journey, hastening swiftly to his own patron, Sainte Foy. He offered her glorious praise, for supported by her power he had been able to overcome a huge enemy force with only a few men.

3.19: How a Pilgrim Was Freed from the Saracens Through the Holy Virgin

Another story we have learned about a miracle accomplished through the wondrous divine providence of omnipotent God is worthy of inclusion in this book.

The servant of a fighting man named Raymond went on a pilgrimage to the Lord's Sepulcher in fulfillment of his own fervent wish. After experiencing the joy of reaching his goal, he was making his journey home when he was captured by Saracen shepherds. They beat him from head to foot with heavy blows and demanded talents of gold from him. Because they couldn't find any on him, they tortured him even more cruelly. Finally they stripped off his sheepskin garment—something that ought to be treated with reverence[48] — and beat his naked body. Then those pagans built a fire and put his clothes and belt into it, so that when it was reduced to cinders whatever gold he had concealed might be found in the ashes. When the captive realized that he was in the hands of murderers, he called on Sainte Foy with tear-filled cries and entrusted himself entirely to her hands.

"Sainte Foy," he said, "celebrated virgin and martyr, up till now I have felt that your support was there whenever I needed it, for through you I have been protected many times from hunger and starvation; I have avoided loss and danger; I have even survived shipwreck and storms at sea. Now as your suppliant, I require your mercy. Rescue me from the cruel savagery of these men."

Shedding aggrieved tears, he continued to implore Sainte Foy in this fashion. As he spoke the fire formed itself into a hollow circle, turning the whirling columns of smoke away from the sheepskin garment thrown over it and preserving it unharmed from the flames. When the uncouth peasant shepherds saw this, they clapped their hands and burst into gales of laughter. Hoping that the deed had come about by chance rather than through the power of God, they left him there and betook themselves to their sheep pens in the mountains. But the freed man rejoiced and leapt in the air because of the great miracle. He took up his clothes, gave to God and the holy martyr the thanks that was due them, and hurriedly completed the journey he had begun.

3.20: How a Little Boy Was Called Back from Death at Millau[49]

It does not seem right to me to pass over a miracle that I know was wondrously accomplished through the holy virgin's outstanding merits, a miracle that a very large crowd of people witnessed.

In the territory of Septimania there is a church of the glorious martyr. It is located in a place known throughout the region as Pallas because of the princely power of those who ruled there. The elders of the monastery had agreed that the venerable golden effigy of the virgin should be carried in procession to this church. En route the procession came to the well-known town of Millau. Instead of entering the town, they set up tents in a grassy meadow lying below it and fittingly placed the sacred image in a pavilion at the center. When the people living nearby heard of her arrival, they rejoiced greatly and approached such a great patron on bare feet and with the highest reverence. Displaying appropriate deference, they said prayers and vows committing themselves and their families to her protection.

But when an inhabitant of their town named Lambert saw this great gathering of people he scoffed at them with foolish jeers, for he had been ensnared by pagan error. He threw insulting abuse upon God's saint and refused to go with the others. The holy virgin, impatient with his wicked recklessness, did not wait long to avenge the injury inflicted on her, but struck soon so that her sharp attack might become an example to all. For suddenly Lambert was reduced to a fool, empty-headed and irrational; he was scarcely able to find the way to his own house. But it wasn't only this opinionated and conceited person that felt Sainte Foy's righteous anger; his small son, resting on his nurse's breast, paid the price of his father's condemnation. One of the child's eyes was afflicted with great pain. First his brow and then his whole head swelled up, causing such great distress that he almost seemed to be quivering with his last breath. When his anguished mother saw how cruelly he was set upon, she ranted and raved uncontrollably and snatched up her son in her arms. Then, filling the entire area around the crossroads with her great cries, she rushed forward to the holy martyr's feet and laid her son there. Asking for his recovery, she shouted in her loudest voice:

"Most glorious virgin of Christ, Foy, holy in name and deed, from heaven now hear the pleas of a wretched woman who, enveloped in intolerable pain, cannot but importune you. Listen mercifully to my cries; I am overcome by immense grief because my only child is dying. Through your kindness have pity on wretched me who suffers grief in my whole body. Let your sacred visitation to this place be for us a health-giving cure, not a condemnation to loss. O glorious virgin, what great crime could my little boy have committed against you, who has not spoken a single word, who can't even talk yet? How can it be that he deserves punishment when he has not committed a single sin? O most holy virgin, either return him to me, or take him to yourself. His death will be my death. O glorious mother, O patron worthy of adoration, I fly to your feet, distraught because the child of my own womb is dying. Do not judge me unworthy of your help. Even if some sin has been wrongly committed against you by his parents, do not crush this innocent child whose purity of life makes him a stranger to every fault of human depravity. Do not deprive me of the sweetness of my son, whom I love in the depths of my heart more than all my desire to live."

While she was forcefully and tearfully carrying on in this vein in the image's sacred presence, someone spoke of her husband's dire situation at home. And so she left the small infant behind. He lay as if he were dead in his nurse's lap in front of the sacred virgin's image. The woman returned home and discovered her husband prostrate on his bed. Cursing and accusing him relentlessly, she forced him to admit his responsibility for the harm that had been done. She pulled him out of his bed and tried to restore him to his previous mental state. Meanwhile the little boy, whom the nurse was holding in front of the most blessed virgin's sacred effigy, appeared to everyone to be dead. All night he lay there, lifeless and unmoving, before the sacred relics. But when the cock had crowed, when this omen of the day to come had caused the first voices to be lifted in prayer, the little boy regained the breath of life and all who were keeping watch over him as if he were dead were struck with a trancelike stupor. After he was reborn in this way, his father confessed his own guilt and appealed for the holy virgin's pardon in an attitude of humble entreaty. And so he too was cured by divine medicine. He completed vows of prayer, took his revived son with him, and went back home happy and healthy.

On that same procession, so many signs of the sacred martyr's powers shone forth that because of their incomprehensibly great number the limited capacity of parchment pages cannot contain them.

3.21: How a Warrior Stole Straw from One of Sainte Foy's Peasants and How a Wicked Horseman Was Struck Down[50]

Pallas, which I mentioned in the last miracle, is overlooked by a castle named Loupian.[51] Once a lord named Bernard the Hairy[52] was besieging that castle. He had erected a palisaded rampart around it and had amassed a force of a thousand horsemen and almost as many foot soldiers. With sword, fire, and plundering they destroyed everything around the castle. When they had recognized that such a siege was at hand, the people of the surrounding area had collected all their belongings and taken them inside the walls of the church at Pallas, leaving behind nothing that could be destroyed except their own huts. So the horsemen, deprived of the hope of plunder, harassed the neighboring places and what they could find they collected and took back to their encampments.

And so it happened that one horseman, driven by necessity, broke into that church and violently snatched a bundle of straw from a peasant. When he began to spur on his horse, laden with the bundle—wondrous to report!—he could not make the horse move from the spot by any means, even though he bloodied both its flanks with the goads of his spurs. He became agitated and even violently angry. He quickly dismounted, grabbed a piece of wood, and began to beat the horse hard on its haunches and flanks. When he mounted the horse again, this time without the straw, he cried out in surprise because the horse moved so quickly—he had never known it to turn around so readily. Then he loaded the straw on the horse again, since he wanted to depart. But just as before there was no way the horse could be moved from the spot.

Perhaps, like Balaam's ass, that horse saw an angel with an unsheathed sword standing in front of him and threatening death![53] For both animals stood immobile while their masters raved at them furiously and beat them cruelly. In both cases, their masters would have been able to kill them more easily than to lead them one step from the spot. But between these two animals, dissimilar in species but not in kind, there was this difference: the ass cried out in human speech against the injuries inflicted on it undeservedly, whereas the horse indicated what it clearly saw only with groans.

What more is there to say? At last that man came to his senses and gave heed to the presence of God's power. He put down the bundle of straw, returned to the peasant the other things he had carried off, and confessed his guilt before the crowd standing there. The horse, freed from its burden, began to move unsteadily in little leaps, as if it wanted to become warm again after bathing by moving around. The peasant understood that he had regained possession of his goods because of a miracle performed through the holy martyr's intercession. He demonstrated his love for her by giving the bundle of straw to the horseman and placing it on the horse's neck. And so it came about through the miraculous dispensation of all-powerful God that he who was completely unable to carry off what had been stolen was easily able to lead away what had been given.

When the horseman rejoined the rest of his companions he disclosed everything that had happened to him, to the wonder of all. But one of them held the great magnificence of God in such little regard that he took two of his fellows with him and broke into the enclosure around the church. He forcibly carried off bread and wine from the monks' provisions and then, catching sight of all the peasants' plowhorses and bedding crowded together there, he said that he would quickly return and swore an oath that he would carry off everything. As soon as he turned away from them, the whole multitude of peasants called on Sainte Foy's protection, for they had committed themselves and their dependents to her safekeeping. And divine power did not allow his wicked plot to reach the stage of execution. He was so swollen with pride that before he returned to his own men he attacked the castle alone. From the spot where he was concealed, the son of the castle's lord struck him down with a lance and the horseman gave up his miserable spirit. Since all acknowledged that this was done through Sainte Foy's intercession, they gave to God and the holy martyr the great thanks due them, and afterward they were preserved from any further disturbances.

3.22: How a Girl Who Was Paralyzed Was Made Whole Again by Sainte Foy

Here is another extraordinary miracle. I believe it would be a sin if I were to pass over it in silence.

Above the torrent called Bromme[54] in Rouergue there is a church dedicated to Sainte Foy. In this parish lived a peasant who had a daughter then about seven years old, paralyzed from her waist to her feet. Encouraged by the great abundance of miracles that had been worked through Sainte Foy, the peasant confidently carried his daughter on a horse-drawn pallet to the holy virgin's shrine. There he lit candles and he spent the night in holy vigil; he did not stop pleading with the holy martyr for her recovery, and he gave the whole night over to praying. When morning came the priest took pains to celebrate mass for the pilgrims, so that through his prayers their safe journey would be more assured.

And so it happened by divine will that while her father was receiving the Eucharist for the common safety of all, the little girl suffered a little more intensely with pain in her limbs, and afterward all the pain had disappeared and she regained complete health. For at the same moment the joints in her back became connected, her muscles stretched out straight, and the soles of her feet were strengthened; in this way her two legs were restored immediately from their paralysis. When they saw this, the whole crowd standing there were filled with great joy. They sang praises to the most high God and the holy martyr, and rejoiced over such a great gift.

3.23: How, for Love of a Warrior, Sainte Foy Restored Speech to Three Mute Men

At about this same time there was another miracle, one so wondrous that it was truly worthy of being added to this book also.

A warrior came to the holy virgin's church to pray and brought with him a young man who from birth had made no human sound. When they had finished keeping the customary vigil through the night, it was dawn: Aurora, rising, left the bed of Tithonus.[55] With dawn's arrival the mute boy spoke clearly, and he bestowed the first fruits of his voice in the act of thanksgiving. The warrior who had brought the boy there rejoiced greatly because of the miracle and offered heartfelt thanks to the holy virgin. Then he hastened home. When a year had passed, the same warrior returned to Sainte Foy's abbey church. This time, as before, he brought a mute man with him and, as before, due to heaven's tender mercies, he took the man back with him fully possessed of the power of speech. And when the same warrior set out for Conques a third time for his usual prayers, he overtook on the road a mute man named Gozmar. Gozmar turned toward him and began to ask alms from him by moving his lips. The horseman seized Gozmar and brought him along to the holy virgin so that he could obtain the favor of a cure for Gozmar, just as he had done for the other two. As he entered the holy church the horseman gave a wax candle to the mute man. He then bowed down in prayer and eagerly entreated God's saint on behalf of himself and his companion. However, when he saw that the man remained mute he brought his prayers to an end and cried out that he was a guilty sinner.

"O blessed virgin," he said, "I confess that my sins require that I be judged unworthy of the kindness you have customarily shown me. Twice in the past I was enriched with the gift of a miracle, twice you brought it about that a happy man went home from your basilica. Now I think that because I am contaminated by some offense, the grace of your usual favor has been withheld from me."

And sadly pondering on these matters, he said, "Let's go to the guesthouse, and after we have had breakfast we'll come back and ask permission to depart."

When they had just about reached the middle of the basilica, by divine command the mute man exclaimed clearly, "First, my lord, I ought to offer my candle because I haven't offered it yet."

When he heard these words, the warrior was overwhelmed by inestimable joy and returned to the holy virgin's altar with a lively step. There he prostrated himself and sang magnificent praises to God and the holy martyr, for they had bestowed their compassion and enriched him with a threefold gift of miracles. God had performed these miracles because of the outstanding merits of His own virgin, the same God Who, before the murder of Julius Caesar, forced a plowing ox to utter in plain speech, "Rome, beware!"

3.24: How a Priest Captured a Pilgrim en Route to Sainte Foy

Yet another miracle remains, and I have decided to end this book by recording it. In the Albigeois there is a castle called Thuriès.[56] As Christmas neared, a fighting man from that castle named Regimbald was coming to Sainte Foy's abbey church. But Regimbald's journey was interrupted by a grievous circumstance: he was taken captive by a priest named Hadimar, who hated him, and confined in chains. Regimbald gave his pledge that he would return to captivity and traveled on to the holy martyr's basilica. There, prostrate on the ground, he made known to her all the bitterness in his heart and the harm he would suffer in captivity. With steadfast prayers he demanded that she come to his assistance. After the feast of Christmas had been celebrated, Regimbald gave himself up to captivity and returned to his chains. But He who "lifts up those who are cast down" and "looses those who are fettered"[57] struck Hadimar from the soles of his feet to the top of his head with a wretched malady so that Regimbald would be freed from the bonds of his chains. Hadimar's sores ran with a discharge so foul that his whole household found it intolerable.

Hadimar freed his captive, who had fulfilled his pledge by returning to him. Then, because he could not walk on the stony footpath, Hadimar went on horseback to the holy virgin's church. When he arrived there, with sincere groans he confessed his guilt to the holy martyr and to all the monks. Then he began to beat himself severely, to expiate the crime to which he had confessed. After he had humbly completed vows and prayers, Hadimar returned home. God's compassion cured him, so that after a modest interval his swelling disappeared completely. Wholly recovered, he purchased provisions for a journey and set out for Jerusalem. God granted him a successful pilgrimage and on his return he came to the holy virgin's abbey church. He faithfully pledged himself to her and to all the monks and from then on he honored his pledge by visiting there frequently.

These miracles should be sufficient in quantity for even the most eagerly attentive reader. But because this little book already contains a collection of a great many miracles, I will treat those that remain in a second book. This fresh start will renew the listeners' powers of attention. They will hear in both books of the astonishing and mighty works of omnipotent God, which He deigned to bring about through His most glorious martyr Foy, to the praise and glory of His own name, that name which is wonderful and awe-inspiring forever and ever. Amen.

The end of the third book.

The Fourth Book of Sainte Foy, Virgin and Martyr[1]

The Chapters of the Fourth Book

The Fourth Book of the Miracles of Sainte Foy, Virgin and Martyr of Christ

4.1: How a Dead Person Was Revived, and Miracles Performed for Him While He Was on His Way to Sainte Foy

Because I have been set aflame by ardent love for the very glorious virgin and athlete of Christ,[2] the unconquerable Foy, I feel compelled to lay claim to the time for writing that I once had and for so long since, have not had. I urgently ask to be aided by the glorious assistance of that martyr, most holy and most beloved of God. Though she has been united with the angelic host in the heights of heaven, the remarkable great works of her miracles shine brightly and make her power known to the whole world, while I stand here and say nothing. For even if she can't show herself to people as a corporeal being, still she manifests herself perpetually through the revealed signs of her miracles. There is no land from one pole to the other where her fame and the praise of her name are not known. And this fame and praise are well deserved, for from her very early youth she had an outstanding character. She was distinguished by the goodness of total chastity, and in all her actions she shone purer than gold. She held fast to the virtues instilled in her. And so she is worthy of these words, "While the king was at his repose, my fragrance sent forth a sweet odor to him."[3]

Truly the fragrance of her sanctity and of her chaste life breathed out a sweet scent to the supreme king sitting on the high throne of the heavens, because she was wholly "the good odor unto God," to use the apostle's phrase.[4] When finally she was burned in the searing fire of her passion, when the alabaster perfume jar that was her body was shattered by the harshest punishments, she became choice myrrh. The court of God was filled with her most pleasing fragrance and sent forth pillars of smoke[5] scented with her most delightful sweetness to all the earth's wide regions.

There the most glorious virgin's magnificent name is received with pious love and there her eternal commemoration is celebrated with the veneration she deserves. Just as the wondrous signs of her miracles bear witness, in the torments of her passion she put aside her body that was made of earth and owed to death and exchanged it for a life far freer. Thus she moves unconfined through the upper air surrounding the earth, and whenever a perilous situation reaches crisis, she is present; she hears and answers those in need who seek her aid. In her presence no illness can inflict harm, for every disease must yield to the balm she applies at the sound of her name. Even Death itself, which once learned how to paint faces with a wan pallor, sparing no one, now must learn a new and different lesson; the holy virgin, called down by supplicating prayers, wishes to warm these pallid faces to their former ruddiness. Indeed in a singular fashion ravenous Orcus[6] is forced to give back uninjured from his bloodstained mouth the bites of souls he has swallowed, bites for which his mouth always gapes so he can stuff his harpy's belly, for he ever craves to sate his insatiable hunger. This virgin, chosen above all others, was enriched by the Lord with such great rewards and honors because, when she was tortured by excruciating pain for love of Him, she wasn't afraid to suffer with patience the final insult of death. Her celebrated reputation, borne through the air to every place on untiring wings, as I have said, urges everyone everywhere who is crushed by any affliction at all to seek safe refuge by calling on her protective power. They know that she hears readily and gives generously.

And so it happened that in the Toulousain a man named Hunald was worthy of receiving a wondrous benefaction from the holy martyr, and he experienced by sight and deed her unexpected and magnificent power. For Hunald had a son whom he sent to keep watch over a herd in the pastures as tradition dictated. After Hunald's son had taken up the duties of a herdsman, he was leading the herd back home one day when the evening star was rising. Through carelessness the boy let one cow wander off into the bushes while he was bringing the rest into the enclosure of the barn. When he saw from the empty place that one animal was missing he went back to the pasture, wandering alone through the gloomy shadows of night, but after most of the night had slipped by while he searched in vain he returned sad and guilty without the cow. He had no idea what to do nor where to turn. He was so thoroughly terrified of his father's fierce sternness that he didn't dare enter the house openly and confess what had happened to him. At last everyone was asleep, and he slipped into bed secretly. While he was tossing to and fro, completely exhausted by his search for the missing cow, the boy was seized by such great pain right then and there that he was sure almost every joint in his body had been dislocated. As this pain grew too strong to bear, he lost the ability to move his limbs and slipped into a coma.

When morning came and Hunald saw that his son was in the grip of such a serious illness, he soon put aside his anger. He began to mourn over his son's imminent death with doleful groans, and then, battered and wracked by great sobs, he implored Sainte Foy's healing aid with loud cries, begging her to restore his son to his former sound health. But his son's whole body remained immobile; it seemed to Hunald that the heat of life barely flickered deep in the boy's chest. Nine days passed while he lay motionless and no light of understanding brightened his eyes. However on the tenth day, which was kept as the Lord's Day, his attendants saw the light of life in the boy's eyes fading away gradually into death and ice-cold sweat ran from his brow and cheeks. A hand pressed against the boy's left side found no life-bearing heartbeat. They recognized by these clear and evident signs that what was left of him had been given to the deep sleep of eternity. What more is there to say? They prepared the body and when the lifeless cadaver had been laid upon a bier they honored it with wails and laments. But the next day when they had conveyed his corpse to the place dug in the ground for his burial, his father, who was unable to endure the loss because of his deep love for his son, embraced the ice-cold body. Hunald's eyes were wet and his entire face was streaked with flowing tears; he filled the whole place with bitter cries. Amid these heart-rending moans he cried out over and over, "Holy martyr of God, Foy."

With tear-filled pleas Hunald implored her to return his son to him, and he repeated this three or four times:

Virgin Foy, beloved of God, renowned light of the world,
You who always bring help quickly to the wretched,
Hear my humble voice, O most holy martyr.
I beg of you, confer as much aid as you can upon a pitiable man.
No one who has been forced by misfortune to seek your favor
Has departed empty-handed. Holding fast to your hand,
I believe, and it is not empty faith, that you are able to do what I wish,
Because God in heaven promised you for this purpose.
Behold, the only son born to me, my sole joy,
Struck down, my only love, my only hope of offspring.
Since he has perished like this, the remainder of my life

Will endlessly prolong my sadness.
But if, virgin of God, you are softened by any plaints of
Wretched ones, and if you are overcome by my plentiful tears,
My son whose limbs we see lying lifeless at his burial,
To his former life, I ask you, now recall.

Lying over the body of the dead boy, Hunald kept on repeating plaints like this and lamenting with great wails. All who were present at the last service of the funeral ceremony were moved by compassion for the weeping man; their faces were flooded with tears and, mixed with the tears, prayers to the very glorious virgin Foy. With one voice they exhorted her, asking that she deign to respond to the invocation of her holy name with a merciful appearance.

And so straightaway—Oh, marvelous to tell!
Foul Death turned back, fled, leaving behind its prey.
And the greedy devourer spewed out its prey from its jaws.
At once the boy's head nodded slowly,
Turned in both directions; Life-giving heat rewarmed his ice-cold
bone marrow,
And suddenly Christ poured his soul into his body.
It flooded through his cold limbs.
Lying there, he was raised up.
He slowly opened his timorous eyes,
And soon he raised up his whole body at once,
And stood on his own feet, using his limbs,
And so he and his father returned home.

When they had seen this, all who were present offered thanks; they wept for joy because of such a great miracle. Glorifying the power of the holy virgin and martyr Foy, they solemnly promised vows and gifts to her from themselves and their dependents. Then they left the church of Saint George[7] where they had gathered to bury the youth and returned home.

Not long thereafter the father of the reborn son and the other members of his household examined him carefully with eager questions. They wanted to know what he had seen during those nine days when he lay ill, unconscious and nearly dead; who had helped him; and how he had come to draw breath again shortly after he had been brought for burial. He was still trembling from his experience, but he took several long, deep breaths and began to answer his interrogators.

"I am going to pass over other things for now and disclose concisely, with the greatest certainty and without any doubt, what happened to me at the very end of my life. My soul had been freed from its corporeal chains and was given over to some very hideous and loathsome attendants, who commanded that I be cruelly dragged to the edge of an enormous pit. I was indescribably afraid, terrified of being hurled into this horrid abyss. I did not know whether to cry out or remain silent, when, behold! a man of bright shining splendor arrived. He was the commander of Paradise, Michael the archangel, as I learned later. I could see him clearly. The glorious virgin Foy stood beside him, a companion on his pleasing journey; she shone with wondrous radiance, brighter than the sun. But when this commander of the heavens caught sight of those who raged implacably, like executioners, against me whom they had been assigned to torture, he said:

'You contrivers of evil, why are you raving so furiously and cruelly in tormenting this new arrival? Why are you going to pitilessly destroy a soul created by the most high God? Stop mangling him now, because God has permitted through this very holy virgin Foy that his soul will be snatched from your power and restored to his body.'

"At the sound of this voice the servants of Tartarus were seized by unbearable terror; they dropped their hands, which were always engaged in doing evil and, shaking with unaccustomed fear, they obeyed the celestial messengers. Without delay, the blessed virgin Foy rushed fiercely into the midst of the torturers' ranks and firmly dragged my soul from their hands. She delivered it to my body lying on the ground and poured it back in to work the miracle that you saw."

After the boy had described in sequence the contents of what was not only a vision but the truth of the matter as well, his father and neighbors undertook a journey. They took with them the boy who had been revived and they directed their course to the holy virgin's monastery in order to offer there the thanks and praise due to her. While they were descending along the steep side of the mountain that stretches its cloud-covered head above the bed of the Dourdou River,[8] where the path is steep and slippery, the son was riding because he had not yet recovered from his illness. His mount's foot slipped; it faltered and struggled for a long time to regain the path, in the process throwing the boy down on his back with a huge crash. And although he could have fallen to his death because the trail was so narrow, he was protected by a miracle of God and the guardianship of the holy martyr and immediately rose up uninjured.

And when the group of pilgrims reached the basilica, with exultant spirits they offered praises to almighty God for bestowing the gift of resurrection that was their reason for coming. They honored the holy virgin, venerating her with the gifts they owed, praising her and proclaiming that she shimmered with the light of the miracle's marvelous powers. When prayer had been completed they went to the guesthouse. That night they prepared their torches and set out for the church to celebrate holy vigils in front of the holy virgin. Hunald's son, whose name was Bernard but who was often called "the resuscitated one,"[9] found the Ancient Enemy lying in wait to capture him, for, in an unforeseen calamity, when he was in the hall he tumbled down a gaping hole that had been covered over by wooden flooring. His companions ran down to him swiftly and found him safe and uninjured; the holy martyr had placed her hand beneath him and it was as if he had landed on soft cushions after a short fall. But on the next day the reverend brothers of this monastery, who had too little information about the power of the previous miracle, took him aside and inquired diligently about the whole sequence of his vision with shrewd industry. Bernard invoked God as his witness, for Whom no secret lies hidden, and asserted that everything had happened just as it is preserved in the preceding narrative.

I do not think I should omit another miracle that Sainte Foy worked for Bernard, the resuscitated one. For in it our virgin's admirable sanctity shines forth magnificently, she who is worthy of being compared in merits to all the saints, our patron Foy. In this miracle she restrains imprudent men to keep them from completing their unlawful and forbidden undertakings.

Because Bernard owed allegiance for the benefaction he had received, he returned to Sainte Foy's basilica about a year later. A man named Garsias from the town of Saint-Orens, commonly referred to as Marciac, accompanied him. Garsias (a name found frequently among the Gascons) was carrying a piece of cloth with him in order to sell it at a profit. This is customary—he didn't start the practice. When he reached the entrance of the church at Lucasine, he was attacked by a robber who stole the cloth. Garsias made light of the theft because of his love for the shrines of the saints and decided to proceed with the journey he had undertaken. But the robber gathered some seamstresses and urged them to quickly make trousers for him from the cloth.

What more is there to say? Divine power was certainly present there, for it changed the cloth so that it was as hard as stone and made the sharp scissors as blunt as if they were pieces of wood. After the miracle had been demonstrated repeatedly, the seamstresses realized that the power of God and the holy martyr was present and was preventing them from cutting the stolen cloth. The thief was utterly terrified by this very powerful sign, and he saved the linen cloth. When the pilgrims returned he sought their pardon for his crime and humbly returned the cloth. They understood that the holy virgin's power had prevailed in this matter and rejoiced with thanks at the restitution of the property.

4.2: About a Flask That Was Left Empty

While all of these miracles were happening, another remarkable deed occurred. Since it was found worthy of praise and wonder, I believe it would be a crime to exclude it from these pages.

Some peasants from the territory of Auvergne were traveling together to the holy martyr's church to pray there. After they had crossed the river Lot and had reached a certain tree which is commonly called *rixiac*,[10] they sat down under its leafy shade. There they divided among themselves the jar of wine that they had brought along to relieve the summer's heat. When they departed they hung the empty flask in the tree under the holy virgin's protection. After they had completed all the prayers they had vowed to say at Conques, the peasants returned on the footpath, for they were concerned to retrieve their wine jar. When they reached the tree they took the jar down from the branches. Marvelous to report, what they had left there as empty they found overflowing with the purest Falernian wine,[11] as if under the autumn sun it had foamed up with a thick froth of fresh new wine from the bottom to the very top. Stunned by such a sight, they recognized it as an act of God through the holy virgin's power, into whose protection they had entrusted this container so that she would preserve it. They made use of this gift that heaven had conferred on them and soon shared it with all the travelers and other people who came upon them. In the holy virgin's honor they poured freely and drank uninterruptedly until the vessel was empty. Then they gave huge proclamations of praises to God and the holy martyr for such a great blessing, returned the vessel to its owner, and joyfully set out for home on the dusty footpath.

4.3: About a Boy Whose Eyes Were Put Out

I do not think that I ought to withhold this miracle in silence, for in it the power of the admirable virgin Sainte Foy shone forth through divine will, power no less praiseworthy than in her other miracles.

In the village of Conques lived a man named Hugh who was the illegitimate brother of a boastful official there.[12] Hugh was thoroughly hated and continually addressed everyone with bombastic pride. Motivated by his insolence and arrogance, Hugh had developed an unbearable hatred for a villager named Benedict. He ground Benedict down with constant abuse and harassed him all the time with cruel attacks. Finally Benedict, who bore this abuse with difficulty, was overcome by fury. He attacked Hugh and killed him, then fled for fear of Hugh's kindred, leaving behind all that he had. His wife also fled and escaped with him, because she did not wish to be separated from her husband. They left behind at home a son almost five years old whom the fugitive parents could not carry with them. When the dead man's kindred saw the little boy and understood that his father, the murderer, had fled—alas! cruel and horrible deed! They were impelled by the same Furies who drove Orestes to slay his mother! They seized the little boy and, disdaining to kill such an insignificant person, they pierced the pupils of his eyes with sharp, pointed sticks and left him half dead.

But omnipotent God, to Whom is left the care of the wretched, was present for this boy abandoned by his parents, and He did not deprive the boy of His usual mercy. For the men of that village lifted him from the ground and carried him down to the church door, and they instructed him that with the others who were sick or injured he should beg alms from the people coming to pray. For several months he sought contributions there. Then one day when the sun was hastening to the west the inhabitants of Conques led him by the hand up to the holy virgin's altar. They eagerly requested of the highly renowned virgin that she deign to provide her customary mercy by granting a miracle for him. But I'll not waste time in long digressions. Just as a tiny little spark of fire set to a dead coal will cause it to brighten slowly until it glows with red heat, light sent down from heaven began to burn through the boy's clouded vision little by little, clearing the eyes that had been extinguished for so long. He reached out to touch the forms of things opposite him as if by the dim light of a dark moon, then he began to cry out with boyish glee that he could see a little. The way he was shouting brought to memory the man about whom it was attested that after his sight was restored by the Savior he saw men who looked to him like walking trees.[13] That little boy was like him, as I say, for with scarcely any delay the light continued to increase and he saw everything so clearly that he both recognized by sight and named whatever was shown to him. Everyone was filled with indescribable joy by this; the air rang mightily with their exuberant shouts; with their voices rivaling one another they made the whole basilica reverberate with declarations of praise. What more is there to say? The people gathered and no one of any sex or age stopped praising the holy virgin. No orator could find the words to describe their applause, their dancing. The boy was reciting the Psalmist's words, "My father and my mother have left me, but the Lord has taken me up,"[14] as the brothers carried him to the blessed virgin's holiest place. They nourished him with monastic support for the rest of his life, until death claimed what was owed and his soul flew up to the heavenly kingdoms.

4.4: How a Prisoner in Chains Went Forth from the Hands of His Enemies a Free Man

Many people know that the castle of Aubin[15] in the Rouergue lies about six miles from the village of Conques. There a warrior named Deodat was holding a man named Rainold captive. Finally, so that Rainold would be compelled by his suffering to agree to a ransom more quickly, Deodat sent him directly to another castle where the conditions of his imprisonment would be worse. But there, in the midst of the tortures he was forced to endure, the captive invoked Sainte Foy's patronage with continuous cries. Then Deodat ordered that Rainold be sent back to him again, for he was planning to employ worse torture. The men who were to escort Rainold put him on a horse, bound hempen ropes about his lower body, and fastened the ropes to the horse's trappings. They tied his hands together behind his back, bound his feet together under the horse's belly, and set out to lead him back to Deodat. When the darkness of night overtook them, they were nearing a wood that lay on a downward slope. The captive had been trying to attract Sainte Foy's assistance with eager cries and was passionately making vows and promises so that she would come to help him. The holy virgin was easily moved by his entreaties, and immediately brought it about that all the bonds restraining his body were weakened. They seemed to be consumed, like the threads of a loom when they are set afire. When Rainold understood how the holy virgin had helped him, he leapt nimbly from the horse, slipped away from his escort, and lost himself in the thick woods. While he lay hidden in the dense woodland, men and dogs tracked him diligently, searching for his scent, but divine protection concealed him and even though the dogs frequently ran right by him he was not discovered.

Since the trackers could not find Rainold, they thought that he had fled the area so they stopped searching. On the Sunday after they had gone away, Rainold, who was weary and hungry after two days in the woods, broke out of his hiding place in a thornbush. In the wavering light he scanned the open fields in all directions, but he saw no one except a herdsman tending grazing cattle. As soon as he saw Rainold emerging from the woodland, the herdsman knew that he was the one who had been sought for two days and had remained concealed among the thornbushes. The herdsman said to Rainold:

"Aren't you that fugitive whom they hunted for two days and couldn't find? Don't delay any longer. Hurry and complete your journey quickly."

When Rainold replied that he didn't know the way, the herdsman first explained to him where he was and then showed him what route he ought to take to avoid being recaptured. With the benefit of such good instructions Rainold reached home safely, and after a short while he hastened to the holy virgin's basilica. With huge acts of thanksgiving he announced to all what a favor she had done for him and, free of the vow he owed, he returned home again with a glad heart.

4.5: A Peasant Who Was Tied Up

The previous chapter tells an especially wondrous miracle. This next one belongs here because it is similar, just as powerful, and not at all inferior in its accomplishment.

In the vicinity of Conques, thieves invaded the shadowy silences of the night and stole livestock from several pens and sheds. They drove the animals with them and hid away in the village that has been called Golinhac since ancient times.[16] On the following Saturday night a peasant named Deusdet who took the theft very badly went out as if he were just looking around and came secretly to Golinhac. There he found a calf that he had reared himself. Deusdet freed the calf by stealth and tried to lead it home, stealing back what had been stolen from him. But before he could get away he was seized along with his booty by the thieves, who had followed him. They led him and his calf back to the place where he had committed the theft. He had a presentiment at the time that it wouldn't turn out well. When they got there, Deusdet's legs were bound with fetters and his arms were tied tightly behind his back with thongs, as if he were the one who had stolen the property of another. He was put in a room on an upper floor. While Deusdet was so barbarously imprisoned, Sainte Foy's name was never absent from his lips. With constant cries he called on her both night and day. But she always shows herself willing to answer the prayers of those made wretched by their troubles. So one day when he was in that state that is neither completely asleep nor fully awake, as prisoners tend to live, the holy virgin wove herself into his dream. She stood there with the face of an angel, radiantly attired, and urged him on with words like these:

"Rise up quickly, I say, because I'm giving you a chance to escape."

Her admonition released Deusdet from his dream-state, and he remembered that the holy virgin had been right there with him. And so he exerted himself, flexing his arms vigorously. His bonds broke apart as if they had been rotten threads and soon he had regained the use of his arms. Then his fetters slid down his legs and fell to the ground. While those who were present looked on, he lifted the fetters to his shoulders and left, free and unbound. Deusdet completed his journey and devotedly offered his tangled chains to the holy martyr. He made uncountable expressions of thanks to almighty God and the blessed virgin, for it was through the aid of her miraculous power that he had obtained his freedom from the nets of his chains. In my opinion such things happened to him because he behaved like a thief on the sacred eve of holy Sunday, daring to violate so holy a night with behavior forbidden even on other nights.

4.6: How a Man Was Liberated from the Saracens

I will not speak of eastern Ausonia, but I must relate the outstanding miracles that have happened so frequently because of the holy virgin's intercession in the territory of western Ausonia.[17] Western Ausonia spreads out into a plain quite favorable for raising livestock. This wide plain is called Segre by the inhabitants, from the river of the same name.[18] In this pleasant place a castle called Calonge can be seen from a great distance. A church of Sainte Foy has been there for a long time. Out of reverence for Sainte Foy, and so that they might always be joined to the holy church of Conques, the leading men of Calonge took charge of sending a letter to the abbot and the rest of the brothers at Conques by their own couriers. The letter said that, because they feared that the Saracens were going to do great harm to them with their constant raiding and wanted protection from danger, the lords of the castle pledged it to Sainte Foy, to be held outright by her. And because there was a great distance between them and the holy virgin's monastery, they established as tribute to her that they would send every year a certain weight of gold to be used in the decoration of her sacred church. And if they were successful in the wars through her intercession, in recognition of the triumphal victory they would send her one-tenth of the spoils taken from the conquered Saracens.

The monks rejoiced greatly that love of their great patron saint had grown up in such a remote part of the world. They gave their full attention to the messenger's words and they considered carefully what would be appropriate to send back to the people of Calonge that would serve to protect their safety. Finally they approved a decision urged by those among them who had greater authority and, along with a letter paying their respects, they sent a banner to Calonge. When this standard was carried before their troops it would invoke the holy virgin's power and the fierce enemy forces would be so afraid that they wouldn't break through the lines.[19] The people of Calonge were greatly heartened by their confidence in this banner. By invoking the holy martyr they consistently slaughtered the Saracen armies in battle, divided the booty and, laden with their share of the spoils, they returned home with the palm of victory. Thereafter they absolved themselves of the debt they had vowed by sending a tenth of the booty to the holy virgin. In this they followed the custom of the patriarch Abraham,[20] who gave the high priest Melchisedech the tithe he deserved after Melchisedech offered gifts of bread and wine to the triumphant patriarch for the victory he had won. And the holy virgin was like Melchisedech, for to earn the thanks of those who had been saved by invoking her name, she had been both priest and willing sacrifice to God on the altar of an iron grill over a blazing hot fire.

In the settlement that had grown up around the castle at Calonge there lived a man named Oliba who was admirable for his directness and honesty. According to the standards of that place Oliba had the means to enjoy an ordinary life. A Saracen from the nearby town of Balaguer had come to Oliba on business. When the Saracen saw how peaceably Oliba lived there, he was completely captivated by a greedy desire to extort a ransom from him, so he found some accomplices as wicked as himself. With them the devilish Saracen stole secretly into Oliba's house, seized him violently, carried him off, and burdened his hands and feet with masses of steel. Then this Saracen was roused by a fury worthy of Tisiphone[21] to a passion greater than a tiger's when its young have been carried off, so that the pains he inflicted could no longer sate him. He pushed Oliba into a narrow seat and surrounded his head with iron spikes set in pieces of wood, so that Oliba could neither eat nor lean against the wall to take a short nap nor lie down to rest his weary body.

But because the captive had often heard of the miracles of Sainte Foy he cried out to her, invoking her name day and night, and he promised that he would put on a monk's habit in the monastery at Conques and would serve her until he died. While Oliba was suffering this cruel torture, out of His own goodness and immense pity God sent His holy warrior to the man who was lamenting and praying. During the shadowy gloom of the night she turned her attention to him from the high summit of the heavens and found him while his eyes were swimming in sleep. She tore away all the iron implements and threw them down onto the ground. Then she withdraw and left him there completely unfettered. But because he was so thoroughly terrified by fear of a horrendous death he didn't dare to believe that escape was in any way possible. On the next day he was bound and subjected to the same torture all over again. Again it was God's will that he be freed by the holy virgin and again, for the third time, he was bound with chains. But God got the better of the tyrant once more; then he saw that he struggled in vain against celestial power and so, under the protection of a truce with the Christians, he led Oliba back home. Oliba spread the news everywhere of the power of this great miracle. Then he left behind all his personal possessions and, just as he had vowed during his torment, he took up the clothing of a monk. Content with one companion, he traveled quickly on foot to the village of Conques. There Oliba showed devout obedience to the Lord and to the holy martyr as long as he lived, until at last death intervened and claimed its due.

Oliba's companion answered to the name of William. When he was a young man William had been struck by a paralysis that left his left hand curved backward and permanently clinging to the side of his body. He could neither raise it to his mouth nor use it for any purpose. While he was still suffering from this wretched deformity, his parents took William to the church of Sainte Foy in the castle of Calonge. They poured out prayers of supplication and immediately they got back their healthy son. Then they returned to the great King and His saint the thanks that were due them.

4.7: How a Warrior Was Freed from His Fetters

There are so many miracles springing up everywhere through the whole world that writing them could have kept even the learned Jerome occupied. I have no choice but to skip over many thousands and attend to rendering in writing only those whose witnesses experienced them either by sense or by sight. The person who told me the story of this next miracle is the very one for whom it happened, for he felt compelled to speak of the monstrous cruelty that had been inflicted on him.

As often happens, a powerful warrior of a very illustrious family, a man named Adalhelm who was lord of the castle of Roche d'Agoux, captured a warrior from Auvergne called Robert and held him for his own purposes. However, since the holy season of Lent was approaching, the captive was allowed to offer as surety his pledge that he would return to captivity. An agreement was reached as to the day that Robert would return, and he was temporarily able to go home. When the feast of the Lord's Resurrection drew near, Adalhelm took some companions with him and went to Sainte Foy's abbey church to pray. His captive Robert heard about this journey and quickly followed after Adalhelm, hoping that through the love of God and the holy virgin he might succeed in gaining from Adalhelm some relaxation of the terms of his captivity. But it was due to a devil's instigation that Adalhelm had been motivated by avarice to seek a ransom. Although during the celebration of mass before the holy altar Adalhelm was humbly implored by the abbot and the monks and many of the faithful, he refused either to release Robert or to reduce the high ransom he had set, on behalf of either God or the holy virgin. Adalhelm, the cause of Robert's misfortune, held to his position so stubbornly that it was as if he had chosen to follow the nefarious example of the Pharoah of Memphis[22] rather than that of the Lord, Who said: "If you do not forgive your brothers from your hearts, My Father will not dismiss your debts."[23]

There was nothing else for the captive to do but give himself up to his former captivity as he had pledged. And so after he returned home Robert again placed himself under prison's sway. Adalhelm, who was as harsh as the cruelest Achaemenid,[24] bound his legs with immensely heavy fetters, completely denied him food and drink for two days and on the third night gave him moldy crusts of very dry bread for sustenance. When Robert wanted to sleep, his bed was bare earth; he had no straw to lie on or bed clothes to cover himself. But in the midst of these brutal torments the wretched man never stopped pleading for Sainte Foy's assistance. More than once the locks on the iron fetters fell open and he was relieved of their weight. But the utterly wicked Adalhelm couldn't have cared less about these amazing demonstrations of Sainte Foy's power. He grew as savage as that tyrant who shut living men up inside a bronze bull and burned them to death.[25] In the top story of the castle Adalhelm constructed a very narrow wooden cage. Then he inserted Robert's legs into "bracelets" so tight that a seven-year-old boy's delicate and slender shin-bones could scarcely fit into them. He thrust his captive into that penitential cage and set watchmen to guard against his flight.

Robert lay there buried in his misery while approaching nightfall only increased the horror of his dark enclosure. Trapped in the loathsome shadows he relaxed his pain-wracked body into a light sleep. Suddenly he saw the glorious virgin glide toward him, shining with the indescribable glow of red gold. She lamented over his suffering and opened her celestial mouth to speak these words:

"Don't delay any longer. Hurry and flee from here quickly. Don't be afraid that you will be hindered by the obstacles of chains and locks, because everything that binds your body has been dissolved."

After she had said this, the holy virgin returned to the citadel of heaven. The captive was flooded with great joy and broke the bonds of sleep at once. Leaving behind the weight of his irons in the castle prison because they were too massive to take with him, Robert opened the little door that had been fortified with bars and bolts. With a mighty leap he jumped over the guards sleeping in front of his prison and left his little cage. Then he found a way out of the tower whose walls were built out of wooden beams and stones joined together without mortar and walked quickly on a footpath to his home. After he had stayed there a short while, Robert went to the monastery church of Sainte Foy as quickly as he could. While all sang praise to God, Robert gave to Sainte Foy the allegiance and the thanks he owed her.

4.8: How Raymond Was Freed from His Fetters and Chain

Just now another miracle very similar to the preceding one demands the service of my pen. Because the deed was so marvelous, I think that it should be honored by being remembered forever.

Many of you knew Raymond for his impious actions, the high rank of his family, and his open displays of arrogant pride. He came from the castle called Montpezat[26] over which his father, the mighty Bernard, ruled as lord. Because Montpezat is near the city of Cahors and Raymond needed an education, he was placed with the canons of that city with the idea that he would choose to become one of them in the years to come. While he was studying there, Raymond was struck by the incurable disease of epilepsy, which troubled him miserably at each new moon. As a result his kindred felt revulsion for him on account of his disability rather than holding any hope for achievement based on his natural talents. Finally Raymond was motivated by all he had heard of Sainte Foy's miraculous powers and went to the holy virgin's shrine. Through her merciful favor he found the cure that he desired. Every year thereafter he eagerly returned to the basilica of the holy doctor Foy to express his gratitude for her immense gift to him.

But Raymond's relatives, both by blood and by marriage, were hunting for him because of deep hatred born of their greed for his patrimony, and eventually they captured him. Then they handed him over to a very well-known man named Gauzbert who considered Raymond his enemy because Raymond had so often inflicted serious abuse on him.[27] Soon came the very holy days of Lent, which, when sincerely observed with temperance and austerity, drive out all of life's sins. Since Raymond was spending these days entangled in a great mass of chains, with all the hardships of a hermit, and utterly parched with thirst, for him they were more a torment than a means of gaining salvation. His food, which came only in the evening, was old bread covered with green mold. It was so foul that he could scarcely wash it down his throat even though he was given nothing else to eat. And because those barbarous men were so intimidated by his fierce strength, they wrapped Raymond in fetters and triple chains as if he were a Gaetulian lion.[28] They left him lying in such a way that no matter how he exerted himself he could move neither hand nor foot. The chain was linked together with strong hooks and painfully restrained his legs and upper arms because it was wrapped around him so many times. It led from his back to the wall of the stone tower, where it passed through to the exterior. There it was made fast with iron bolts on the outside in such a way that by no force—unless possibly by continuous filing with sharp saw-blades—could Raymond be freed.

Nevertheless, all through these afflictions the words "Sainte Foy" were always on his lips; not a single moment passed in which he did not call on her. When Raymond had survived five weeks of this severe regimen, that day shone forth which gladdens the hearts of all people throughout the world on account of the Lord's triumphal entry. It is celebrated with palms and all kinds of flowers and with ineffable transports of joy. Although the general joy of this day spread in every direction, it brought no happiness to Raymond. But almighty God perceived the ruthless stubbornness of his savage torturer, Gauzbert, and through the holy virgin's intercession He was moved to be merciful, for His compassion is always available to those in despair. While Raymond was soothing his pains in a wretched sleep, God sent to him from heaven a young man gleaming with wondrous splendor, who addressed him with words like this: "Raymond, are you awake or asleep?"

Raymond was in the middle of a pleasant dream, and it seemed to him that he responded like this: "Who, I ask, are you, lord?"

"I am that Stephen who some time ago was stoned by the Jews and thereby earned my place among the citizens of heaven.[29] I was sent and come to you for this reason: to lead you swiftly to Sainte Foy."

Raymond asked him where the magnificent virgin was.

"Rise," the distinguished martyr responded. "You're not deluded by a dream. If you follow me without hesitation, you will see her of whom I speak."

As for Raymond, it seemed to him that, as the wondrous vision urged, he followed the holy martyr Stephen who was leading the way, and then the martyr positioned him above the bridge over the Dourdou at Conques (see Figure 11) and spoke sweet and reassuring words like these:

"O my son, direct your gaze above this mountaintop wrapped in clouds and regard the bright light of God that you see shining there. For in the midst of that great splendor the most holy virgin and glorious martyr Foy shines forth, surrounded by the outstretched hands of the angels. This reveals very clearly the honor owed to her on her own merit. This is she of whom what was said in the Song of Songs can truly be believed — that she is beautiful among the daughters of Jerusalem, filled with charity and love; when the queens saw her they praised her in the citadel of heaven.[30] When she climbed up to the heavens, crowned with the triumphal laurel, the heavenly citizens admired the marvelous gleam of her sanctity and spoke in this way: 'Who is she who ascends like the glistening dawn, fair as the moon, bright as the sun, awesome as an army ordered in ranks?[31] She is chosen for her excellence, truly sanctified, truly set at the head of the virginal choirs next to the mother of God, who alone has no equal.'"

When Raymond heard these words he rejoiced in this high praise of the holy virgin and he lifted up his watchful eyes to the vision on high. He saw a fiery globe sparkling with intense brightness, in the midst of which the beautiful virgin shone forth. She spoke to the angels that surrounded her:

"The place that you see is adorned with my bones. I ask you to sanctify it with your right hands."

The angelic host willingly gave their assent to the virgin's request and raised their shining right hands to give the sign of the venerable cross. Consecrated by the power of this sign, this place was filled with the grace of complete sanctity. While these truly marvelous and lofty acts were taking place, behold! suddenly a misty fog rose up from the river's depths and a stormy whirlwind enveloped Raymond as he stood on the bridge. It drenched his clothing with falling drops.

Astonished by this sight, Raymond woke abruptly from the dream. Immediately he began wringing his garments in his hands for they were running with water, just as he had seen in the vision. As he was patting himself all over with his hands he realized that the entire tangle of chains had been dissolved from around his body. Next he found that the little door, which had been so securely bolted that night, stood wide open. Then Raymond understood that the vision in which he had seen the water was a true vision,[32] and immediately his mind was occupied with the decision whether he should leave or not. Soon with determined daring he jumped headlong over the barrier formed by the men guarding him and ran quickly down the stairs. Passing right through the midst of the guards sleeping there, he came down to the great hall of the castle. While he was standing there in great agitation and uncertainty at last it occurred to him that, although he couldn't convey his chains to the holy virgin's basilica because of their great weight, at least he could carry off the chessboard hanging there as evidence of his escape. After he had grabbed it he threw himself headlong over the wall, which was higher than he was tall, landed without injury, and sped away on bare feet.

The rough mountain path wreaked havoc on his feet and he soon sank to the ground. Then he saw the shape of a woman standing opposite him and holding a pair of shoes in her right hand. She addressed him in this way:

"Are you that Raymond whom Sainte Foy just now freed from the chains of prison?"

When he acknowledged that he was, she immediately offered him the shoes to relieve his journey, saying:

"Take these and escape from these parts as fast as you can, while you still have a chance."

Alerted by this gift that was both a favor and a comfort to him, Raymond thought hard and came to understand that the woman was nothing other than the holy virgin's presence. But while he was exploring this in his mind she suddenly vanished and was nowhere to be found. Nonetheless, Raymond took heart from the urgings of his great patroness and completed the escape he had undertaken. His pursuers could not touch him because Sainte Foy was protecting him. And in this way he rushed unseen through the midst of his enemies and came to the city of Cahors.

There he was eager to offer the thanks he owed to the protomartyr

Stephen[33] who had, as it were, led him to his escape. And because he had been weakened by the long period of fasting and by his flight, instead of going on to Conques Raymond sent a candle to Sainte Foy, as large as he could afford, in gratitude for the rescue she had provided for him. Finally, on that night when the Lord's betrayal took place—at once our salvation and the ruin of the Jews—while Raymond was in the sacristy of Saint Stephen's Cathedral in Cahors preparing the lection assigned to him for reading the next morning, he fell asleep and was resting there quietly. Sainte Foy blended into his troubled sleep as if she were the sun breaking through the mist of a cloudy morning. She seemed to scold him with (as he thought) angry words:

"You most dull-witted of all people, have you been so perverted by idleness that you are not going to come to the holy place of my relics during these holy days of Easter and offer me your usual acts of thanksgiving there? Why are you wasting time? Throw off the bonds of delay, take up the chessboard that is the physical proof of your liberation, set out swiftly on the footpath for Conques, and celebrate the joyous feast of Easter there."

Deeply moved by this vision Raymond overcame the weariness of sleep, and in a state of terror he told what he had been commanded to do in his dream both to Gerald, coadjutor of the bishopric of Périgueux, who happened then to be on his way to Toulouse, and at the same time he told it to Bernard, bishop of Cahors.[34] When they heard Sainte Foy's instructions they ordered that the commands be translated into deeds and not put off by any contrived delays whatsoever. What more is there to say? Content with only one attendant, Raymond eagerly took up the journey and carried out the imperious virgin's mandates. Completing the journey he had undertaken, he arrived at the oft-mentioned place carrying the chessboard with him and prostrated himself in prayer, offering what he had thought out in a humble murmur. When he had finished praying and had impressed the sign of the holy cross on his forehead and heart he addressed the people there and told them what had been done for him miraculously through the holy virgin while he was wrapped in chains. The small crowd of people, both men and women, listened in silence. Among them was the son of the above-mentioned Gauzbert, who by chance was with a group of his fellow warriors who had come there to pray. He was absolutely dazed by the sight of Raymond in the center of the crowd, wondering how he could have been freed from the bondage of so many chains. And equal amazement gripped Gozfred at this sight: he saw his own chessboard which Raymond had carried off to Conques offered to the holy virgin as evidence of the miracle!

Then all recognized that divine power had been at work and they turned to declarations of praise, glorifying the power of the holy martyr Foy bestowed upon her by the Lord, Who grants every kind of miracle because of her holy merits.

4.9: How a Warrior Was Captured by His Enemies and Miraculously Freed

There still remains one miracle that belongs with those I have just related. It is an achievement for which I think we ought to sing as much praise to the glorious virgin as she receives for her other miracles, although the manner in which it was accomplished was somewhat different.

Many of you know the castle of Salignac in the region of Périgord.[35] A warrior named Bernard from that castle fervently loved the powers of Sainte Foy and so he customarily returned every year to her shrine.[36] One day as he hurried off to honor Sainte Foy he fastened the sign of a pilgrim to his wallet and set out alone on his usual route. He was heading for the place where his fellow pilgrims were staying because he planned to travel along the pilgrimage route with them the next morning. The time of day had come when the sun had already buried its head beneath ocean's waves, when behold! Bernard, who was alone on the road, met with Archambaud, his mortal enemy, accompanied by five armed men. They took Bernard prisoner and refused to let him go even though he called on Sainte Foy. But lest it seem that he had poured forth his prayers into the wind, while they were taking him away Sainte Foy's power gave Bernard a means of escape: she led his own brother to him. For in the confusion of the thick, dark night Bernard's brother and a companion, his squire, had taken the wrong road. Moving quietly and hidden by darkness, they unexpectedly came upon Bernard and his captors and, alarmed, asked who they were. Bernard recognized his brother's voice and cried out from among his captors that his brother should bring him help. But his brother was so intent on freeing Bernard that he launched an all-out attack, one against five. Forgetting himself and his dependents, he did not hesitate to put himself in harm's way and gave no thought as to how large the enemy force was. Though Bernard was unarmed he ran boldly towards Archambaud and flung out his hands to seize him. At that very moment, due to the wondrous power of God that was present because Bernard had called upon the holy virgin, his enemy's lance leapt forward into Bernard's right hand. Armed with this lance he fought as well as Jonathan had once battled against the Philistines.[37] And so with his brother fighting beside him Bernard turned his enemies to flight, and he and his brother held the middle of the field. They were the victors, rejoicing over their triumph in a righteous fight. Soon Bernard joined his traveling companions and went on to Sainte Foy's basilica to thank her for the gift she had given him.

And many times thereafter Bernard trusted in this lance to defend himself and was not afraid to fight with a few men against a great many, for he knew that he had received his lance from an enemy's hand through Sainte Foy's miraculous power and she would always be there to help him. A long time afterward he offered this lance to the holy virgin in witness of the miracle and to the present day it is used for displaying all kinds of banners.

And now I have said enough about the freeing of captives. The multitudinous host of various kinds of miracles seems to be growing without bounds. Thus the value of my work lies in choosing them in such a way that I extract their essence. I don't do this so that a small portion of my life may be adequate to include every single one of them, but because the habit of drinking water from a great sea may soothe the longing of thirsty people with a sweet drink. Still, may these miracles always resound in praise of the Omnipotent One Who, glorious in His own saints, deigns to confer so much help on mortals through the wondrous goodness of His own holy martyr Foy.

4.10: About a Wounded Warrior[38]

So that my narrative will be arranged in the best sequence, I must follow these astonishing and great miracles of liberation with the wondrous miracle related in this chapter.

In the region of the Albigeois two warriors were waging a grievous war. As the fierce battle led to mutual slaughter, some won the palm of victory; others were sent down to the portals of Leucata.[39] In such a battle strength gains ground, timidity retreats. For after the battle was joined the fighting was hand to hand. The weapon being wielded was the iron sword, with which the combatants both inflicted and suffered many wounds. A warrior named Rigaud had entered into this battle. After he had killed countless numbers of the enemy, he failed to parry a blow. His opponent's sword pierced through his right arm and buried itself deep in his side. After this severe wound his arm was so paralyzed and numb that he felt no pain when a red-hot iron was placed in his hand, though this experiment was tried rather often. Rigaud fell into such a depression because of this that he wanted to die rather than to drag out a disgusting and useless life with his body in such a shameful state. He had abandoned his life as a fighting man and completely given up the practice of riding a horse.

While he was in this state Rigaud's lord was utterly consumed with finding a way to help him. He had sponsored Rigaud with his own resources from the time Rigaud first took up arms to his belting as a warrior, and had taken his wounding very hard. According to his usual practice this lord went to the holy virgin's shrine. There, in the evening, he and a great many of his companions were preparing to go from the guesthouse to the church. Their candles were lit and then a strong gust of wind blew out every one of them, leaving behind wavering threads of smoke. After the candles had been lit again, Rigaud's lord, who had been looking for an omen of Rigaud's recovery, said:

"Let this be an utterly clear and evident sign for us that our Rigaud will recover his health: that all the other candles will be blown out by the wind, and only this one that I lit for him will stay lit all the way to the holy virgin's basilica."

And so it happened. The lord completed his vows and prayers and soon returned home. He told Rigaud about the sign he had been shown and he advised Rigaud to seek out the holy virgin's abbey church himself with confidence that he would be healed there. Although he had his doubts, Rigaud undertook the journey and sought the holy virgin's mercy. While he was keeping the holy vigil before the tomb of her sacred body he became drowsy, let his eyes close, and slipped into a very deep sleep. As he rested there quietly, though no person spoke, he heard a voice speaking words like these:

"Why are you drowning in sleep? Get up as fast as you can and protect yourself quickly with the sign of the cross."

After the voice had warned him a third time, Rigaud leapt to his feet in terror. He forgot his weariness and lifted his previously paralyzed right arm in the air, for he was eager to do what the voice had commanded. Then he understood what he had done and recognized that through God's mercy the power of Sainte Foy had given him back his former health. The joyous man roused up his companions to tell them about his unexpected gift, and all were filled with great joy on account of the healed right arm.

4.11: About a Thick Forest of Leafy Trees

I believe that this miracle is indeed worthy of being remembered, for the great amazement of all who live nearby stands in testimony to it.

Once Arnald (of blessed memory), bishop of the church of Rodez, decided to convene a council[40] and he announced that many saints' relics from the various parts of his diocese must be brought there to give more authority to the council. That is how it happened that Adalgerius (worthy of remembrance), the august abbot of Saint Foy's monastery,[41] sent messengers to a warrior named Bernard Astrin.[42] They asked Bernard to give the abbot the leafy branches of a forest from which they would build a pavilion suitable for Sainte Foy. But Bernard's intense greed boiled over into words and he answered that he had already given many trees *gratis* to a great many saints. Sainte Foy was infinitely richer than the others. Therefore he was not going to give her the branches without some payment, no matter how small. After Abbot Adalgerius heard this, an agreement was reached with Bernard that the abbot would authorize seven sous for the work of setting up the bowers. And so the woodcutters cut down the leafy timber in the place where they were directed. With the branches to provide shade, they made a canopy over the platform where God's saint, the virgin Foy, was placed and where she shone with the light of many miracles.

Sainte Foy wanted to show that the worst thing, for both the body and the soul, is greedy desire for money. After the harsh winter is over comes the time when damage to the trees is repaired with new growth and the woods are covered with a cloak of leaves. Sainte Foy caused the part she had paid money for to stand unchanged. The trees whose branches had been cut showed no regrowth, although the rest of the trees all around seemed to be restored to a pristine state and displayed branches thick with sprouting twigs. And so it is up to the present day.

I conclude that this deed should be interpreted in this way: the holy virgin forced the trees that she purchased and paid for to remain as they were with no new growth. For according to the law the purchaser owns things sold to that person outright, but things that are loaned to another person out of reciprocal friendship should eventually be returned to their owner. Once the wood had been offered in a business deal and the money had been paid, this holy businesswoman had acquired it for her own use. If she didn't want to return it, that is entirely her affair. Of course it seems that she had no need to keep it, but I understand her lesson to be this: that savage greed should be uprooted everywhere and the cause of God placed ahead of wealth.

4.12: About a Girl Who Was Paralyzed

At another time, a girl who had lost the use of all her limbs was carried from the town of Cayssac[43] in order to acquire the gift of divine mercy through Sainte Foy's renowned intercession. But those who were bringing her were indifferent to her fate and abandoned her on the opposite bank of the river that flows past the craggy shores where Conques[44] is located. She sought alms from those who passed by. As she lay there without shelter, her face and body were touched every night by wild animals as she herself later testified; she had no strength to hold them off either with her hand or with a staff. Since no one took pity on her and carried her to the monastery, she remained for many days in this wretched state. Finally it was God's will that the senior monks of the monastery be moved to mercy. They ordered that she be carried to the monastery on a pallet. For a long time she could be seen lying there at its main entrance, at the most "beautiful gate of the temple," in the same way that the lame man later healed by Peter once sought alms from those entering the Temple to pray there.[45] But finally from heaven God's holy virgin Foy became another Peter. Toward evening of the day which is adorned with the glory of leafy branches and palms,[46] the paralyzed girl was lifted up from the ground and walked to the holy virgin's tomb. She was completely healed; her feet bore her weight firmly. The people standing there were filled with great joy on account of this marvelous deed and with one voice they praised almighty God, Who deigned to invest His own warrior Foy with so much power through all the splendor of her miracles.

4.13: How a Paralyzed Man Was Healed

Here is another miracle quite similar to the last one. It seems to me worthy of being inserted on the page waiting before me.

With his parents' help, a person named Humbert was brought from the Agenais so that he might gain the holy virgin's favors. His mother's livid nature had sent him forth from her womb in a condition in which his lower body, from the kidneys down, lay lifeless. He lived there for a great many years, supported through the compassion of pious people, when finally, after the solemn feast day of the Holy Mother of God's Assumption, he was visited by divine pity. On the night after the feast he was keeping vigil before the glorious martyr's shrine along with many others, when intense pains shot through his useless limbs and he began to wail and cry out. But even in the midst of these pains he did not stop bellowing out his prayer to Sainte Foy; he sobbed as he begged her to cast her merciful gaze upon him. Suddenly there was a cracking sound and his twisted limbs were stretched out straight. Through his invocation of the holy virgin the disabled body he had dragged around since he left his mother's womb was now healed. And so he cast aside the crutches of a paralytic, which he had formerly used when he needed to go somewhere, and moved across the ground leaping like a grasshopper. Now he took pleasure in running through the crowds, scampering nimbly to and fro.

4.14: How a Warrior Was Cured of Blindness Twice

A man named William of the castle called Carlat,[47] a valiant warrior from an excellent family, suffered a head wound. As a result his eyesight faded and then he became completely blind, but after he appealed to Sainte Foy he found eye salves effective and regained his sight. Some days later one of his warriors was brawling with another member of William's household. While the man was advancing on his opponent with a staff, intending to stab him in the eye, William stepped between them, ignoring the danger and receiving the blinding wound himself. And so while he was trying to do good William suffered injury. Streams of blood poured from the wound, and William felt such pains in his head that he could scarcely lift it from his bed or even open his eyes. In great distress and despairing of a recovery, he turned again to his usual source of help and with heartfelt sighs he urged Sainte Foy to come to his assistance.

"O most holy virgin Foy," he said, "your healing powers surpass the medicines of the most skillful doctors. Why did you want such a horrible and dreadful thing to happen to me? You should have protected the sight you gave me from every assault. What good did it do me to get back my sight when cruel misfortune has again taken it away from me? But since this is where things stand, give back what you gave me before. O blessed virgin, you deserve to be proclaimed with every praise. Let your abundant pity reach out to the afflictions of the oppressed. Do not abandon your own, for without you an inescapable fate lies before me. Turn your most compassionate eyes to me and incline your open ears to my prayers. And when you have once again felt pity for the wretched straits in which I find myself, soothe my sightless eyes with the salve of your mercy."

When William had brought his plaints to an end he said that he would not touch any sustenance, neither food nor drink, until he had moistened his eyes with water blessed and consecrated by the majesty of Sainte Foy.[48] Hearing this, a member of William's household quickly went to the holy virgin's basilica, which was a day's journey from Carlat. Then, turning his lord's commands into swift action, he returned with the blessed water. When this was poured over William's head the pain went away, but his sight was still very dim. Since the feast day of this great virgin was drawing near, William himself went to Conques to keep the holy vigils. He arrived seven days before the feast and spent his nights at the foot of her tomb, praising God.

After the solemn mass on the actual day of the feast, William was being led from the church. It seemed to him that he could make out human shapes as one does in the wavery light of dawn, but he couldn't really tell who they were. Then he returned to the altar and fell prostrate at the feet of the sacred majesty. As he lay there, little by little light filled his eyes and he saw every object clearly. All the common people congratulated William because of the gift of this outstanding miracle, and they sang the praises of the great works of God and Sainte Foy whose astonishing miracle they had been privileged to see.

4.15: About a Blind Widow

Great bishop Front,[49] you rightly deserve to be called
The splendor and leading light of all Aquitaine.
Apostle, follower of Peter, the first known
To carry your teacher's lessons to western soil.
When you spoke, doctrines of holy law radiated from you,
Doctrines that emptied pagan temples and illumined holy churches.
In this little book that spreads the holy virgin's glory to the whole
  world,

It is proper that your distinguished name be included.
For you, potent with miracles and visible through signs,
Deigned to ennoble it with your own gift.
You demonstrate that your home is known to be
A place that the holy virgin illumines with her goodness.

A woman from that place was mourning inconsolably for her lost spouse. She wept every day, wearing out her eyes with her tears until they clouded over in blindness. Because of this she wandered from one saint's relics to another's but gained nothing; she remained blind for nine years. One night while all the lamps were dark and she was deep in sleep the woman was admonished to hurry to Sainte Foy's monastery church, for the gift she had been seeking elsewhere would be given to her there without delay. After she awakened, she clung faithfully to these instructions. She did as she had been ordered and came to Conques with some companions. Throughout the night they spent in a hospice there they insistently and urgently pled for Sainte Foy's help. First a pain like an unbearable migraine headache[50] began to pound her head, and like a Bistonian woman who had drunk deeply of wine[51] she rolled her head back and forth on her bed without stopping. Finally a boy led her by the hand to the holy virgin's abbey church and there she soaked the dust with streams of tears. But, wondrous to see! and contrary to nature, her tears turned to blood, which flowed down in waves and lay in red clots on the ground. After this gush of blood stopped, a tiny spark of light gradually began to light her eyes and she distinguished the shapes of things inside the church. Before sunset she could see everything clearly. Her fervent praises to God and the holy virgin moved others to join her, so that the joy of the gift granted to her became a source of joy for all.

Thus, Great Father, the holy virgin sent her foster-daughter back to you,
The woman whose grief and bitter love had dimmed her eyes.
Hail to you also, jewel among priests. For so great a gift
To your ally above the stars, we thank you.
As topaz is well set in reddish-yellow gold,
So mention of you gleams in this *Panaretos*.[52]
With your companion, the renowned and bountiful virgin,
You reign with the Lord in the heavens above forever.

4.16: About a Warrior Who Repeatedly Opposed the Holy Virgin

How often Christ's warrior and noble champion was gentle to her enemies and how she sometimes struck them with terror, I have not spelled out fully in the pages of the preceding books. The proper measure of her punishment brings most people to repentance, but for some it comes, although later, in the form of severe condemnation. For she was already well instructed in the learned celestial doctrine to which the citizens of heaven subscribe, and she knew well to heed the meaning of both of these precepts: the one that says, "Do not let yourself always be prepared for vengeance" and the other that insists, "Render a retribution to the proud."[53] The wise virgin keeps to the middle road between the two, for she is easily appeased and often restrains her hand from taking vengeance on those who repent. But after the time for being indulgent has passed, she looses her hand once and for all to smite those who have abused her patience. And those whom she has once pardoned she destroys by smiting them even more harshly when they become negligent. Now I'll show you why I said these things, so pay attention for a little while.

The castle of Belfort[54] is known to many because it is very close to the village of Conques and its barbarous master, named Hector, preyed ruthlessly on the holy virgin's lands. He even dared this wildly reckless act: he put the monks' servants to death by the sword. That holiest of days shone forth, the day of the glorious martyr's triumph, which all should celebrate. Many people flocked together from various places to observe the festivities of this day. Even this tyrant Hector came among them, not out of desire to celebrate the feast, but rather out of desire for a lady whom he followed everywhere, burning unashamedly with lewd passion for her. He led her to a remote section of the monastery and made her sit there so he could enjoy seductive conversation with her. But because uncountable numbers of people had flocked together for the joys of this great festival, many a great lady was there to whom it was proper to defer, particularly since they belonged to more noble families and held higher and more powerful titles. Hector, blinded by lust, pushed them out of his way with his hands and sometimes used his fists. The warriors who were keeping order during the festival grew disgusted with his shameless arrogance. Together they rushed toward him and attacked him furiously. Exchanging blows of the fist, each side injured the other. In the midst of this morally offensive turmoil an uproar arose from the people, and their frenzied shouts brought disorder into the holy shrine. It occurred to one of the monks that they ought to carry the majesty of the holy virgin out of the sanctuary to subdue these savage evil-doings and bring down her heavy fist on Erinys, the greatest of the Furies, who was venting her rage there. When this was done, the furor subsided through the holy martyr's power and without threat of death or bodily harm to anyone the clash quieted down. But that heinous butcher had been perverted by a serpent's bile and anger. When he saw that his villainy had been repulsed, he stole secretly out of the monastery with his men and led his enemies' horses out of the stables. He fled with them to his castle. Later, although unwillingly, he returned them.

In the midst of the fighting and uproarious turmoil something wondrous happened, appropriate to the occasion, and it seems to me that it should be remembered. As I said, the holy virgin's golden effigy had been brought out to calm down this evil and blasphemous outburst. From the neck of the effigy hangs a crucifix delicately carved from ivory and adorned with gold. One of the combatants, who was shoved by his attackers, threw out his hand toward the sacred effigy and, unaware of what he was doing, he tore the crucifix from the neck of the image and threw it down to the ground. As soon as the bearers noticed this they immediately returned their holy burden to the sanctuary and, deeply saddened, secured it there. After the turmoil had been subdued and the candles had been lit, the monks turned the place upside down looking for the crucifix. They gathered up the pieces scattered on the pavement and put them in a locked room. But when the rites of the feast had been completed and before they went to the refectory to eat, they came back again to see the broken body of the image. They blamed the whole shocking affair on Sainte Foy's negligence. Still distressed, they took the pieces of the shattered *corpus* and laid them rever ently on the cross, which had itself been repaired and polished.

He Who told the raging Jews to destroy the temple of His own body, which He would rebuild after three days,[55] did not delay the restoration of this figure after the monks left. With His power the Supreme Maker, through the intercession of His own warrior, Foy, joined together the broken limbs of the *corpus* in such a way that even under close examination no trace of a scar could be found. It seemed to me that because when Our Savior spoke about the rebuilding of His own body He made no mention of nails, that is perhaps why when He restored this *corpus*, His own image, He failed to replace the little nails that fasten it to the cross. I know that it was not a matter of His inability to replace the nails, since He can do greater things. When they discovered the restored *corpus* the senior monks were flooded with great joy. They rejoiced because of so great a gift, offered thanks, and were free to enjoy a sumptuous meal.

But if anyone is eager to know what happened to the man whose haughty arrogance caused this, I can tell you that he was discovered in illicit lust, and afterward, because they had been disgraced, his own wife and children threw him out. For many years the wretch lived like Cain as a wanderer and a fugitive, enduring a life filled with afflictions and insults. Sainte Foy gave him over to the punishment he deserved for his wickedness, for he had always acted wrongfully against her, not only in this one offense against heaven but in many other misdeeds as well.

4.17: About a Warrior Who Had a Shriveled Hand Caused by a Wound

Earlier I wrote the story of a warrior wounded in war and healed through Sainte Foy's power.[56] The subject of this chapter was also healed, but in a different way.

This warrior followed a man named Gerald from a very noble family of the Rouergue on a military expedition against the inhabitants of Quercy. Once when he leapt into the fray to break up a fight he suffered a serious wound in his side from a lance. He was treated by the unskilled hands of physicians who erred in bandaging the wound too quickly.[57] In so doing, they trapped putrefying, congealed bloody matter inside his body and it began to infect his internal organs. And since the confined fluid inside him had no outlet it raged on the inside and his body swelled up on the outside. The young man was distressed by pain and constantly called out for Sainte Foy's help. But finally one night after he had laid down his decaying body to rest and was enjoying a soothing, deep sleep, it seemed as if he lay on the pavement before the holy virgin's altar at Conques and appealed to Sainte Foy to help him. And he thought that as he was praying Christ's champion herself appeared to him, carrying a rod in her hand. He increased his tear-filled plaints, and said:

"Most gracious patroness, filled with kindness and mercy, help wretched me while the heat of life still flows through my putrefying body and a thin pulse beats in the depth of my heart, before I lose the light of this world for the final end. I know that you can open and close the roads to hell to save your devotees."

She turned her countenance, ever clear and bright, toward him for a moment and touched his wound very gently with the rod she carried in her hand. At so healing a touch, bloody matter soon burst forth as if a sharp knife had cut into the wound. The pavement was covered with a vile, putrid fluid. When he recoiled in disgust at the rancid foulness she, the most patient of doctors,[58] spoke these gentle words:

"Don't be fearful, son. To those of us who perform the duties of doctors it is the rottenness of villainous souls, not the putrefaction of human flesh, that is foul. I have come here to confer the gift of healing on you. And therefore I charge you that, after you have rejoiced over your recovery, you must go immediately to Conques and give thanks to the holy Savior for the favor you have been granted and before the tomb of my body give me the praises I deserve."

After she had spoken she faded into the celestial breezes. But the man was shaken by the vision. He woke up abruptly and carefully recalled the holy doctor's words. He could feel the thick clots of bloody matter that had burst out of the open sore swollen up around the wound. Now he softly touched his side with his hand to find out what had actually happened. As he passed his hand over his body, he recognized that the vision had been true. Once the wound had been opened to purge the concealed poison and the pain had been emptied out, he was restored to good health. And so he went to Sainte Foy's basilica to offer her deserved praise.

4.18: How a Mule Was Revived

Now I am eager to have your attention so I can tell you, in a few words, about something that was recently and miraculously accomplished on the journey to Saint Peter, prince of the apostles, by the glorious handmaid of Christ.

In the province of Italy called Lombardy a warrior of the Rouergue named Garbert overtook a warrior from Poitou riding ahead of him. The latter was quite distinguished both in his lineage and in his military prowess, and after they had exchanged greetings and paid their respects to one another Garbart joined the Poitevan's company for the journey. They pursued many different topics of conversation and entered into a discussion of all Sainte Foy's great works, in which the warrior from the Rouergue bestowed great praise on her miracles. And the Poitevan listened to his stories with great wonder and applause. When they had arrived at an inn in the village of Saint Domninus,[59] the Poitevan's mule, which he cherished, fell seriously ill. By the following day it seemed barely alive. But Garbert remembered the magnificent deeds Sainte Foy sometimes worked for animals like this one, and he asked whether a remedy had been used to treat the mule. When the answer came back that nothing at all had been done, he replied:

"Didn't you hear what I told you yesterday about Sainte Foy? Send her gold in good faith and your animal will recover immediately."

Without hesitation the Poitevan took a Byzantine gold coin from his money bag and gave it to Garbert to carry to the holy virgin. But Sainte Foy kept back her hand for the greater glory of her own power. She did nothing for the mule while it was alive and certainly did not restore it to good health. What more is there to say? The rising dawn urged them all to hasten on their journey. The dead mule was dragged out of the stable and a price was paid only for the value of the hide. As they continued on the road, both men were sorrowful: the one had taken the gold as security for the mule's life; the other had lost the animal and had to suffer the loss. The warrior from the Rouergue was distressed and filled with shame for boasting of Sainte Foy's powers, and because of his disgrace he wanted to return the gold he had received. But as he was reaching out to hand it back, behold! suddenly he heard something behind him, the sound of something following them, and a clatter as if a horseman were pursuing a runaway animal. And so he looked back and in the distance he saw the mule running away from the exhausted innkeeper, and when the mule spotted Garbert it ran even faster. When Garbert saw this, he cried out, "Sainte Foy!" in an astonished voice and kept the gold that he had wanted to exchange for his shame. Finally, after the mule had been caught, they asked the innkeeper to describe the animal's resurrection. He exclaimed in wonder:

"O how fortunate you are to have such a great virgin as your patroness! Through her omnipotent intercession, not only do you gain the salvation of your souls, but even your bodies are cared for by her great medicines. This virgin, holy in deed and power, does not permit you to suffer misfortunes even if it comes to the resurrection of animals. This animal that you see was stretched out on the ground, its teeth bared, completely lifeless. It came to life in the hands of its skinners and sprang up from the ground with a sudden leap. So it got away from us, transformed and ready to serve you."

When they heard this, the whole column of pilgrims burst out in exclamations of praise. Their voices rivaled one another and made the air resound with the cry of "Sainte Foy." Then the Poitevan warrior returned to the innkeeper eight pieces of silver, which was the payment for the hide, and they went joyfully on to the holy shrines of the Apostles. After they returned home, they paid the votive gold and gave heartfelt thanks.

4.19: How the Same Thing Happened to a Poor Man's Little Donkey

Since the subject is bringing animals back to life, there is another miracle that deserves to be included at this point. It is a miracle that the Lord deigned to work wondrously in the village of Conques through the most precious intercession of Sainte Foy, and it happened to an animal very similar to the one that was the subject of the previous chapter.

One of the servants of the brothers who worthily served God there, a married man, had a small donkey, and with its help he earned his livelihood selling a variety of merchandise. But that beast of burden was afflicted with a very serious disease, and its approaching death threatened a loss for its master. He was very sad because the donkey was his only protection against poverty. He offered the holy martyr a candle for the protection of its life and before her sacred body he recited many prayers for its health in a faint whisper. But all his murmuring was futile; his prayers had no effect; death prevailed. Final death possessed his animal; he cried out to the whole church that this would be his ruin. He dragged the donkey out into the public square to be a meal for wild animals and birds. And while the hide was being torn away from one rear leg, the other was being cut with a sharp knife. But remembering his humble circumstances the man kept on repeating to Sainte Foy in a whining voice that she might have come to him more quickly in his misfortune. And sometimes his words were soft and soothing, but most of the time he scolded her with harsh words full of blame:

"Most powerful helper of wretched people, lady and holy virgin, blessed Foy, up till now you have been my encouragement and my most faithful patroness. Hear me, most wretched of men, and save me from falling into dire poverty. I was nourished by the sacred breasts of your kindness. Till now you cherished me under the cloak of your compassion and you deigned to preserve me from many distressing disasters. In you alone is my hope, in you my salvation, in you the safest asylum from all my pains and troubles. Illustrious Lady, if you watch over the great palaces of the wealthy, if you alleviate their troubles again and again, if you willingly answer them when they call upon you, why shouldn't you protect with your right hand the small possessions of poor people and especially of your own servants? I know that you are truly able to restore my useful animal to life, for you are the miracle worker who has been proclaimed for reviving many animals."

And after he had said these words, interspersed with great bursts of tears, he left the cadaver and went quickly back to the holy martyr's church, taking a candle. As soon as he had lighted it, the cold limbs of the dead little donkey grew warm again with its own life force, or something very like it; wondrous to report! it stood up again on its feet. Oh, reader, whoever you are, how you would have been faint with astonishment at this, how you would have been captivated by wonder, had you seen this four-legged creature standing and displaying the sign of its death, the hide hanging from its hooves! Are there people so stony-hearted that they would hold back tears of joy at such a sight? The holy virgin consoled the sorrowful man and returned the property he needed for his business. She did not desert this grown man in his distress when she had known him as a nursling at her nurturing breast. This is the way, Sainte Foy, your mercy hurries to reach those who call on you in their distress, the mercy that has so often been demonstrated in many miracles, to the praise of your name.

But perhaps someone is uneasy about the little hide that was left hanging. Sainte Foy's wisdom is not that found in a book of herbal medicine;[60] her power comes from the will of heaven. Just as her great works add to her glory, she also elevates her name through small favors.

4.20: How a Woman Was Cured of the Offensive Blemishes of Warts

How effective Sainte Foy's most laudable power has been both in the greatest and in the smallest matters is demonstrated by the testimony of so many miracles. Of these, I have not hesitated to recount faithfully the ones that were told in my presence and attested to by many witnesses, because my writing benefits future readers. I may be criticized because of the way I have written up these works so far, that is, that I have slighted them with such brief treatment when their greatness made them suitable for more eloquent orators than I. But I feared that I might be overwhelmed by the number of miracles springing up and leave some entirely untreated. And so I have preferred to touch on most of them in passing and on the surface, for the edification of my listeners, rather than to hold onto each one out of garrulous verbosity and as a result to offer small matters as if they were great. The ones I have already written seem to be of such a character that the reader may have in them the pleasure of a succinct discourse and through them the holy virgin, that famous, miracle-working martyr, may be made known to the whole world. For they are not, in my opinion, the kinds of things that will bore readers because they are drawn out excessively or repel those unfamiliar with Sainte Foy because their brevity makes them obscure. For how could a carefully crafted story produce receptive listeners if their willingness to listen and learn is spoiled by a cloud of blind ignorance? It is true that "faith comes by hearing,"[61] and hearing is instructed through words. Therefore it is worthwhile that suitable words pass from the narrator's mouth so that listeners' hearts are caressed with honeyed sweetness and they easily grasp the content. That is enough of this topic. Now I need to return to the holy virgin's outstanding deeds and record them with my pen.

Since she had been very young an adolescent girl of a wealthy and high-ranking family had had a growth on her right hand that neither crushed juniper nor the milky juice of tithymal[62] had been able to cure. Because she had reached puberty and was at the right age for the bridal bed, she was given in marriage to a nobleman. When she was at table she covered her hands with her veil to hide the clusters of warts. And because she lived near the holy virgin's abbey church, she obtained her wish to be taken there to pray with her lord. When she arrived there and began her prayers her very great concern about her warts kept coming back to her mind, and she pursued this subject during the whole time that she kept the vigil in prayer. When morning came they had completed the prayers that they vowed to say there and so they set out for home. Reaching the cloud-covered mountain top, they paused on bended knee to pay their respects courteously once more to the blessed and glorious virgin and with resolute prayers they asked her to remember their petitions. When they arose from praying they made the triumphant sign of the holy cross over their foreheads and hearts. In this way they humbly requested a blessing on their return journey. But when the girl look at her wart-covered right hand, marvelous to report! she found it as smooth as if it had never been disfigured by rough warts. If it is not blasphemous to say so, her hand was like the hand of Moses, which was afflicted with the swelling of elephantiasis in order to enforce belief in the Lord's teachings, and regained its former smoothness by divine will.[63] But in a wondrous way the surface of her hand looked very delicate and rosy in color, as if it were newly healed after the application of some effective medicine. Seized by astonishment and joy, the young woman hid the visible gifts of healing from her husband. After she returned home she removed her hand from her bosom and found it as completely healed as if it had always been sound. No blemishes marred it. When they saw this, her husband and the rest of her relatives congratulated her because of the blessing conferred on her and with astonished voices all joined in praise of Sainte Foy whose power is poured out in so many miracles.

But, oh, inscrutable wisdom of the heavenly Artificer, Who polished to smoothness the high promontory of the heavens and made the broad spaces of the earth rough with uneven heaps of mountains, for what reason, what purpose did it serve, that after the blemishes of warts were removed from her right hand, they were transplanted to her right foot? I know that You have made nothing without a purpose, since Your unquestionable Providence cannot be turned aside from the direction It takes. All that exists is within Your gaze.

After her cloak had been removed and her personal servant had taken off her anklets, the mountainous crop of warts became visible which, through God's will, Sainte Foy had thoroughly eradicated from her hand. When she had told her husband about this, both of them gladly returned to Sainte Foy at the morning's light. There they honored their vows and gave her their praises because of the healing she had brought about. But this Avigerne, for so she was called, who had been given a wart-covered foot, was always grateful that her own body offered proof that she could use for the rest of her life to proclaim the powers of Sainte Foy.[64]

4.21: About a Wicked Peasant

In honor of Sainte Foy, a monk named Deusdet built a church out of wood in a place called Sardan in the Bazadais.[65] It was a simple frame covered with boards. It wasn't much to look at, but it was filled with heavenly power. Peasants frequently passed by in front of the church when they were going to cut down the forest to create new fields for cultivation, and they bowed humbly in honor of the holy place. But one of them who had been led to take the path of error began to scold them, saying:

"I'm amazed that you've descended to such foolishness. Every day you pray at this oratory, and you ask that it grant you salvation. But I think you would be as likely to get salvation from a doghouse!"

This wretch had not understood that divine glory flourished there because it had been made holy by its dedication and because the holy virgin was invoked there. It seems that he was like those heretics who don't understand the mystery of spiritual grace, so they deny that the water in the baptismal font is able to change its natural properties and assert that it always stays exactly the same. They need to know and understand that there are two aspects to the sacrament of baptism—the water in the baptismal font and sanctification—and it is when they are conjoined that the sacrament is imbued with power. And in the same way, out of a material building and a spiritual sacrament one body is made in the edifice of holy Mother Church.

This man was lamentably mistaken because he followed their error and as punishment he was forced to believe in something that, had he been of sound mind, he would have to reject. For heaven's vengeance did not long tolerate his impious words. It threw him down prostrate on the ground, this man who spoke with such proud arrogance against God's work. With his knees pulled up to his chin he rolled around in the dirty sand; he had lost his mind. Those nearby were thunderstruck when they saw what had happened. They beat their bared breasts with their fists and joined together in praising God. Then they lifted the pitiable man in their arms and carried him well into the church; united in purpose they devoted themselves to prayers for his recovery. Finally, while they were keeping the vigil with him on the following night, they sensed that because of their prayers Sainte Foy's ready kindness had descended to him. And just as she had cast this haughty and proud man down to the depths, so now in turn she raised him, lying humbly before her, back to his erect stature. After they had seen this, all who lived around there begin to give the place more reverence, and they believed without a doubt that Sainte Foy's power flourished there.

4.22: How the Holy Virgin Healed a Man's Household and Herds of Various Illnesses

At Saint-Martin-de-Belcassé in the Toulousain is some land that a farmer named Arnold usually worked with oxen. He told me himself that whenever troublesome things happened to him Sainte Foy often turned them around and caused his affairs to prosper and that she protected him from many misfortunes. When a servant in Arnold's household fell seriously ill and was near death, as usual Arnold hastened to seek Sainte Foy's aid, which he had put to the test in many troubles, and he reminded her of all the good she had done him in the past:

"O glorious virgin, O easily moved divine majesty Foy, I have always been certain that you would answer my prayers to you and I have never felt that you were adverse to me. You have the power to do what you want. Grant me your heavenly favor for the physical illness of this dependent of mine. He is seriously afflicted and is breathing his last breath. Lady, prevent his life from slipping away and pour strength back into his weak body. When he is restored to me as I ask, you will have begotten great happiness as well as eternal praise for your power."

Arnold had not yet finished speaking when Sainte Foy, knowing his faith, granted a recovery to the sick man. Almost immediately thereafter Arnold's wife took to her bed with a very high fever. While Arnold was begging for Sainte Foy's customary mercy, a heavy, trembling sweat broke the fever.

And then in that part of the country the corruption of the air infected the grasses and springs with a deadly pestilence. A violent plague fell on Arnold's pastures, and his neighbors' fat cattle frothed at the mouth and choked to death. Arnold's best ox was among the animals still living. When he saw that it had the same disease, for its dewlaps had begun to swell and its belly was heavy, he ordered a slave[66] to skin the animal with a sharp implement because he knew from experience that its death was inevitable. Meanwhile the disease progressed rapidly and the animal's breath was clouded with vapor; the skinners made ready and hastened to the work. But while something delayed them a bit the peasant, who had called his wife, said to her: "Ha! What have I been thinking?

Believe me, all vestiges of good sense have left us, wretched as we are,
Insight and understanding have fled.
I don't know what I should do, what I should want or reject,
I'm not seeing things clearly as I usually do.

But it seems to me that we ought to do one thing that will at least help to protect the rest of our animals: we must make a candle the length of this dead animal and in Sainte Foy's honor we must keep a light before her altar hereafter."

So the humble woman trustingly stretched out a wick so that it extended to the full length of the ox's dead body ready for skinning. And at that moment the heat of life flowed into the cold body. First the ox gradually raised its head, and then the fortunate animal rose to its feet, shook itself, and left behind every trace of its disease. And after the recovery of this one, the cure immediately spilled over onto the rest of the herd, so that not even one in the whole herd was lost.

4.23: How a Warrior Was Tormented by the Irregular Shifting of His Intestines

Behold! I cannot keep silent about a brilliant remedy like this one.
I believe she deigned to play a remarkable joke.
Bountiful Foy offers celestial cures for all
Whom bitter illness torments in various ways.
And she claps her hands with delight when she finds some worthy remedies
That neither the son of Phoebus,[67] nor people around the Black Sea,
Nor the cloven right hand of Chiron[68] mixed for the ailing.
She doesn't scrape away diseases with an iron hook,
Or twitter old witch's songs over rotting wounds,
But wields all her power with a potent command.
Prison-caves stand open, breached strong-rooms gape,
Iron fetters melt like ice in the sun,
Scourges have no power to harm, at the advent of this virgin.
Even fierce Death, now frightened, takes cowardly flight,
And sighs at the loss of the prey snatched from its jaws and
Restored to life, and sighs again at being forced to return the ancient ones after they had lived their last day,
When they had been carried off at the appointed time.
I believe that Tartarus[69] itself will not lack these endless tears
Because of unwanted and frequent plunder,
For the esteemed virgin snatches them away and leads them to the light.
She enrolls as citizens in heaven those whom harmful life had long ago turned to criminals through hateful deeds.
She remembers everything about devotees who offer her prayers and vows.
And even if something was brought to her only once, she is mindful of this allegiance,
And comes to the rescue whenever that person asks, his whole life long.
The merciful virgin feels a bond with her devotees.

She dares to go to the Throne which she is always near,
Where the high-thundering King of Kings sits.
Through gentle words she apportions rewards and tempers wrath.
She reconciles those who are accused, and conveys them to the high heaven.
She, their fellow citizen, garbs them in sacred white,
And she makes colonists for the eternal homeland above the stars.

And now that I have sung a few things in epic verses about the holy martyr's exceptional stature in heaven and great glory on earth, my purpose urges me to return my attention to the miracles that remain.

In the Auvergne there was a bold warrior who had been waylaid by misfortune. During the periods between the old moon and the new a portion of his intestine left its proper place and ruptured into his scrotum with a great roaring of his bowels. He wore himself out with his laments over this condition and often prayed for death so he wouldn't have to endure it any longer. Eventually he was demoted from horseman to foot-soldier. Then he consulted his wife, who knew of his problem, and, trusting her advice, he decided he should ask for Sainte Foy's kindness in the matter. Although his wife raised many objections and yielded only reluctantly, he put into action the desire that had taken shape in his mind and went to the holy virgin.[70] There he prostrated himself in tears before Sainte Foy's sacred body. Over and over again he repeated his reason for coming to her, and poured out heartfelt prayers for the recovery of his health. He spent that night before Sainte Foy's relics, but he was worn out from the intensity of his praying and fell asleep. Then he saw that the holy martyr was with him. She addressed him very modestly, the way a virgin would, with the words: "Are you sleeping?"

When he answered that he was, the blessed virgin went on to say this: "You should know that although I have cured serious ailments caused by many different diseases I've never been called upon at all to treat the kind of problem you bring to me. But you shouldn't leave here without some advice. Pay attention and I'll explain to you how you will be healed. Do you know the blacksmith who lives near you?"

He replied that he knew the man well, both his name and his appearance, and she went on: "Go to him straightaway and ask him to take up the hammer he would use to pound a mass of iron heated in the furnace till it is glowing white. Then put the part of you that is suffering on his anvil and tell him to strike his most powerful blow. This will quickly give you the recovery you desire."

At these words the man woke up. Stupified and incredulous, he thought she was surely mocking him. He debated for a long time in his noble heart about what such a vision could mean. Finally he returned home, having made up his mind to die. Without telling anyone he went to the blacksmith and secretly told him what Sainte Foy had instructed him to do. And when he had heard it, the blacksmith's heart sank. He swore that he would not perform this fantastic practical joke:

"Believe me, my lord, these weren't the words of a healer but of some joker. If you are naive enough to follow this advice, you could be accused of your own murder. And I will never enact such an evil crime, for I am completely convinced that you will meet an instant death with this."

The reply came that the blacksmith would stand blameless for any punishment resulting from the blow. Then the blacksmith retorted that he feared the penalty the man's kin might exact from him because his blow had caused the man's life to end in pain. Soon the warrior had convinced him that none of these things would happen to him. What more is there to say? His swollen scrotum was stretched out over the anvil and his diseased genitals were prepared for the blow. Soon the blacksmith flexed his muscular arms and swung the enormously heavy hammer high into the air. When the warrior saw what awaited him he was struck with incredible terror, slipped backwards, and lay prostrate, as if all his bones had been broken in a fall to his death. And in this headlong fall, wondrous to report! all at once his herniated intestines were sucked back inside so completely that they never ruptured again for the rest of his life. So he came out of it in good shape, for he was cured without being cauterized with a hot iron or taking any potion as a remedy. And Sainte Foy's joke, if I may call it that, was quickly going to become a miracle that people would marvel at ever after. That is how he was relieved of his weighty burden; that is how his harsh disgrace ended. That is how, instead of the terrible horror of death, the cured man was flooded with great and indescribable joy to the praise and glory of the holy martyr.

No one should think that this is simply something to laugh at, something that I made up, for I introduce here as my public witness Robert, abbot of the monastery of Chanteuge, a man whose venerable white hair attests to his integrity. He is the one who related this to me, because the man to whom it happened was very far away and did not come here afterwards where I could have seen him. The man from whom I heard it is not the kind of person who fills people's ears with absurd flattery or fictitious foolishness; whenever he speaks, he speaks the truth. Ultimately, where there is doubt about an informant like him, there is distrust about the good works of God.

4.24: How a Craftsman Working on the Church Miraculously Escaped Lasting Harm from the Weight of Huge Stones

The miracle that I am going to tell now has lain in silence for so long that it is like a piece of buried iron; when unearthed it is covered with scaly rust, if I may use this expression. It seems to have been neglected because new miracles keep happening and I have been working hard to write them up. But, however it happened, the memory of something so wonderful should not disappear due to my negligence, and putting it here seems to be the right way to complete the sequence of the preceding miracles. Just as a boundary stone establishes the limits of a field, this miracle completes the second book, which is already long and must now be brought to an end. And even though this miracle occupies the last place in this book it deserves no less praise than the rest, because after heavy sorrow it gave us the joy of an unexpected cure. The eyewitness to this miracle is a monk named Sallust, who is still with us at the present time.[71] He is outstanding for the integrity of his life and his character.

Obeying a command from the abbot, Sallust took with him thirteen pairs of oxen and went to the mountain where stonecutters were diligently cutting the stones to be used in building the monastery. In the wagon he was going to bring down stones for the architraves[72] and massive foundation stones. And while they were descending the steep mountainside with a wagonload of stone, they came to a thicket of thorn bushes. These had been cut not long before and their very sharp thorns were now growing back. In this critically dangerous moment the branches of the thorns obstructed the motion of the wheels by catching in the spokes and brought the wagon to a halt. Hoping to free it, all the men put their shoulders to the axle, which was smoking between the hubs on account of the heavy weight. They rushed to help in whatever way they could. Hugh, who was in charge of the operation, hurried into their midst with a large pole, which he leaned on with all his strength, straining to release the wheel stuck fast in the bushes.

But his foot slipped and he fell under the wagon. The whole vehicle passed over his lower legs, dragging Hugh behind it through the branches for about six paces.

When they saw what had happened, everyone threw aside their tools and ran frantically to Hugh. Consumed by both shock and surprise, with one voice they called for Sainte Foy's help. They quickly freed him from danger, removed his shoes, and found the bone of his leg curved back like a sickle. Lamenting wildly at this, they invoked the medical assistance of Sainte Foy. Then the injured master mason[73] himself grasped his bowed leg with both hands and straightened it as easily as if it were made of warm wax. Then their sadness turned to joy; then tears fell to the ground in their great happiness. As soon as he saw that he had been healed by the holy virgin's power, Hugh eagerly leapt up to complete the job that was underway and led the load of rocks all the way down to the glorious virgin's basilica. After the stone had been set down on the ground, Hugh sang over and over again the acts of thanksgiving he owed to the glorious virgin, for it was through her powerful miracle that his body had come through this crisis.

This miracle, which was so prodigiously accomplished by God through Sainte Foy, lay in utter silence for so long because the structure erected out of these stones has arches with gaping fissures in them and threatens to fall into ruins. How this happened I do not know, but perhaps it is similar to what I have learned from the writing of Saint Gregory, bishop of Tours, about the church of Saint Antolianus, martyr of Clermont.[74] For, as Saint Antolianus related to one of the faithful in a vision, his church stood in a place where the remains of many saints had been dug out. And so it was gaping with cracks and collapsed down to its foundations, as God wished. I have noticed that our church is in almost the same condition as that one, so I passed over the miracle worked during the conveying of its stones until now. But so much for this.

Thanks to divine grace, a very splendid accumulation of so many miracles has been spread over the whole world through the outstanding merits of Christ's most glorious virgin and martyr, the wondrous Sainte Foy, that their very number warns against continuing this book. It is not that there is a dearth of miracles to write up, for they are always piling up all around me. But those that are not included in this volume I want to prepare more fully for a third volume, if I should live long enough to write it.

Indeed, there are so many signs of this virgin's powers that, scattered as they are through the four corners of the world, they cannot be gathered together. Furthermore, they are so numerous that they cannot be contained in pages. With God as her navigator she penetrates all the seas and illuminates all regions. She herself is fully equal to the merits of all the saints in the wondrous brightness of her powers. The Lord has led her to rise like a gleaming sun and to shine from one pole to the other of a world grown decadent. Her brilliant rays illumine the entire earth, which blooms with miracles; immense numbers of people flourish from her miracles every day. Even the deep recesses of Erebus[75] lie open as she leads souls out of the underworld. Her miracles are very abundantly spread over many different lands, where they occur even more frequently than in that place where her most sacred relics are revered.[76] Moreover the numbers of suffering people who come to her sacred shrine get the cures they wish for — the blind, light; the tormented, deliverance; those dry with fever, quiet rest; the crippled are set erect; the sty-afflicted receive medicine; epileptics regain their health; and those who despair of life are restored swiftly. When she is invoked she crushes the strength of armies and provides remarkable victories for her devotees, for she strikes harder than weapons; she contends more forcefully than strong men.

Like Elijah, she opens the heavens closed by human faults; like Peter, she raises the lame up from their pallets; like Paul, she makes fair the dark clouds of the sea; like Nicholas, she stills wild tempests; like Martin of Sabaria,[77] she raises the dead. She is the equal of any citizen of heaven in every kind of miracle, for the very essence of sanctity radiates from her. Without doubt she is an intimate acquaintance of the mother of God, because the dazzling whiteness of her virginity places her in the forefront of the virgin saints, and the laurel-crowned glory of her Passion places her at the head of the chorus of martyrs. Blessed and powerful, she is virgin most precious, pearl of Paradise, joined with the chaste body of the heavenly spouse in the celestial bed-chamber, bright lamp of the world, most watchful patroness of peoples, glory of virgins, flower of martyrs, praise of angels, ornament of the heavens, salvation of the country, force of the Church, plunderer of Gehenna and door of the closed heavens, strongest for the healing of diseased bodies, sweetest remedy for the weak, most invincible protection of the distressed. She not only gives strength to feeble limbs, but what is more, she wipes away the filth of sin. She obtains pardon of the charges against us from God in heaven, and she is a faithful translator who brings the prayers of suppliants to the ears of divine mercy.

I devoutly exhort her most glorious powers, asking that she who performs such excellent miracles here on earth will deign to raise me from the sepulcher of my faults, for I am now almost dead to God because of my sins. I ask that in that dreadful moment of resurrection she will move me from His left hand, stripping from me the miserable cloak of a goat, and place me at His right hand, where I will be garbed in clothing of white wool and where she is exalted with a crown. And may she bring me a wedding garment and enroll me as a guest at that wedding banquet which the wise virgin herself, bearing a lamp burning with the oil of exultation, shall enter to partake of its sumptuous feast, and she shall reign with Christ, in Whom, with the Father and the Holy Spirit, is honor and dominion forever and ever. Amen.

Other Miracles of Sainte Foy[1]

C.1: [How a Thief was Resurrected][2]

. . . evildoers, she would remove many from the noose of destruction that they deserve. Through the holy virgin his pardon was granted and he was brought back to breathe the same air as the rest of barbarous humankind. He opened his eyes, which had been closed in death, and when he had regained his strength he immediately burst out with these words, which he punctuated with many a tear-filled sigh:

"Miserable people, what are we doing? Why are we taken in by the hollow seductions of this world? What we can see amounts to nothing, but what we cannot see is Truth. Behold, passionate desires for transitory things are disguised snares for our feet! Behold, our pride prepares our future ruin, for nothing but our deeds accompanies us on that journey! Blind greed runs unbridled toward every kind of downfall. How it is tortured with wretched flames and excruciating pain! Oh, my beloved friends, cast off this death-bearing plague, for if in your ignorance you are seduced by greed's enticing suggestions here on earth, you will be turned away from the rewards of eternal life that only the just enjoy. Hasten to help me, I beg you! The most glorious virgin Sainte Foy would have hurled me into the eternal abyss had I not been protected by the merciful assistance of the archangel Michael and the apostle Peter.

The day before yesterday I carried off a heifer that belonged to one of her peasants. She took up his case and brought a charge of accusation against me. No one argued on my behalf. And when she saw that I was losing my case she threw in the matter of the money that I unjustly stole from the relatives of the dead man. This nearly dispatched me to Tartarean exile.[3] Through the intervention of the two saints I mentioned I barely made it back here where you see me now, where my purpose is to give satisfaction for the harm I caused and the injuries suffered through my misdeeds. Don't forget the amends I am making for my crimes. Ever since I was very young you have granted me mercy when I pled for it. I need it now, because unless you feel compassion for me I will be thrown into eternal ruin with no hope of escape. I warn you to refrain from such deeds as mine, lest the snare of death overtake you, the snare of utter ruin into which indifferent people fall, for they will be cast down into that sulphurous secret place where there is no relief. Love justice, flee avarice, speak the truth, keep the peace, and work no evil upon your neighbor. If you do these things, you will be blessed."

Then, as it became clear to them that he had been rescued from a great horror, he again described the vision he had seen, point by point, and deep sighs from his heaving chest forcefully showed how terrified he had been. He never stopped urging them to throw off their love of worldly goods and, his face moist with tears, he entreated them to be content with their own incomes and stop seizing the property of others. He would not have returned to this world from the other place, he told them, except to offer his experience as a serious lesson that would wrench them away from their depraved actions.

After these words and many other pleas, he surrendered part of his inherited property to the holy virgin to be held by her forever. He did this to gain her pardon for his crimes and his friends served as witnesses to guarantee that it would be done. In reparation for the cruel death of the peasant and the ransom he unjustly collected from the man's relatives, he obeyed the priests' decrees that recompense should be made of an agreed-on portion of his own wealth. In this way he would be freed from the lingering stain of his crimes and could avoid the tortures that he would otherwise suffer. And so that he would not commit more crimes that would be even worse, after he received the grace of this absolution the Lord commanded that he lay aside his robe of flesh, and his liberated soul soon soared into the upper air.

If anyone feels uneasy and doubtful about this story, you should know that I learned about it from witnesses who claimed they had been there.

C.2: How a Warrior Who Laid Waste to the Holy Virgin's Land Perished by the Sword[4]

Since the glorious martyr never stops working all kinds of miracles, I am trying hard to rise to my duty as a writer. In this I rely on her support, for even my love for such a great virgin can wring from the dryness of my feeble intellect only a meager drop without her aid. Her deeds are filled with such great sweetness that the inner mind takes delight in hearing them, as if they were the highest pleasures. And the more her deeds capture the imagination, the more eagerly do I thirst to hear more of them on account of their great worth. For in her deeds both the wondrous splendor of her powers and the grandeur of her great sanctity shine forth, offering very clear object lessons to a great many people. What people have such hard hearts that the things I tell of do not inspire them to repent of their evils?

As I've just related, a thief committed crimes and received a heavy sentence as punishment. If he had not been released through the intercession of the leading saints of heaven, the holy virgin would have cast him down into the jaws of the eternal abyss. But the man who is the subject of my next story was not found worthy of a single protector, and so he had to suffer painfully the punishments that he deserved.

I am speaking about a man named Arnold; according to the firm testimony of many people, he lived in the Agenais. This savage usurper didn't hesitate to claim lands his daughter-in-law owned and had given to Sainte Foy herself. And, to top off such great treachery, like an enemy he plundered everything the holy virgin possessed that was near his own property, taking farm animals and household goods as spoils. He was so swollen with arrogant pride that he even made a rash attack on the church of Saint Michael located on the hill of Cailles, which belonged to the holy virgin.[5] He seized the wines stored there, which were under the holy virgin's protection. The impious man poured them into his own cellars. Brother Deodet, who served as an obedientiary at that church, greatly mourned this loss.[6] He informed the abbot and the other senior monks of it, and he was gently persuasive in advising them to call on Sainte Foy's help in the matter. But because it weighed so heavily upon his own anxious heart, the following night while he was asleep Deodet saw the holy virgin beside him. She parted her rosy lips and spoke words like these:

"Don't be sad or distressed. The Lord has been moved by your prayers and He will preserve your safety and destroy your enemy at once."

Now Deodet was joyful because the vision had comforted him. The next morning he told the brothers all that had been said to him in the dream, for they had also become deeply concerned about the insolent acts committed against them.

Immediately thereafter, this Arnold was going somewhere with his men at dusk. He was spotted by his enemy, Isarn, who had laid an ambush and was spending the whole night waiting there. Totally unaware of this, Arnold fell into the ambush and a great many of his men were wounded while the rest were captured. Isarn followed Arnold as he fled for shelter to the very church of Sainte Foy that he had ravaged. And there in accordance with the just judgment of God Isarn killed Arnold with his sword; there grim Death was ready for him because of his crimes. This is like the fate of wretched Jezebel whose body was thrown to dogs as plunder. For she stained Naboth's vineyard with her warm blood, the very vineyard that this most wicked of women had dared to seize after Naboth had been slain through her deception.[7]

C.3: How a Madman Was Cured

Many of you have seen the church called Campagnac.[8] Once a man happened to come there who was possessed by an unclean spirit and had wandered for a long time in the forests and mountains. As he rolled his wild eyes all around he caught sight of the altar, rushed headlong at it, quickly grabbed the cloth lying over the altar table, and threw it to the ground. When the officials of the church saw this they shouted at the madman and immediately called down on his behalf the mercy of God and of Sainte Foy, in whose honor the church had been dedicated. And then, so that the Enemy would be driven out of him through the holy virgin's intercession, they lit the candles. Soon thereafter, wondrous to see! blood flowed from his hollow throat and then he vomited up the hidden evil spirit, which was not strong enough to resist the divine command. When they saw this, all who were there praised the might of heaven, which gives Sainte Foy her power and adorns her with remarkable miracles.

C.4: About Men Who Came from Different Regions to Lay Waste to Sainte Foy's Land, and About a Wondrous Vision

Midway between Albi and Cahors lies the church of Sainte Foy in Belmont,[9] whose safety had been made the responsibility of a warrior named Amelius Guy. Amelius had made bitter enemies of two other such men and although they were from different regions they were united in their hatred of him. Once it happened that on the very same day both of them rode out on their horses to plunder Amelius's lands, but each was unaware of the other's plans. Each had decided that because Amelius's own land had been devastated by repeated raids they would find easy plunder on Sainte Foy's property, where the inhabitants of the surrounding territory had taken refuge out of fear. What more is there to say? They readied their weapons and prepared to do battle; from one direction came Raymond of Albi, from the other direction Arnold of Cahors, each accompanied by as many fighting men as he could muster. But as they advanced from both directions nearer and nearer to Sainte Foy's land something wondrous happened, and there is no doubt that the might of God brought it about. After Arnold had spent almost the entire night on his horse he saw in the distance, in the misleading light of early dawn, what he thought was a host of armed men marching into battle. He was deeply disturbed by this shadowy sight, for he thought that Amelius was about to attack him. He acted at once to avoid being destroyed by what he imagined to be true. But as dawn began to outline the face of the land, he caught a glimpse of a military force on the opposite side of the mountain. It was moving to attack him; he could see heads in their chain-mail lined up in battle-formation.

Arnold shouted, "To arms, to arms," raised his banners and rushed headlong into battle, uncertain as to what the outcome might be. It was a brutal contest; brave men fell on both sides. Since neither side retreated, many men were thrown to the ground in the bloody slaughter. Finally the men from Albi were triumphant, and the very few men from Cahors who remained turned and fled, surrendering the battlefield to the victors. But they were soon struck by shame and overcome by deep sorrow for their slain comrades. With a bold spirit they formed up their lines and thus emboldened they returned to the Emathian fields.[10] These men from Cahors were burning to renew the danger of battle to make good their ill-omened loss. When they rushed into the field where the lamentable battle had taken place, they found that the victors were busily stripping the corpses. The men from Cahors attacked savagely and fought with every trick of war. Now it was their turn to drive their enemy to flight and to gain the spoils, both from their own fallen dead and from the vanquished. The men from Albi didn't know where to turn in their perilous flight, so they ran for protection to the castle of Amelius Guy, the very man for whom they had laid an ambush the night before. And so Sainte Foy delivered them into his hands, in the same way that once the king of Samaria received thieves through the hand of Elijah.[11]

The inhabitants of the castle were filled with immense joy to see this, and they repeatedly sang great proclamations of praises to almighty God and to their own highly renowned martyr Sainte Foy, for without loss of their own blood they captured the very men whose frequent raids had caused them such trouble. After they had submitted themselves to Sainte Foy the men from Albi returned home, fully understanding that it was through the terrible power of God and the holy virgin that they had suffered such heavy losses of their own men.

Immediately thereafter, that Raymond who had taken the lead in the foolhardy action was struck by the spear of God's wrath. His whole head swelled up and dissolved into disgustingly foul-smelling rottenness. He died a cruel death and sent his soul down to the pit of Tartarus. The men of Cahors rejoiced over the happy result of the second victory, but thereafter they came to repent their imprudent attempt. They decided to seek pardon and chose as their representative William, a leading official of the church of Saint Stephen Protomartyr.[12] They went on bare feet to the most glorious virgin Sainte Foy's basilica, devoutly confessed their offenses against her, and asked for remission of their sin. They celebrated holy vigils before the virgin's Majesty, which deserved their reverence. There they offered many acts of thanksgiving to her and then returned home.

C.5: About the Monks' Grainfields

Here is another miracle that the holy and excellent martyr worked recently. I do not think I ought to consign it to oblivion through my neglect, for many witnesses attest that it was a good and true miracle.

The place where the church mentioned above is located is very good for raising cattle, for it abounds in lush pastures. A warrior named Aichard was working a great hardship on those who farmed its lands, for he allowed his large herd of horses[13] to graze in the peasants' standing crops and meadows. Finally Aichard was worn down by the peasants' persistent complaints and ordered that the intruding mares should be driven away. But he kept one mare there, which he especially cherished and thought better than the rest because of her plump body and muscular neck. This horse continued to damage the crops badly, even those of the monks, both by eating them and by trampling them. The peasants were deeply offended by the way their neighbor was injuring them and began a constant clamoring for Sainte Foy's help.[14] They persisted in asking her to drive this pest away from their fields. Then a wondrous thing happened! One day when the horse was standing in the middle of a grassy meadow it bloated so badly that its belly burst and its entrails fell to the ground. Its empty body shook the earth as it collapsed; like wretched Arius once, this victim of divine justice lay there with a burst stomach.[15] When the peasants saw this astonishing miracle they recognized that it was the work of Sainte Foy's avenging power, which doesn't allow the arrogance of criminals to rejoice very long.

V.1: How a Peasant Was Freed from a Demon

I have almost fulfilled my purpose in writing this work and intend to bring it to a conclusion right away. Therefore I must disregard the ill-will of this decadent age I live in, because my heart clings fervently to these words from Holy Scripture: "Vengeance belongs to Me, and I will repay."[16] Shall I love any among the faithful who doesn't offer praises to such an eminent virgin, when Christ deigns to work miracles before my eyes because of her privileged position? Therefore if it pleases the Lord to cause something, it should not shame His servant to speak of it and even to portray it. And so, although the present generation fails to obey God's will, even for them I will investigate the miracles that I have yet to write up for this book.

There was a peasant who was possessed by a demon. His name has now slipped from my memory, for the huge number of miracles and the scarcity of writers has meant that some things are forgotten or left out that are nonetheless worthy of the attention of the faithful. This peasant was raving wildly and running all over the place, endangering his life by the way he dashed along steep mountain ridges. Often he even threw himself off the high cliffs and plummeted downward onto the dangerous rocks of the chasm below. How sad it is that the Enemy of humankind has dominion over us again and again! And while this Enemy befriends the faithless, he lures the minds of the good into danger of eternal death.

After this peasant had raved madly for quite some time, he was taken to several shrines of the saints. Finally his arms were tightly bound and the disturbed man was led to Conques. It is necessary to note that here the faithful revere Foy not out of a general esteem for religion; rather, this holy virgin of Christ is a focus of popular devotion due to her miracles. When the possessed peasant reached Conques and his chain was loosened, he plunged without any hesitation into the dreadful, raging waters of the Dourdou

River. It seemed as if nothing could cure him, but his mother finally suggested the gift of a simple beast of burden, a donkey. And then the invading demon was put to flight and the man was completely cured.

Do you understand how this happened? There is no doubt that through the gift of a foolish animal that which is most foolish of all was driven out.

V.2: A Similar Miracle About a Girl

Recently a young girl affected with the same illness was brought to us by her parents to seek our virgin's help. They had heard of Sainte Foy's glorious actions from afar and since they were secure in their faith they were eager to test her and show her worth. But when they got to Conques the girl persisted for several days in the same wild raving state. She hid wherever she could and frequently ran away to conceal herself in secret places. She lost the comfort of friends because, as usually happens, they found it very tedious to care for someone afflicted in this way, and so they left her treatment to the celestial doctor. And then the girl became so violently insane that a young female relative of hers was forced to leave her; as I often saw myself, the mad girl would unexpectedly appear and try to knock her relative down with stones. Thus the mad girl was stripped of absolutely all companionship and afflicted herself with every possible torment, running to and fro all around the rocky ravines. Then through divine will she was finally forced to return to the church. It was the second Saturday before Easter. Due to the harsh treatment she gave to her body she was in pain and completely debilitated, so she was resting quietly in this holy place for a bit. Then suddenly all who were there saw her vomit blood and slump to the ground as if she were dead.

And when she lay there so peacefully, as if in quiet repose, a cry rose up from everyone there. All together we shouted out that she had regained her health through Sainte Foy's intervention. As if these voices had awakened her she quickly got up from the ground, stretched out her arms to heaven, and cried out in a frightful voice that instilled horror in us all. And so those who had begun to rejoice became confused and sad. When she had been raving this way for quite a while, she was summarily thrown out of the holy place, for no one could bear her savage violence, especially since she had begun to gnash her teeth endlessly. Finally she regained her senses and sat inside the church again in the midst of a great many people. She rejoiced because she was healed. It is often the case that when an unclean spirit is departing from people it is not afraid to drive them mad one last time.

When the girl was rejoicing and in high spirits, it suddenly occurred to her that she should return to the sanctuary and offer her thanks to the holy virgin. But when she came to the door that is called the Iron Grills she found it barred, as it often is. From the depths of her heart she called on Sainte Foy and instantly the door was opened through divine will. All the people rejoiced over the double miracle and swiftly began a celebration on account of Sainte Foy's ability and power. As for us, we happily praised the King of Glory, Who never stops glorifying His own handmaiden with so many miracles that even while I write I am sure that she lingers in our village.

V.3: How a Warrior Wounded by an Arrow Was Healed Through Sainte Foy

The force that splits humankind into feuding factions, which is characteristic of our decadent age, always opposes my work. For this is an age in which people incline toward what pleases them and place little value on what might be beneficial. Today's language abounds in unrestrained profanity; shame can't even set limits on it. And it is obvious that, if people's words do not reveal upstanding moral character, then their consciences are undoubtedly ungoverned as well, for as a certain poet is supposed to have said,

"Behavior shapes the heart."

But, oh, what shameful filthiness, what impudent wickedness, what intolerable sensuality! For when it happens that shame is dismissed, modesty also disappears, and when wantonness is embraced, good character is cast aside. And worst of all, when reverence goes, religion is lost as well. But it is not fitting that I linger over such things any longer, because the lips that are going to speak of Sainte Foy's surpassing goodness ought to be made absolutely free of any memory of unclean thoughts. So now I shall do what is waiting to be done.

It is a widely held opinion that the castle of Filigières[17] has strong ramparts and a massive defensive force, but actually defenses like these provide losses for those who rely on them more often than they bring joy. And although the inhabitants may not seem to be overconfident, again and again they are deceived by their trust in strong fortifications, for such defenses attract and must then be able to withstand the hatred of warriors and the envy of a ferocious army. The lord of this castle, a man named Giselfroy, went one day to another castle. With him he took a force of armed men, hoping not only to besiege it but, if they were equal to the task, to overrun it. But after they had arrived there, bravery and ability began to show themselves on both sides.

Then a siege engine is built against the walls; each of the military
arts is prepared for the task:
Now a battering ram, now a high mound, now a rampart next to
the castle.
Now a catapult flings large stones that hiss through the air.
Now also a tortoise,[18] now, right now they're making their way,
now a wheel turns;
Now, the scaling-ladders are in place; they're trying to overrun the
castle.

And when the enemies joined in battle, as often happens, victory yielded to each in turn. A warrior of Filigières named Mathfred, with his companions at his back, moved rapidly from one place to another driven by the fury of battle.

Around he went; he encouraged, he maneuvered, he armed and equipped his men.

For a moment the joy of victory seemed within reach; then it seemed as if Mathfred had dared this courageous act in vain. For each one of the combatants strongly desired to fight fiercely so that afterward he might be spoken of everywhere and enjoy the advantage of winning his lords' gratitude. Perhaps these warriors had heard that in the camps of Marathon it was considered a great disgrace not to have a wound. For on the bodies of brave men a very large scar is a praiseworthy thing. Therefore among the bold defenders of the people Mucius stands out because of his mutilated arm.[19] And when Pompey the Great took Caesar's fortification by surprise, among so many unscarred faces one-eyed Sceva is said to have been well-adorned.[20] It is difficult, so difficult, to earn the praise that comes from enduring without giving way. On the other hand, in those who are cowardly and faint-hearted, as are the wicked, strength lies inert. Fortune indeed errs in favoring such people.

Then a huge wave drove the swift sail forward,
And swelling, violent tempests shook the outspread seas.
Hostile night covered his eyes, while he was about to rage violently,
The way that a lion does, when it tastes of human blood.
For he did not know that he was led by the wicked fates,
Like a tigress pained by the loss of beloved cubs.

Immediately a skilled archer lay in wait for Mathfred. He carefully aimed his curving bow, released the hissing arrow, and wounded Mathfred severely in the middle of his cheek, beneath his eye.

He can already discern what cost worldly concerns exact.

The arrow had plunged in so deeply beside his nose, under his cheekbone, that only the bloody shaft could be seen. This meant that he was in a very dangerous situation. Finally the shaft was torn out, but the arrowhead was left behind inside the wound. Doctors were summoned at once, but the conclusion of their collective expertise was that they knew of no way to extract the arrow lodged inside his head without endangering his life. This was the opinion offered by experienced physicians. In fact the situation would not improve until someone had enough faith in his abilities to open the wound further by drawing back the skin and flesh surrounding it. But they thought it was rash to try to heal him in this way and to draw out the arrowhead, no matter how much care was taken. Then one of the doctors, who thought he knew more than these dilettantes, grabbed up a cautery and probed the wound with it to determine whether he could use it to come in contact with the arrowhead. Seeing he made no progress, he gave it up as a useless task. He was uncertain as to what would happen because the arrowhead was so deeply buried, so after this attempt he thought of his own reputation and was thoroughly afraid because his knowledge had been completely useless.

A day passed in this way; all lost hope of Mathfred's recovery. Despair, the darkest of all emotions, slipped into Mathfred's heart. In the midst of this unhappy state of affairs, the wife of the lord Giselfroy was inspired by heaven to follow after the wounded man's wife and speak to her. She saw that the woman was overcome by sorrow and was suffering the pain of great anguish, and she felt deep compassion for her.

"I see that you are deeply devoted to your husband. If your actions carry out my words, he will regain the health you despair of and the joy you wish for will fill your heart."

Mathfred's wife promised to follow her instructions, and the woman added:

"We all know that the holy virgin Foy, the lady of the town of Conques, heals unfortunate victims like this. When those who invoke her have faith there is no doubt that she effects a cure. If you plead with her devotedly and from the bottom of your heart to help you in your misfortune, and if you are completely firm in your conviction, I am sure you will rejoice because you will have won what you sought."

Immediately Mathfred's wife poured forth such a prayer from the depths of her heart. Focusing her whole being on her request, she invoked Sainte Foy and made vows to her. And, believe me, her hopes were not dashed. As soon as the prayer reached heaven, Sainte Foy immediately warded off the danger and the suffering man fell asleep at once. He lay quietly as if he were awaiting the celestial doctor's help. When they saw that he had fallen asleep they decided to call back the physician and ask whether he would now venture to do what he had been unwilling to risk before. Now what the poet said was shown to be true:

"Persistence conquers all."

And not only will he rejoice soon, he will also give the sad attendants a reason to rejoice.

Then the miraculous physician descended from the high heaven,

She saw the injured man lying there awaiting his death, whenever it might be. While he lay quietly and had fallen into a deep sleep, the mortal doctor inspected the wound. Behold! he rejoiced to see that the arrow, which had penetrated all the way to the chamber of Mathfred's brain, as I said, had moved and now lay at the opening of the wound. Then he gently lifted it out, the danger was gone, and everyone relaxed. They glorified Sainte Foy with praise, and because of their noise Mathfred, who had now escaped the risk of death, was forced to wake up. Once he was awake he began to ask why the people gathered there were making such an unusual racket. They were filled with joy and quickly explained to him what had happened. Then they showed him the piece of metal that had caused him such grief. But he didn't believe them, for he feared that they had seen his sadness in the face of approaching death and were just trying to cheer him up. Then his wife hurried in, determined to make him believe what had happened, and repeated the story over and over. But what need is there of words? He quickly regained his strength and made the journey to Conques. He rejoiced all the way here and when he arrived he told the story of the miracle to everyone who had flocked together to hear it. At once we sang praises to God and as a sign of the miracle the arrow was suspended from the paneled ceiling.[21]

A.1: How a Young Man Was Raised from the Dead by Sainte Foy

There is a town in the Toulousain that I know very well; the people who live around there call it Colomiers.[22] In that town there was an abundantly wealthy man who was a powerful member of the mid-ranking nobility, for there were many below him and relatively few above him. He was recognized as the leading man of the town. This man had taken a wife, a very gracious and well-bred lady, who had borne him one son named Raymond. He brought up his son with the greatest care, for Raymond was his sole heir and he expected that this boy would be the precious consolation of his life, a universal feeling among humankind.

Raymond passed through boyhood and adolescence and became a young man. His parents had every reason to hope for his great success even though they were a little cautious in their expectations. And what could be more painful for them, now that he had been with them so long and stood on the brink of a successful adult life, than to lose him to harsh Death? But when he reached that stage of his life he fell ill, and his illness grew more serious until he showed all the signs of imminent death. He had used up all his strength, for it had been exhausted by his long illness. Intense medical attention was of no avail; the dying youth breathed his last breath. As his miserable parents gave in to their grief, their neighbors heard of his death and came to help. They arranged for the burial service and lifted the body from the bed where it lay to prepare it for burial. But his mother, who was like all women in being more sensitive to suffering, was tortured by her anguish.

She ripped her clothing and tore her hair,
So wracked with pain that she was speechless, she threw herself to
the ground,
But after recovering her breath she broke her long silence.
She heaved a great sigh and spoke barely audible words like these:
"Wretched me! Why should I live when with my son is dead?
Since my son is gone from me, only death can console me.
Wretched pain! Would that my flesh had never brought you forth,
You who deserved to survive your mother."

And while she was giving voice to this pain that had struck her to the heart and was crying out in her sorrow, she at last remembered the powers of Sainte Foy, for the people in the Toulousain were spreading accounts of a great many of her miracles just then. And so she repeatedly called upon Sainte Foy, seeking a relief for her suffering. Why should I delay longer? The body was placed on a bier, lifted up, and carried to the church for the Commendations, the various services that must be conducted on behalf of the dead concluding with the burial. But when the people who had carried the bier lowered it to the pavement, his mother began again with tears and sighs as if she had not yet mourned her son at all. She cried out repeatedly that if Sainte Foy returned her son to life, she promised that he would serve the saint. And she swore that each year she herself would bring two gold coins to Conques as an offering for his resurrection, just as if it were tribute that she owed under the law.[23] She said:

Sainte Foy, comfort me, for I am wretched and grieving.
Through you, powerful virgin, may I win what I beg for.
Examples of your miracles reveal to us
That through your goodness you have the power to bring what I ask.
And so I implore you to return to me my son who has been deprived of life,
Or I beg that death may take my own soul.
If you give him back, he will serve you for all time,
He will come himself to the church at Conques and to you,
And it will be like a law for him, promised with a vow, that every year
He will give you two gold coins as a votive offering.

And so when she had completed this prayer, punctuating it with cries and moans, the bier shook and the youth arose under the astonished eyes of all who had gathered for the burial services. His mother put aside her mourning clothes and reclaimed the garments of a virtuous widow. And I also saw afterwards that Raymond came to Conques and offered at the altar of the most blessed Foy the gold coins that his mother had promised for his recovery.

A.2: How a Saracen Was Taken Prisoner, Freed Through Sainte Foy's Intercession, and Became a Christian Who Called Himself John[24]

As I write down the many stories of the most blessed Foy's miracles, I am eager to recollect one particular miracle which would seem utterly impossible if the Lord, Who wishes the powers of His own chosen ones to become known through their numerous miracles, had not proclaimed and attested that all things are possible for those who believe in Him. He said: "If you say to this mountain, be removed and be cast into the sea, and if you have no doubt in your heart, it shall be done for you,"[25] and, "All things whatsoever you shall ask in my name, I shall give you."[26]

Near Jerusalem there lived a pagan man, a Saracen, who was a strong and willing warrior. Once while he was serving in the war, he was in the field called Aretha, about a mile from Damascus. There he had the upper hand, but then—as God's judgment required, because God scourges everyone whom He takes as a son,[27] but most of all because He wanted to magnify the glory of the virgin Sainte Foy, as will be plainly clear in what follows—the Saracen was captured along with many of his companions and led to a city called Galiba. There he was thrown into prison, closely guarded, and tightly bound with iron chains. An oppressively heavy chain was wrapped around his neck many times and pulled down to bind his legs and feet, weaving in and out in such a way that he was completely entangled in it. Moreover, his enemies demanded from him one thousand five hundred of the gold coins that we commonly call *besants*. Since they wanted to force him to give in and pay this ransom quickly, they withheld all food and drink from him for three days.

Another prisoner who was being held outside the Saracen's cell was the only one there who knew of the virgin Sainte Foy's reputation. This man came from Aquitaine and like many others had come there to wage war. When he saw that the pagan held captive inside was in despair because of his great anguish, he began to explain that a virgin named Sainte Foy was known to possess such great powers that she cured the blind, healed the sick, freed the enchained, and even called the dead back to life. Therefore he privately advised the Saracen that, if he were to plead for her help, he could be confident that through her kindness he would escape. When the Saracen heard this he knelt at once, though he could scarcely bend his knees on account of his fetters. He invoked the Holy Virgin's patronage with words like these:

Oh merciful virgin Foy, whose name is so potent,
Have regard for this wretch, if what I hear is true.
For I see that the King of Heaven cherishes you.
Since you have such great power, I beg you to save me.
I beg you to grant that this heavy weight of iron is carried away
through your help.
I shall find a church, I shall receive the water of baptism,
And I vow that I shall abandon the world and become a monk,

And that I shall go to visit your church clothed in goatskin,
If you deliver me, safe and free.

When he finished speaking, the chains burst asunder and he stood free of the iron bands. But it still seemed as if making his escape would be very difficult, for the prison had been built like a fortified cage. It was reinforced with iron on every side: chains and strips and bars of iron bound it tightly. And in addition the two Saracens who were assigned to guard him stayed on top of the cage night and day. But the prisoner had the greatest confidence in Sainte Foy's power, so he applied his strength to lifting up his prison door with his shoulders and head. As he threw open the door his guards, who were lying nearby, were knocked to the ground. Then he brought out the fetters that had bound him and carried them to the outer door of the house. When he found that it was securely barred, he walked through the whole house until he came upon an extremely narrow opening which was closed with a large rock placed against it on the outside. He pushed hard and succeeded in shoving it out of his way. Then he escaped unharmed. He sent the fetters that he carried away with him to a church that a brother named Robert had built in honor of Sainte Foy on the bank of the Euphrates River.

And when he returned to Jerusalem he became a Christian, just as he had promised God and Sainte Foy. His baptismal name was John, replacing the name of Iron Man that his military strength and skill had earned him. John put on a monk's habit and a hair shirt; then he hurried to search for the monastery at Conques. When he had traveled as far as Constantinople, he told the Emperor Michael everything that had happened to him.[28] And while John was telling the court about his great miracle, behold! the man from Aquitaine who had been a prisoner, as I mentioned above, arrived unexpectedly. This was the very man who had proclaimed Sainte Foy's miracles to John while he was held in prison. He said that he himself had also been released from captivity through Sainte Foy's patronage. From their testimony the emperor was convinced of the great miracle and began to congratulate them. Then he sent them on their way rejoicing at their great good fortune.

John came through Aquitaine to Sainte Foy's monastery at Conques. There he offered her the thanks he owed for the favor she had conferred on him and explained to all what had happened to him through the holy virgin's intercession. Then in the presence of us all and in witness of this miracle, he hung in front of the martyr's tomb the hair shirt he had worn.

A.3: How a Man Named Arnold Was Captured by the Saracens and How Sainte Foy Freed Him Along with His Companions

Among the countless throngs of saints I know that some are of higher merit than others, and I believe that the most blessed Foy easily stands out as even more remarkable among them all. My faith affirms this, but not as a personal opinion based on favoritism; rather it is the great multitude of her miracles that commends her excellence to me. Of these, I am now going to set forth one before the eyes of all, which I consider so great and so praiseworthy that it leaves no doubt as to the magnitude of her compassion.

There was a man called Arnold from the fortified town of Cardona, which is located in Spain, near the border.[29] Arnold had heard of the holy virgin's miracles, incomparable in their powers to those of other saints, and had planned to go to her sepulcher in Aquitaine to pray there. But he postponed the journey, which would have been unpleasant because of the harsh winter, and set aside his plan until a later time when the weather would be fair. Meanwhile he pursued his business interests by traveling with some companions to a city in Spain called Balaguer.[30] But when he had finished his business and started for home Arnold and his companions were captured by pagans. First the pagans robbed them of their money, and then they began to divide up their prisoners so as to sell them in a distant region. They cast lots to distribute the prisoners among themselves, and four of them, including Arnold, went to four warriors as booty. As they traveled, two of the warriors went some distance ahead for quite a while in order to ask where they would be able to sell their prisoners at a higher price. Of the other two, who had been left behind with the captives, one led them with his sword unsheathed and the other followed with a lance at their backs. A single massive chain was wrapped and knotted around each of the prisoners' necks, linking them together, and their hands were manacled in the same way. While Arnold and his companions were being dragged along in this wretched state their captors broke the long journey midway to rest, and both they and their prisoners fell asleep. While they were deep in sleep, Sainte Foy appeared to Arnold and said: "Are you sleeping, Arnold?"

Answering her, he asked who she was. The blessed virgin replied:

"I am the martyr Foy. You had planned to visit the place where my relics are enshrined and for that reason I have come to free you. Get up and release those who were taken prisoner along with you. Understand that I freed you first, for I have broken the chain that was around your neck and I have opened the manacles."

As this vision dissolved the pagans awoke, roused their captives, and forced them to continue the journey they had undertaken. As they were moving along, Arnold revealed the vision to each one in turn and by invoking the blessed virgin he persuaded his companions that there was no need to despair. Arnold wanted to rise up against the brigands himself at once, but the other three made a plan that involved waiting until time for their meal when all their hands would be freed; they feared that one man alone would not be able to overcome their two guards successfully. When they came to a fountain, their hands were freed so they could eat. And so when they had seated themselves Arnold, whose neck and hands were free, took a deep breath and called on the blessed martyr's aid. As tears poured down his face he repeated these words and others like them:

Now is the time to remember your wretched ones, faithful virgin,
Hear our prayers; bring your merciful aid.
Whoever offers you suitable vows in devoted prayer,
Receives your help without delay.
You bring protection to the fearful and health to the sick,
No one remains in want who wholeheartedly asks you for help.
We are terrified; make us safe and free,
Rip away the chains of our sadness.

After he had spoken prayers like this he took some very deep breaths, and then, trusting in the holy martyr's power, he sprang up. Then he seized the lance usually carried by the warrior who went behind them and tore that man's face open with a fierce slashing motion. As he was falling to the ground another of the prisoners named Goodson kicked him so hard in the chest that he had no breath to call out. Then the other two fell on him and wrenched away his soul. The other warrior, the one who went ahead of them carrying a sword, saw what had befallen his companion and fled swiftly on his mule. With his comrades who were still chained by their necks, Arnold went into the woods and there he broke their chains.

Once freed, they retraced their steps until they came to the Ebro River, which they had crossed by boat while they were being led as captives. But they feared that they would be recognized if they approached the crossing, so they turned back. They found another place and implored the blessed virgin to protect them while Goodson led the way, took them across one at a time on his shoulders, and set them all ashore on the far bank. After they completed this crossing they traveled for eight days through pagan lands as safely as if they had been natives of the country. They were protected by their continual invocation of blessed Foy and reached Christian territory without any danger. Once they had returned to their own country they carried their chain wrapped around their necks to show their deep humility. And in this way they came to the holy virgin's church, where they made a great spectacle for all, returned their thanks to her, and left her their chain.

A.4: How Another Young Man Was Raised from the Dead

In Normandy there is a village called Ramis, where a man who was living a secular life stood out among his neighbors for his illustrious lineage, his high office, and his abundant wealth. He was at the peak of his prosperity, for he had been graced with a most fitting marriage partner and was fortunate in the procreation of sons. He devoted himself to supervising their care and expended great effort in bringing them up, because he deemed that the greatest part of his own happiness rested in this, which was the natural purpose of all humankind.

After this father had diligently completed his parental task and, as time passed, his sons grew up and reached the prime of their lives, unforseen tragedy befell him. One by one, over a period of time and to a variety of illnesses, he lost these children whom he had cared for so lovingly. Although he was deeply immersed in his sorrows over these losses, he had not been robbed of every consolation. For out of all his sons one had survived and, because he was the only one, his father cherished him all the more. His presence greatly eased his father's suffering. But none of the frail things of this life stays the same for long, for many misfortunes persistently intrude themselves. And so it was that this young man fell victim to the same fate that had struck the rest of his brothers whom he had survived. Wracked by high fever, his life reached its end: he died. His father was struck through and through with immense grief—grief beyond description. He sank to the ground as if he were dead and withdrew totally within himself, forgetting everything. Grief weighed as heavily on his mother. When their relatives and neighbors heard of it, they quickly gathered there to share the suffering and console his parents with comforting words and to attend the dead youth's funeral services. But they couldn't be comforted and only gave way more completely to grief. Finally those who had come there conceived a singular plan and tried to persuade the grieving parents that they should all beg for a miracle from Sainte Foy, for they knew that in the wondrousness of her miracles she excelled all the saints. The father and mother regained their composure a little and agreed to their friends' plan. Then, shaking with sobs and in such distress that they were scarcely able to speak, they joined with with all those present in this lament for their pain:

As you shine brightest among the saints in high heaven,
Look upon us crying out to you, virgin Foy.
We know that you are radiant with virtues and potent with power,
And so we beg your help.
Do what we ask, show yourself to us,
Lift our pain and and fulfill our desires.
We beg you: do what you can, return him for whom we weep, we implore you.
Here are his mother and his mourning father themselves, asking this of you.
Raise him up, alive, whom we know lies dead,
Return the life that dark death rushed in and carried away,
So that we may praise and glorify your miracle,
Which that good fame will ascribe to your intercession.

While they were crying out such words and more like them in clamorous voices and sighing from the depth of their hearts, behold! the dead body shuddered, and the boy whose grave was even then being prepared and over whom the grave cloth had already been drawn, called his parents and openly proclaimed to all that he had been recalled to life through Sainte Foy's intercession. When those present saw that wondrous miracle they were equally dumbfounded and filled with joy. They believed that what they had heard about the holy virgin Foy was true beyond any doubt, and they proclaimed that her miracles completely deserved their renown. Not much afterwards the young man's father and mother pledged to go to the monastery at Conques. When they had arrived there, they offered for the health of their son the golden collar that hangs over the holy martyr's altar.

R.1: [Since the fragment begins in mid-sentence, no title is preserved]

. . . through Sainte Foy's magnificence. For while all were entreating Sainte Foy's power,

Soon Thierry, who had been commended to such a great power
And was ill, emitted a roar that shook his whole body,
And he regained consciousness as a healthy man. He lifted himself into a sitting position;
He who had been mute, behold! he spoke,
And he honored the name of reviving Foy,[31] which he had not known,
Exclaiming happily, "Quench your sad tears;
I tell you truly that a martyr and renowned virgin
Called powerful Foy granted that I have now escaped the decisive moment of death;
The corruption of disease withdrew from me.
I know that whatever health remains in me she will strengthen;
Therefore now render eager thanks to her at once
And before long I shall arrange to visit her honorable temple.

Thus the old man Thierry, recovering from his illness, proclaimed to all those gathered around listening to him both the power and the name of Sainte Foy virgin and martyr, whose reputation he had never even heard of when he had been a healthy man. Therefore it cannot be doubted that the heat of life had completely left this man, since after he had been resuscitated he spoke about things of which he had no knowledge as long as he lived in his body. For I have heard that it frequently happens that people at the moment of the soul's departure are proved to have acutely perceived many things that were hidden from them while the soul was weighed down by its fleshly body. Gregory also describes this more fully in his book, *The Dialogues*, where he discusses the acuity of the soul. The case of Thierry also offers evidence that is satisfactorily consistent with this, because it is confirmed that something Thierry was unaware of during his whole lifetime he recognized through the acuity of his departed soul, and this was made manifest when his soul was returned to its own body through Sainte Foy's merits.

And so Thierry was obedient to his vow, and even before he had regained his bodily strength horses conveyed him to Conques and he came into the corporeal presence of Sainte Foy herself to give her his thanks.

R.2: [The space for the title is left blank in the manuscript][32]

I was particularly eager for this next story to be included in the abundant number of Sainte Foy's miracles. It would be thought of as totally impossible if we didn't know that the Lord, Who wishes the powers of His own chosen ones to become known through their numerous miracles, hadn't said, "The works that I have done you shall do, and greater than these you shall do."[33]

Near Jerusalem there lived a certain man, a Saracen, who was a strong and willing warrior. Since he opposed divine law, he often persecuted Christians by waging war against them. But finally God's mercy intervened: the man renounced his pagan superstitions, hurried to be baptized, and became a Christian. Moreover, he took the name John in baptism; formerly because of his strength and boldness in war he had been called Iron Man. Now, reversing himself, John transferred to the pagans the hostility toward superstitious infidels that he had exercised against the Christians and, trusting in God's help, he undertook to attack the infidels more fiercely and exhausted them with his relentless assaults.

Once while John was serving in the war, he was in the field called Artha, about a mile from Damascus, where he was striving against the enemy with all his might. But finally he lost the upper hand; God's judgment required this, for God "scourges everyone whom He receives as a son."[34] And most of all God wanted to magnify the glory of Foy, holy virgin and martyr, as will be plainly clear in what follows. John was taken captive along with many Christians and led to a city called Galiba. There he was thrown into prison, closely guarded, and miserably bound with iron chains. An oppressively heavy chain was wrapped many times around his. . . . [the fragment ends here].

L.1: How Two Peasants Were Freed After They Had Been Captured by Arabs in Spain

I think it would be unforgivable if I refused to discuss the kind of thing the Maker's goodness brings about constantly to the honor of this great virgin.

A peasant named Gumfred, native to the region of Girona, was at work digging in the vineyards with a close associate of his named Raymond when they were both captured by Saracens and taken to the city of Tortosa. This is not surprising, for it is well known that the Spanish Arabs are characterized by such treachery that people everywhere speak of them as bringers of misfortune. By this people refer not only to the way these Arabs commit every kind of disgraceful act but also to their inclination toward perversity. This is what Horace said about similar people in his day: "It is bad to let a dog taste the spoils."[35] In their base nature these Saracens are just like brute animals and they will commit any disgraceful act for filthy profit. If anyone who reads this finds it incredible, the story I am going to tell next will make it clear.

Gumfred and Raymond had been held in chains for about four years and had to labor at public works every day. At night they were weighed down with iron shackles and kept in a trench that had been dug out, rather like a bear pit, where they were heavily guarded. Their lives were miserable. Between the pain from injuries they had suffered and the horrible torments inflicted by their guards, they constantly passed sleepless nights, waiting patiently for the profound suffering of another day. But Gumfred continually called upon Sainte Foy, for he once had happened to overhear people praising her merits. To evoke her pity for him, he endlessly cried out from the depths of his heart:

Foy, sacred virgin, you deserve reverent praise,
And fame among the dwellers in heaven,
You are a martyr rich in glorious merits,
Eternal spouse of the eternal King.
We beseech you, respond favorably to our prayers,
And free us from this dark prison.
Do not let a race deserving of perpetual ruin
Forcibly subject us to their dominion.

While Gumfred and Raymond were undeservedly suffering this cruel treatment, the first days of February came, a time when the Saracens celebrated one of their detestable festivals with a pagan ritual. Dedicated to the pursuit of pleasure, these Saracens decided that it would be the greatest fun to run their prisoners through with a sword. But then they became caught up in the celebration of the festival and in the very entertaining buffooneries of some actors. Immediately divine will through the goodness of Sainte Foy brought it about that the watchman at the prison, who was longing to immerse himself in the pleasures of the festival, consoled himself with wine and sleep and left open the trench he was guarding. Then Gumfred, who had been instructed in a dream, addressed his companion with words like these:

"Since we decided specifically to call on Sainte Foy to save us from this misfortune, all that is left for us to do now is to get out of here as quickly as possible with her protection. Let me remind you that she told me herself it was time to rouse ourselves from our lethargy and flee."

Then they noticed that divine power had loosened all the chains and fetters that restrained them. In response to their pleas for solace, the holy virgin's aid brought a way of leaving that foul abyss. Once they were free of their bonds they attempted their escape, deciding to face whatever might happen. They declared that they would rather die following divine guidance than endure the threat of death constantly. So these happy men completed their escape and for a while they encouraged one another by speaking frequently of God's generosity to them; then suddenly it seemed that their joy had been destroyed by fear. If they had not called on Sainte Foy and she had not hurried to help them, there is no doubt that their attempt would have been in vain. For at a distance they caught sight of those sons of evil advancing toward them on horseback and immediately they begged their great saint and guide to defend them. They separated from one another and ran in different directions, but their escape was blocked. Gumfred hid himself beneath an overhanging rock, waited patiently through the day until it was night, and moved on under cover of darkness. As soon as the daylight that could give him away began to return he quickly found another hiding place, and he kept going this way, traveling at night instead of by daylight. On the third day he reached Tarragona, where faithful Christians received him very warmly. On the two days since his escape he had not eaten anything, so he was completely weakened by this long fast, but a variety of sumptuous dishes restored him. From Tarragona Gumfred arranged to go first to his own home to reassure his family, and then he decided to bring his praises to Sainte Foy as best he could. And when he came here I saw him myself and I rejoiced. As for Raymond, with whom he had escaped, Gumfred said that he didn't know what had happened to him. But since Foy can be summoned even by infidels, surely the sacred virgin delivered her devotee once and for all and didn't allow him to become entangled in such a situation again.

L.2: How a Man Named Peter Was Freed from His Chain and Bonds

The goal of this text is to make known to all the sublime worth of our virgin, to the praise of our Maker, as it is always His wondrousness that is proclaimed in such a great miracle as this.

Once a warrior (I'm not certain of his name) from the castle called Najac[36] [see Figure 7] in the peasants' language, was setting an ambush for his enemies when he fell into one of the traps that they had laid for him. He fell backward and didn't see what was happening, for he couldn't see where the snares were. And so it is true that "he who prepares a pit shall fall into it by chance."[37] These enemies took the man captive, wrapped him cruelly in chains, and took him to the castle of Montirat,[38] as it's called. There he was bound with enormous fetters and weighed down with a huge chain. And as he considered his situation, he was sure that this endless torture would soon result in his death. He constantly called upon Sainte Foy, asking with heartfelt prayers that she hurry to help him. But after he had kept this up for a long time and was still no better off he lost hope. Certain kinds of people reveal their character at a time like this: if they decide to commit themselves to something they take it on with great eagerness, but when they think that their exertions are in vain they abandon the whole effort at once. And so it was with the imprisoned man: he could no longer see the point of praying without any result, so he abandoned what he should have finished. He quit when he should have persevered, and instead he brooded anxiously about his ransom. Although his faith had penetrated to heaven, it had not yet imprinted itself deeply on his heart because he had begun to turn away from his effort to gain divine attention, as such people do.

But that night he fell asleep and the holy virgin forcefully reminded him with words like these:

"I am kindly disposed to you because you did well to solicit my help so fervently in your unfortunate circumstance. Now your mind is far too lukewarm, and I don't think you have much faith that you'll be saved. But your more recent performance won't wipe out the impact you made with your first fervid prayers, so get up quickly and you'll be able to leave here without danger."

The man woke up, but he didn't take the vision seriously, so he went back to sleep. The blessed virgin again came to him and spoke to him insistently. She used the same words as before, telling him that he should leave and that he should not think so much about his fear of being caught. Nonetheless the man rejected the vision that required such courage of him and remained completely convinced of his own opinion about his situation. But holy Foy will fight for what she has begun to set right until she achieves her end, so that afterwards her goodness will be proclaimed. She came to him a third time and chidingly warned that he should get out of there, for trouble was at hand. Now the man roused himself, for he remembered that he had been greatly blessed with a vision. He had a strong feeling that help was on the way and immersed himself in turning over in his mind what he should do. While he was pursuing such thoughts, which were weighing very heavily on him, he was so filled with anxiety that his body was shaking as he tried to make a plan. Then all at once he felt that the fetter on his right foot had fallen off completely; his foot was no longer burdened with a massive weight. He listened intently and looked all around but no one could see him, for the dark of night covered everything. He didn't delay but hurried to do what he had to do. Nonetheless, if the blessed virgin in her kindness hadn't come to his aid he would have been frustrated in his purpose. He lay surrounded by the seven men who were guarding him and, given this impediment, he did not know how to complete his escape. But it's clear that whoever receives the saint's approval will also feel her support. However he was vastly outnumbered by the guards lying next to him and he was hampered in moving his left leg.

But he had received the help and the insistent cajoling of the glorious martyr, so he immediately rose up from his bed carrying the loosened fetter in his hand. He took the key to his chain, for he had happened to see where it was kept when one of the guards put it there. Again he was safeguarded by her protection and helped by her promise to assist him. He unlocked the chain at once and, still carrying the fetters, climbed down a ladder woven out of hazel branches. That night he hid in the thick darkness offered by a nearby woods and waited to see what would happen next. But the guards were terror-struck as soon as they understood that he had escaped. They brought lamps, lit torches, and set out to scour every little path in the woods. And so they spent a sleepless night struggling to prevent a divine miracle. When they could no longer deny that their efforts were fruitless they returned to the castle. Finally Peter grabbed up a hard stone and smashed the fetter that still shackled him. Then he completed the journey he had begun. Immediately this happy man came to Saint Foy's glorious sepulcher and offered his weighty fetters to us in fulfillment of his promise. And when he had discharged his vow in this fitting way, he quickly went home rejoicing.

L.3: How an Elderly Man Who Had Lost the Use of His Arms and Legs Regained His Health and Strength

I am not going to avoid the judgments of people who find fault any longer, although I feel the sting of their threatening abuse. Even if what I write doesn't deserve praise, I'll praise good writing when I see it. And so I congratulate myself with an overflowing heart that I am unaffected by either the anger of my attackers or the envy of my defenders. But I'll pass over such comments for now and get on with my story.

Robert, count of Rouergue,[39] who was the strongest and most highly praised of men, was staying in Rodez once when he fell victim to a debilitating disease and nearly died. He came to understand that none of the medical treatment he was receiving was effective, and in fact it was believed that there was no treatment available to humankind that could cure him. Therefore he decided to seek out the unparalleled medicine of the unparalleled virgin, for he believed that through her he could win heaven's favor. And so his spirits and his hopes were raised and he looked forward to an improvement in his condition. Moreover since he was a very wise man, as everyone thought, he took the step of sending some of his own men to Conques. They urgently requested that a considerable number of the monks come to Robert so that through their witness and privileged position he could achieve what he desired deep in his heart. For although Robert was married he didn't seem to make use of his wife as an advisor. She was still a child and, even when she had completed her childhood years, in her heart she cared only for herself.[40] Therefore Robert determined to consult his senior advisors and to reveal the secret in his own heart to Sainte Foy's witnesses when they had been summoned. When they had been brought in, he said:

"Since the attentive care of mortals hasn't found the cure to this illness, I intend to request the health-giving aid of your great virgin. If, through her intercession, Christ is kindly disposed toward me and brings me the assistance of a cure, I shall place under her authority my church located in the diocese of Auvergne, which the locals call Tanavelle.[41] And finally, I shall treat liberally those subject to my authority who are under her law and shall protect them in every way."

And since he was not ashamed to say this, I am not displeased to report it. It was wondrous the way the words of his pledge were followed by the gift of his health. Almighty God granted his prayer and cured him to provide an example for people to follow. It is clear that that is why he hadn't been cured before and why his cure didn't come about a long time afterward. And then since Robert had received his cure he discharged his vows and faithfully kept his promises.

A little later, the holy virgin's glorious image was carried in procession to the church at Tanavelle. It was a custom of our senior monks that when a very welcome gift enriched the monastery with the benefices of churches or the outstanding addition of manors, the shrine of the relics was borne to that place to put it under her protection. In this way the virgin claims these things for herself and the presence of her body subjects them to her forever. When the monks saw that such a procession should be undertaken, they sought the approval of the senior monk. While the relics were being carried to Tanavelle with as much pomp as the monks could muster, the populace came running from every direction, rejoicing greatly. Each person who was sick or physically impaired was carried to the procession as it passed, and several of them were restored to their former good health at once. The reason I have explained all this is so I can tell this story:

By the third day word of the procession had flown out to multitudes of people. A crowded assembly of men and women had gathered, and a great number of young people from Brioude[42] rushed in to join them. I suspect—may I be pardoned for saying this—that our virgin will be thought to be haughty, for it could easily be seen that she was the equal of Paul and even of Peter, save for the reverence due his apostleship, because she made a lame old man walk again.[43] What more is there to say? She is extolled with praise fit for angels, she performs miracles in the manner of the apostles, she is adorned with the glory of the martyrs, she participates fully in the great joyfulness of the confessors, and she is among the company of the virgins, with whom she delights in the vision of the Lamb. And though I might say that there are regions somewhere on the earth where word of her has not reached, I surely doubt that her marvelous deeds are unknown anywhere. But why have I decided to delay what I promised to write by saying these things? Let me return, then, to the story I was telling.

While the boisterous group of young people from Brioude were passing by the village of Massiac,[44] they came on an old man who was very decrepit and extremely aged. From his youth he had been unable to use his arms and legs. In addition he suffered from a condition that had developed at the same time, namely that his limbs were stiff and unbending; he could neither move them to walk nor sit with any comfort. Since he suffered from such a physical impairment and had to struggle with it every day, he lacked any means of support and patiently joined the ranks of poor beggars. When he heard that his companions were hurrying to the holy virgin's procession, he turned to his faith in her and wanted to put to the test what he had heard about her long before. But since he couldn't walk, he eagerly asked them to take him to her and to expose him to the favor of her miracles, which could end the misfortunes governing his life. Through God's will his companions believed that he could be cured. They were deeply moved by his plight, so they prepared a beast of burden to transport him, placed him on it, and conducted him to the town of Talizat.[45] They quickly heard from people who were coming back from there that the stewards of the holy image who had brought it to the region had already decided to return to Conques. They hesitated, not knowing what to do. Because they were uncertain about trusting faith, they made a bad decision. They made up their minds to set the lame old man down where he was, so that they might more easily hurry to the saint, who for them was not Faith but a martyr, or at least a virgin.[46] And so he was left alone without shelter, but not without help. Glorious virgin Foy, our devout faith, here is this man in need of your care; his case has been reserved for your remedies. Bring it about that he receives what he faithfully seeks.

When the man realized all at once that he had been left without any assistance, I believe that he began to be very sad, not unreasonably, and he became thoroughly upset and distressed by sorrow. Who could describe today the tears that he shed as he began to pray to Sainte Foy? But unless I'm wrong the divine power from heaven that glorifies our virgin was with him. Behold, old ways, oppose this new power, if you please. Apostle of great power,[47] I ask you, who is like our virgin in glory, excepting those of your rank? This young girl, our virgin, spreads before us greater works than yours. Great God works miracles for her not by the shadow of a body and, even better, not by a word or the laying on of hands, nor by a belt as Paul is believed to have done.[48] But when she is called on from far away by name only, the presence of her blessing is felt instantly. I have an abundance of other examples, but I don't want to criticize these persons with such great powers any further, persons to whom we believe that power over heaven and earth has been granted, lest I be called a detractor of the saints, which I am not.

But let's see what our man did. As he ceaselessly called on Sainte Foy, immediately through God's will the old man stood up straight, his feet firmly on the ground. He wasn't tottering around, as usually happens in such cases, since what he asked from Foy he received firmly through his faith. The new, old man came to us swiftly and nimbly on his own feet — for we were about two miles away from him — so that he could tell us what had happened. When he arrived there we all listened to him lovingly, as was fitting. With us, the happy man rendered thanks and praise to God and the holy virgin. And so that he could add physical proof to his assertion that he had been cured, he still had some signs of his former malady. But in addition proper witnesses were found, namely, the people who had taken him to Talizat. It was easy to see that he walked with quivering steps and it was not surprising, since he was not accustomed to running and the length of the journey had exhausted him. He helped to carry the holy virgin's reliquary with his aged hands, which he was using as if they were new although it was clear beyond a doubt that they were spotted with age. Who would not be astounded, who would not marvel at such a sight? Some were struggling with tears because they found it worthy of weeping over, but others, who found it a pious sight for rejoicing, raised joyful voices. Those who were there with me and saw this sight are proper witnesses to the miracle. And they are eager to glorify God, Who is wondrous in His saints[49] and glorious in His works, Who so magnifies Sainte Foy that her reputation spreads to the four corners of the three-part earth.

L.4: How Christ Deigned to Work the Same Miracle for Two Men to the Praise of Our Virgin[50]

Since I'm striving to write the outstanding deeds of the outstanding virgin, I must still set about to put the remainder into an appropriate style so that my writing may become an example to future generations, an exhortation to those who are well-disposed, a punishment to the spiteful, and for me may it result in a reward. Before I could undertake even the beginnings of a theme, for my mind was not yet reflecting deeply and skillfully on my purpose, something happened that was unforeseen. It astonished me, but then it didn't. Who has been able to avoid the maliciousness of envious mortals and their minions? But what is so marvelous and worthy of mention is that such people don't shudder at the deaths of those in whose steps they seem to follow, as Cicero says in the *Philippics*.[51] It doesn't matter because, as Augustine says, where the knowledge of eternal and immutable truth is absent, virtue is false even in a person of the best character. Solomon spoke with foreknowledge of divine words when he said: "For the generation that shall come afterward shall not rejoice in them, but this is vanity and vexation of spirit."[52] For, indeed, if these envious mortals don't remain silent and I achieve what I have attempted, I believe that they will be sorry. Now let me turn my attention to the story I intend to tell.

And since I have heard how one warrior who was imprisoned was freed through divine intervention it pleases me to compose a similar story about two others, even though the circumstances are not the same.

In the district of Rouergue where the virgin glorious in her miracles dwells and where her body is revered, two warriors proud in their lineage, excellent in their reputations, and noted for their wealth, were taken captive, as happens often. They were wretchedly dragged off and led to the castle of Montmurat,[53] which is strongly fortified, people say, so they wouldn't find any chance to escape. One of them was called Bego, the other Arnold. Afterward, I remembered that I had seen both of them frequently. After Bego and Arnold had been conducted to Montmurat, they were imprisoned in the extremely unpleasant manner typical for such men. And their restraints were even harsher than usual, for they were bound together, one of each of their legs in a single set of fetters. And to add to this continuing torment, they were closely guarded as well. They had been in this situation for quite some time and had devised no clever strategies for escaping; their understanding was confused and their ability to reason grew dull under such strict confinement. In their grief they could not imagine that anyone would help them. But finally their minds cleared. They had even lost their ability to recall their one safe refuge which, with all due respect for the faith, I would say is the virgin Sainte Foy, whose praises the human mind cannot encompass, she who is moved by prayers and does not refuse to bring assistance to people everywhere who hasten to her. Both prisoners remembered her at the same time and both began to pray to her incessantly. Their repeated prayers were accompanied by floods of tears. Her name never slipped out of their thoughts, even for a moment, as is almost always the case for people in combat or suffering some kind of extreme danger.

And so while they were calling upon her with constant prayers and insistently begging that she remember them and help them, behold! one night the glorious virgin appeared to one of them in a vision and said:

"Because you have decided to exhort me more than others with your persistent pleas about your trouble, out of my innate compassion I won't refuse to help you get what you don't really expect, but fervently desire."

She continued, "So be prepared, for tomorrow your vows will not be in vain. From the very moment that my mandate comes to you, you won't have to fear anyone. Hurry to do immediately what it charges you to do to free yourselves. As you are leaving this place terror will not pierce you to the heart, and you will even walk the public road. Neither by accident nor by design will anyone trouble you."

Then the man awakened, certain that it had been a true vision and believing in words of such great reassurance. He immediately began to explain to his companion in suffering what he had seen or, more precisely, what he had heard. And when he had finished, their joy was so great I cannot describe it. They glorified the great works of God, Who is hope of the faithful, faith of believers, Who hears the pleas of the humble and does not despise the voices of those trusting in Him.

They spent the whole next day in anticipation, and by the time evening was approaching they had begun to lose their fervor and to despair. Then two men who were known for their biting wit came to the castle and happened to turn aside to stay the night there. The first was from Conques, the other was a native of Carlat.[54] Their coarse humor is so well remembered everywhere that I am not going to hand down their names to posterity. I think they ought to be omitted because the disgraceful acts of reprobates remain as vivid as the deeds of the good for those who come after me and enjoy the account in my writing. When these two had arrived they unsheathed their swords, for this is typical behavior for such people—seriousness is completely missing from their actions. Play-acting, they ran about all around striking wildly here and there and shouting madly, "Quick, get out of here, degenerates! Flee, lazy bones! Clear off, you miserable creatures! The lord[55] has entrusted your property to us!"

The prisoners were startled by these voices, for they recognized who the men were, and they waited in amazement to see how things would turn out. Then they moved quickly to take advantage of the disturbance and busily did as they had been instructed from heaven, with no fear at all of recapture or injury. Each encouraged the other, and they went over the plan several times. Each declared that because it was commanded from heaven nothing could interfere with it, and they both agreed that they ought to put themselves in the hands of divine protection. And when it was near sunset yet fully light, the prisoners, still joined by the bolted fetters, left the tower where they had been inhumanly imprisoned. They escaped according to the divine plan and made all possible speed in doing it. As they were leaving the castle they met several people who were conducting their business affairs, but a divine miracle clouded their minds so that they took the two to be part of their own group rather than strangers. And when they had begun to gain some distance from the castle the escaped prisoners came on Hector, the lord of the castle, but they didn't flee in terror since they knew their heavenly guide was assisting them from above. Hector was with some of his own men and was supervising a project and assigning tasks to see that it was carried out. As Bego and Arnold passed by no one said a word to them, since they hadn't been recognized; Hector was turned away from them and didn't even see them.

Finally, doing as the virgin had told them, they walked on the public path, for they weren't vulnerable to an enemy ambush. In this way they didn't have to worry about stumbling on sharp rocks or into crevices, or finding detours around such difficulties. Then by chance or, rather, by divine influence, they came to the Lot River. They couldn't find a boat, but since night was near they waded across and returned home without further complications. When they had arrived there, they immediately broke the bolts of their heavy encumbrances. In their joy they scarcely endured one day's wait before they hurried to Sainte Foy, on bare feet as is proper, and offered her the great weight of iron along with their immense thanks.

L.5: How William of Reims Was Cured of a Paralytic Disease

Since I have been prompted by my great love for the holy virgin Foy, I am trying to narrate the signs of her miracles, and I depend on the most reliable assistance so that I may be found suitable to accomplish this. Therefore, good God, I feel compelled to send away unexpected witnesses to other miracles, even though they speak the truth, and to investigate more fully (relying on dependable witnesses) the miracles I've seen with my own eyes.

A native of Reims called Guy, who put great trust in the things of this world and was totally absorbed in his life as a warrior, decided that his son William should be taught to read and write. Since Guy had a great number of children, both sons and daughters, he chose this one to serve the Lord. But the minds of worldly people are always changeable and mutable; Horace spoke truly when he said: "You may drive nature out with might and main, nevertheless she will return again."[56]

Guy took the son whom he was going send for his education and instead enrolled him in a military life. And since people seek to make others like themselves, Guy did not hesitate to get his son entangled in the false values of this world. But divine power always has pity for human misfortunes; no one is beyond the reach of God's vengeance, but more importantly no one is beyond the reach of His kindness. In this case it was first necessary to apply a father's corrective rod to this young man who belonged to Him, as you shall read in what follows. It is well known that young men devote themselves to entertainments and spectacles. They live in the present, scorn the past, and give no thought to the future. Like an unbridled horse, William involved himself in the pursuits of his fellows and feverishly chased after the delights of this world. While he was caught up in such activities and avidly sought his pleasures, it so happened that the commander under whom William was serving took him along when he went on a distant expedition against his enemies. The commander was determined that they should remain there, and after several days they fell prey to two constant evils: starving for lack of food they grew ill, and benumbed by the cold they sat in a stupor. One day after he had been tormented by hunger for quite some time, William ate some rye bread. After he had gulped it down he wept freely, realizing all the more clearly what suffering lay ahead of him. Finally he was driven by his hunger to eat poisonous things. In his desperation he gently caressed what it was injurious even to touch. Then, full to bursting with this deadly food, he fell into a deep sleep and further weakened himself by lying there without moving in the intense cold of the night. By midnight William was burnt up with fever and ravaged by thirst, as the poisons raged through his body and threatened to destroy the very marrow of his bones. He was completely unable to endure such intense thirst so he was driven to drink the slime in a stagnant pond, which was as filthy as cups filled at the Phlegethon.[57] He had given himself to the destruction of encroaching death. Suddenly sweat began to pour from his thoroughly enfeebled body, his stomach swelled up, the color of his face changed, and little by little his limbs began to contract terribly. Not even the physicians could decide whether his condition ought to be called dropsy or paralysis. As time passed and William was under the constant care of doctors, the part of his body from the kidneys upward regained its normal functions. The rest was completely lifeless. His parents were moved to sorrow and shame by such a great misfortune, for they were considered to be eminent among their fellow-citizens because of their great wealth, their large retinue, and the amount of property they controlled. Yet they had no choice but to rely on the medicine of God alone.

Then one day, content with only one horse and attended by two servants, William set out without his father's knowledge to visit saints' shrines wherever he could find them. He wanted to obtain a cure of his serious illness through the love of Christ's faithful, for no hope was being held out to him that he would recover through means available to humankind. Or, if he was not to be cured, he wanted to hasten his death through the hardships of travel. For it is said that members of the nobility deliberately prefer to exile themselves and leave home rather than to be viewed with disdain by their kin. Therefore William made himself a continual exile, and he wandered all through not only Frankish and Germanic, but also Celtic and Belgic and even Ligurian regions. He went on to Italy, turned around, and planned next to see Ireland and all of Spain. He had not yet touched the borders of the region of Conques, although he had already made a passage through the Rouergue. As I will describe fully and clearly, the celebrated honor of this miracle awaited Sainte Foy, the glorious virgin who was adorned with a singularly privileged martyrdom—*pace* all the other saints. And so when William was returning from the shrine of Saint James he went to Toulouse, and he turned aside from the outstanding virgin's monastery as if he were avoiding her, because of fear of the rough terrain and the rugged journey. He decided to go to Limoges so that Martial, an outstanding confessor of God, might grant his prayers. There William had to do without the help of his servants, for they fled secretly and left him behind; his only recourse was the providence of almighty God. Alas, the wickedness of servants! If they aren't restrained by harsh masters and if shrewdness doesn't prevent them from escaping, there isn't the least bit of loyalty in them.

While William was delayed in Limoges, one night it seemed to him that he was in the place where the blessed virgin rests. When morning came, he sought advice from the townspeople as to what he should do. All agreed that if he went to Conques and implored Sainte Foy with prayer she would confer her help on him, for she almost always comes to the assistance of all who invoke her. William found some help for his journey and set out. While he was spending the night as a guest at some castle he lost the horse he had been riding. For his companion, who had plotted out their journey as if he had divine guidance, stole away in the night, unseen by all, and left behind this helpless devotee of Sainte Foy. For a price that seemed low to him William purchased another mount. Then he refused all companionship and crossed the steep mountainsides alone on his way to the holy martyr's shrine.

Ah! celestial virgin, spouse of the eternal King, now is the time to remember the outstanding favors of your miracles and how much the whole world magnifies your praises.

After William arrived at Conques he persevered in prayer for two days, but on the third day he became disheartened and decided to leave. When he had gone some distance, he came to his senses and it occurred to him that he ought to go back; now hope joined him, faith fortified him, love strengthened him. On his return he had himself positioned before the clay of Sainte Foy's holy body, and he called on her to remember him in her compassion. At once he was transported, as if he were in an ecstatic trance. He lost all sense of himself and awaited what God intended. All at once his skin split open, the structure of his muscles firmed up, blood ran down everywhere; the sick man immediately regained his health and stood on his feet. I learned this from none but William himself, who told me that he had spent four years in his paralyzed condition. He returned praises to God and extolled the holy virgin highly, as she deserved, for it was through her kindness that he who had come a sick man departed a healthy man. And so William returned home joyfully, and he who previously had been borne on the feet of others now was not afraid to return on his own feet.

L.6: How Sainte Foy Brought a Dead Man Back to Life

Although I follow the path of my predecessors according to custom, even if my stride is not equal to theirs, and I rely upon the kindness of the illustrious Foy, not only have I been afflicted by the hypocrisies of my enemies' hatred but because of the slanders they have launched against me I have been hampered in my writing. I hadn't been torn to pieces by the attacks of abusive people until I began to be involved in pursuits like this. For very frequently it happens through twists of fortune that the wickedness of criminals governs and virtue not only is judged to be worthless but, for shame! it is thrown beneath the feet of its detractors and punished as befits despicable crimes. I wouldn't have believed it possible that a citizen of the celestial homeland, our Foy, could be derided by such bold attacks. And so I would like to have my say on this question:

You who are potent with consummate power and gleaming with goodness,
Always our greatest glory, our honor, our aid, our hope,
Our light, our remedy, our salvation, you whom time does not restrict,
Virgin Foy, remember my humble prayers,
Grant me the ability to scorn the spiteful hearts of men who rant at me
And to perceive truth, so that it may always grow.
Repress the deceitful, curb the habits of the enemy,

Lest he conquer the one who proclaims your praises.
I am often tormented by evils; may your solicitude always be
vigorous against them
And help me to ascend to the starry kingdom with you.
Hear me with rapt attention, faithful virgin,
And may you prevail now and and through the ages and forever and
forever.

But since I take the approach of frequently mixing my grievances with my praises for such a great virgin, perhaps it may seem that I'm straying from the plan I've set out. That's why it seems appropriate that I, the writer appointed to this task, should have no regard at all for the nonsensical histrionics of my critics. And finally I am obliged by the precepts of my teacher not to seek the approbation of my critics for appropriate praise of God. But let me speak of these things elsewhere and turn now to what was brought about by Foy's charity.

Recently the most powerful men here in the territory of the Rouergue devoted their efforts to the building of a castle at the enclosure for animals that is called the castle of Aigremont.[58] The dissension between the lord of Aigremont and the lords of another castle was nearly endless. Isn't it strange? Wavering and mutable fortune torments the leading men of the world and leads these wretched people down the slippery paths of pleasure by a devious road. Only in a kingdom with the highest and best ruler would it be impossible to find a moral fall equal to this. But let me return to what I started.

In the ongoing strife, the enemies of Aigremont were striving to overrun that castle with a strong force of fighting men. During this attempt, something happened that brought sorrow to the attackers, although afterward it caused us to rejoice. The men of Aigremont organized their defense against their attackers, and since they believed that the castle was well fortified they concentrated on protecting the ramparts, hoping to win some praise for its name through their valor.

When they saw their enemies turn their backs, the defenders rejoiced greatly. The flight of their assailants augmented the defenders' bravery. The battle became heated and each side threw all its forces into the fight. Whenever the battle chanced to favor one side, the other drew on its resources to renew the attack. In this way the men defending the ramparts of Aigremont, even if they didn't want to, immediately tried to attack their enemies' backs with bows and with *balistas*.[59]

Then fortune brandished her grim visage.

When the situation had reached this point, one of the attackers, Bernard surnamed Gerald, turned his back to flee. A *balista* took aim at him and drove an arrow deep into his head. Near death, Bernard was carried home by his companions who survived. Of course, this sign always marks fugitives: since they turn their backs to flee the only scars they bear are on that part of their bodies.

Great God! when they told his mother how seriously wounded Bernard was, for they believed that his situation was as hopeless as escape from a labyrinth, her own heart bled for her son's injuries and she didn't know what she should do.

Then in her grief she clawed at her face, loosened her thinning hair,
And tore her clothing from her breast,
In her distress she knew not what to do.

Meanwhile their friends, who were deeply concerned and able to think more clearly, discussed what ought to be done in this disastrous situation. But their sadness had cast such a pall over their minds that, as often happens in such circumstances, their views moved futilely back and forth: some thought it prudent to consult doctors, others feared his death, and some clung to the hope that he would recover. Finally a doctor was summoned; assiduously,

He called up all his knowledge of the sciences, he stared
contemplatively into the quiet night,
He studied the skies, he repeatedly felt the patient's pulse.[60]

But when he noticed that particles of Bernard's pierced brain were emerging from the wound made by the missile, he lost hope right away and said that there was nothing he could do.

Bernard lay in this unfortunate condition for almost three months. Nothing had helped him and he was certain that death was near, so he made a heartfelt appeal to Sainte Foy. Almost all his friends had drifted away and his only hope was God's providence. He prayed that God would take pity on him and come to his aid; he repeated this prayer over and over. And after a few days had passed in this way, his strength faded little by little as the end approached. His disease grew worse and death made good its threat. And so Bernard's lifeless body was laid on a bier, the funeral ceremonies were conducted in the usual way, and each person came up to bid a last farewell, lamenting and speaking a few words.

Now our Foy took action. Now she showed why she waited to answer the prayers of his friends and of Bernard himself and to restore to him the pleasantness of this life. Now she showed what she could do when faced with the opposites of death and life. Bernard's mother, scarcely alive herself, raised her voice and begged for a munificent gift from Sainte Foy in words like these:

Holy virgin Foy, my hope cries out to you now
To help me, spouse of the supernal King.
Behold my son, always the center of my life,
Lies dead. In his misfortune he was beset by a bitter calamity.
I pray you, give him back to me through your sacred power,
Let sad death depart, and happy life rise again.
Do as you have done so often in driving out the sorrow
Of those who are sad.
Banish fear,
Do not suffer grief's presence,
Return him to joy,
Blessed virgin.
For this we shall extoll you,
As you deserve,
With faithful hearts,
With songs of praise.
Be quick,
Splendid martyr,
Learned teacher,
To answer our prayers,
Completely.
With devout minds
We think it worthy
To believe in you.
And the world shares our faith.
God granted you power,
To give life,
And to overcome death.
Hear our prayers,
Faithful virgin,

Be merciful to us,
Deliver us from our despair.

And while his mother wept copiously and besieged heaven with her incessant, pleading prayers, our virgin could not bear these pitiable and tearful laments. She reached out her hand to a great undertaking,[61] revealing the power she customarily wields. Even if she comes back wearing her golden headband again and again, nevertheless the vessel that she fills at the fountain of miracles is not yet exhausted. And therefore it will be very easy to call out to the holy virgin, "Return, O Sulamite woman, return that we may behold thee."[62]

They kept watch with the body the day he died and the next day to give his friends time to gather and to prepare a proper funeral.

When Hyperiona[63] had poured light on the fleeing stars a third time
She unveiled great joy about to reach his friends.

At once Sainte Foy's interceding power was there, she who was about to give them all a reason to have faith in the life to come.

How often my Foy has broken the law of Avernus.[64]
The Thracian[65] showed respect when he visited Pluto's[66] kingdoms,
But she shatters laws when she goes there and demands the return of her prize.
The gates of Tenaria lie open and he departs from Erebos,[67]
Then they flee the shadows, the barred doors of Hell are opened,
Death also quakes when it abandons its own laws in this way,
Thus the victrix conveys supernal souls to the upper air.

All was reversed as those who were present at the funeral and had stayed for the burial exchanged their sorrowful weeping for tears of inexpressible joy. Within a few days Bernard had completely recovered, and he rejoiced that he had been cared for by the holy martyr's protection. Therefore he took seriously the general opinion that he should go quickly to Conques, give her his verbal thanks, and offer her the linen cloth that had shrouded his dead body and the hand-coverings that we call *guantos*[68] in the peasant language. For there may have been ill-will on the part of envious people who were, as so often is the case, endeavoring to disparage this outstanding miracle; why they should denigrate everything I don't understand, for I know of no better way to establish the truth of a miracle for all and to glorify God Who reigns forever.

I avow truly that Bernard came here and that I and others saw him and wondered at the miracle. Who has the ability to give worthy utterance to the praises of this miracle when he sees such great things worked through Sainte Foy? But to dispell any disbelief, the winding-sheet hangs in front of the holy image as a sign of the miracle to this day.

The end of the miracles of this virgin.

Translatio: The Translation of Sainte Foy, Virgin and Martyr, to the Conques Monastery

Prologue

The King of the Heavens is magnificent and eternal. Thus, before the beginning of the world the Father, Whose rule is absolute and Whose wisdom is indescribable, marvelously saw beforehand the end of all creatures along with with their beginning, although they did not yet exist. That is the way He chose those who were later going to be His own Christians. They were the ones who took up the saintly way of life from earliest childhood and contemplated divine mysteries with the inner eye. The privilege of faith had given them great power and they persevered steadfastly during martyrdom, for they disdained the tyrannical laws and cunning enticements of pagans and, above all, they showed contempt for every kind of torture. Thus their stubborn persecutors, who threatened them with death, could not bend them to acknowledge false, pernicious idols, whether their approach was soothing or harsh. Rather these extremely brave athletes, who fought in the name of Jesus their champion, held fast to the end in the combat of the pilgrimage that is this life. They returned to their homeland with an outstanding victory and received rewards from their Lord for a successfully completed campaign.

To insure that their victory should be as well known to those who live on earth as it is to heaven-dwellers, God, that same glorious Arranger Who is Himself without beginning, saw to it that there should be a succession of writers, trustworthy men who loved Christ, who would write about their outstanding triumphs and palms of martyrdom, as well as their miracles. When such writings are handed down to succeeding generations they provide examples of the right way of life and embodiments of religious teaching.

In contrast to these men, who practiced their occupation so well, I am ignorant even among my contemporaries and the lowest of all. I could never be counted as one of their number. And although I have no lively style of elegant, rhetorical writing to rely upon, nevertheless I have been compelled to act, more out of my devotion than my abilities. Pen in hand, I dared to write the title "Translatio," undertaking thereby to tell of the Translation of one of Christ's virgin martyrs named Foy, whose deeds were as noble as her name. But my meager talent was an abiding weakness that threatened to confound me, and I have been slow to begin. Now I am filled with mystical inspiration and I shall start to write, relying on my own powers as I set out. I say *my* powers, which are not comparable to those of illustrious men. They have no fear of sailing out into the depths of a sea of uncountable numbers of books in great triremes whose folded linen sails spread wide in the breezes of the south wind. The fierce winds of the north, which blow fiercely, do not trouble them, nor are they terrified by the menacing ocean swells. Such a mind makes full use of the rapid winds when setting its course; it is like a swift ship that flies over the waves as the rowers carry out the oarsman's commands.

My poor little boat, on the other hand, stays within a pole's length of the shore. It lacks sails and is rowed along by my own sweat, sticking to the safety of calm waters. And in this way I advance little by little toward the goal I have set myself; out of exhaustion I stop now and then.

And so, reader, don't look for artful accomplishment in this work, nor the locution of elegant refinement, nor the vastness of the rhetorician's eloquence. But recognize the poverty of a rather narrow and unsteady talent which, as I said above, has been involved in this endeavor more out of devotion than ability. Nevertheless, the High Creator is assisting me and the goodness of God is instructing me and refreshing me with help. Therefore I desire to fulfill the vow I made of my own free will and to complete this task, and I shall not refuse to do as I promised.

Chapter 1

In the time when Diocletian and Maximian held the scepters of Romulus's realm, they raged against Christians with tyrannical fury. As a result, to the very borders of the Empire, that is, from the Eastern to the Western Seas, persecution of the faithful was cruelly carried out in each and every city by that heinous criminal Dacian, who was directed by their edicts. During that calamitous period, it happened that as this wicked governor was traveling across to the western borders he entered the city of Agen. And when a relentless investigation of Christ-worshipers was undertaken, the first to fall into the vicious hands of this most villainous torturer was a virgin of the noblest stock, but even more noble in her sanctity, the handmaid of God, Foy, an inhabitant of that very place. When he did not succeed in compelling her to worship idols, Dacian subjected her to the fiery grill and scorching live coals. Then, along with Caprais, Prime, Felician, and several others, she gladly achieved her martyrdom by means of a bodyguard's sword.

But Christ's flock, still small and meek at that time, was concerned about the martyrs' bodies. Secretly, because they were afraid of the cruel pagans, the Christians gathered up Foy's sacrosanct body with care and attention and took it to an unlikely and unsuitable place for burial.

Many years later, when all the pagans' murderous frenzy lay in the distant past, a holy man named Dulcidius, who had been elevated to the high office of bishop, put everything else aside to build a church outside the wall of Agen in a suburb to the north. He consecrated it to the heavenly Bridegroom and secondarily to the veneration of the holy virgin. In a visionary dream Dulcidius was admonished from heaven not to delay in transferring the saints' bodies from their neglected and inappropriate resting place to the site consecrated by the Lord. Dulcidius separated the bodies. The most blessed virgin Foy, who surpassed the others in her palm of victory, he commended with the greatest honor to a precious mausoleum, carved from marble, inside the basilica. Letters briefly spelling out the title of her *Passio* were carved on it to transmit the truth of history down to the present. And Saint Caprais was brought down inside the city walls to a church founded there and very carefully placed in a sarcophagus, also of marble, with similar honor.[1]

The bride of Christ and martyr, Foy, had begun to shine forth with great miracles, for she was giving sight to the blind, restoring hearing to the deaf, curing those possessed by the devil, and driving out all kinds of infirmities from various invalids. In fact the Lord had crowned Foy as queen of such brilliant miracle-working power that her fame resounded not only through neighboring cities and regions, but also through the four quarters of the earth. Because she was adorned with excellent miracles, Foy herself, daughter of heaven and most sacred virgin, was proclaimed by every people far and wide as the most famous and the most glorious. Therefore within a short time pious assemblies of people frequently came together at her tomb, and great crowds of people with various afflictions were brought from all around. God miraculously glorified that greatest of martyrs through them, for all had their health restored. Unimpaired and rejoicing, they returned from there announcing the great deeds of God and the virgin.

The city of Agen is located in Lower Gaul, through which the Garonne River flows. But in the triple division of Gaul this third, to differentiate it from the other two, is called by the name Transalpine and Lower Gaul.[2] In that same province of Gaul is a monastery called Conques, which was established in a valley enclosed on all sides, completely surrounded by rugged mountains and shaded by woods to the south. The monastery extends to two stadia in length.[3] The contours of the place form a shape that resembles a mussel shell,[4] and it is understood that its name originates from this. That very monastery was destroyed once to its foundations by an army of Saracens, when they came with hostile forces to devastate almost all of Europe.[5] As a result the royal charters holding that the monastery was a diocese of its own were scattered and destroyed. A few years later, at the command of Emperor Charles the Great to his son Louis, who was crowned and elevated into his kingship while his father was still living, the monastery's privileges were written anew by Louis's order, and it was honorably restored from its foundations. From then until the present time there has been a reputable community of monks in the same monastery. Their predecessors were sustained by the harsh practice of the ascetic life, which in their successors, as may be observed clearly every day, is amplified zealously by increases in good virtues.

Often these highly honorable men spoke together about the prodigious miracles of the virgin who has been praised earlier in this text.[6] Meanwhile an opportune suggestion caught their interest and unexpectedly there was a reason for them to consider how they could bring it about that the most holy martyr's body would come into their possession for the salvation of the country and the redemption of many people.[7] Therefore they summoned a monk named Arinisdus, who had been assigned to a parish of that monastery in accordance with the Fathers' common practice, to provide religious guidance for its church. Arinisdus was prudent in council, quick-witted, and outstanding in every aspect of his character. Since he was perfectly suited to the task, the monks worked out the entire sequence of the proposed matter and, as it was necessary, they cleverly worked out how, if fate should assent, it would be accomplished openly. After the plan was completed they sent Arinisdus to Agen with a guide for his journey.

Possessed of such a secret, Arinisdus arrived in Agen, turning over various ideas in his mind. As the matter had demanded, he had shrewdly looked into everything for himself. He lived there in the garb of a pilgrim, as befitted a stranger, and conducted himself with every caution. He took pains to keep discreetly secret anything associated with his mission. He arranged for a place to live, pretending that he would be a permanent tenant, and lived there in apparent simplicity. To all he truly displayed his attachment to a devout way of life. In fact, while he was keeping up such an exemplary life, he quickly made a strong positive impression on the inhabitants of Agen because he lived a visibly chaste life and they began to feel that he was one of them. In fact the clergy received him not only in friendship but also in companionship. In return, after he became well known among them in the usual way, because he displayed every kind of virtue and was flourishing through the exercise of his skillful talents, this lover of divine law hardly let matters rest there. He made himself useful everywhere, surpassing all others in patience and humility, and yielding obedience to all in everything. Since this praiseworthy concord of character and behavior was clearly very pleasing to all, after some days they unanimously agreed to promote him to guardian of their church.[8]

Thereafter he pursued this ecclesiastical duty in a proper and orderly manner and gave fitting attention to it. He continued and increased his activity as a doer of good works and a teacher of others. Nevertheless, his secret—the reason he was there—had outlasted both successes and adversities; it had not vanished from the depths of his own heart. But because easy access to this desirable treasure—and therefore the means of acquiring it—was not given in a short period of time due to fear of adverse fortune, Arinisdus put the fulfillment of his vow into abeyance. He kept his place among the brothers, awaiting an opportune day.

Meanwhile his anxious mind labored incessantly, and in the depths of his heart he was consumed with formulating a plan for gaining the access he needed to carry out such a difficult task. Then on the great feast of the Lord's Epiphany, all convened as usual to eat the common meal after the celebration of Mass had been completed. Arinisdus had strenuously demanded that they grant him freedom from attending to certain legally required monastic duties so that he could guard the church, lest by chance, as often happened, something ill-fated should come about on such a joyful feast day. They unanimously yielded to his decision and judged that they had acted wisely in this. While they lingered over their festive meal for a long time, Arinisdus, who placed his trust not in himself but in the Lord, approached the sacred virgin's burial place without hesitation. But the covering stone remained immobile because it was held firmly in place by iron seals. Arinisdus didn't know how to lift it intact, so he struck it at the foot. The tomb partly opened and he very diligently gathered up the most sacred body. Lifting it out of the tomb very reverently, he put in into a small sack that was very clean, exalting and magnifying God.

Chapter 2

After this Arinisdus waited tensely for the silence of the night. Then he summoned his companion for the journey and, taking their divine gift, they set out swiftly for home. As day broke the next day, the guardian, when sought, was found to be missing and the tomb, when visited, was found empty of the body, its precious treasure gone. Then a huge tumult arose among the populace; astounded, they gathered in crowds, questioning one another about what had happened. And, as is often the case in a distressing situation, rumor spread the news quickly through the crowd and made it known to all the people of that region. Therefore the whole city congregated at the virgin's sepulcher. When they determined that the holy remains were not there, all of them were deeply afflicted with extreme, heartfelt grief. They were struck by such great sorrow that there was no room in their minds for consolation. But even though they were consumed with grief at their own misfortune, they didn't forget its cause. Some of the equestrian order[9] prepared for a journey and set out in hot pursuit of the fugitives carrying off that holy treasure.

Meanwhile, every member of the Agen clergy was piling reproaches on himself for this mischief. And the rest of the population reviled them no less, blaming them for setting a stranger, who came from so far away, in authority over themselves. Furthermore, they had preferred this foreigner so much, while having less esteem for local people who were suited to the position. However, after the endless outpourings of words and countless laments, they formed a plan. They agreed unanimously that if fate should return the fugitives to their hands they would either hang them from the gallows or blind them. Therefore they sent a powerful search party along the route leading from Agen to the region of Conques. But God in His mercy wished to protect His servants, lest they should suffer total destruction. The pursuers went in a completely wrong direction, traversing the Garonne River by boat and hurriedly crossing over into Gascony. Through God's will they were plunged into such witlessness that just when they thought they were nearing the fugitives and readied themselves for a fierce attack, they were moving farther and farther away because they were traveling in the opposite direction.

When the pursuers regained their wits and recognized that they had been deluded in taking the wrong road and had labored in vain, they returned to Agen, deeply shaken and dejected. They reported the sequence of things that had happened to them en route. The inhabitants of the city were again agitated about the calamity and directed the search party to set out once more in pursuit of the fugitives. They thought that with swift horses the searchers might be able to make up for the earlier delay and succeed in their efforts. The pursuers traveled with excessive speed and, one day at dawn, fortune unexpectedly brought both parties to a place called Lalbenque.[10] There the pursuers found the man who had carried off the sacred body, along with his companion, sitting under a shady tree to catch their breath. But although they were staring right at him with a fixed gaze, nevertheless God's power was present there in a miraculous way. For, although they were looking at a fellow countryman as well as a favored citizen whom they had seen on a daily basis at home and with whom they had spoken daily, it was as if their seeing eyes had been blinded, for they recognized him neither by inspecting his height nor by hearing his voice.

They questioned him closely, as if he were a stranger, as to whether he had seen a man of the description they had made known. With deceptive words he swore to them that he had seen absolutely no one anywhere like that. Of course this man of God was completely terrified that during this interrogation he would betray himself, so he feigned an identity. Then he stretched his exhausted body on the ground as if to rest and turned his face to the earth, so that he wouldn't be recognized. After this he left his companion behind and continued his journey through Quercy with the sacred relics.

The pursuers went to the city of Cahors and stayed there for a day. They searched into any trace of the matter astutely and industriously, hoping that by chance some line of investigation would occur to them that would yield useful information. They didn't fail to inquire diligently as to how far they should take which road or where the roads went. Finally, as they sensed that they were exerting themselves in vain, they anxiously discussed what ought to be done in this awkward matter. At last, agreeing among themselves that it would be more advantageous, they made a definite choice to go back to Agen: "Therefore let's return. Perhaps, the virgin's powers prevented any departure from there, for people believe she would not allow herself to be carried away from us and transferred to another place." After they had agreed to this they turned back, and when it turned out otherwise than they had hoped, at least they arrived home, having been proved false in every inquiry and in their own hope.

On their arrival the search party reported to the lay magnates of Agen. The unwelcome news that the holy martyr's body had not been recovered from farther away resounded in their ears. Having suffered such a grievous loss, they concurred in the opinion that nothing would be more useful than to bury this calamitous event in silence. For if their shame and disgrace were divulged to the people, the blame for the misfortune would be imputed to their inexperience and ignorance. But the sacrilege—a fortunate one, if it is permissible to say so—couldn't be hidden for long; it was revealed soon thereafter and became generally known everywhere.

Meanwhile, in his anxiety Arinisdus sped up his flight, for he was terrified of his pursuers. Since he had been protected by the shield of God's compassion, he had been permitted to avoid the bloodthirsty hands of his enemies. Constantly driving himself to keep up an inhuman pace, Arinisdus hid from view when he was traveling through a village called Figeac. But there was a blind man there who had received divine revelations in dreams that he would be cured of his blindness when the holy virgin passed by. He knew of the arrival of her body because he had received a presentiment from God. He reached out boldly and demanded to be healed and, when he touched the veil covering the body, he suddenly regained his sight. In fact, not only in the case of this man but also in a great many other miracles that were worked during her passage, this mighty virgin was elevated by the Lord. To avoid writing at great length I shall omit them, but I should say that more miracles would have been worked through her if her bearer had not been engulfed by such distressing terror that his enemies' violence would annihilate him, that he left every locale in headlong flight.

The bearer of the holy relics feared that if he were caught and punished the great treasure he was carrying might be damaged in the process. Therefore he especially asked the man who had been cured not to reveal it right away. Arinisdus said that no matter how much the healed man considered that it had truly been accomplished, he should by no means make it known until Arinisdus had returned home, lest by chance someone should put a stumbling-block in his way that would cause him injury. And in his joy the man who had received the gift of sight praised and magnified God and the virgin and easily agreed to his prayers of entreaty. And when this discussion had been brought to an end, the servant of Christ pressed forward with all his energy, directed his course to the place already mentioned above, that is, to Conques, and reached it as swiftly as possible. It was not far away, but only about twelve miles from Figeac.[11]

Word of Arinisdus's impending arrival reached Conques, and when this bearer of the holy secret was nearing their vicinity all the monks of Conques walked out some distance towards him. An appropriate procession including the rest of the crowds of the faithful went to meet the most sacred martyr; with a cross, thuribles redolent with aromatic odors, and all the rest of the divine pageantry, the blessed virgin was received by all with worthy honor, the happiest hearts, and willing minds. After these rituals of praise had been completed properly and devoutly, they returned with hymns and songs of rejoicing, and they bore the body of Christ's most blessed martyr, with the highest honor and glory, into the church dedicated to the holy and highest Savior Jesus Christ. And they very carefully and reverently set it in the most fitting place under the most diligent guard on the 19th day of the Kalends of February [January 14]. This was at the time when Charles the Less, King of the Franks, was ruling; the princes under his authority unjustly conspired against him and deprived him of the royal throne. They placed the crown of the kingdom on Eudes, duke of Aquitaine and chose him to rule in place of Charles.[12]

In fact, on account of their reverence for the virgin the very devout people of Christ chose the abovementioned day of the Translation as their most festive day forever, a day surpassing all others in complete joyousness of true faith. The Christian community of that whole land observe that day annually in praising God since that time, and now, and in the future. Totally transported by spiritual joy, they adorn it with every kind of ornaments of sacred worship and celebrate the festivity once more. Therefore from that day until the present people from everywhere very frequently gather in great multitudes at the church of Conques in order to visit the relics of Christ's holy martyr. Unless you see it with your own eyes it is difficult to believe the report of how many come and return in closely packed multitudes. In some instances the size of the monastery does not suffice to contain them suitably, although it is of very great magnitude. There they customarily observe the nocturnal offices with candles and after completing prayers and the mass they joyfully return home.

It was inevitable that this enclosure for pious, gentle monks, who followed the example of Christ's servitude and the tradition of holy father Benedict, could not continue to bear the continuous onslaught of such populous crowds. Due to the serious discomfort and restlessness of the people, the monks themselves enthusiastically lent their support to the building of a new church. This was in the days of Stephen, venerable bishop of Auvergne, one of the cleverest of men.[13] With his counsel and most especially at his urging, a basilica of the greatest beauty was built next to the monastery; it was constructed from its foundations in a very little time. The sacred virgin's body was to be entrusted there to a tomb that would provide easier access for all those who constantly came to Conques to see it. Therefore, when the edifice of the oratory had been completely finished according to the architect's design and consecrated by the abbot's legitimate blessing,[14] the notable dignitaries of the land, who were of course wise as well, gathered together. The more guileless and worthy among the monks were chosen, men who would be suited to the purpose of removing Christ's holy martyr from her resting place and bearing her with the deepest humility to the newly built church.

When these highly meritorious men anxiously approached her glorious body, they started to lift it with every effort of religious awe. But, due to the wondrous act of Christ the Supreme Creator, it had such great weight that it remained fixed in place, staying as steadfastly immobile as a mountain. Of course those men feared that they were not worthy enough to have touched this holy object. They resolved to chastise themselves with fasting and prayers, but when they returned it became clear that the task was not to be completed in this way. In fact they ascribed their failure to accomplish the deed to an unlawful fault of moral weakness, so they again gave themselves over to the mortification of daily fasting. Then they tried a third time, but their labor made no progress at all in accomplishing what needed to be done. They feared that if they exceeded a third attempt, someone would think the men of this monastery with such a famous and lofty name were stuffed with foolishness or that they would suffer some measure of punishment, not without cause. Therefore they withdrew completely from any further attempt to carry that holy body to the aforementioned place.

Then, of course, they recognized that what they had tried to do was unlawful and forbidden to them by God's command. They undertook to have a reliquary made, which was thereafter placed next to the high altar of the Savior Jesus Christ mentioned above.[15] It was fashioned with marvelous workmanship and made a great display of gleaming red gold and scintillating gems. The most worthy virgin, sealed beneath it, rests there happily in Christ and there is no doubt that she is constantly visited there by countless people. In this place the Lord certainly exalts her through meritorious miracles in so many different ways that her acts of healing are manifested for all those who are ill, as well as those afflicted with various evils. Heaven has glorified her in such a way that daily she ascends from miracle to miracle. The outstanding deeds and miracles of this virgin, who is filled with wise understanding, are so incredibly varied that no brief telling does them justice. We have assumed that they do not have to be inserted here and, since they have been recorded, we pass over them entirely. But if anyone is an avid peruser of books and ardently longs to acquire written accounts of them, let that person read thoroughly the book of her miracles.

What tongue, O loving reader, what weight of elegance suffices to reward in a worthy enough fashion such an outstanding martyr of Christ? Or what capable philosopher will prepare a thousand kinds of songs to the praises of all of her merits? Assuredly the pursuits of the Academy,[16] powerful in its own virtue, should pass away, for all the rhetorician's skill is unable to express the pinnacle of her glory. O thoroughly blessed virgin, dweller in Paradise, companion of angels, when you were placed in the flesh you thirsted, panting in your heart for Christ. Like a warrior you fought for Him and in valorous triumph you completely conquered the enemy. Above the stars you brought your noble trophy and received as Spouse Him for whom you thirsted. O how joyously deserving is this pearl, and O how great and inestimable is her miracle! Her soul has earned the embrace of God's Son in heaven, her relics were carried from another place, desirous of possessing a home specially assigned to her own name, so that this place should not be without a sacred mystery. For just as she has been united as spouse with the heavenly Bridegroom in the starry halls on high, so in her little dwelling here below she was united with her relics. And just as she who is beloved should never leave her lover in heaven, neither should any place be empty of love for them.

Hail, renowned daughter of Zion, O bountiful Foy, foster-daughter of the heavenly Jerusalem, gleaming forth among the choruses of virgins like a rose and lily. O day to be reverenced, day to be cherished, day to be proclaimed, on which such a great flower was offered into the light of this world. O exceedingly happy land of Conques, adorned with the relic of such a gem and of such a lantern, you shine brightly with her lightning; rejoice and applaud, clothed with such a light, which gleams above the ether like the sun among the stars. O sublime ornament of the earth, crown of martyrs, lustrous among virgins, shining with a countenance as beautiful as the brightest star, you come forth from the bridal chamber of the King as fair as the rosy dawn; rejoice, most noble girl, for your beauty has merited Christ as lover, the true Sun, whose splendor and beauty outshine the brilliance of heaven and all the brightness of a summer day. To the Unbegotten, to the Son, His Only-begotten, and to the Holy Spirit, the Paraclete, honor and glory alike through eternal generations of generations. Amen.

God the beginning of all things that are, to you glory and a song of
    praise;
You, Who fixed in place the globe of the world, and the abyss.
Your beauty is seen in all created beings;
Scarce otherwise you shine greatly and wondrously in the saints.
For you the virgin Foy disdained the best things of the world,
Scorning Dacian, she conquered over whips, the sword, the grill;
And brought back a noble banner over the triumphant ether.
The city of Agen, flooded with a red wave of blood,
Was the first to cherish her body, but afterward bemoaned its loss.
Now the soil of Conques enjoys the presence of these sacred limbs,
And this renowned land sparkles with the rays of such a star,
And raises a shout of joy to Christ the Lamb, offering Him double
    and triple praises,
Who granted this highest splendor as their reward.
Hail, star, Foy, you who are the greatest of heaven's citizens,
O hope, grandeur, salvation, power, flower, glory and starbearing
    light, you who reign with the Lord in heaven's halls,
Lift up . . .

[In the *Acta Sanctorum* the next five lines of the Latin are omitted because the editor couldn't make sense of their meter and syntax]

Wherefore, pious virgin of God, hasten to assist an insignificant
    Creature, made of dust and therefore mortal,
And do not let an image of Christ be vanquished by the weight of
    flesh,
But return as ethereal spirit, victorious, to the stars,
Where there is eternal peace and true light without end,
And the scepter-bearing high-throned One reigns, and to these
    heavenly kingdoms,
Make us, King of Kings, arise piously on high,
Where we shall dance for You with magnificent praise through the
    ages.
And this may the Father, the Begotten, and the bountiful Spirit
    grant.

The Song of Sainte Foy

A prose translation from the Provençal by Robert L. A. Clark[1]

1. I heard a Latin book about the old times read under a pine.[2] I listened to it in its entirety, to the end. There was no meaning that it did not render clearly. It spoke of the father of King Licinius and of the lineage of Maximin.[3] These two tormented Christians just as a hunter does stags in the morning: they led them to prison and to death. They left them dead on their backs, lying in the fields like criminals. Their neighbors did not bury them. This was around the time of Constantine.[4]

2. I heard a song that is beautiful to dance, which was on a Spanish subject.[5] It was not in Greek speech nor in the Saracen tongue. It is sweeter and more delicious than a drop of honey or any spiced drink prepared by man. Whoever says it well in the French style, I believe that it will be to his great profit and that it will so appear in this world.[6]

3. All the Basque country and Aragon and the country of the Gascons know what song this is and if this story is true. I heard it read by clerks and scholars, by very good ones, as the *Passion* in which one reads these lessons shows it.[7] And if our melody is pleasing to you, as the first tone guides it, so will I freely sing it to you.[8]

4. You have long and quite often heard it said that Agen was a very rich city, closed in with walls and moats. The Garonne flows past it on one side. The people from there were very bad; they lived in sloth and idleness. Not one of them abstained from the great sins, the man of reason no more than the fool,[9] until God, moved to pity them, saved them on the cross and delivered them from the Devil.

5. The people would have been beautiful if only they had been healthy in spirit. Their hearts were infirm because they were pagans. They abandoned God and rushed to the temple; they covered it with gold from Córdoba. Each offered there the ring from his hand; he who could do no more, a piece of bread.[10] It would have been better to give it to a dog. They did all their works in vain. Ah, why were they not Christians!

6. King Solomon told the parable of the apple tree that is born in the bush, which the thorn bush encloses with thistle and hawthorn all around: there at the summit it brings forth flowers and then apples of good quality.[11] The Gascon pagans were evil, they who rejected God in heaven. Their shadow stifled this young plant about whom we sing this song. And yet God took sweet and good fruit from it.

7. The lord of this city had great domains in abundance.[12] As much as he was able, he took leave of that sin and loved God greatly in secret. You will hear how God honored him and what a precious good He gave him. He gave him a daughter of such great worth that her name, sent by God, was Foy, and she was raised in chastity and preserved her holy virginity. By her God has greatly honored the world.

8. Her body was beautiful and small in size; even nobler was her reason that was within.[13] Her eyes were pretty and her face white, and the wisdom of her heart was worthier still. Before she was twelve years old, she did such a deed as is pleasing to God: she took martyrdom so very harsh, as you are reading and singing. O God! this world is so greatly honored by it!

9. The honor that she had from this world was worth no more to her than mud.[14] Her heart was with God in heaven, and His service was very pleasing to her. It will not stop, so I believe, until she pays God Himself with her death. By this the Devil is put to dismay.

10. She had great country estates and strong castles and furs of wild animals and buttons and precious rings on her fingers and well-made vessels of gold and silver. She feared that these were an evil snare that the black Devil had made for her. With her wealth she nourished the poor and the lepers. She made herself poor, like a beggar, and remained faithful to God, Who was more pleasing to her.

11. After having gowns with bordered sleeves, for God she placed herself in great poverty. She left the others of her train and boldly endeavored how she might seek God. Do not believe that He will not reward her for always wanting to be His servant and His faithful chambermaid and for seeking how she might offer herself to Him, for this is the way of righteousness.

12. I must tell you about these pagans, how harshly they treated the Christians.[15] When Saint Adrian was killed, Diocletian was king.[16] He was king of the Greeks and the Romans, and held Spain and the mountains of Cerdagne.[17] Licinius was his oldest son; and, when he was born, he gave him schoolmasters. This old dog rose up against God; he killed His saints with both hands. Now he has fallen quite low and lies beneath a thousand devils. Maximian was his peer.[18]

13. They carried out their business together. They held their idols too dear and commanded that they be worshiped and honored by land and by sea; and they chose a wicked criminal—that is, Dacian—God save us from him! They sent him to govern that kingdom and to take and burn the Christians and to treat them harshly and bitterly.

14. And then he came into Agen! He was a man who had no good sense.[19] Everywhere he went about doing such deeds by which we know that he offended God. He worshiped the Devil and sold men and ambushed and captured Christians. Some he put to the sword and others he hanged and many of them he burned in the flame, and he sought to do this very often.

15. When they heard that Dacian was coming, this was a great joy for the pagans. They raised up their idols on their temples and they displayed their ornaments in the squares. This was a bad and a vain show, the idea of a fool and a madman. And then they talked about the Christians:

16. "Lord, why have you taken so long, after you conquered this kingdom? You should have visited it before our people abandoned their faith. A damsel has preached to us that there is a God in trinity who is good. Whoever prays to the gods of our temple she calls mad and out of his mind. If this is not severely punished, you will lose this land and this city, for everything is hers by inheritance.

17. "What our people tell you, let not wrath nor forgetfulness make you forget it. This damsel has insulted us; she places us in affliction on her account. Her lineage has always nurtured us, and she has wickedly abandoned us. Let her not find support in you if she does not shamefully renounce the god in whom she believes. She has truly taken us to be fools; her hostility has greatly disturbed us. And you are dead and completely shamed if her neck does not bleed for it, as you had done to Saint Felix."[20]

18. He sent people to look for her right away and ordered that she not be harmed: "Lead her to me gently by the arm, and tell her what I'm doing here. And I will promise her such great treasure that I will rid her of all ill intentions. I'm a very skilled hand at this."

19. His men then tried to outrun each other. They came to the place where she was. They did not even give her a proper greeting but rather menaced her very much. And she controlled herself without her heart's wavering, for she had one that was worthy and strong. And she prayed God that through His strength He would help her in her great need, for she had placed everything that was hers in His care.

20. She raised up her voice and commended herself to the Holy Cross. She did not value the fools more than she would a nut, neither their commerce nor their trade. For in hell, in the deepest pit, great harm will come to them for their sloth, for in that place there is a very bitter spring.

21. Then she crossed herself with three fingers[21] and prayed to God, who made this world: "God, who has kept me from all evil habits, if you come to my aid now, you will do what is good, because you said to your people: 'When you have great need, if you tell me so, you will see me at once.' Lord, I pray you to help me. I beseech you to guide me so that, as I believe, Lord, you may take my soul."[22]

22. Dacian's bailiffs took her and led her to him in the middle of the square. He called a publican who was dressed in camlet:[23] "Go, take her gently by the right hand and lead her into the temple. Let her offer incense to the god Sylvanus and pray to Diana and the god Janus."[24] She cared no more about this than about a dog, nor did she concern herself with this pagan. Her heart was firm and strong and healthy, and she held God in heaven to be her sovereign. This is what all Christians must do.

23. When the day began to wane, he ordered that she be beaten and struck. He had the harshest prison opened, and ordered that she be dragged therein. Then the madman uttered a sigh such as the peasant does when he is going to die. He went to bed but could not sleep any more than a man who wants to take flight. He who fostered him made him feel great anguish.[25]

24. The next morning he began to prepare the trial and ordered her to come before him: "Now, damsel, I want to hear what lineage you wish to serve." She spoke, and she knew how to tell him this: "I want to abandon myself to our God, and, in that which I know best how to choose, there is nothing that I so admire.[26] If I do not have Him, I cannot be saved. There is nothing I love so much, I will not lie. With Him I wish to find laughter and joy."

25. Then he called to her with great love: "Remove yourself completely from this error. Choose a great honor: you will have it, and then a greater one. You have a body of gracious bearing; you seem to be the daughter of an emperor." The damsel answered at once: "You speak mockery and dishonor. I do not want to change lords. The Lord who made me—Him I believe and adore. Whoever loses Him may fear Him."

26. Now hear whether the fraudulent traitor struck her a severe blow: "Your ancestors venerated Diana as do all our people. If you leave this youthful foolishness and agree to do as I desire, I will give you a diadem of gold and clothing of true purple. A hundred damsels will follow you, and a thousand outfitted knights."[27] She answered him and did not lie: "God forbid that I should be tempted by a fool. I prefer to die or to hang in the wind rather than to enter into your protection. Whoever consents to this has lost God.

27. "In health or in suffering I will be faithful to God, as has been my wont. For this let no one praise nor blame me: I want neither Diana nor Jove, nor do I embrace Minerva, nor do I wish to turn my eye there. When you raised them up on this temple and embellished them so, all this you did through pride. Each of the supports of a wine press, fashioned with an axe in the forest, would be worth more.

28. "Whether I am ill or healthy, I will not pray to your Diana. May a Christian woman never do this, because in truth it is certain treason. Every day of the week the Devil is ever ready to steal praises. If each of you offers

him a frog and makes incense for him from the smoke of wool, he will show hell to you—be assured of it."

29. When the stinking wretch heard that she would not change her intention, he became mad as a snake. His eyes rolled in his head and he gnashed his teeth, and then he swore his great oaths: "Your head will be bloody for this, or the fiery flame will burn you, as you have heard it did Saint Lawrence."[28] She was not at all frightened by this and said in words most fitting: "May you be a traitor if you have spoken one false word!

30. "May God never let me see the day when I adore Asclepius or Saturn.[29] For in hell, in the deepest pit, with many others who are of the same sort, they do battle within the flame. They do not have a pleasant stay there. I do not want such a god at all.

31. "God, our Lord full of glory, is powerful over all things. From heaven He descended here below for us and made of Himself a most ingenious man: He healed the sick and lepers, and gave us baptism in water. His precious body was taken; the Jews killed Him through envy. He destroyed dark hell; from there He freed His own whom He knew to be worthy. I would like to have Him as a spouse, whatever quarrel I might thus make for myself with you, for He is so beautiful and full of love for me.

32. "His name is Adonai: so He said to Moses. In truth, He is so powerful that, of all that He commanded, nothing failed. And from them who serve Him with a good heart, He withholds not their just reward. He sought humility and good, and to His faithful friends He gave honor. And to them who cast their lot with Him, He gives their share in heaven and, when they die, He places their souls there. I think that He will do so for me, for I have always loved Him since I first heard of Him."

33. Now you can hear how the demon answered her at once: "I swear to you by the gods of this temple's tower and by those to whom I make sacrifice that you will pay dearly for this outrage: you will lose your head." Then he had one of his servants come who made him an iron grill. He placed her on it over the hearth, her chaste and pure body completely naked; he made her a fire of walnut and of other wood from the orchard. She did not attach the value of one denier to this, for all her thoughts were with God and she was the daughter of a knight.

34. The people wept and grieved. For the damsel they raised a great cry: "Ah! such youth, so quickly undone without any crime that we have heard!"[30] And then they repented greatly of the harm they had done to God through their forgetfulness, and to Him they were converted, and many of them died as martyrs; and they begged Him to guide them Himself.

35. The whole city was filled with sorrow. The good men fled on all sides. Even Saint Caprais, whom it did not please, stayed hidden above in a rock. From there he saw a great miracle that God made on the furnace where the body of the saint lay roasted and burned on the iron grill: a winged angel came there from heaven, white as a dove is in the year of its birth; when the angel fluttered over the fire, the blaze went cold. May no one ever believe anything I say more than this.

36. This angel that came there, hear what a great treasure he there brought: a gold crown that shone more than does the sun when it is at its zenith. He covered her body, which was completely naked, with a cloth of beaten gold. No one, young or gray-haired, saw this, except Saint Caprais, her friend, who always remained faithful to God.

37. When the wretch saw the blaze dead and the fiery furnace extinguished, he then felt great despair because she made so lightly of it. And he cried out in a loud voice to his men: "Let her not keep even a part of her head, my men, for she does all of us great harm."

38. The people let out a sigh on account of such suffering, which they saw her endure without any crime. Were a person to reach the age of one hundred, he would never suffer more greatly. The Basques from Aran[31] cried out, saying: "Let her not depart from here alive on any account!" Pulling her from the fire, they stood her up on end. One of them raised the flashing sword. He gave her such a blow on the head with the blade that he took her head completely off, as Herod had done to Saint John.

39. The body remained, truncated and severed in the way that the sword had killed her. The angels took joy over her soul; in joy and laughter they carried it away. All paradise was joyous on account of it and the saints who are seated therein. I speak the truth, so I believe, if I have not been mistaken through forgetfulness, for I have questioned wise men and I have learned this from scholars. I take Saint Denis as my witness.

40. Now you will hear sorrowful news: her blood made a great stream in the earth. The living dared not bury her because the wicked one forbad it by his power. They made her a nest in the earth as the ostrich makes in summer. And then they cried very piously because they could do nothing more fitting. They remained sorrowful and wretched; they had great fear that the evil would return and were in anguish like fugitives.

41. She remained in this sepulcher as long as this affliction lasted. Her flesh smelled good as it aged; no worm made even a scratch in it. On her head the stain of her blood appeared; it was red all around the neck. This madman was dead who harmed God's own. The world recovers naturally: all good returned to its full measure, and the fool suffers in his flames.

42. As the pagans' situation got worse, the Christians' got altogether better. Then Saint Dulcidius took matters into his hands and for God he applied himself in his bishopric. He had the hard marble prepared where the saint would lie securely. He skillfully engraved the cover: there he made an inscription of the martyrdom. Then on a very dark night two monks made an opening in it; they took the body out with great care. They have her, holy and pure, in Conques, and they read this in writing.

43. This place is truly blessed where God brings such a powerful saint, for He makes great miracles through her and most pleasant dispositions and little jests. Gerald, a badly tonsured priest, tore out the eyes of his intimate,[32] Guibert; then, a year after he had lost them, God gave the light back to him through her. If a blind or mute person comes to her, or someone greatly stricken with illness, or if someone is held in prison or in misery because of war, when that person turns to her, be he young or gray-haired, if he has repented of his sins, joy and salvation will always come to him. Now I pray to you, my Lady, that you help me.

44. I want to tell you, before I stop, how God killed these cruel men.[33] They wanted the vain praise of this world; this was their joy and their pleasure. Their work was treachery and fraud; they were worse than you hear here. They destroyed Emmaus Castle and the work of Saint Nicholas.[34] They commanded the ports where the ships were, and on land renown was theirs. Hell took them, which is very deep; they lie there low as beams. Dacian is shut in with them, and King Herod and Archelaus. The blue sulfur smoke torments them.

45. To these sinful men hell and heat are due. But God held them above others on purpose and allowed them to be emperors and placed them as judges of this world, so that they would kill the best men. If He had not given power to the worst men, there would not be such praise for the saints. They sent to Him such flowers whose color is beautiful in heaven. Sweet and pleasant is their odor, and the person who smells it falls in love with it and in that person's body its strength increases.

46. Maximian was a traitor to God and Diocletian was like a lion. They were worse than the other Jews and did worse than the Philistines.[35] The Jebusites were allied with them and the Arabs and the Perrizites. The Armenians held their entire fief from them and the Amazons and the Pygmies, the Hermaphrodites and the Hebrews and the Corbarins and the Amorites. I am very sorrowful that the Maccabees were not in power, because they would have stood in their way.[36]

47. Maximian had a miserly heart and one could not have faith in him. He gave Constantine his daughter in marriage so that he could better ruin him.[37] The latter held Marseille on the sea and was very prudent and courageous. He loved the lady and held her dear, and she could not have loved him more. Then the old man began to think how he could drive them from the kingdom, but this was an evil thing to arrange.

48. He had his son Maximin arm;[38] he told him to go send for his army. People of this sort armed themselves: there came the Danes and the Navarrians, the Negroes and the Moors and the sons of Hagar and those of the tribe of Issachar. There came the men of Kedar and all those from the kingdom of Shalmaneser.[39] Together they began to ride and to agree on their plan to go and destroy Marseille.

49. He sent his letters and couriers, sent for those who held fiefs from him: he sent for the Bulgarians, the Greeks and the Chaldeans, the Marcomanni and the Macrobians. There came the Satyrs with the Idumeans, the English and the Scots with the Canaanites.[40] Saint Maurice led the Thebans to him: these were men whom God loved. The traitorous Jew betrayed him: he killed the saint himself, which is terrible to say.[41] If Judas Maccabaeus had been there, Eleazar or Timothy, or if Samson the Nazarene had been there or Joshua or Zacchaeus the Less, I do not think the game would have been his.

50. There he killed Christians to his heart's content. Sixteen thousand and six hundred died there. You would have seen the field red and bloody! A great many left their youth there. The Rhône swelled with the flowing blood: high was the bank that was not touched by it.

51. Then he set a very treacherous ambush that would let him catch Constantine. The latter recognized his ruse and mixed a similar concoction for him. He ambushed his men immediately, took the old man from them, took him to Marseille before their very eyes, and threw him in prison like a wretch. His daughter gave him treatment such as one must not give one's father: she had him strung up dead in the wind.[42]

52. Diocletian was on the steps of his palace. He was angry and knew not why. Before him a thousand Slavs practiced fencing all around.[43] His heart was swollen, and to this traitor nothing that they did was good. He looked far off: in a field he saw a young man riding. When the latter was before him, Diocletian addressed him. The man did not refuse to tell him all he knew, for he saw that he was angry as a lion:

53. "You have lost the companion for whom the barons esteemed you. In truth, he has been killed in prison by his own daughter's treachery." When Diocletian heard such cruel news, he tore his beard and mustache. His heart burst near his lungs.[44] His soul had need of a guide: behold! they are both with Pharaoh and are bound like thieves. Their guards are very evil dragons; every day they burn them like a firebrand. Their names are not fitting for a song, except in a pimp's tale, for they were traitors and criminals.

54. He is a fool who strives so greatly to make his lineage nobler through evil deeds. To these men's sons God gave this fate: few were the days that they did not attack each other.[45] In Rome a crow announced that the two of them would fight a great battle. The combat was joined on a footbridge.[46] Hauberks were of no use there, no matter how strong the mail, nor laced helmets nor any other armor.

55. He who was struck through the visor lost all his blood through his neckpiece. Behold the two kings, dead on the straw, each wrapped in a sheet. God burned this line like the fire does a torch; you will never see even their remains. And if they are dead, may it be of no concern to you, for I do not value it at a farthing! I have had enough of singing about them.

Notes

Introduction

1. For an introduction to manuscripts containing hagiographic materials, see Philippart, *Les légendiers latins*.

2. Head, *Hagiography and the Cult of Saints*, 14. For an introduction to hagiography, see Aigrain or Wilson.

3. See my essay, "The Saints in Medieval Culture," for a more detailed discussion of trends in the study of hagiography, which concludes that "the saints were active participants in virtually every aspect of medieval life, both public and private. The study of the saints seems to have moved from the notion that hagiographic materials deserve little attention because they are repetitive and boring to a situation in which the same materials are seen from an exhilarating variety of perspectives" (26).

4. For an overview, see Brown, *Cult of the Saints*.

5. For a detailed examination of this process, see Bisbee, *Pre-Decian Acts*.

6. For an excellent introduction to the medieval understanding of miracles, see Ward, *Miracles and the Medieval Mind*.

7. During the Middle Ages and until the French Revolution, the province in which Conques is located was called Rouergue. When France was reorganized into departments, the same geographical entity was renamed Aveyron. It is sometimes still called Rouergue with reference to traditional or historical features. For the history of this region, see Enjalbert and Cholvy, *Histoire du Rouergue*.

8. For a discussion of fragments of a Crucifixion in repoussé that may date to the Merovingian period, see Dominique Taralon, "*Le reliquaire*". For the Latin text of the chronicle see *Chronicon monasterii Conchensis*. Amy Remensnyder's *Remembrance of Kings Past* (forthcoming from Cornell University Press) evaluates this and other foundation stories of medieval monasteries in southern France.

9. For general background on the Carolingians, see Riché, *The Carolingians*.

10. Book 1, lines 224–301, of *In honorem Hludowici Pii*, edited by Edmond Faral in *Ermold le Noir*. For discussion of Ermoldus and interpretation of the poem see Godman, *Poets and Emperors*, and Godman, "Louis 'the Pious.'"

11. On Pippin I see Collins, "Pippin I"; on his gifts to Conques and their import, see esp. p. 370.

12. Beginning in the late eleventh century, the monks copied their charters, the originals of which were lost during the Revolution, into one large manuscript, which is in the collection of the Société des Lettres, Sciences et Arts de l'Aveyron. I am grateful to the archivist, M. Pierre Lançon, for allowing Kathleen Ashley and me to examine it. For an edition of the *Cartulary* see Desjardins, *Cartulaire*, and for

interpretation, analysis, and corrections to Desjardins, see the various writings of Gournay.

13. For a thorough analysis of this document, see Wolff, "Notes sur le faux diplome de 755."

14. Jean-Claude Fau suggests an alternate scenario for the acquisition of Foy's relics. Pointing out that Viking raids up the Garonne River were frequent in the years around 866, he surmises that the relics of Foy may have been taken to Conques deliberately for safe-keeping (*Rouergue roman*, 86). On relic thefts in general, see Geary, *Furta Sacra*.

15. See Boehm, *Medieval Head Reliquaries*; Hubert and Hubert, "Piété chrétienne;" Solt, *The Cult of Saints*; and Solt, "Romanesque French Reliquaries."

16. Future citations to specific chapters in the *Book of Sainte Foy's Miracles* will be in the form 1.1, etc.

17. See Vielliard, 48–50. A new edition of the *Pilgrim's Guide* is in press; see Gerson, et al, *The Pilgrim's Guide*.

18. See Duby, "The Origins of Knighthood," in *The Chivalrous Society*, 158–70.

19. See Bonnassie, "Les forteresses."

20. Paxton, 31. This essay offers an excellent overview of scholarship on the Peace. Duby's essay is available in English in *The Chivalrous Society*.

21. On this term see Hubert and Hubert, "Piété chrétienne," 253.

22. Camille, *Gothic Idol*, 223. On this point see also Belting, *Likeness and Presence*.

23. See Kendall, "The Voice in the Stone," for a summary of various opinions regarding the date of the tympanum and for his own argument in favor of completion by the early date of 1110–1115.

24. The tympanum makes an especially strong impression because of its size (6.73 m wide by 3.63 m high), its relative closeness to the ground, the depth of the carving, and its strikingly good state of preservation.

25. See Quentin, *Les martyrologues*, 261–62, 483.

26. Saltet, "Étude critique."

27. See Mandach, "Contribution" and "Le rôle." Mandach's analysis of the *Passio* is part of a larger argument that a medieval text was often polyvalent, that is, intended to be used in a variety of ways.

28. On preaching in the vernacular in this period see Töpfer, "The Cult of Relics," 53.

29. Hubert and Hubert, "Piété chrétienne," 265 (my translation).

30. Sigal, *L'homme*, 14.

31. Sigal, "Histoire," 244.

32. For an excellent introduction to Bernard of Angers, which focuses on Bernard's "position on oral and written culture," see Stock, *Implications of Literacy*, 64–72.

33. Remensnyder, diss., 355.

34. MacKinney notes that "former students at Chartres rhapsodized over bygone days at 'the Academy of Chartres' under their 'Socrates,' Master Fulbert" (*Bishop Fulbert*, 23), but stresses the lack of evidence to substantiate Fulbert's role in formal instruction and comments, "It is constantly necessary to stress the fact that

the dominant purpose of Fulbert and his school was not the advancement of the liberal arts, but the training of young clergymen in orthodoxy and morality" (24). Richard Southern emphasizes, however, that Fulbert "was able, by his sensitivity to what was going on round him, by his encouragement, and his genius for drawing men to him, to make the school of Chartres the most vigorous in Europe" (*Making of the Middle Ages*, 197). On the later school of Chartres see Southern's essays, "Platonism" and "Humanism."

35. For a recent study devoted to Hubert, see Fanning, *Bishop*.

36. Head, *Hagiography*, 18.

37. Remensnyder, diss., 355.

38. Gournay, *Étude*, 398.

39. For a discussion of the translation of Sainte Foy's relics in the context of relic thefts in general, which were rather common in the high Middle Ages, see Geary's *Furta Sacra*.

40. The only manuscript preserving this text does not give it a title. The French philologists who edited the poem assigned it a French title, *Chanson de Sainte Foy*, rather than one in Provençal, and it is by this French title that the *Song* is conventionally known. In the original the saint is called "Fides." For a thorough study of the *Song*, see Zaal, *"A lei francesca"*.

41. For a later vernacular version of Sainte Foy's *Passio*, see "The Life of Saint Faith" in Cazelles, "The Lady as Saint," 182–203. Cazelles translates into English a portion of an Anglo-Norman French poem about Foy written by Simon of Walsingham between 1211 and 1216.

42. Durliat, *La sculpture*, 44–79.

43. Dunn, *Gallican Saint's Life*, 145.

44. The only manuscripts discussed here are those containing miracles of Sainte Foy that are translated in this book. Other manuscripts include only her *Passio*, or one or more of her miracles, but they are too numerous to be described in this book.

45. Gournay, *Étude*, 398.

46. Their contents were published by Bouillet in "Un manuscrit inconnu."

47. Lemaître, "Notes sur les manuscrits," 268.

48. Gournay, *Étude*, 398.

Passio

1. October 6 is Sainte Foy's feast day.

2. There is no historical documentation of Caprais other that the *Passio* itself. By the twelfth century local tradition was calling him the first bishop of Agen. This legend may have been constructed to aid the canons of the church of Saint Caprais in a struggle with the bishop and cathedral chapter in Agen. See Wands, *Romanesque Architecture*, 15.

3. There is some scholarly agreement that there was a historical person named Fides who was martyred in Agen, but probably in the third century rather than the early fourth, as the texts generated by her cult insist (Benedictines of Paris,

"Sainte Foy," 146). At the time Agen was a wealthy Gallo-Roman city that boasted an amphitheater, among other public buildings. Located on the Garonne River, Agen was on the route between Rome and Bordeaux, an important administrative center to which it was connected by a major Roman road.

4. The text in the oldest manuscript, the one in Montpellier, does not name the prefect, saying instead that the author was unable to learn his name. The Benedictines of Paris (146–47) suggest that this indicates a considerable gap between the events and this text. A number of Spanish martyrdoms, most notably that of Saint Vincent of Saragossa in the early fourth century, were attributed to Dacian, who is not otherwise documented. The naming of Dacian in the Paris manuscript (lat. 5301) is the only mention north of the Pyrenees and was undoubtedly influenced by the Passions of Spanish martyrs (see Gaiffier, "Sub Daciano Praeside," 396).

5. The words here are *lectum hereum*, but other versions of the *Passio* use the term *craticula*, identified by Gillian Mackie as "a wheeled grill on which meat could be cooked, but which in the context of martyrdom was prepared as an instrument of torture and, perhaps, death" ("New Light on the So-Called Saint Lawrence Panel," 55). For an illustration of a *craticula* see the mosaic in the mausoleum of Galla Placidia, Ravenna, of a male martyr usually called Saint Lawrence but identified by Mackie as Saint Vincent of Saragossa.

6. Later versions add other people who were moved to follow the examples of Foy and Caprais; among them were two brothers, Prime and Felician, and a group known collectively as the Holy Innocents. A very late addition to the number of these martyrs was a supposed sister of Foy called Alberta.

7. Some scholars conclude that this version of the *Passio* was composed before Foy's relics were moved to Conques, since later versions omit praise of Agen.

8. This concluding passage appears to be in the wrong place.

9. According to Wands (*Romanesque Architecture*, 16), a local tradition holds that "the bodies of Foy and Caprais were thrown into a pit or swamp on the outskirts of the city where the chapel known as 'le Martrou' now stands."

10. Wands suggests that "Dulcidius was bishop in the first half of the sixth century, with his episcopacy ending before 549" (*Romanesque Architecture*, 18).

11. Caprais's relics were also transferred to a separate church built in his honor. On these churches see Wands.

Letter and Book One

1. *Scolastico*. In discussing the use of this word in this text and in Angers, Fanning comments, "the meaning of *scholasticus* here seems to be only the general term 'schoolman' or teacher" (*A Bishop and His World*, 70).

2. Bernard's gift to Fulbert is his collection of Foy's miracles. He wrote this letter to introduce and justify his project.

3. For Fulbert's letters and poems see Behrends, *Letters and Poems*; for discussions of the School of Chartres see MacKinney, *Bishop Fulbert*, and the various publications of Richard Southern.

4. Hubert, bishop of Angers from 1006–1047, founded the school at the Cathedral of Saint Maurice that later became the University of Angers. Fanning calls this act "the most important innovation concerning the cathedral carried out by Hubert during his episcopacy. . . . The foundation of such schools in the west of France was common during the later tenth and eleventh centuries. This development, in which Bishop Fulbert of Chartres played a major role, was shared by Angers" (*Bishop*, 69).

The date of Bernard's arrival in Angers was probably 1010 (see Remensnyder, diss., 355); Fanning's date of 1012 (69) is not consistent with the evidence in the *Book of Miracles*.

5. Literally, "not only sense for sense, but even word for word." As Thomas Head points out, Bernard "neatly reversed a common *topos*" (*Hagiography*, 73) for the act of translation, described as "not word for word, but sense for sense" (83).

6. Most scholars agree that this miracle must have taken place about 983. For another translation of 1.1, see Geary, *Readings*, 346–50.

7. *Pagus*, the local unit of Carolingian administration.

8. The cartulary (no. 215) names a Gerald who was priest of Castailhac and made a donation to the monastery at about the end of the tenth century. Gournay (*Étude*, 247) suggests that he is the person discussed in this story and that his donation may have been an act of penance.

9. Gerald had stood as Guibert's sponsor at his confirmation, an act which created a bond of spiritual kinship between them, that of godparent and godson. See Lynch, "*Spiritale Vinculum*," 181–204, esp. 194–95.

10. The word *romeus* derives from the local dialect word *roumieu*, which developed to describe pilgrims to Rome and was then extended to become a general term for pilgrim.

11. This is a typical example of the antisemitism that became pervasive in medieval Europe in the high Middle Ages; see Moore, *Persecuting Society*.

12. The implication is that Gerald had a wife or mistress whom he suspected Guibert of "debauching." It was not unusual at this time for a priest to be married or to keep a mistress, though a reform movement aimed at this practice was launched by the mid-eleventh century; see Brundage, *Law, Sex, and Christian Society*.

13. 1 Kings 17: 6.

14. Claire Wheeler Solt suggests that Guibert's vision corresponds to the state of the reliquary-statue at that time, that is, that it "probably had a painted wooden head at this time as do all known Auvergnese madonna reliquaries, some of which were reveted with metal except for the hands and face" (Solt, diss., 51–52). As Solt points out, the statue was renovated during Guibert's lifetime and could have received its present head of gold during that renovation.

15. Present-day Espeyrac, about fifteen kilometers west of Conques.

16. The solidus (sol) or silver penny was the basic coin of medieval Europe; the term denarius (denier) refers to the amount of silver in a coin but was also used, as here, interchangeably with solidus. An obolus (obol) is half a solidus.

17. In Hildegard of Bingen's understanding, there was a physical connection between immoderate sexual pleasure and blindness. In her *Causae et curae*, "Hildegard warned that those who discharge their seed in lust risk blindness, whereas

those who do so moderately will not be harmed, and she later gives a recipe to cure men and women whose inordinate libido has led to eye trouble" (Cadden, *Meanings of Sex Difference*, 87).

18. Sigal (*L'homme*, 76) describes a similar miracle performed by Saint Benedict. A paralytic peasant was cured by Benedict, but suffered a recurrence of his ailment every time he succumbed to the sin of fornication.

19. John 14: 12–13.

20. Located northwest of Conques and now known as Le Monastier, this castle complex included a church and a monastery founded by Saint Calmilius. By the late eleventh century the monastery owned a bust-reliquary of its second abbot, Saint Chaffre (Théofrède), martyred in 732. On the bust-reliquary, see Boehm, *Medieval Head Reliquaries*, 231–39.

21. Pons was count of Gevaudun in the late tenth century; thus Gerbert was acquainted with a member of one of the noble families dominant in the region.

22. Ps. 35: 7 (36: 6).

23. Ps. 146: 9 (147: 9).

24. The cartulary of Conques (no. 40) mentions a man named Bonus-filius who made a donation to the monastery at Conques at the end of the tenth century.

25. According to 1.23, Gerald was a vassal of Raymond II, count of Rouergue.

26. Sigal (*L'homme*, 96–97) notes that there are numerous examples in the eleventh and twelfth centuries of the vow of a candle the length of the body, of a part of the body, or of an animal and that early examples can be found in the writings of Gregory of Tours.

27. A *vicinia* (region) is a subdivision of a *pagus* (district).

28. Matt. 10: 33.

29. Luke 9: 26.

30. Bergand is named in documents dated 958 (no. 292) and 964 (no. 434) in the cartulary of Conques.

31. Aubin is about fifteen kilometers southwest of Conques.

32. The *Psychomachia*, an allegorical poem describing a battle between personified Virtues and Vices, was written at the end of the fourth century by the Christian Roman poet Prudentius. It was standard reading for Benedictine monks, who were required by the Benedictine Rule to read at least one book each year.

33. For a discussion of this miracle story in relation to a representation on the Conques tympanum of a *miles* falling from his horse into hell, see Little, "Pride Goes Before Avarice." Little sees pride as "the characteristic sin of the feudal and hierarchic age, when property was for the most part not liquid and power was not yet predominantly associated with money" (16).

34. The castle of Cassagnes (comm. Goutrens) is mentioned in the cartulary of Conques (nos. 14 and 15).

35. Molières (comm. Escandolières) is mentioned in nos. 125 and 257 of the cartulary of Conques.

36. *Benedictus*, his name in Latin, means "blessed of God."

37. This section is composed in hexameters.

38. Bonnassie, "Forteresses," 21, assumes that these steps were cut in the face of the rock on which the castle was built.

39. In the Sélestat manuscript, these lines are in fact written as verse.

40. This is Le Puy en Velay.

41. See John 8: 47.

42. Ps. 15: 9.

43. Bernard refers to Silvester I, pope from 314–335, whose legend credits him with the resurrection of an ox.

44. Gerbert taught in the monastic school at Reims. He had a theoretical knowledge of medicine and knew some ancient medical treatises. See MacKinney, *Bishop Fulbert*. I have not found further information on Berengar or Azolin.

45. Ps. 134 (135): 6.

46. This is the Guy of 1.2, who had been responsible for blinding Gerbert.

47. Ps. 33: 22 (34: 21).

48. The Latin word is *Saliencium*.

49. See Ps. 34 (35): 8.

50. This diatribe is apparently directed at the violence against which the Church launched the Peace of God movement; see Head and Landes, *Peace of God*. For another translation of this chapter, see Geary, *Readings*, 350–51.

51. Castelnau-Bretenoux Castle is on the northern border of Quercy.

52. Alos is also described as a farm (*mediam curtem de Alans*) in the cartulary of Conques (no. 480). The same document confirms the donation of Alos (Alans) to the abbey of Conques in the tenth century by a woman named Deda, presumably the same person as the Doda mentioned here.

53. Penne Castle, today in ruins, was built on high rocks above the left bank of the Aveyron River, in Tarn.

54. Raymond I, Count of Rouergue, died in 961. In his will of that date he made important donations to the monastery at Conques. Bernard claims that he was murdered while on pilgrimage to Santiago de Compostela. He and his wife, Countess Berthe (mentioned in 1.28), were the parents of Raymond II, Count of Rouergue, who fought against the Muslims in Spain in 985. Raymond II, who died in about 1008, is also mentioned in 1.23 and 2.5. On the history of the counts of Rouergue in this period see Bousquet, *Le Rouergue*, and Lewis, *Development*.

55. This donation is documented in the cartulary (no. 17) and was made between 998 and 1010. For an analysis of the events recounted in this chapter, see Dunbabin, *France in the Making*, 226–27, who says that Pallas was in Narbonne. Gournay, however, locates Pallas, which is no longer extant, a little further north, between the towns of Mèze and Loupian, on the bank of a lake named Thau. Pallas is also the locale of 3.20 and 3.21.

56. Several documents in the cartulary dated 1012 (nos. 102, 160, 178, etc.) refer to Airad as abbot; Gournay suggests that the events in this chapter took place in 1013.

57. If this is the same procession that is the subject of 2.4 and 3.20, then the reliquary-statue was also part of the procession.

58. The person sitting in judgment, though named Bernard, is surely not Bernard the Hairy.

59. *Tartareae furiae*. The Furies are the goddesses of vengeance in Greek and Roman mythology. Bernard associates them with Tartarus, or hell.

60. This passage is written in hexameters.

61. Bernard indulges here in the rhetorical device called "ubi sunt" (where are they now?).

62. According to Russell (*The Devil*, 248–49), Zabulon (from *diabolos*) was used as a name for the devil. The reference here would then be to Lucifer's usurpation of God's throne and the subsequent fall of the rebel angels to become the devils of hell.

63. Though Bernard doesn't name the place, it must have been Aurillac, which is about 57 kilometers north of Conques. The golden statue of Saint Gerald had only been made recently when Bernard wrote. It was made in the time of Abbot Adrald, whose abbacy began after the death of Gerbert of Aurillac, that is, after 1003. It does not survive. For another translation of this chapter, see Geary, *Readings*, 351–52.

64. Bernier or *Bernerius* had become master of the School of Angers by 1025 (Fanning, *Bishop*, 70).

65. The use of the word *scholasticus* may imply that Bernier is a teacher in Bernard's school at Angers.

66. The cartulary (no. 244) indicates that Adalgerius was dean under Abbot Airad. Charters of 1019 show that by then he had become abbot, and the chronicle of Conques claims that he ruled over both Conques and Figeac. He is also mentioned in 1.34.

67. Hubert and Hubert ("Piété chrétienne") note that this is the oldest attested usage of the word *majestas* to refer to a reliquary-statue.

68. In his note to this passage, Bouillet (*Liber miraculorum*, 52) identifies this Bernard as a son of an Aquitainean nobleman named Hugh. Bernard studied at Fleury, became abbot of Solignac before 979 and abbot of Beaulieu in the Limousin about 984. It appears that, under the name Bernard II, he became bishop of Cahors in 1005.

69. According to Bouillet (*Liber miraculorum*, 56), William Taillefer, Count of Toulouse, had taken Arsindè as his first wife about 975. The same story, but giving the countess's name as Delfonsa, was told in rhymed verse in the local dialect. The poem, dated variously to the eleventh and the thirteenth century, is edited and translated into French in Cantalausa, *La Chanson de Sainte Foy*.

70. Dunbabin (*France in the Making*, 105) uses this miracle as an example of the need of noble marriages for heirs: "The benefits of marriage, however great, could not be stabilized unless heirs were born. At this, tenth-century West Frankish aristocrats were not notably successful. The Flemish counts managed to keep the succession going by the skin of their teeth; and Richard the Justiciar was the only Burgundian duke of the century to produce a male heir. It was much the same in the south. One of the first miracles attributed to St Foy of Conques was that she helped the wife of count William III of Toulouse to conceive, in return for the gift of golden bracelets. In this case, the saint made doubly sure by allowing Arsinde two sons."

71. Austrin of Conques, who is mentioned in this miracle, also appears in the cartulary (nos. 23, 32, 33, 365, 366) in documents that allow the events described here to be dated shortly before 1013. Austrin and Avierne, his wife, were generous benefactors of the abbey according to the cartulary, which also mentions four of their children. Avierne appears as well in 4.21.

72. *Incolae loci*. Elsewhere in Bernard's writing *locus* appears to refer specifically to the monastery, but it is not clear here whether he means that the people who refer to some of Sainte Foy's miracles as *joca* are only the peasants or all the people who lived in that place, monks included.

73. See 1.4. Gerald lived at Vialarels, near present-day Decazeville.

74. This would be Raymond II, count of Rouergue from 961–1008; see 1.12.

75. The monastery undoubtedly collected beeswax as rent from its tenants and sold the wax to pilgrims in the form of candles they could offer to the saint.

76. This story is cited by Barral y Altet ("Définition," 406–7), among other scholars, as evidence that there was a metalworking shop at Conques. It is likely that a number of the objects still in the treasury at Conques were made in this workshop.

77. Gimon is named in documents in the cartulary dated from 930 (no. 291) to 959 (no. 405).

78. Matt. 7: 21.

79. Mercurius of Caesarea, a Roman soldier, was beheaded at the order of the Emperor Decius because he was a Christian. "According to the Eastern legend, one hundred and thirteen years later St Basil invoked the aid of St Mercurius against Julian the Apostate, and he was made the instrument of divine wrath. For Mercurius appeared from the heavens, girded with a sword and brandishing a spear, with which he transfixed and killed the infidel emperor" (Thurston and Attwater, *Butler's Lives*, 4: 421).

80. Bernard refers sarcastically to David's slaughter of the giant Goliath, for which David was rewarded, not punished.

81. Belial appears in the Hebrew Bible as a name for the Devil. For the derivation and uses of the term, see Russell, *The Devil*, 188.

82. Sigal (*L'homme*, 274) offers a natural explanation. Since the candle was kept near the statue, its heat would cause the metal to expand. After the candle went out the metal would make a sound as it cooled. Remensnyder (diss., 374, n. 147) cites other miracles in which a candle in front of relics or an altar relights itself, but notes that in none of these is the saint viewed as playing or joking.

83. Ps. 4: 5.

84. Lauranson-Rosaz notes, "Bishop Arnaud, the organizer of this synod, was mentioned in 1025–31, but he probably succeeded Deusdet [the previous bishop] (latest mention 1004) considerably earlier" ("Auvergnat Origins," 127). Bernard must have been writing this chapter in about 1012. For another translation, see Geary, *Readings*, 352–53.

85. For a discussion of the image reliquaries see Boehm, *Medieval Head Reliquaries*; see also Solt, "Romanesque French Reliquaries."

86. This plain is to the north of Rodez, that is, on the side closest to Conques, and at the foot of the high outcropping on which Rodez is built.

87. The Latin terms are *maiestas* (majesty) and *capsa* (reliquary box). Saint Marius was a bishop of Clermont; his majesty was brought from the abbey of Vabres near Rodez; the majesty of Saint Amantius (Amans), an early Christian bishop of Rodez, was brought from his monastery there; Saint Saturninus, known in French as Sernin, was the founding bishop of Toulouse.

88. Bertha was the wife of Raymond I, count of Rouergue, and the mother of Raymond II; see also 2.5.

89. For another translation of this chapter see Document 5 (pp. 331–2) in Appendix A of Head and Landes, *The Peace of God*. A note there indicating that Foy's relics were stolen from the monastery of Figeac is incorrect.

90. Since Bernard heard this story in 1013, it must have taken place in about 1008.

91. A similar use was made of the votive chains that accumulated at Vézelay.

92. The dedication to Saint Peter was apparently carried over to the Romanesque church that replaced the one Bernard is describing; three capitals in the south crossing are carved in relief with scenes from the life of Saint Peter.

93. According to Bouillet and Servières (*Sainte Foy*, 493), Broussadel is a simple farmstead in the commune of Saint-Georges in the Cantal. The name Aimon was the hereditary name of its owners for three centuries and occurs in documents as early as 1025.

94. Castelpers is in southern Aveyron. The castle was on a rocky escarpment overlooking the confluence of two rivers, the Céor and the Giffou.

95. Judg. 20.

96. Greek legend gives the name Sardanapalus to the last of the Assyrian kings (who lived in the seventh century B.C.E.) and describes him as especially effeminate, which would explain Bernard's reference to his feather bed. Actually the last Assyrian king, Assurbanipal, was especially fierce.

97. Ps. 112 (113): 4.

98. Adalgerius is also mentioned in 1.13.

99. The *Life of Martin of Tours*, written by Sulpicius Severus in the 390s, was one of the most frequently read works of hagiography in Middle Ages.

100. For a discussion of the northern elite whom Bernard cites as his friends and patrons in this chapter, see Remensnyder, "Un problème," 355.

101. Hubert of Vendôme was bishop of Angers from 1010 to 1047. Here Bernard refers to him as *juvenis*, which usually is translated "youth" or "young man." Bernard is writing some years after Hubert's consecration in 1006, so the use of this word might seem incorrect. With reference to this passage Fanning comments, "This is not a precise word, for in the twelfth century, a *juvenis* was an adult and could be used to describe a soldier until he was married and sometimes even beyond. In the thirteenth century, it could refer to the time of a man's life between the ages of twenty and forty. Its usage in the eleventh century is not known so well, but it could be consistent with the later evidence" (*Bishop*, 17). He assumes that Hubert was born ca. 980–985.

102. Bouillet (*Liber miraculorum*, 87) says that Gauther is mentioned as bishop of Rennes between 1014 and 1030.

Book Two

1. Gournay points out that this may be the first occurrence of the word translated here as "townsman" (*quidam burgensis illius ville*): "Il se peut donc que la

toute première mention d'un bourgeois en Occident ait désigné un habitant de Conques" (*Étude*, 212).

2. This description gives valuable information about the tenth-century church, which must have had a bell tower at the western entrance. Above the entrance was a vaulted chapel dedicated to Saint Michael, and above that the gallery with the bellropes.

3. Luna was at the south edge of Liguria, a province on the northwest coast of Italy centered on Genoa.

4. Córdoba had been conquered in 711 during the Arab invasion of Spain; after 756 it was the capital of the western caliphate. The Berbers are inhabitants of North Africa and the Saracens are Muslims.

5. This is Count Sancho García of Castile, who was fighting on the side of the imam Sulaymān ibn al-Hakam against another pretender to the caliphate whose followers were called Alabites. This battle took place in 1009.

6. Lethe, which means oblivion in Greek, is the name of a figure in Greek mythology as well as of a river in the underworld whose waters erase human memory.

7. The story of Raymond's long absence, adventures, disguised return, and recognition would appear to owe something to the *Odyssey*.

8. This must refer to Adalgerius; see 1.13.

9. This golden reliquary was probably a lidded box or châsse. Its contents were most likely to have been Sainte Foy's bones, though some scholars have argued that it contained relics of Christ, reported by the chronicle of Conques as belonging to the monastery. The identity of the Charles the Great (*Karolus magnus*) said to have been the donor is also in question. Some favor Charlemagne, others Charles the Bald. For a thorough discussion of the question of Conques' possession of relics of Christ, see Remensnyder, *Remembrance of Kings Past*.

10. Richard Landes assumes that this was Psalm 150, "Praise the Lord with harp and timbrel," which would certainly have been appropriate (Landes, "Popular Participation," 196).

11. On this kind of ritual activity see Ashley and Sheingorn, "An Unsentimental View."

12. The cartulary contains numerous documents written by monks of the abbey who presumably learned their skills at the monastic school.

13. Luke 13: 11–13.

14. John 5.

15. Ps. 40: 4 (41: 3).

16. The history of the abbey is somewhat confused in this period. Apparently for much of the tenth century and into the eleventh one person held titles of both bishop of Clermont and abbot of Conques and appointed another person to live in the monastery and administer its property. Bego appears to have been one of the bishop-abbots, with his nephews serving under him as administrators of the abbey. The events described here seem to have taken place in the early eleventh century. Some interpreters suggest that this bishop and his nephews may be recognized on the tympanum of the abbey church as the three monks roped together next to a bishop or abbot kneeling in front of a demon.

17. Gourdon is northeast of Conques, on the border between Quercy and Périgord. The town is built on a terraced hillside at the top of which this castle once stood.

18. Since Raymond II died about 1008, mention of his approaching death would seem to place this story somewhat before that date. There is a similar story in the posthumous miracles of Saint Benedict. When Count Odo of Orléans intended to allow his army to pillage property belonging to the monastery of Fleury, Benedict appeared to a monk in a dream and promised to protect the monastery if the monks would pledge to follow his Rule. Soon after, Odo died. For a discussion of this miracle see Head, *Hagiography*, 12.

19. *Remeos*; see 1.1 and note there.

20. According to Bonnassie, "Forteresses," 20, the term *fines castelli* here means the boundaries of the territory over which the holder of the castle held sway.

21. William V, or the Great, count of Poitou and duke of Aquitaine from 990 to 1030, was a close friend of Fulbert of Chartres, Bernard's teacher.

22. Beatrice was the daughter of Richard I, duke of Normandy and her brother was Richard II, called the Good, also duke of Normandy.

23. In late Roman times the "indiction" referred to assessments of goods required to support the army. A cycle of indiction was a fifteen-year period and the numbering of the indiction was used to date the financial year.

24. This statement would place these events in 1020.

25. *Romeos*; see 1.1 and note there.

26. Ps. 139: 6 (140: 5); Ps. 7: 17 (7: 16); Isa. 51: 17.

27. Raymond II died in about 1008 (see 2.4) and Bernard collected this miracle in 1020, so the event recorded here happened sometime between those dates.

28. See 1.22.

29. Conques is thirty-nine kilometers from Rodez, the seat of the count of Rouergue.

30. The servants (*servitori*) of the monks mentioned in this chapter are presumably lay servants who lived in or near the monastery.

31. See 1.28.

32. For an analysis of this chapter, see Ashley and Sheingorn, "An Unsentimental View"; Töpfer, "The Cult of Relics."

33. See 1.26.

34. Ps. 50: 19, 21 (51: 17, 19).

35. Bernard's brother may have been the Robert who became abbot of Cormery in the Touraine in 1047.

36. 1020.

Book Three

1. In spite of this claim, scholars do not assign the rewriting of the *Passio* to the author of Book Three of the *Book of Miracles*.

2. "*omnium virtutum liber.*" The word *virtus, virtutis* means both power and

miracle. I have translated it here as "power" to account for the inclusion of the Passion.

3. This couple can be identified as Roger I de Tosny and his wife Godehilde. Godehilde bore Roger several children and later married the Count of Evreux. Bouillet (*Liber miraculorum*, 129) quotes a charter from Conches in which she describes herself as follows: "I, Godehilde, Countess of Evreux, formerly wife of Roger de Tosny." Roger went to Spain in 1034 to aid the King of Aragon, Sancho the Great; he apparently made a pilgrimage to Conques then. The church Goteline built for Sainte Foy was in Conches-en-Ouche; the present church there was built in the fifteenth century. On the Tosnys, see Musset, "Aux origines."

4. This must be Richard II, duke of Normandy from 996 to 1026.

5. The term used here, *propiciatorium*, is used in the Vulgate Old Testament to refer to the place above the altar in the Temple where God is present. It is often translated into English as "mercy-seat." Since at Conques the reliquary-statue of Sainte Foy stood above the high altar, the use of this term here compares Sainte Foy's presence in the form of her relics with God's presence in the Temple. The author of Book Three of the *Book of Miracles* uses this word several times.

6. Roger was killed in a feud about 1040.

7. Saut-du-Sabot or Saut de Sabo; in this place there is a high falls in one of the branches that flow together to form the Tarn River.

8. Saint Salvius lived in the sixth century. The primary source for his life is Gregory of Tours's *History of the Franks*.

9. This castle, which does not survive, was in the far southern part of Auvergne, near Chaudes-Aigues.

10. This is probably the Bernard Feval de Vallelas who appears in a document in the cartulary (no. 441) dated about 1020–1030, according to Gournay, *Documents*, 175.

11. This is an Arab dinar. Such coins apparently reached Auvergne from Islamic Spain via Christian Catalonia.

12. Siger was lord of the castle at Conques. His hostility toward the monastery, and his subsequent ruin, are related in 3.17. He is surely the same man who appears in several documents in the cartulary with dates in the 960s. The castle seems to have been located on a rocky outcropping in the village of Conques above the place where the rivers Ouche and Dourdou flow together. There are still some ruins there, as well as a chapel, now abandoned, that was once the castle chapel dedicated to Notre-Dame, later the chapel of Saint Roch, and more recently that of Notre-Dame de la Salette.

13. Bonnassie, "Forteresses," 18, 20 states that in this text the word *oppidum* used here means castle.

14. Gen. 40.

15. According to Bouillet (*Liber miraculorum*, 136), Belfort was about nine kilometers west of Conques. It is also mentioned in 4.16.

16. This castle, which was in southern Auvergne southeast of St.-Flour, no longer exists.

17. Girbert was internal abbot between 996 and 1004; these were among the years when Bego was external abbot; see 2.5.

18. See 3.1.

19. This word refers to a man who lives twice (*bis vir existens*) because he was resurrected from the dead. According to Bouillet and Servières (*Sainte Foy*, 536) this is the name Romans called Hippolytus after he was returned to life; it was also used for Lazarus.

20. 4 Kings 4: 8–37 (2 Chron. 4: 8–37).

21. Gournay, *Documents*, 35, suggests that the usage "our Romans" indicates the monk's knowledge of and identification with classical culture—"humaniste avant la lettre." Due to his education at Chartres, Bernard of Angers, the author of Books 1 and 2, would have had such knowledge. Apparently some of the monks at Conques were also well educated.

22. Montagrier lies about 25 kilometers northwest of Périgueux. The castle, now gone, overlooked the valley of the Dronne, which is a tributary of the Isle.

23. No. 394 in the cartulary, dated around 1019, also refers to this castle (*castellum de Aurosa*).

24. The writer takes this story from Gregory the Great's *Dialogues* 1.10.

25. Ps. 35 (36): 7.

26. Miremont is about 25 kilometers northwest of Clermont-Ferrand. The lords of Miremont made significant gifts to the monastery of Sainte Foy at Conques in the eleventh and twelfth centuries.

27. Today called Entraygues-sur-Truyère, this town is located at the confluence of the Lot and the Truyère rivers.

28. The Latin, "quod vestrae fraternitati in promptu est," suggests that this text is addressed to a monastic community to which the writer does not belong, but there is no further evidence as to the identity of either writer or intended audience.

29. North of Conques is an area called Cantal where there was an active volcano in prehistoric times. Lava flows formed level areas where the soil was enriched as the lava decomposed. The plateau referred to here is one of these areas.

30. Pierrefiche, which is in Cantal, is mentioned in no. 307 of the cartulary.

31. This is Belmont-Sainte-Foi in Lot, equally distant from Montauban, Cahors and Villefranche-de-Rouergue; it is also mentioned in C.4.

32. According to the cartulary (no. 548), La Fargue was a dependency of the church at Belmont.

33. It seems reasonable to assume that Reinfroi's fifty horsemen were cured as well, but the text does not say so.

34. This must have been the court of William Taillefer, count of Toulouse.

35. See note to 3.7.

36. If the events of this chapter took place at about the time of the preceding chapter, that would be 996–1004.

37. Now in ruins, this castle was about 20 kilometers southeast of Conques. In this period it belonged to the counts of Rouergue.

38. *Propiciatorium*; see 3.1.

39. Vergil, *Aeneid* 2.354. See also 3.16.

40. "The *balista* . . . was a kind of large crossbow. Its operation depended on the tension created by drawing back a string, exactly as a bow is drawn. . . . Such machines could also be operated by making springs out of twisted ropes, creating

force by torsion, as had been done in antiquity. *Balistas* were commonly used to shoot arrow-like missiles or bolts." (Bradbury, *Medieval Siege*, 250).

41. Orcus was lord of the underworld in Latin mythology. He appears in Vergil's *Aeneid*, a text that the author of Book Three quotes elsewhere; see 3.15.

42. This castle and its inhabitants are also mentioned in 3.4.

43. Prov. 18: 2.

44. Ps. 36 (37): 28.

45. The Latin is "elephantino morbo ulcerosa pena dampnatur crudelissima."

46. Literally, "joined himself to her in marriage" (*in matrimonium sibi copulavit*), but the implication is cohabitation rather than a formal marriage ceremony.

47. Sigal, *L'homme*, 47–48, notes that relics were seldom sent to battle because of the danger of loss or damage. He cites other examples in which standards were employed instead and comments: "Ces étendards de saints étaient évidemment chargés d'une valeur symbolique: marcher sous la bannière du saint, c'était être conduit par la saint lui-même, mais il semble que l'étendard était considéré pratiquement comme une relique."

48. The sheepskin ought to be treated with reverence because the garment is a symbol of pilgrimage.

49. In this chapter the narrator returns to miracles worked during the procession to Pallas that probably took place in 1013 and is described by Bernard of Angers in 1.12. Bernard referred to these miracles in 2.4. 3.21 also takes place at Pallas.

50. The frequent use of *ac* and *quod* in this and the next chapter suggests that they may have been written by a different author.

51. There are remains of the castle surviving.

52. Bernard the Hairy is also mentioned in 1.12.

53. See Num. 22.

54. The Bromme River passes through deep gorges as it flows south into the Truyère about twenty kilometers north of Entraygues-sur-Truyère. The abbey at Conques owned a number of properties near the Bromme.

55. Aurora (Greek Eos), was goddess of the dawn in Greek and Latin mythology; Tithonus was her consort.

56. Ruins of the castle of Thuriès still exist. It was located on a high ridge overlooking the Viaur River, near Pampelonne and roughly halfway between Rodez and Albi.

57. Ps. 145: 8 (146: 7–8).

Book Four

1. The manuscript (Sélestat 22) does not contain this title, which has been added here for consistency.

2. The term "athlete of Christ" refers to a martyr as a participant in a contest in which the martyr champions the cause of Christ. It was commonly used in the early Christian period.

3. Song of Songs 1: 11. The Song of Solomon or Song of Songs was

frequently interpreted by medieval exegetes as a dialogue between Christ the king and his lover, the human soul.

4. 2 Cor. 2: 15.

5. This is a reference to Song of Songs 3: 6, "Who is she that goes up by the desert, as a pillar of smoke of aromatical spices, of myrrh, and frankincense, and of all the powders of the perfumer?"

6. See note to 3.16.

7. There is a place called Saint-Georges southeast of Toulouse and about forty kilometers north of the Spanish border, on the Aude River. Saint-Orens and Marciac (see the next chapter) are nearby.

8. The Dourdou flows past Conques at the bottom of a deep gorge before joining the Lot about seven kilometers further on.

9. The Vatican manuscript calls him "Virbius." See note to 3.8.

10. The name of the tree is given in the local dialect; its exact meaning is not known.

11. The Falernian territory, a region at the foot of Mount Massicus in Campania, was known to the Romans for its wine.

12. *Vicarius*; During the Carolingian period a *vicarius* was the representative of a count or viscount and was a public official with judicial powers. Gournay says that, although this term had this very specific meaning during the Carolingian period, by the eleventh century it was most often used in a very general way to indicate someone to whom power had been delegated ("vague représentant de n'importe quel pouvoir," *Étude*, 335). It is not clear which usage is intended here.

13. Matt. 8: 24.

14. Ps. 26 (27): 10.

15. This castle is also mentioned in 1.5.

16. Golinhac is about seventeen kilometers east of Conques and overlooks the Lot River.

17. Ausonia is a poetic name for Italy used, for example, by Vergil in the *Aeneid*. Here eastern Ausonia means Italy and western Ausonia refers to Spain.

18. The Segre, a tributary of the Ebro, crosses Catalonia as it flows southwest out of the Pyrenees.

19. The banner of Sainte Foy is put to a similar use in 3.18.

20. Gen. 14: 18–20.

21. Tisiphone was one of the Furies or Erinys. They are spirits associated with punishment and vengeance in Greek and Roman mythology; they work by disturbing the mind.

22. The author refers to the ruler of Egypt, whose capital city in biblical times was Memphis.

23. Cf. Matt. 18: 35.

24. Achaemenes was the founder of the Persian dynasty called the Achaemenids, which ruled from the 7th century B.C.E. to 330 B.C.E.

25. The reference is to Phalaris, tyrant of Acragas in sixth-century B.C.E. Greece, who was known for punishing his enemies by roasting them alive in a hollow bull made of bronze.

26. Montpezat-de-Quercy is in Tarn-et-Garonne.

27. Bonnassie ("Forteresses") identifies Gauzbert as the castellan of Castelnau-Montratier in Lot, based on an entry in the cartulary (no. 347) referring to a *Gauzbertus de Castello Novo*.

28. A lion captured on the coast of North Africa is called a Gaetulian lion.

29. Acts 7–8. Stephen is considered to be the first Christian martyr.

30. Cf. Song of Songs 6: 8.

31. Cf. Song of Songs 6: 9.

32. *Horoma*, the Greek word for vision, is found, for example, in the Passion of Perpetua and Felicity 10.1; see Halporn, *Passio Sanctarum Perpetuae et Felicitatis*.

33. The term "protomartyr" refers to Stephen's status as the first Christian martyr.

34. Bernard II was bishop of Cahors from about 997 to about 1028; Gerald became bishop of Périgueux in 1037. Gournay dates the events in this miracle to about 1025–1030.

35. Salignac Castle stands on a high rock near the Dordogne River in the village of Salignac-Eyvignes, near Sarlat. The present castle there was built between the twelfth and seventeenth centuries.

36. *Propiciatorium*; see note to 3.1.

37. See 1 Kings 14: 13.

38. Bouillet (*Liber miraculorum*, 194) suggests that the title of this chapter would accord better with chapter seventeen and vice versa.

39. Leucata is a promontory on the south of the Ionian island of Leucas, from which, in ancient times, criminals were thrown into the sea in a yearly ritual.

40. This is the synod referred to in 1.28. It may have been called in relation to the Peace of God movement. Since Arnald died in 1031 this chapter must have been written after that date.

41. Abbot Adalgerius is also mentioned in 1.13. His presence dates these events to about 1019.

42. Bouillet (*Liber miraculorum*, 196) suggests that this may be the same person as the Austrin mentioned in 1.22.

43. Cayssac is about nine kilometers northeast of Rodez.

44. This is either the Dourdou or the Ouche, a mountain stream that empties into the Dourdou below Conques.

45. Acts 3: 2.

46. Palm Sunday.

47. Though the castle has been destroyed, the high cliff called the rock of Carlat provides a commanding view of the Cantal mountains. It is about sixteen kilometers southeast of Aurillac and thirty-five kilometers northeast of Conques.

48. This probably refers to water in which the reliquary-statue had been washed. It was not uncommon for healing powers to be ascribed to such a liquid, wine more frequently than water; see Sigal, *L'homme*, 49–53.

49. This miracle about a woman from Périgord apparently inspired the writer to compose a poem in honor of Saint Front, the legendary founder of the bishopric of Périgueux. Tradition held that Front was sent to Gaul by Saint Peter; this would make him the father of Christianity in the area and explains why he is referred to as "great father" in the poem that ends this chapter.

50. The Latin is "dolor intolerabilis migraneo."

51. The Bistones were a Thracian people. The word "Bistonian" was used as a synonym for "Thracian." Thus, the reference here is to the Thracian Bacchantes, who celebrated the festival of Bacchus with wild reveling.

52. For this term, see the prologue to Book Three.

53. Ps. 93(94): 2.

54. See 3.5.

55. Matt. 26: 61.

56. See 4.10.

57. This topos goes back at least to Augustine, who, "in recounting miracles of healing he claimed to have seen at first hand, provided emphatic and detailed accounts of the previous failure of skilled physicians to cure those subsequently healed by supernatural means" (Siraisi, *Medieval and Early Renaissance Medicine*, 9).

58. The notion of the saint as doctor probably derives from the notion of Christ as doctor. Siraisi notes that "Saint Augustine had developed the idea that Christ himself was the true physician, that is, the physician primarily of souls but also of bodies" (9).

59. In modern times this village is called Borgo San-Donnino. It is about twenty-four kilometers from Parma.

60. The reference could be to any one of a number of herbals in circulation in this period.

61. Rom. 10: 17.

62. This is a kind of spurge, a plant or bush with a bitter, milky juice that is often known for its medicinal properties.

63. Exod. 4: 6–7. The Latin here is "elephantico tumore."

64. This may be the same person as Avierne, the second wife of Austrin of Conques, who was the subject of 1.22.

65. Gournay dates these events to the second half of the eleventh century based on the mention of the monk Deusdet in a document in the cartulary (no. 50).

66. This is the only occurrence of the word *mancipium* in the entire *Book of Miracles*.

67. Phoebus is another name for the sun god Apollo, who fathered Asclepius, a god whose primary function was healing.

68. In Greek and Roman mythology Chiron was one of the centaurs, beings whose upper body was human and whose lower body was that of a horse. Chiron was thought of as a kindly old man with considerable medical wisdom.

69. Kendall points out that "Roman poets borrowed the masculine form *Tartarus* from Greek [Tartaros] as a synonym for Hades" and that its use in the form *Tartara* (Greek neuter plural) in the inscriptions on the Conques tympanum (which he dates 1105–1115) "is indicative of the cultural level of the abbey of Conques" ("The Voice in the Stone," 167).

70. Although his wife's attitude sounds contradictory, perhaps she wanted her husband to pray to Sainte Foy but felt that his condition was too serious for travel.

71. Several monks of this name appear in the cartulary in documents of the first half of the eleventh century.

72. In the system of the classical orders of architecture, the term architrave

refers to the horizontal band resting directly on the capitals of columns; it may also refer to the moldings around windows.

73. The Latin is *magister*; Hugh was clearly a person of some authority who had a range of duties and appears not to have been a monk. For a discussion of the skills and responsibilities of the master mason, see Coldstream.

74. Gregory of Tours, *Glory of the Martyrs*, chapter 64.

75. Erebus was the personification of darkness in Greek religion; here the name is used as another word for hell.

76. The author may be insistent on this point because it ran contrary to common opinion in the eleventh and twelfth centuries. According to Sigal (*L'homme*, 63) it was generally thought that miracles normally occurred in the places where relics were found and that the greater the distance the more extraordinary the miracle.

77. Sabaria, in the Roman province of Pannonia, was the birthplace of Martin of Tours.

Other Miracles

1. This title has been supplied. Under it are grouped miracle stories not found in Sélestat 22. Their sequence follows the relative dates of the manuscripts in which they occur.

2. The beginning of this chapter is lost. The title, which is descriptive of the contents, was supplied by Bouillet.

3. That is, to hell.

4. According to Gournay (*Étude*, 31) this miracle took place in the second half of the eleventh century.

5. The cartulary (no. 49) mentions a church of Sainte-Foy-des-Cailles. There is a place called Saint-Martin-des-Cailles near Penne d'Agenais, the site of a historic castle now in ruins.

6. If this is the same person as the Deusdet mentioned in 4.21, the events in the story can be dated to the second half of the eleventh century.

7. 3 Kings (1 Chron.) 21; 4 Kings (2 Chron.) 9: 29–37. For evidence as to the interest in Jezebal in this period, see Ziolkowski.

8. Campagnac is about forty kilometers east of Rodez. The church there was formerly dedicated to Sainte Foy.

9. Belmont-Sainte-Foi is also mentioned in 3.14.

10. This is a reference to Emathia, a region in Macedonia known for its warlike people. Cf. *dux Emathius* as a cognomen for Alexander in Ovid, *Tristia*, 3.5.39.

11. 1 Kings: 20.

12. This is the cathedral of Cahors, which is dedicated to Saint Stephen.

13. The Latin is *pothniadarum grex*, literally, herd of those from Potniae, which is the name of a village in Boeotia. It was surrounded by pastures that either drove grazing animals mad or killed them.

14. Based on the use of the word *clamoribus*, Lester K. Little cites this incident as an informal use of the "clamor," a ritual of malediction, excommunication, or

anathema, and notes that it is unusual to find the "clamor" as far south as Conques (*Benedictine Maledictions*, 146–47).

15. Eusebius describes the death of Arius in *Historia Ecclesiastica* 10.4, to which Gregory of Tours refers in his *History of the Franks*. Gregory writes, "Arius himself, who, according to the historian Eusebius, lost his entrails in the lavatory" (9.15); and "Arius, that evil man, the founder of that evil sect, lost his entrails in the lavatory and so was hurried off to hell-fire" (3, prologue).

16. Heb. 10: 30.

17. Since the author gives no information about the location of this castle, it has not been identified.

18. A tortoise is a wooden covering for the protection of besiegers.

19. The author refers to the Roman story of Gaius Mucius Scaevola, who demonstrated his ability to withstand pain by holding his right hand in the fire.

20. Cassius Sceva, centurion, who lost an eye and received several other wounds, did not leave his dangerous post, to which he had been assigned by Caesar, in the battle of Dyrrachium where Pompey was victorious.

21. In this manuscript this chapter ends with the concluding paragraphs of 4.24 that bring Book Four to an end.

22. Colomiers is west of Toulouse, about ten kilometers from the city center.

23. The dedication of her son to the saint and the promising of an annual offering are discussed by Sigal (*L'homme*, 115) as typical examples of personal devotion to a saint, which could range from literal servitude to a yearly donation.

24. This story is reworked in the partially preserved R.2 (see below).

25. Mark 11: 23.

26. John 14: 13.

27. Heb. 12: 6.

28. This could be Michael IV (1034–1041), Michael V (1041–1042), Michael VI (1056–1057), or Michael VII (1071–1078).

29. Cardona, in Catalonia near the French border, was a walled town with a castle.

30. Balaguer is in the western part of Catalonia, not far from Lerida.

31. The Latin phrase, "Fidis almae," is reminiscent of the Roman "O Fides alma," used of nurturing goddesses like Ceres and Cybele.

32. This is a reworking of the contents of A.2. Gournay notes that it contains much more of the spirit of the Crusades, "reconnaissable à son hystérie meurtrière" (*Étude*, 314).

33. John 14: 12.

34. Heb. 12: 6.

35. Horace, *Satires*, II., 5.

36. Najac is in Aveyron, not far south of Villefranche-de-Rouergue; the present castle, in ruins, was built in the thirteenth century, but there was an earlier castle on the site, which was built late in the eleventh century; see Delmas, *Aveyron*; Mathieu, *Najac*.

37. Cf. Prov. 26: 27.

38. Montirat is between twelve and thirteen kilometers from Najac.

39. Robert, count of Auvergne, acquired the additional title of count of

Rouergue on the death of his first wife's father in 1053. His wife, Bertha, was the great-granddaughter of the Countess Bertha mentioned in 1.28. On her death in 1066, Robert married Judith, daughter of the Count of Melgueil. A charter in the cartulary (no. 46) confirms the donation recorded in this miracle of Robert's gift of the church of Tanavelle to Conques in 1058.

40. The note to the French translation in Bouillet and Servières (*Sainte Foy*, 611) indicates that the Latin text here seems to say that it is the count who is still a child, but that both the context and the fact that this phrase corresponds exactly with a passage in Sidonius Apollinaris (*Epistolae*, book vii, letter 2) indicate that it refers to his wife.

41. Tanavelle is about seventy kilometers northeast of Conques.

42. Brioude is about 110 kilometers northeast of Conques.

43. Cf. Acts 3: 1–11.

44. Massiac is about fifteen kilometers southwest of Brioude, that is, in the direction of Tanavelle.

45. Talizat is about eleven kilometers north of Tanavelle.

46. Here the author puns on Foy's name, saying that if they had had faith in her they would have understood that she was faith. Puns on Foy/faith continue through the rest of this chapter.

47. The author addresses his words directly to Saint Peter.

48. Cf. Acts 19: 12.

49. Ps. 67: 36 (68: 35).

50. Since this miracle is about the freeing of prisoners, not about healing, it must not have been intended to follow the previous chapter.

51. Cicero's *Philippics* are a series of fourteen orations he wrote against Marcus Antonius.

52. Cf. Eccles. 4: 16.

53. Montmurat is about fifteen kilometers northwest of Conques.

54. Carlat is also mentioned in 4.14.

55. The Latin word *dominus*, in this context, could be understood as either lord of the castle or Lord God. The whole speech has a double meaning.

56. Horace, *Epistles*, I, x.

57. The Phlegethon is one of the rivers of Hades.

58. The Latin text reads, "cingna animalium Aeri Montis dicebatur." Gournay points out that the words "cingna animalium" (enclosure for animals) refers to a Celtic wall of at least one thousand years earlier that has since been rediscovered. It extended several kilometers and enclosed the top of the hill. The enclosure functioned as a refuge for both people and their domestic animals in the case of raids. The castle of Aigremont, apparently of the usual type for the Rouergue, must have been built inside that enclosure.

59. See note to 3.15.

60. Some knowledge of astrology was part of a physician's training. He may also have consulted a "sphere of life and death," a device "based on the magical virtue of numbers and astrology" that was "used for the purpose of finding out whether a patient would live or die" (see Sigerist, 292).

61. Prov. 31: 19.

62. Song of Songs 6: 12.

63. Hyperiona is another name for Aurora, goddess of the dawn.

64. Avernus is the underworld.

65. A reference to Orpheus, who went to the underworld to bring back his wife, Eurydice, and won her back by playing his lyre so well that he entranced Hades himself. Orpheus looked back as Eurydice followed him out of the underworld and thereby lost her again.

66. Pluto is another name for Hades, lord of the underworld.

67. See note to 4.24.

68. *Guantos* means gloves in the local dialect.

Translation

1. As Wands points out, the details given here about the locations of the two churches, "correspond to the present location of both churches, to the local tradition of their passions, and to a hypothesis on the location of the walls of the early medieval town" (*Romanesque Architecture*, 53–54).

2. This author displays his erudition with this rather confused version of Julius Caesar's famous line on the division of Gaul into three parts.

3. One stadium is 606 feet, 6 inches.

4. The Latin word is *concha*.

5. Although the chronicle written by the monks of Conques in the late eleventh century claims this to be true, there is no independent evidence of it and no historical circumstance that would substantiate such a claim.

6. The reference is to Sainte Foy, not the Virgin Mary.

7. For a general discussion of relic thefts, as well as an analysis of the circumstances surrounding the theft of Sainte Foy's relics by the monks of Conques, see Geary, *Furta Sacra*.

8. The Latin word translated here as "church" is *monasterium*, but according to the notes in the *Acta sanctorum* this word was commonly used at this time for any church whose clergy lived communally. For a discussion of the duties assigned to the guardian of the church, see Sigal, *L'homme*, 123–26.

9. *ex equestri ordine*. The author again displays his erudition by attributing to Agen the class structure of ancient Rome.

10. Lalbenque is about sixteen kilometers southeast of Cahors and approximately halfway between Agen and Conques.

11. It is actually about forty kilometers from Figeac to Conques.

12. There is lack of agreement as to the identity of this Charles, and thus as to the date of the translation of Foy's relics. For an argument that he is Charles the Young (or the Child), ruler of Aquitaine from 855 until September 29, 866, and that the translation took place in 866, see Geary, *Furta Sacra*, Appendix A. For a summary of scholarship on the question, favoring the argument that he is Charles the Fat and that the translation took place in 882 or 883, see D. Taralon, *"Le reliquaire de Pepin"*, Appendix I.

13. Stephen II was both bishop of Clermont and abbot of Conques from 942 to 984.

14. The abbot who ruled the monastery on site at this time was either Bego II or Hugh. In 1876, during the restoration of the choir of the abbey church at Conques, the foundations of a rotunda made of small dressed stone were uncovered just beneath the pavement. Jean Hubert identified these foundations as the remains of the tenth-century oratory described here, but does not accept the story of the immoveable body as authentic (Hubert, "Le plan de l'église de Conques au Xe siècle").

15. The text is not sufficiently detailed to determine the form of this "theca mirificae machinae", and scholars do not agree on the interpretation of these words. Some argue that it was a lidded box, a châsse, but others point to the text's careful indication that the saint was sealed beneath it. Dominique Taralon (*"Le reliquaire de Pepin"*, 32) suggests that it was a canopy, a baldachin, erected over the altar that itself contained the relics.

16. *Achademicum studium*. This reference to Plato's Academy displays the author's familiarity with Greek as well as Latin antiquity.

Song

1. The translator's goal has been to produce a text that remains as faithful as possible to the content and tone of the original without sacrificing clarity or readability. The past tense has been used uniformly in those passages where the Provençal switches back and forth between present and past. The translation is based on Hoepffner's edition in Ernest Hoepffner and Prosper Alfaric, *La Chanson de sainte Foy* (hereafter referred to as *SF* with the corresponding volume number). Also consulted was the edition by Antoine Thomas, *La Chanson de sainte Foi d'Agen: Poème provençal du XIe siècle*. The *Song* is untitled in the manuscript.

2. This Latin book, the contents of which are briefly indicated here and developed in *laisses* 44–55 of the poem, is almost certainly Lactantius, *De mortibus persecutorum*, ed. and trans. J. L. Creed (hereafter *DMP*) (*SF* 2: 28–29, 81n). The unique manuscript of this text (now Paris, Bibl. nat. Colbertinus, 2627) was in the abbey of Moissac. The pine as a place of assembly is a commonplace in Old French epic poetry (e.g., *Chanson de Roland*, lines 114, 165, 168, etc.).

3. The *Song* has, erroneously, Diocletian as Licinius's father (see *laisse* 12 below) and Maximian as Maximin's (see *laisse* 48). The pairing of Diocletian and Maximian also occurs in the *Translatio*, cap. 1. For a concise presentation of the historical background, see Creed's introduction to Lactantius, *DMP*, xv–xxv.

4. Constantine I, first proclaimed emperor at York in 306, sole emperor from 324 to 337.

5. Alfaric (*SF* 2: 30–35, 83n) identifies this *canczon* as the *Passio metrica sanctorum Fidis et Caprasii* (*Biblioth. hagiogr. lat.* 2938) and reprints the Bollandists' edition of the text (*SF* 2: 183–197). Zaal concurs, characterizing the *Passio metrica* (hereafter *PM*) as a text destined for chanting accompanied by liturgical dancing (*"A lei francesca"*, 7–10, 22). The reference to the subject matter as "Spanish," which

has baffled scholars, may simply mean that Foy's cult enjoyed wide popularity on both sides of the Pyrenees in the second half of the eleventh century when the poem was composed. Note the further references to this region in the next *laisse*.

6. The French style (*a lei francesca*) was presumably the style of chanting, similar to the style of delivery for epic poetry, that was used for such hagiographic texts in the vernacular as the *Vie de saint Alexis* (Zaal, "*A lei francesca*", 137–152).

7. This is a reference to the *Passio sanctorum Fidis et Caprasii* (hereafter *Passio*) from the liturgical office of Sainte Foy (*SF* 2: 45–49, 86n). Cf. pp. 33–38 above.

8. The reference to the first tone is presumably to the practice of liturgical chanting (Zaal, "*A lei francesca*", 1–22, 132–136).

9. Lit. "the fool more than the man of reason."

10. Alfaric notes (*SF* 2: 89n) that the offering of jewelry to pagan idols is the counterpart of such offerings made to Foy, a frequent motif in the *Book of Miracles* (1.17–22).

11. Song of Songs. 2. 2–3, freely rendered.

12. In the *Passio* Foy's parents are said to be noble but not lords of the city; in the *PM*, only "excellentes" (line 15). The central part of the *Song*, which recounts Foy's trial and martyrdom, draws extensively on the *Passio* and *Passio metrica*. Several of the more direct borrowings from these texts will be noted. For a detailed analysis of textual borrowings, see the notes that accompany Alfaric's translation of the poem into French in *SF* 2.

13. *Passio*, cap. 2: "Pulchra erat facie sed pulchrior mente."

14. *PM*, line 16: "Sed res mundanas ducens ut stercora vanas."

15. Cf. *Translatio*, cap. 1 (pp. 264–68 above).

16. Saint Adrian was martyred under Diocletian in Nicomedia ca. 304 (*Acta sanctorum* Sept. 3: 218).

17. The region of Cerdagne is in the eastern Pyrenees.

18. Diocletian appointed Maximian Herculius as his "Caesar" in the West in 285 and then elevated him to the rank of Augustus, or emperor, the following year. Diocletian launched the great persecution of Christians in 303.

19. *PM*: "Dux igitur vanus, ratione carens, Dacianus / venit in has partes" (lines 18–19).

20. Saint Felix was martyred at Girona ca. 304 under Diocletian and Maximian; according to tradition it was on the order of Dacian (*Acta sanctorum* Aug. 1: 22–28).

21. Foy crosses herself both in the *Passio* and the *PM*, but neither text includes the detail of the three-fingered gesture. This was, according to the *Dictionnaire d'archéologie chrétienne* (3: col. 3143), the customary practice until the thirteenth century.

22. Cf. Foy's prayer in the *PM*, lines 32–41.

23. "barracan": according to Du Cange ("*Boracanus*" and "*Barracanus*"), a thick wool cloth with silk fringe, similar to camlet.

24. Diana is the only pagan god mentioned in the *Passio* and the *PM*.

25. An obscure line, the best interpretation of which is probably Alfaric's: Dacian's anguish is caused by his doing his master's, that is, the Devil's, bidding (*SF* 2: 289n).

26. Cf. *PM*, lines 47–48.

27. *PM*: "Et tibi praebebo, si te mactare videbo, / Servos, ancillas, thesauros, praedia, villas" (lines 53–54).

28. Lawrence was a Roman deacon and martyr who died probably in 258.

29. The *Song* has the Greek form "Asclepi," as does *DMP* 33 in an unrelated passage.

30. Cf. *PM*, lines 100–103.

31. The valley of Aran is in the central Pyrenees. Hoepffner notes that the inhabitants were not Basque but Gascon (*SF* 1: 311n).

32. "druz." Cf. *Book of Miracles* 1.1, where Guibert is said to be Gerald's blood relative, household servant, and godson.

33. Diocletian and Maximian Herculius.

34. Saint Nicholas of Myra. Alfaric cites a ninth-century Latin life of the saint (N. C. Falconius, *S. Nicolai acta primigenia* [Naples, 1751], 112–126) in which he is arrested and imprisoned under Diocletian and Maximian (*SF* 2: 151n). The reference to the two emperors as the destroyers of "Emmaus Castle" has not been elucidated.

35. The Roman emperors are "Jews" (see *laisse* 49) because they persecute Christians the way the Jews were held to have persecuted Christ.

36. The *Song* draws on several sources for the names of the various cohorts in the emperors' armies: the Old Testament (Jebusites, Perrizites, Hebrews, Amorites); the *Etymologiae* of Isidore of Seville (Amazons, Pygmies, Hermaphrodites); and the *chansons de geste* (the Armenians fight for Baligant in the *Roland*, 3227; a Saracen is named Corbarin in *Ogier le Danois*, 2333).

37. Maximian's plotting against Constantine is recounted in Lactantius, *DMP* 27–30.

38. The *Song* conflates Maximin Daia and Maxentius. The former was appointed Caesar by his uncle Maximian Galerius, emperor in the East, and became one of the four emperors upon the latter's death in 311. Maxentius was the son of Maximian Herculius, emperor in the West. He likewise became emperor in 311, along with Licinius and Constantine.

39. To names derived from the Old Testament (Hagar, Issachar, Kedar, Shalmaneser) and epic poetry (Danes, Negroes, Moors) are added the Navarrians. The presence of the latter alongside the Moors is perhaps an oblique reference to the complicated political alliances of the Reconquest in Spain, which entered a crucial phase in the second half of the eleventh century.

40. Further use of names from the Old Testament (Chaldeans, Idumeans, Canaanites) and Isidore (Marcomanni, Macrobians, Satyrs).

41. Maximian, the "traitorous Jew," betrays Saint Maurice and his legion from Thebes (in Egypt) in the *Passio* of Saint Maurice (Migne, *PL* 50: 827–832).

42. In 310 Maximian was forced to commit suicide after his plot against Constantine had failed; he chose death by hanging (*DMP* 30.5–6).

43. The Slavs are mentioned in the *Roland* (3225), as is fencing (113).

44. Diocletian had in fact abdicated in 305 and died between 311 and 313—according to Lactantius, of hunger and anguish (*DMP* 42.3).

45. The "sons" are Licinius and Maximin. The historical Licinius and Maximin

Daia were, in fact, rival emperors in the East. Maximin Daia committed suicide in 313 after an unsuccessful attack against Licinius.

46. The battle of the Milvian Bridge was fought in 312 between Constantine and Maxentius. Maxentius was killed in the battle. Two years later Constantine defeated Licinius, thus becoming sole emperor in both parts of the Empire.

Bibliography

1. Primary Sources

Acta Sanctorum, October (6), ed. J. Ghesequière, III, 269–300; and *Acta Sanctorum*, October (20), ed. J. van Hecke, VIII, 815–28.

Behrends, Frederick, ed. and trans. *The Letters and Poems of Fulbert of Chartres*. Oxford: Clarendon Press, 1976.

Bouillet, Auguste. "Un manuscrit inconnu du *liber miraculorum sancte Fidis*." *Mémoires de la Société Nationale des Antiquaires de France* 58 (1899): 221–33.

——, ed. *Liber miraculorum sancte Fidis*. Collection de textes pour servir à l'étude et à l'enseignement de l'histoire, fasc. 21. Paris: Alphonse Picard et fils, 1897.

Cantalausa, ed. *La Chanson de Sainte Foi. Un Miracle de Sainte Foi*. St-Cyprien-sur-Dourdou: Éditions Dadon, 1985.

Chronicon monasterii Conchensis. In J.-L. E. Bourret, *Saint Martial de Limoges, premier apôtre et fondateur de l'église de Rouergue*. Rodez: Carrère, 1895.

Desjardins, Gustave, ed. *Cartulaire de l'abbaye de Conques-en-Rouergue*. Documents Historiques Publiés par l'École des Chartes. Paris: Alphonse Picard, 1879.

Fabre, Augustin, ed. *La Chanson de sainte Foy de Conques*. Rodez: Éditions de la Revue Historique de Rouergue, 1940.

Faral, Edmond, ed. and trans. *Ermold le Noir: Poème sur Louis le Pieux et épitres au roi Pépin*. Les Classiques de l'Histoire de France au Moyen Âge. Paris: Champion, 1932.

Gerson, Paula, Jeanne Krochalis, Anne Shaver-Crandell, and Alison Stones. *The Pilgrim's Guide to Santiago de Compostela: A Critical Edition of the Codex Calixtinus and A Catalogue of Monuments*. 3 vols. London: Harvey Miller, 1994–.

Halporn, James W. *Passio Sanctarum Perpetuae et Felicitatis*. Bryn Mawr, PA: Bryn Mawr College, 1984.

Hoepffner, Ernest and Prosper Alfaric. *La Chanson de sainte Foy, Fac-similé du manuscrit et texte critique, introduction et commentaire philologiques par Ernest Hoepffner*. Vol. 1. *Traduction française et sources latines, introduction et commentaire historiques par Prosper Alfaric*. Vol. 2. Publications de la Faculté des Lettres de l'Université de Strasbourg 32–33. 2 vols. Paris: Les Belles Lettres, 1926.

Lactantius. *De mortibus persecutorum*. Ed. and trans. J. L. Creed. Oxford Early Christian Texts. Oxford: Clarendon Press, 1984.

Martène, Edmond and Ursin Durand, eds. *Thesaurus novus anecdotorum*. Vol. 3. Paris, 1717: cols. 1387–1390.

Thomas, Antoine, ed. *La Chanson de sainte Foi d'Agen: Poème provençal du XIe siècle, édité d'après le manuscrit de Leide avec fac-similé, traduction, notes et glossaire*. Classiques Français du Moyen Âge. Paris: Champion, 1925; rpt. 1974.

Vielliard, Jeanne, ed. *Le guide du pélerin de Saint-Jacques de Compostelle. Texts latin du XIIe siècle, édité et traduit en français d'après des manuscrits de Compostelle et de Ripoll.* (Codex Calixtinus, liber quintus) Paris, J. Vrin, 1984.

Ziolkowski, Jan M., ed. *Jezebel: A Norman Latin Poem of the Early Eleventh Century.* Humana Civilitas 10. New York: Peter Lang, 1989.

2. Secondary

Abou-el-Haj, Barbara. "The Audiences for the Medieval Cult of Saints." *Gesta* 30 (1991): 3–15.

Aigrain, René. *L'hagiographie: ses sources, ses méthodes, son histoire*. Paris: Blond et Gay, 1953.

Ashley, Kathleen and Pamela Sheingorn. "An Unsentimental View of Ritual in the Middle Ages Or, Sainte Foy Was no Snow White." *Journal of Ritual Studies* 6,1 (Winter 1992):63–85.

Aubert, Marcel. *L'église de Conques*. Paris: Henri Laurens, 1939.

Barral y Altet, Xavier. "Définition et fonction d'un trésor monastique autour de l'an mil: Sainte Foy de Conques." In Claude Lepelley et al., eds., *Haut Moyen-Âge, Culture, Éducation et Société. Études Offertes à Pierre Riché*. La Garenne-Colombes: Éditions Européennes Erasme, 1990: 401–408.

Belting, Hans. *Likeness and Presence: A History of the Image Before the Era of Art.* Trans. Edmund Jephcott. Chicago: University of Chicago Press, 1994.

Benedictines of Paris. "Sainte Foy: Vierge et martyre (IIIe siècle?)." *Vies des saints et des bienheureux selon l'ordre du calendrier avec l'historique des fêtes*. Paris: Éditions Letouvey et Ané, 1952. Vol. 10: 145–55.

Bernoulli, Christoph. *Die Skulpturen des Abtei Conques-en-Rouergue*. Inaugural-Dissertation, Basel. Basel: Birkhäuser, 1956.

Bibliotheca hagiographica latina antiquae et mediae aetatis. Subsidia Hagiographica 6. Brussels: Société des Bollandistes. Vol. 1 (1898–99): 441–44.

Bisbee, Gary A. *Pre-Decian Acts of Martyrs and Commentarii*. Harvard Dissertations in Religion 22. Philadelphia: Fortress Press, 1988.

Boehm, Barbara Drake. *Medieval Head Reliquaries of the Massif Central*. 2 vols. PhD dissertation, New York University, 1990.

Bonnassie, Pierre. *La Catalogne du milieu du Xe à la fin du XIe siècle: Croissance et mutations d'un société*. Toulouse: Association des Publications de l'Université de Toulouse-Le Mirail, 1975.

———. "Les descriptions de forteresses dans le Livre des miracles de sainte Foy de Conques." *Mélanges d'archéologie et d'histoire médiévale en honneur du Doyen Michel de Boüard*. Geneva: Droz, 1982: 17–26; translation in *From Slavery* 132–48.

———. *From Slavery to Feudalism in South-Western Europe*. Trans. Jean Birrell. Cambridge: Cambridge University Press, 1991.

———. "Du Rhône à la Galice: Genèse et modalités du régime féodal." *Structures féodales et féodalisme dans l'Occident méditerranéen (X^e–Xiii^e s.). Bilan et perspectives de recherches. Colloque international organisé par le C.N.R.S. et l'Ecole fran-*

çaise de Rome, oct. 10–13, 1978. Collection de l'École Française de Rome 44. Rome, 1980: 17–44; translation in *From Slavery* 104–31.

Bonne, Jean-Claude. *L'art roman de face et de profil. Le tympan de Conques*. Paris: Le Sycomore, 1984.

Bouillet, Auguste and L. Servières. *Sainte Foy, vierge et martyre*. Rodez, France: E. Carrère, 1900.

Bousquet, Jacques. *La sculpture à Conques aux XIe–XIIe siècles: Essai de chronologie comparée*. Lille: Serv. de repr. des thèses, 1973. 3 vols.

———. *Le Rouergue au Premier Moyen Âge (vers 800–vers 1250)*. Vol. 1: *Les pouvoirs, leurs rapports, et leurs domaines*. Archives Historiques du Rouergue XXIV. Rodez: Société des Lettres, Sciences et Arts de l'Aveyron, 1992.

Bradbury, Jim. *The Medieval Siege*. Woodbridge, Suffolk, Rochester, NY: Boydell Press, 1992.

Brown, Anne Murray. *The Golden Majesty of Saint Foy at Conques*. M.A. thesis, California State University at Long Beach, 1982.

Brown, Peter. *The Cult of the Saints: Its Rise and Function in Latin Christianity*. Chicago: University of Chicago Press, 1981.

———. *Society and the Holy in Late Antiquity*. Berkeley and Los Angeles: University of California Press, 1982.

Brundage, James A. *Law, Sex, and Christian Society in Medieval Europe*. Chicago: University of Chicago Press, 1987.

Cadden, Joan. *The Meanings of Sex Difference in the Middle Ages: Medicine, Science, and Culture*. Cambridge: Cambridge University Press, 1993.

Camille, Michael. *The Gothic Idol: Ideology and Image-making in Medieval Art*. Cambridge: Cambridge University Press, 1989.

Cazelles, Brigitte. *The Lady as Saint: A Collection of French Hagiographic Romances of the Thirteenth Century*. Philadelphia: University of Pennsylvania Press, 1991.

Coldstream, Nicola. *Masons and Sculptors*. Medieval Craftsmen Series. Toronto: University of Toronto Press, 1991.

Collins, Roger. "Pippin I and the Kingdom of Aquitaine." In *Charlemagne's Heir: New Perspectives on the Reign of Louis the Pious (814–840)*. Ed. Peter Godman and Roger Collins. Oxford: Clarendon Press, 1990: 363–89.

Cowdrey, H. E. J. "The Peace and the Truce of God in the Eleventh Century." *Past and Present* 46 (1970): 42–67.

Dahl, Ellert. "Heavenly Images. The Statue of St. Foy of Conques and the Signification of the Medieval 'Cult-Image' in the West." *Acta ad archaeologiam et artium historiam pertinentia* 8 (1978): 175–91.

Delmas, Jean. *Aveyron*. Le Guide des Chateaux de France 12. Paris: Hermé, 1981.

Denny, Don. "The Date of the Conques *Last Judgment* and Its Compositional Analogues." *Art Bulletin* 66 (1984): 7–14.

Duby, Georges. *The Chivalrous Society*. Trans. Cynthia Postan. Berkeley: University of California Press, 1977.

———. *Rural Economy and Country Life in the Medieval West*. Trans. Cynthia Postan. Columbia: University of South Carolina Press, 1968.

Dunbabin, Jean. *France in the Making, 843–1180*. Oxford: Oxford University Press, 1985.

Dunn, E. Catherine. *The Gallican Saint's Life and the Late Roman Dramatic Tradition*. Washington, DC: Catholic University of America Press, 1989.

Durliat, Marcel. *La sculpture romane de la route de Saint-Jacques: De Conques à Compostelle*. Mont-de-Marsan: Comité d'Études sur l'Histoire et l'Art de la Gascogne, 1990.

Enjalbert, Henri and Gérard Cholvy, eds. *Histoire du Rouergue*. Toulouse: Privat, 1987.

Fanning, Steven. *A Bishop and His World Before the Gregorian Reform: Hubert of Angers, 1006–1047*. *Transactions of the American Philosophical Society* 78, Part 1. Philadelphia: American Philosophical Society, 1988.

Fau, Jean-Claude. *Conques*. Les travaux des mois 9. Saint-Léger-Vauban: Zodiaque, 1973.

——. *Rouergue roman*. 3rd ed. La nuit des temps 17. Saint-Léger-Vauban: Zodiaque, 1990.

Fichtenau, Heinrich. *Living in the Tenth Century: Mentalities and Social Orders*. Trans. Patrick J. Geary. Chicago: University of Chicago Press, 1991.

Forsyth, Ilene. *The Throne of Wisdom: Wood Sculptures of the Madonna in Romanesque France*. Princeton, NJ: Princeton University Press, 1972.

Fros, Henricus, ed. *Bibliotheca hagiographica latina antiquae et mediae aetatis*. Subsidia Hagiographica 70. Brussels: Société des Bollandistes, 1986: 334–36.

Gaiffier, Baudouin de. "Liberatus a suspendio." *Études critiques d'hagiographie et d'iconologie*. Subsidia Hagiographica 43. Brussels: Société des Bollandistes, 1967: 227–32.

——. "Miracles bibliques et vies de saints." *Études critiques d'hagiographie et d'iconologie*. Subsidia Hagiographica 43. Brussels: Société des Bollandistes, 1967: 50–61.

——. "Les revendications de biens dans quelques documents hagiographiques du XIe siecle." *Analecta Bollandiana* 50 (1932): 123–38.

——. "'Sub Daciano Praeside': Étude de quelques passions espagnoles." *Analecta Bollandiana* 72 (1954): 378–96.

——. "Un thème hagiographique: le pendu miraculeusement sauvé." *Études critiques d'hagiographie et d'iconologie*. Subsidia Hagiographica 43. Brussels: Société des Bollandistes, 1967: 194–226.

Gaillard, Georges. *Rouergue roman*. La nuit des temps, 17. Saint-Léger-Vauban: Zodiaque, 1963.

——. "Une abbaye de pélerinage: Sainte-Foy de Conques et ses rapports avec Saint-Jacques." *Compostellanum* 10 (1965): 691–711.

Gauthier, Marie-Madeleine. *Highways of the Faith: Relics and Reliquaries from Jerusalem to Compostela*. Secaucus, NJ: Wellfleet, 1983.

Geary, Patrick J. *Furta Sacra: Thefts of Relics in the Central Middle Ages*. Princeton, NJ: Princeton University Press, 1978; revised ed. 1990.

——, ed. *Readings in Medieval History*. Lewiston, NY: Broadview Press, 1989. Rpt. 1991.

Godman, Peter. "Louis 'the Pious' and His Poets." *Frühmittelalterliche Studien* 19 (1985): 239–89.

——. *Poets and Emperors: Frankish Politics and Carolingian Poetry*. Oxford: Clarendon Press, 1987.

Gournay, Frédéric de. "Aperçu sur les données du cartulaire de Conques." *Revue du Rouergue* n.s 21 (Spring 1990): 5–26.

——. *Les documents écrits de l'abbaye de Conques (IXe—XIIIe s.)*. Université de Toulouse-Le Mirail. U.F.R. d'histoire. D.E.A. (Mémoire). sous le direction de Pierre Bonnassie, Sept. 1992.

——. *Étude du Cartulaire de l'abbaye de Conques (actes postérieurs à 1030)*. Université de Toulouse-Le Mirail. Mémoire de maîtrise sous la direction de Pierre Bonnassie, October 1988. 2 vols.

Grémont, Denis. "Le culte de Sainte Foy et de Sainte Mary Madeleine à Conques au XIe siècle d'après le manuscrit de la Chanson de Ste-Foi." *Revue du Rouergue* 23 (1969): 165–75.

Head, Thomas. *Hagiography and the Cult of Saints: The Diocese of Orléans, 800–1200*. Cambridge: Cambridge University Press, 1990.

Head, Thomas and Richard Landes, eds. *The Peace of God: Social Violence and Religious Response in France around the Year 1000*. Ithaca, NY: Cornell University Press, 1992.

Hearn, M.F. *Romanesque Sculpture: The Revival of Monumental Stone Sculpture in the Eleventh and Twelfth Centuries*. Ithaca, NY: Cornell University Press, 1981.

Heffernan, Thomas J. *Sacred Biography: Saints and Their Biographers in the Middle Ages*. New York and Oxford: Oxford University Press, 1988.

Hubert, Jean. "Le plan de l'église de Conques au Xe siècle." *Bulletin de la Société Nationale des Antiquaires de France* (1948–1949): 240–44.

Hubert, Jean and Marie-Clotilde Hubert. "Piété chrétienne ou paganisme? Les statues-reliquaires de l'Europe carolingienne." *Christianizzazione et organizzazione ecclesiastica delle campagne nel'alto medioevo: Espansione e resistenze*. Settimane de Studio del Centro Italiano di Studi Sull'alto Medioevo 28. Spoleto, 1982: 235–75.

Kendall, Calvin B. "The Voice in the Stone: The Verse Inscriptions of Ste.-Foy of Conques and the Date of the Tympanum." In *Hermeneutics and Medieval Culture*, ed. Patrick J. Gallacher and Helen Damico. Albany: State University of New York Press, 1989: 163–82.

Landes, Richard. "Between Aristocracy and Heresy: Popular Participation in the Limousin Peace of God, 994–1033." In Head and Landes 1992: 184–218.

Latouche, R. "Sainte-Foy de Conques et le problème de l'or aux temps carolingien." *Annales du Midi (Hommage à F. Galabert)* 68 (1956): 209–15.

Lauranson-Rosaz, Christian. "Peace from the Mountains: The Auvergnat Origins of the Peace of God." In Head and Landes 1992: 104–34.

Lemaître, Jean-Loup. "Note sur les manuscrits conservés de l'abbaye de Conques." *Scriptorium* 41 (1987): 264–71.

Lewis, Archibald R. *The Development of Southern French and Catalan Society, 718–1050*. Austin: University of Texas Press, 1965.

Little, Lester K. *Benedictine Maledictions: Liturgical Cursing in Romanesque France*. Ithaca and London: Cornell University Press, 1993.

——. "Pride Goes Before Avarice: Social Change and the Vices in Latin Christendom." *American Historical Review* 76,1 (1971): 16–49.

Lynch, Joseph H. "*Spiritale Vinculum*: The Vocabulary of Spiritual Kinship in Early Medieval Europe." In *Religion, Culture and Society in the Early Middle Ages. Studies in Honor of Richard E. Sullivan*, ed. Thomas F. X. Noble and John J. Contreni. Kalamazoo, MI: Medieval Institute Publications, 1987.

Mackie, Gillian. "New Light on the So-Called Saint Lawrence Panel at the Mausoleum of Galla Placidia, Ravenna." *Gesta* 29 (1990): 54–60.

MacKinney, Loren C. *Bishop Fulbert and Education at The School of Chartres*. Texts and Studies in the History of Medieval Education 6. Notre Dame, IN: The Medieval Institute, University of Notre Dame, 1957.

Mandach, André de. "La 'Chanson de sainte Foy' en occitan: chanson de geste, mystère ou 'théâtre de danse'?" *La vie théâtrale dans les provinces du Midi*. Actes du II° Colloque de Grasse, 1976. Ed. Yves Giraud. Paris: Éditions Jean-Michel Place, 1980: 33–43.

———. "Contribution à l'histoire du théâtre en Rouergue au XIe siècle: un *Mystère de Sainte-Foy*?" In *La vie théâtrale dans les provinces du Midi*. Actes du II° Colloque de Grasse, 1976. Ed. Yves Giraud. Paris: Éditions Jean-Michel Place, 1980: 15–31.

———. "Le rôle du théâtre dans une nouvelle conception de l'évolution des genres." In *Stylistique, rhétorique et poétique dans les langues romanes*. Actes du XVIIe Congrès International de Linguistique et Philologie Romanes, vol. 8, Aix-en-Provence, 1983. Aix-en-Provence: Université de Provence, 1986: 27–46.

Mathieu, Georges. *Najac: Son histoire*. Paris: Girouette, n.d.

Moore, R. I. *The Formation of a Persecuting Society: Power and Deviance in Western Europe, 950–1250*. London: Basil Blackwell, 1987.

Musset, Lucien. "Aux origines d'une classe dirigeant: les Tosny, grands barons normands du Xe au XIIIe siècle." *Francia* 5 (1978/77): 45–80.

Paxton, Frederick S. "History, Historians, and the Peace of God." In Head and Landes 1992: 21–40.

Philippart, Guy. *Les légendiers latins et autres manuscrits hagiographiques*. Turnhout: Brepols, 1977.

Poulin, Jean-Claude. "Fides." In *Lexikon des Mittelalters* 4. Munich/Zurich: Artemis Verlag, 1987: cols. 434–435.

Quentin, Henri. *Les martyrologes historiques du Moyen Âge*. Paris, 1908.

Remensnyder, Amy G. "Un problème de cultures ou de culture? La statue-reliquaire et les *joca* de sainte Foy de Conques dans le *Liber miraculorum* de Bernard d'Angers." *Cahiers de la Civilisation Médiévale* 33 (1990): 351–79.

———. *Remembrance of Kings Past*. Ithaca, NY: Cornell University Press, forthcoming.

Riché, Pierre. *The Carolingians: A Family Who Forged Europe*. Trans. Michael Idomir Allen. Philadelphia: University of Pennsylvania Press, 1993.

Russell, Jeffrey Burton. *The Devil: Perceptions of Evil from Antiquity to Primitive Christianity*. Ithaca, NY: Cornell University Press, 1977.

———. *Lucifer: The Devil in the Middle Ages*. Ithaca, NY: Cornell University Press, 1984.

Saltet, Louis. "Étude critique sur la passion de sainte Foy et de saint Caprais." *Bulletin de Littérature Ecclésiastique* (Institut Catholique de Toulouse) 1 (June 1899): 175–90.

Sheingorn, Pamela. "'For God is Such a Doomsman': Origins and Development of the Theme of Last Judgment." In David Bevington et al., *Homo, Memento Finis: The Iconography of Just Judgment in Medieval Art and Drama*. Early Drama, Art, and Music Monograph Series 6. Kalamazoo, MI: Medieval Institute Publications, 1985: 15–58.

———. "The Saints in Medieval Culture: Recent Scholarship." *Envoi: A Review Journal of Medieval Literature* 2.1 (Spring 1990): 1–29.

Sigal, Pierre André. "Un aspect du culte des saints: Le chatiment divin aux XIe et XIIe siècles d'après la littérature hagiographique du Midi de la France." In *La religion populaire en Languedoc du XIIIe siecle à la moitié du XIVe siècle*. Cahiers de Fanjeaux 11. Toulouse: Privat, 1976: 39–59.

———. "Histoire et hagiographie: Les *Miracula* aux XIe et XIIe siècles." In *L'historiographie en Occident du Ve au XVe siècle*. Actes du Congrès des Historiens Médiévistes de l'Enseignement Supérieur, Tours, 1977. Fasc. spécial des *Annales de Bretagne* 87 (1980): 237–57.

———. *L'homme et le miracle dans la France médiévale (XIe–XIIe siècle)*. Paris: Cerf, 1985.

Sigerist, Henry E. "The *Sphere of Life and Death* in Early Medieval Manuscripts." *Bulletin of the History of Medicine* 11 (1942): 292–303.

Siraisi, Nancy G. *Medieval and Early Renaissance Medicine: An Introduction to Knowledge and Practice*. Chicago: University of Chicago Press, 1990.

Solt, Claire Wheeler. *The Cult of Saints and Relics in the Romanesque Art of Southwestern France and the Impact of Imported Byzantine Relics and Reliquaries on Early Gothic Reliquary Sculpture*. PhD dissertation, Catholic University of America, 1977.

———. "Romanesque French Reliquaries." *Studies in Medieval and Renaissance History* ser. 2 vol. 9 (1987): 167–236.

Southern, Richard W. "Humanism and the School of Chartres." In *Medieval Humanism*. New York and Evanston: Harper and Row, 1970: 61–85.

———. *The Making of the Middle Ages*. New Haven, CT and London: Yale University Press, 1953.

———. *Platonism, Scholastic Method, and the School of Chartres*. The Stenton Lecture, 1978. University of Reading, 1979.

Soutou, André. "Localisation géographique de la chanson de sainte Foy." *Annales du Midi* 82 (1970): 109–22.

Stock, Brian. *The Implications of Literacy: Written Language and Models of Interpretation in the Eleventh and Twelfth Centuries*. Princeton, NJ: Princeton University Press, 1983.

Taralon, Dominique. *"Le reliquaire de Pepin" du Trésor de Conques*. Mémoire pour l'obtention de la maitrise d'histoire de l'art. Université de Paris-Sorbonne Paris IV—Art & Archeologie. Année Universitaire 1988/1989.

Taralon, Jean. "La majesté d'or de Sainte-Foy du trésor de Conques." *Revue de l'Art* 40–41 (1978): 9–22.

———. *Treasures of the Churches of France*. New York: Braziller, 1966. Translation of *Trésors des églises de France*. Paris: Hachette, 1965.

Thibout, Marc. "La légende de sainte Foy peinte sur le mur de la sacristie au transept de l'église de Conques." In *Mélanges offerts à René Crozet*, ed. Pierre Gallais and Yves-Jean Riou. Vol. 2. Poitiers: Société d'Études Médiévales, 1966: 1367–70.

Thurston, Herbert J. and Donald Attwater. *Butler's Lives of the Saints*. 4 vols. Westminster, MD: Christian Classics, 1987.

Töpfer, Bernhard. "The Cult of Relics and Pilgrimage in Burgundy and Aquitaine at the Time of the Monastic Reform." In Head and Landes 1992: 41–57.

Vergnolle, Eliane. Review of Durliat, *La sculpture romane de la route de Saint-Jacques. De Conques à Compostelle*. *Bulletin Monumental* 149 (1991): 130–34.

Wands, Frances Terpak. *The Romanesque Architecture and Sculpture of Saint Caprais in Agen*. 2 vols. Ph.D. dissertation, Yale University, 1982.

Ward, Benedicta. *Miracles and the Medieval Mind: Theory, Record and Event 1000–1215*. Philadelphia, PA: University of Pennsylvania Press, 1982.

Wilson, Stephen, ed. *Saints and Their Cults: Studies in Religious Sociology, Folklore and History*. Cambridge: Cambridge University Press, 1983.

Wolff, Philippe. "Notes sur le faux diplome de 755 pour le monastère de Figeac." In *Figeac et le Quercy: Actes du XXIIIe Congrès d'études régionales organisé à Figeac les 2–4 juin 1967 par la Société des Études du Lot*. Fédération des Sociétés Académiques et Savantes Languedoc—Pyrénées—Gascogne, 1969: 83–122.

Zaal, Johannes W. B. *"A lei francesca". Étude sur les chansons de saints gallo-roman du XIe siècle*. Leiden: Brill, 1962.

Index

University of Pennsylvania Press
MIDDLE AGES SERIES
Edward Peters, General Editor

F. R. P. Akehurst, trans. *The* Coutumes de Beauvaisis *of Philippe de Beaumanoir.* 1992

Peter L. Allen. *The Art of Love: Amatory Fiction from Ovid to the* Romance of the Rose. 1992

David Anderson. *Before the Knight's Tale: Imitation of Classical Epic in Boccaccio's* Teseida. 1988

Benjamin Arnold. *Count and Bishop in Medieval Germany: A Study of Regional Power, 1100–1350.* 1991

Mark C. Bartusis. *The Late Byzantine Army: Arms and Society, 1204–1453.* 1992

J. M. W. Bean. *From Lord to Patron: Lordship in Late Medieval England.* 1990

Thomas N. Bisson, ed. *Cultures of Power: Lordship, Status, and Process in Twelfth-Century Europe.* 1995

Uta-Renate Blumenthal. *The Investiture Controversy: Church and Monarchy from the Ninth to the Twelfth Century.* 1988

Daniel Bornstein, trans. *Dino Compagni's* Chronicle *of Florence.* 1986

Maureen Boulton. *The Song in the Story: Lyric Insertions in French Narrative Fiction, 1200–1400.* 1993

Betsy Bowden. *Chaucer Aloud: The Varieties of Textual Interpretation.* 1987

Charles R. Bowlus. *Franks, Moravians, and Magyars: The Struggle for the Middle Danube, 788–907.* 1994

James William Brodman. *Ransoming Captives in Crusader Spain: The Order of Merced on the Christian-Islamic Frontier.* 1986

Kevin Brownlee and Sylvia Huot, eds. *Rethinking the* Romance of the Rose*: Text, Image, Reception.* 1992

Matilda Tomaryn Bruckner. *Shaping Romance: Interpretation, Truth, and Closure in Twelfth-Century French Fictions.* 1993

Otto Brunner (Howard Kaminsky and James Van Horn Melton, eds. and trans.). Land *and Lordship: Structures of Governance in Medieval Austria.* 1992

Robert I. Burns, S.J., ed. *Emperor of Culture: Alfonso X the Learned of Castile and His Thirteenth-Century Renaissance.* 1990

David Burr. *Olivi and Franciscan Poverty: The Origins of the* Usus Pauper *Controversy.* 1989

David Burr. *Olivi's Peaceable Kingdom: A Reading of the Apocalypse Commentary.* 1993

Thomas Cable. *The English Alliterative Tradition.* 1991

Anthony K. Cassell and Victoria Kirkham, eds. and trans. *Diana's Hunt/Caccia di Diana: Boccaccio's First Fiction.* 1991

John C. Cavadini. *The Last Christology of the West: Adoptionism in Spain and Gaul, 785–820.* 1993

Brigitte Cazelles. *The Lady as Saint: A Collection of French Hagiographic Romances of the Thirteenth Century.* 1991

Karen Cherewatuk and Ulrike Wiethaus, eds. *Dear Sister: Medieval Women and the Epistolary Genre.* 1993

Anne L. Clark. *Elisabeth of Schönau: A Twelfth-Century Visionary.* 1992

Willene B. Clark and Meradith T. McMunn, eds. *Beasts and Birds of the Middle Ages: The Bestiary and Its Legacy.* 1989

Richard C. Dales. *The Scientific Achievement of the Middle Ages.* 1973

Charles T. Davis. *Dante's Italy and Other Essays.* 1984

William J. Dohar. *The Black Death and Pastoral Leadership: The Diocese of Hereford in the Fourteenth Century.* 1994

Katherine Fischer Drew, trans. *The Burgundian Code.* 1972

Katherine Fischer Drew, trans. *The Laws of the Salian Franks.* 1991

Katherine Fischer Drew, trans. *The Lombard Laws.* 1973

Nancy Edwards. *The Archaeology of Early Medieval Ireland.* 1990

Margaret J. Ehrhart. *The Judgment of the Trojan Prince Paris in Medieval Literature.* 1987

Richard K. Emmerson and Ronald B. Herzman. *The Apocalyptic Imagination in Medieval Literature.* 1992

Theodore Evergates. *Feudal Society in Medieval France: Documents from the County of Champagne.* 1993

Felipe Fernández-Armesto. *Before Columbus: Exploration and Colonization from the Mediterranean to the Atlantic, 1229–1492.* 1987

Jerold C. Frakes. *Brides and Doom: Gender, Property, and Power in Medieval Women's Epic.* 1994

R. D. Fulk. *A History of Old English Meter.* 1992

Patrick J. Geary. *Aristocracy in Provence: The Rhône Basin at the Dawn of the Carolingian Age.* 1985

Peter Heath. *Allegory and Philosophy in Avicenna (Ibn Sînâ), with a Translation of the Book of the Prophet Muḥammad's Ascent to Heaven.* 1992

J. N. Hillgarth, ed. *Christianity and Paganism, 350–750: The Conversion of Western Europe.* 1986

Richard C. Hoffmann. *Land, Liberties, and Lordship in a Late Medieval Countryside: Agrarian Structures and Change in the Duchy of Wrocław.* 1990

Robert Hollander. *Boccaccio's Last Fiction: Il Corbaccio.* 1988

Edward B. Irving, Jr. *Rereading* Beowulf. 1989

Richard A. Jackson, ed. *Texts and Ordines for the Coronation of Frankish Kings and Queens in the Middle Ages.* 1994

C. Stephen Jaeger. *The Envy of Angels: Cathedral Schools and Social Ideals in Medieval Europe, 950–1200.* 1994

C. Stephen Jaeger. *The Origins of Courtliness: Civilizing Trends and the Formation of Courtly Ideals, 939–1210.* 1985

William Chester Jordan. *The French Monarchy and the Jews: From Philip Augustus to the Last Capetians.* 1989

William Chester Jordan. *From Servitude to Freedom: Manumission in the Sénonais in the Thirteenth Century.* 1986

Donald J. Kagay, trans. *The Usatges of Barcelona: The Fundamental Law of Catalonia.* 1994

Richard Kay. *Dante's Christian Astrology.* 1994

Ellen E. Kittell. *From* Ad Hoc *to Routine: A Case Study in Medieval Bureaucracy.* 1991

Alan C. Kors and Edward Peters, eds. *Witchcraft in Europe, 1100–1700: A Documentary History.* 1972

Barbara M. Kreutz. *Before the Normans: Southern Italy in the Ninth and Tenth Centuries.* 1992

E. Ann Matter. *The Voice of My Beloved: The Song of Songs in Western Medieval Christianity.* 1990

A. J. Minnis. *Medieval Theory of Authorship.* 1988

Lawrence Nees. *A Tainted Mantle: Hercules and the Classical Tradition at the Carolingian Court.* 1991

Lynn H. Nelson, trans. *The Chronicle of San Juan de la Peña: A Fourteenth-Century Official History of the Crown of Aragon.* 1991

Barbara Newman. *From Virile Woman to WomanChrist: Studies in Medieval Religion and Literature.* 1995.

Joseph F. O'Callaghan. *The Cortes of Castile-León, 1188–1350.* 1989

Joseph F. O'Callaghan. *The Learned King: The Reign of Alfonso X of Castile.* 1993

Odo of Tournai (Irven M. Resnick, trans.). *Two Theological Treatises:* On Original Sin *and* A Disputation with the Jew, Leo, Concerning the Advent of Christ, the Son of God. 1994

David M. Olster. *Roman Defeat, Christian Response, and the Literary Construction of the Jew.* 1994

William D. Paden, ed. *The Voice of the Trobairitz: Perspectives on the Women Troubadours.* 1989

Edward Peters. *The Magician, the Witch, and the Law.* 1982

Edward Peters, ed. *Christian Society and the Crusades, 1198–1229: Sources in Translation, including* The Capture of Damietta *by Oliver of Paderborn.* 1971

Edward Peters, ed. *The First Crusade: The* Chronicle of Fulcher of Chartres *and Other Source Materials.* 1971

Edward Peters, ed. *Heresy and Authority in Medieval Europe.* 1980

James M. Powell. *Albertanus of Brescia: The Pursuit of Happiness in the Early Thirteenth Century.* 1992

James M. Powell. *Anatomy of a Crusade, 1213–1221.* 1986

Susan A. Rabe. *Faith, Art, and Politics at Saint-Riquier: The Symbolic Vision of Angilbert.* 1994

Jean Renart (Patricia Terry and Nancy Vine Durling, trans.). *The Romance of the Rose or Guillaume de Dole.* 1993

Michael Resler, trans. Erec *by Hartmann von Aue.* 1987

Pierre Riché (Michael Idomir Allen, trans.). *The Carolingians: A Family Who Forged Europe.* 1993

Pierre Riché (Jo Ann McNamara, trans.). *Daily Life in the World of Charlemagne.* 1978

Jonathan Riley-Smith. *The First Crusade and the Idea of Crusading.* 1986

Joel T. Rosenthal. *Patriarchy and Families of Privilege in Fifteenth-Century England.* 1991

Teofilo F. Ruiz. *Crisis and Continuity: Land and Town in Late Medieval Castile.* 1994

Steven D. Sargent, ed. and trans. *On the Threshold of Exact Science: Selected Writings of Anneliese Maier on Late Medieval Natural Philosophy.* 1982

Pamela Sheingorn, ed. and trans. *The Book of Sainte Foy.* 1995.

Robin Chapman Stacey. *The Road to Judgment: From Custom to Court in Medieval Ireland and Wales.* 1994

Sarah Stanbury. *Seeing the* Gawain-*Poet: Description and the Act of Perception.* 1992

Robert D. Stevick. *The Earliest Irish and English Bookarts: Visual and Poetic Forms Before A.D. 1000.* 1994

Thomas C. Stillinger. *The Song of Troilus: Lyric Authority in the Medieval Book.* 1992

Susan Mosher Stuard. *A State of Deference: Ragusa/Dubrovnik in the Medieval Centuries.* 1992

Susan Mosher Stuard, ed. *Women in Medieval History and Historiography.* 1987

Susan Mosher Stuard, ed. *Women in Medieval Society.* 1976

Jonathan Sumption. *The Hundred Years War: Trial by Battle.* 1992

Ronald E. Surtz. *The Guitar of God: Gender, Power, and Authority in the Visionary World of Mother Juana de la Cruz (1481–1534).* 1990

William H. TeBrake. *A Plague of Insurrection: Popular Politics and Peasant Revolt in Flanders, 1323–1328.* 1993

Patricia Terry, trans. *Poems of the Elder Edda.* 1990

Hugh M. Thomas. *Vassals, Heiresses, Crusaders, and Thugs: The Gentry of Angevin Yorkshire, 1154–1215.* 1993

Ralph V. Turner. *Men Raised from the Dust: Administrative Service and Upward Mobility in Angevin England.* 1988

Mary F. Wack. *Lovesickness in the Middle Ages: The* Viaticum *and Its Commentaries.* 1990

Benedicta Ward. *Miracles and the Medieval Mind: Theory, Record, and Event, 1000–1215.* 1982

Suzanne Fonay Wemple. *Women in Frankish Society: Marriage and the Cloister, 500–900.* 1981

Jan M. Ziolkowski. *Talking Animals: Medieval Latin Beast Poetry, 750–1150.* 1993

This book has been set in Linotron Galliard. Galliard was designed for Mergenthaler in 1978 by Matthew Carter. Galliard retains many of the features of a sixteenth-century typeface cut by Robert Granjon but has some modifications that give it a more contemporary look.

Printed on acid-free paper.